Transitional Justice and Rule of Law Reconstruction

This short and accessible book is the f rst to focus exclusively on the inter -
relation between transitional justice and rule of law reconstruction in post-
conf ict and post-authoritarian states. In so doing it provides a provocative
reassessment of the various tangled relationships between the two f   elds,
exploring the blind-spots, contradictions and opportunities for mutually-
benef cial synergies in practice and scholarship between them. Though it is
commonly assumed that transitional justice for past human rights abuses is
inherently conducive to restoring the rule of law   , differences in how both
f elds conceptualize the rule of law, the scope of transition and obligations to
citizens have resulted in diver gent approaches to transitional criminal trial,
international criminal law, restorative justice and traditional justice mechanisms. Adopting a critical comparative approach that assesses the experiences
of post-authoritarian and post-conf   ict polities in Latin America, Asia,
Europe and Africa under going transitional justice and justice sector reform
simultaneously, it argues that the potential benef ts of transitional justice are
exaggerated and urges policy-makers to rebalance the compromises inherent
in transitional justice mechanisms against the foundational demands of rule
of law reconstruction. This book will be of interest to scholars in the f elds of
transitional justice, rule of law, legal pluralism and peace-building concerned
by the failure of transitional justice to leave a positive legacy to the justice
system of the states where it operates.

Pádraig McAuliffe is a lecturer in human rights law at the University of
Dundee. His research interests are primarily in the f   elds of transitional
justice, rule of law reconstruction and international criminal tribunals. He
has published in a number of journals in the f eld of international law.

'This is a bold and nuanced scrutiny of the international system's approach to
transitional justice and the much vaunted rule of law project. Dr McAuliffe
should be congratulated for this well-researched book which should be a
must read for not only scholars and researchers in transitional justice and
peace and conf ict studies, but also policy-makers in the international
system.' Dr. Hakeem O. Yusuf, Senior Lecturer, University of Strathclyde and
author of *Transitional Justice, Judicial Accountability and the Rule of Law.*

Transitional Justice and Rule of Law Reconstruction

A contentious relationship

Pádraig McAuliffe

LONDON AND NEW YORK

First published 2013
by Routledge
2 Park Square, Milton Park, Abingdon, Oxfordshire OX14 4RN

Simultaneously published in the USA and Canada
by Routledge
711 Third Avenue, New York, NY 10017

First issued in paperback 2015

Routledge is an imprint of the Taylor & Francis Group, an informa business

British Library Cataloguing in Publication Data
A catalogue record for this book is available from the British Library

Library of Congress Cataloging in Publication Data
A catalog record for this book has been requested

ISBN13: 978-1-138-93007-0 (pbk)
ISBN13: 978-0-415-66814-9 (hbk)

Typeset in Garamond
by Cenveo Publisher Services

This book is dedicated to Denise, who made every day of writing this a pleasure

Contents

1 Transitional justice and rule of law reconstruction

Between ambition and modesty

1.1 The role of ideas in transitional justice

In examining the relationship between transitional justice and rule of law (re) construction,[1] this book proceeds from two premises. One might be characterized as ambitious and the other as modest. The f rst, more ambitious premise, is that in transitional justice, ideas matter a great deal. To the extent that this book examines why the relationship between rule of law reform and transitional justice is contentious, it is hoped that a better understanding of the strains and complementarities between them can and will inform a better practice. Theory is important in all areas of law and politics because the ideas enunciated f lter into the world in all kinds of ways. However, there is reason to believe the impact of ideas is heightened in the f eld of transitional justice because of the inf uence of a highly mobile international coterie of practitioners and scholars who deploy to transitional states and can implement ideas circulating because their role in supranational or ganizations and NGOs gives them inf uence over government policy.

> Transitional justice operates through the actions of a series of groups: policy-makers who plan and implement the institutions; victim groups def ned by commissions or courts; the lar ger citizenry implicated, but not named, by a f nal report or court decision; scholars who write the literature about specif c country contexts or the phenomenon in general; and practitioners who work for nongovernmental or ganizations (NGOs) that consult on the possible manner of transition.[2]

Kritz exaggerates only slightly when he contends that a government's transitional justice policy 'often depends less on well-grounded and proven policy considerations than on whether the junior member of staff writing the policy memo has some experience with the South African TRC or another transitional justice process',[3] but he highlights a salient fact that animates much of this book – how scholars, advocates and practitioners think about and experience transitional justice can have a large impact on how it is practised and its relationship to other socio-political phenomena. The parameters of transitional justice are often def ned by what international donors at supranational, bilateral or international nongovernmental or ganizations (INGO) levels are willing to pay for.[4]

INGOs (within which dedicated transitional justice or ganizations can be categorized),[5] in particular, are highly inf uential through the development and transmission of norms, standards and principles through world-wide networks to states, inter-governmental organizations and national bodies, and then entreating these actors to conform to them. [6] Mixing advocacy with operational work, human rights and transitional justice NGOs not only formulate the issues, but also def ne how those issues are resolved, using their moral appeal, investigative missions and national NGO partners to pressure states to comply with their programmes. [7] The academy and applied interest are equally inf uential – historically, ideas outlined in papers, conferences or the f eld about how transitional justice can be practised often amount to self-fulf lling prophecies of what will be done in future, even if the success antici-pated does not follow as inevitably . Though legal and human rights theory have traditionally been dominant in the f eld, newer, more holistic approaches require a refreshed trans-disciplinary mindset. [8] Characterized by some as a rendezvous discipline,[9] transitional justice scholarship draws on anthropo-logical, developmental, economic, feminist and sociological critiques to addresses the fresh dilemmas and opportunities the idiosyncratic ecologies of transition present. One of the criticisms this book makes is that the scholar - ship has not drawn suff ciently on perspectives from rule of law reconstruction.

The history of transitional justice, therefore, is the history of interactions of scholars, human rights activists and policy-makers who have always asserted the centrality of ideas. [10] What we now know as transitional justice was initially structured as a f eld at an Aspen Institute conference in 1988 on state crimes, and much of its subsequent development f nds its roots in conferences, seminal monographs and special editions of dedicated journals.[11] The prime example of the triumph of ideas is what Lutz, Sikkink and Walling have called 'the justice cascade',[12] where they argue that the endeav-ours of a transnational transitional justice advocacy network successfully opposed the def ance of recalcitrant governments and stimulated a rapid shift toward effecting compliance with recognized human rights norms. [13] They argue that ongoing norm penetration, public debate and pressure that human rights activists can muster at international and domestic level have mitigated the unwillingness of nascent democracies (who care about what other states are doing and global normative trends) to deal with human rights abuses of the past. The putative justice cascade has been characterized as the work of NGOs acting as activists, advertisers and pressure groups, starting with the efforts of small groups of activists domestically and mushrooming into a transnational network that fundamentally changed the environment in which state actors work. [14] The cascade ar gument probably claims too much. Statistical analysis conducted in recent years suggests that states are no more likely to conduct trials than they were 30 years ago, [15] that use of truth commissions is declining in relative terms [16] and that amnesty remains the most popular mechanism applied.[17] Politico-military balances still tend to dictate the parameters of accountability,[18] while civil society will often get involved after pacts are agreed, the *ancien régime* has f ed or power is shared, and even then remains weak.[19] Even the strongest forms of both transitional criminal trial (the ad hoc tribunals) and truth commission (the South African Truth and Reconciliation Commission (TRC)) respectively represent glosses for military inactivity[20] and security-based blackmail[21] more so than the triumph of an accountability norm. Instead of a justice cascade, there instead appears to exist a justice balance between sometimes contradictory policies like accountability and amnesty. The greatest impact of norm socialization is observable not in causal terms of whether a given mechanism is pursued or not, but rather in qualitative terms of how those mechanisms operate once established.

The cross-fertilization of ideas between these actors has helped develop ideas of good practice among the proliferating transitional justice mechanisms,[22] while the consolidation of both TRCs and criminal trials as policy tools contributed towards the increased eagerness to consider an adaptable continuum of strategies over the previous binary choice between the two. A noticeably more holistic, multi-mechanism, context-specif c approach has become the norm. W ith the consolidation of transitional justice came an accelerated process of contagion learning, where policy-makers in one context appropriated the knowledge and methodologies accumulated in previous transitions.[23] As transitional justice enters a 'do everything, engage everyone' era,[24] a restorative paradigm of justice concerned with the individual, the family and the local community has shared parity with more statist-legalist approaches.[25] The theory and practice of TRCs has become more sophisticated, requiring victim-centred consultation, detailed terms of reference, qualif ed staff ng, impact assessment and follow-up.[26] Many of the restorative principles these practices f ow from were the product of retrospective explanatory theories outlined by scholars to compensate for the trade-offs of realpolitik,[27] who subsequently went on to constructively def   ne the normative expectations of these mechanisms. Similarly, in response to criticisms of the operation of the ad hoc tribunals, victims emer ged in transitional criminal trials from their earlier instrumentalization to become one of the main constituencies of prosecution, consultation became the paramount virtue of accountability planning, and outreach has become imperative.[28] Practitioners in all forms of transitional justice employ the enormous body of soft law developed in the last two decades on issues like impunity, indemnif cation of victims and truth.[29]

The failure of transitional justice to integrate with rule of law reconstruction this book examines is surprising when one considers how fruitfully it has interacted with other peace-building efforts. For example, much progress has been   made in integrating transitional justice with Disarmament, Demobilization and Reintegration (DDR) and Security Sector Reform (now bundled with Justice as SSJR). For many years, these issues were treated separately as security sector debates became synonymous with military and police, but over time it became apparent that the security issues could not be considered in isolation from matters of accountability   . For example, the unchecked power and weight of many militaries complicated efforts at accountability in Latin America, while Liberian soldiers were afraid to demobilize due to rumours that their ID benefit cards might be employed to bring them before the Special Court for Sierra Leone. The realization that transitional justice and DDR/SSJR could be both mutually re-enforcing and mutually destructive spurred institutional and doctrinal innovation coalescing around three common objectives: accountability , building of instructional capacities and non-reoccurrence. [30] By 2005, transitional justice and DDR had become explicitly merged in places like Colombia and a Security Sector Reform and T ransitional Justice Unit has been established within UN Department of Peacekeeping. Similarly, research and practice has begun to examine the gender dynamics of transitional justice which long went over - looked.[31] Its re-orientation evolved from a growing realization of the gendered nature of peace agreements negotiated by men after wars conducted by men which disregarded the needs of women. The masculinist emphasis in transitional justice on regime change between male-dominated parties and factions and the emphasis on 'extraordinary' violations of civil and political rights and war crimes obscured victimization that occurred at the intersection of gender and socio-economics. As the inability of trials and TRCs to respond to the different experience of women in war and repression was acknowledged and as cognisance was taken of the notable rise in levels of family violence that occurs after peace negotiation, initiatives began to address these issues. Similarly, the acknowledgment that the existing modalities of transitional justice have failed to address the structural injustices that lie at the root of conf ict has prompted searches to make it effective through distributive justice at macro-level and through considering how people seek and experience justice after mass atrocity in the context of everyday life at micro-level. By contrast, thinking on the relationship between the rule of law and transitional justice has attracted less innovative thinking and gone underanalysed, largely because this relationship has always been presumed to be mutually-benef cial. On the other hand, the link between transitional justice and DDR or gender were less intuitively apparent, resulting in conscious efforts to reform theory and practice. To summarize once more, how transitional justice is interpreted at legal and policy levels has a fundamental inf uence on how it is implemented and what objectives are given priority.

As Chapter 2 examines in great detail, rule of law reconstruction actors have similarly proven responsive to the arguments of scholars and practitioners as they learn from the examples of the Law and Development era of the 1970s, post-Communist reconstruction and failed peace-missions in the 1990s and the Millennial transitional administrations. In short, much of this book is dedicated to examining how scholars, activists and practitioners in both transitional justice and rule of law reconstruction think about these f elds, and does so on the presumption that a transitional justice praxis that operates with a greater awareness of the opportunities and contradictions that f ow from their simultaneous operations is a better praxis. That such an inquiry is necessary may seem strange. T ransitional justice and rule of law reconstruction have been mainstreamed at the same time and in many of the same contexts. This parallel growth in rule of law reconstruction and transitional justice responds to our intuitions that the processes are related and mutually re-enforcing. De Greiff notes that 'scholars lar gely agree about both the centrality of the concept and about the usefulness of transitional justice measures in efforts to re-establish the rule of law'. [32] Ndulo and Duthie outline a relationship between transitional justice and judicial reform that operates at three levels – judicial reform can constitute an element of transitional justice, it may facilitate transitional justice, while transitional justice may contribute to judicial reform. [33] The necessity of cooperation between the international justice and development communities was formally recognized at the Kampala Review Conference of the ICC in the summer of 2010 and at a follow-on high-level conference in October of that year where practitioners from both spheres acknowledged a need to co-operate in integrating international criminal justice into traditional rule of law programmes. [34] Examples of mutually-benef cial co-operation are legion. For example, we see how the arrest abroad of General Pinochet stimulated the Chilean courts to reform [35] or where reform of Criminal Division of the Court of Bosnia and Herzegovina enabled widespread transitional trials.[36] At the same time, there are obvious opportunities for co-operation given that both processes generally operate simultaneously. For example, it is not uncommon to see the hope expressed:

> With integration [of justice sector reform and transitional justice],
> redundancies can be avoided and syner gies can be tapped. For example,
> backing for a witness protection and support system needed for interna-
> tional criminal law trials could also benef t initiatives on domestic abuse,
> sexual violence, corruption, drug traff   cking, or or ganized crime.
> Criminal investigators who have undergone specialized training in inter-
> national criminal justice may also receive advanced training in securing
> crime scenes, forensics, or taking witness statements – skills that will
> boost capacity of the criminal justice system across the board. [37]

Furthermore, processes of accountability after war or repression will often highlight def ciencies in the rule of law and can serve as an impetus for rebuilding the judiciary, and vice versa.

However, mutually benef cial symbiosis is more apparent on paper than on the ground. Concern has been expressed that it is often the same 'small pool of talent' that will undertake both tasks [38] and that the burden of external assistance for dealing with past human rights abuses will fall not on the international justice community , but rather the traditional rule of law development organizations on account of their larger network of international organizations, aid agencies, and other donor and implementing bodies. [39] While transitional justice has sometimes stimulated benef cial reform, it can also have the opposite effect – in Kenya, justice NGOs began to give up on campaigns to use a national tribunal to pursue justice for post-election violence when the use of the International Criminal Court (ICC) appeared more immediately feasible.[40] Fear has been expressed that activities (such as transitional justice) that are popular and well-funded may be 'cherrypicked' to the detriment of strengthening the justice sector as a whole.[41] The conceptual confusion between transitional justice and rule of law reconstruction that Chapter 2 examines presents a signif cant danger that transitional justice will absorb a signif cant slice of foreign funding that might otherwise go towards justice sector reform. Observers see costly transitional justice projects being pitched f nancially against justice sector reform activities such as training of new judicial actors, repair of courthouses or infrastructure and coming out victorious.[42] The most criticized example of this is the International Criminal Tribunal for Rwanda (ICTR) in Rwanda where donor commitments for justice sector reconstruction in the f rst f ve years after the genocide was an estimated US\$10m per annum, while the ICTR budget was US\$90m per year.[43] It has been suggested that the Haitian domestic justice system has suffered because donors refused to fund ordinary trial processes because they had committed to a truth commission, [44] while it is alleged that of the US\$140m Guatemala received for transitional justice, roughly 3 per cent went to the criminal courts.[45] A further risk is that transitional justice activities will draw off human and material resources. Even though problems of insecurity and violent crime are generally worse after transition than before,[46] the systemic effect of transitional justice proceedings may be to displace ordinary but urgent legal disputes by relegating them to the back of the court queue.[47] Posner and Vermeule posit a cost-benef t analysis, arguing that the net effect is a loss to the transitional state if the displaced 'ordinary' crime proceedings would have made a greater overall contribution to the new regime's welfare than the transitional justice proceedings.[48] Such calculations have long troubled observers. As van Zyl argued in the South Africa context, '[i]f the police and prosecuting authorities were to devote a signif cant share of their resources to dealing with human rights violations, many of which happened a decade or more ago, the country would almost certainly lose the current battle against ongoing crime'. [49] These examples of how transitional justice can both augment and detract from rule of law reconstruction are the key theme this book explores.

Notwithstanding the presumed links between the felds, there is an evident lack of cross-fertilization of ideas between the rule of law reconstruction and transitional justice communities. The interaction of scholarship, advocacy and practice in both sectors is subject to a set of assumptions that lack coherence and depth. As Stromseth, W ippman and Brooks suggest, the question of whether and how accountability processes can contribute to the development of domestic justice systems and the construction of the rule of law generally is 'surprisingly underanalysed' academically.[50] To date, the two f elds have been treated mostly as two separate areas of interest in both academic analysis and in UN peace-keeping practice.[51] Call notes that analysis of post-conf ict judicial reform has failed to address the role of those responsible for past human rights abuses while research on the latter has focused more on past atrocities than rebuilding justice systems for the future.[52] In the immediate context, this blind-spot may be a particularized example of the 'familiar but self-deceiving separation of law , human rights, truth commissions and reconciliation from questions of nation-building' that has persisted in transitional justice notwithstanding its accumulation of projects and goals.[53] Both van Zyl and Lambourne note that surprisingly little analysis has been devoted to the interaction of transitional justice and post-conf ict peace-building,[54] while Kritz observes 'too much bifurcation between transitional justice and the construction of the rule of law'.[55] This is the product of the widely observed professional balkanization that typically aff icts rule of law reconstruction missions where different experts and agencies with divergent mandates and different institutional dynamics concentrate intensely on their core competencies, producing hyperfocused approaches that fail to add up to an integrated and effective whole.[56] The presumption appears to be that there will be a complementary overlap between the two areas of activity, but given the failure to think through their inter -relation, there is a signif cant risk of 'underlap' where incoherence results from the cacophony of projects.[57] One of the recurring images referred to in rule of law literature is that of the gleaming, newly-erected courthouse built by justice sector reformers without any trained professionals to work in it or any community consciousness of its purpose.[58] Because issues of post-conf ict justice are commonly hived off as a separate and specialized issue,[59] all too often transitional justice resembles that courthouse, an impressive edif ce isolated from ongoing development and perhaps even substituting for real reform.

The challenge of co-ordination is a permanent feature of UN peace-building missions as they embrace a plurality of goals through different agencies. For example, the UN entrusts its rule of law work to the United Nations Development Programme (UNDP), United Nations Off ce on Drugs and Crime (UNODC) and Department of Peacekeeping Operations (DPKO) and gives the lead on transitional justice to the Off ce of the High Commissioner for Human Rights.[60] This co-ordination problem is exacerbated by simultaneous operations of non-UN agencies. The hasty, ad hoc and reactive manner in which these missions must deploy in practice often operates to preclude reasoned co-ordination between transitional justice practitioners and those engaged in wider rule of law reform. NGO reports note how in the DR Congo, rule of law development off cials had no awareness of pledges made in relation to justice on their behalf at the Kampala Review Conference or how justice sector reconstruction off cials in Cambodia had no interaction with the

Extraordinary Chambers trials of the Khmer Rouge.   [61] Though judicial
reform and the Special Court for Sierra Leone started simultaneously , there
was little interaction between the Court and broader rule of law reconstruction.[62] These actors, then, are the policy-makers to whom work will be of
most utility. I envisage two core audiences for this book. One is made up of
scholars, practitioners and observers of transitional justice; the other consists
of their counterparts in justice sector reform broadly understood. Though the
distinction between the two is crude, as the above examples of dissonance
suggest, there are individuals and groups that are identif able as rule of law
practitioners and others that are identif able as transitional justice actors,
even if there is occasional cross-over. These actors are to be found in the forty-
plus UN agencies, departments and funds in the wide spectrum of peace-
building activities running along the 'Mogadishu line' beyond ceasef re
monitoring and full transitional administration of society such the UNDP ,
DPKO and the Rule of Law Assistance Unit. These activities have been
grouped in three baskets – the rule of law at international level, the rule of
law in conf ict and post-conf ict situations, and the rule of law in long-term
development.[63] This work may also be of use to the operations of the EU and
Council of Europe, multilateral or ganizations like the Or ganization for
Security and Co-operation in Europe (OSCE) and Bretton W oods institutions, bilateral donors such as the Department for International Development
(DFID) and the United States Agency for International Development
(USAID), aid agencies and of course national actors working in, or at the
intersection of, transitional justice and the wider panoply of rule of law
operations at international, national and grassroots levels. However , professional balkanization is only the or ganizational form of a wider problem,
namely that activists and theorists in both communities have fundamentally
different conceptions of what the rule of law means and requires in post-
conf ict and post-authoritarian transitions. As this book examines, neither
group may have much knowledge of key debates in the opposite f eld. This
lack of common ground means there is a risk some sections of the book will
read either as opaque or excessively introductory for one or other group. I
have tried to avoid this, while keeping both readerships in mind.

1.2 The failure to integrate transitional justice with rule of law reconstruction

Beyond professional Balkanisation, the failure to integrate perspectives from
rule of law reconstruction and transitional justice might equally f ow from the
frequent assumption in academic literature that accountability for wrongdoers
from the prior regime or conf ict automatically contributes to building the
rule of law in formerly lawless or repressive states.[64] As Chapter 3 examines in
detail, rule of law reconstructors have long been aware that international actors
instinctively attach the concept of the rule of law to other concepts such as
democracy, justice, equality and human rights, with the consequence that form

becomes secondary to generalized and politicized notions of good? Transitional justice undoubtedly tends to judicialize politics,[66] but one sees in the literature a presumption that this automatically conduces to constru cting a sustainable domestic rule of law. Transitional justice occurs most often in states transition-ing to Western-style 'rule of law' democracies, or purporting to do so. The teleological impetus of transitional justice has led theorists and practitioners in the f eld to conf ate the rule of law and mechanisms to facilitate transition to a liberal polity, viewing them in some cases as virtually synonymous when in reality they are two very different concepts. It has above all led to some regrettable anomalies and the mar ginalization of the bread-and-butter rule of law issues which in the long term do as much, if not more, to advance peace-building as truth, accountability or restorative justice. For example, while we readily accept the potency of successor trials to communicate political messages about human rights to divided communities and reorient court processes to this task, we ignore the more obvious potency of such trials to communicate how criminal procedure is supposed to work. While it is presumed that trials of war crimes or genocide will help ground the rule of law, we forget that these crimes have little or no relation to the ordinary crimes that ordinary citizens will now rely on the courts to resolve after the conf   ict. Both international criminal law and localized, grass-roots processes are valorized by their respec-tive enthusiasts for their distance from the state justice system and manifest ambivalence about whether the state justice system should have a leading role in reckoning with the past. It is imperative that these blind-spots be brought to light by questioning the presuppositions and omissions in the literature.

Diagnosing a gap in the literature is not the same as f lling it, but progress has been made. The UN Secretary General'   s seminal *Rule of Law and Transitional Justice Reports* in 2004 and 2011, as the name would suggest, identif ed the interdependence and potentially mutually-reinforcing nature of the two f elds, making clear that development of domestic judicial capacity is every bit as essential to peace-building as transitional justice. [67] While the UN has developed its own literature in the area, [68] the academic response to its commendable but broad-brush recommendations has either been sluggish or non-existent, with notable exceptions. Stromseth, W ippman and Brooks have addressed the position of transitional justice within broader rule of law efforts.[69] A diverse edited volume by Call examines the interaction of the two areas, though it failed to establish a robust, empirical connection between justice for past abuses and the quality and accessibility of justice in the future.[70] Kerr and Mobekk ur ge the integration of transitional justice with rule of law reform[71] while Bassiouni has called for a guiding principle based on 'sustainable justice', def ned as a level of domestic justice compatible with the building and maintenance of a viable state legal system.[72] Post and Hesse argue that efforts to enforce international law should be subordinate to promoting the rule of law itself,[73] but dedicated treatment of the relationship between transitional justice and justice sector reform in journals is limited.[74] Pertinent studies of how justice system actors view the impact of transitional justice on domestic systems are rare, and most actually precede the f rst *Rule of Law and Transitional Report*.[75] More detailed examination of the interaction of judicial reconstruction with transitional processes can be found in discrete works on hybrid courts, complementarity and to a lesser extent traditional/ local justice mechanisms, all of which will be examined in later chapters. What is striking about even these is the failure to examine in depth the rich literature on rule of law theory in the context of post-conf ict reconstruction. Observations and recommendations still tend towards the superf cial. This book is a conscious attempt to bridge what Stromseth identif es as the gap between transitional justice and rule of law reform by answering her call to 'explore systematically how accountability processes might, concretely , contribute to forward-looking rule of law reforms'.[76]

The second premise of this work is that even if the links are better under - stood, a hitherto unprecedented modesty about the importance of transitional justice to the rule of law is most apt for constructive reform. Even greatly improved interaction of transitional justice and rule of law reconstruction will have a relatively minor impact on the emer ging processes of peace and democratization. Over time, there has been a slow but far from universal acceptance that transitional justice 'claims too much', creating panacean expectations that dissolve into inevitable disappointment. [77] Rule of law reconstruction was similarly held out in the past as a solution to almost every international policy problem from democratization to development to stabi- lization,[78] but appears to have gone much further in tempering this initial hubris with more realistic expectations of what can be achieved in post- conf ict/authoritarian ecologies that are even more inhospitable than those of generic developing states.[79] Within the universe of peace-building, rule of law reconstruction is a necessary but far from suff cient component of a successful transition to a functioning polity, while transitional justice is but one of many considerations in rebuilding the rule of law. Success in any f eld will largely depend on starting conditions, history and more recent economic, social and political legacies peculiar to each transition.

In the international human rights community, the assumption that transi- tional justice is critical to restoring legality has long been an article of faith[80] However, while most scholars and advocates of transitional justice assume that the question of transitional justice 'presents the very f rst test for the establishment of the rule of law',[81] peace-builders and rule of law practition- ers are considerably more circumspect. Though they generally accept that ending impunity is desirable in grounding the rule of law,[82] the use of trials, truth commissions, lustration or restoration can only ever amount to merely one element of a wider rule of law reconstruction programme, and far from the most essential. The contention that transitional justice can help ground the rule of law has generally been well-argued, but rarely put into the broader context of other factors that can promote and nurture the rule of law . Rule of law reconstruction is something of an umbrella term incorporating a wide range of essential tasks like writing or re-writing national constitutions, restructuring the organizational framework of the courts, re-imposing law and order, drafting laws, improving institutional facilities for justice, human rights and anti-corruption mechanisms, creating procedures for training, selecting and disciplining judges, lawyers and police and improving links with subnational and traditional legal processes. One sees in Security Council Resolutions five basic clusters of meanings attributed to the rule of law , namely law and order, ending impunity, resolving the meta-conflict through law, protecting human rights and establishing principled governance.   [83] Transitional justice may in some circumstances complement or help achieve these rule of law ends, but equally may be of only tangential importance to others and may even hinder, obstruct or contradict some of them. Transitional justice may affirm the rule of law or strengthen it but will not create it.

To simplify grossly by adopting Berlin's fox-hedgehog metaphor, transitional justice practitioners and scholars tend to view the rule of law through the lens of a single defining idea (an almost exclusive focus on legal and non-legal responses to human rights abuses, albeit broadly understood), while rule of law practitioners are foxes who, of necessity , must know many things. [84] While the transitional justice literature has viewed its mechanisms as fundamental to the prospects for the rule of law since the divisive peace versus justice debates that characterized the field in its early days,[85] it is often treated parenthetically (or not at all) in some of the main works on peace-building and rule of law reconstruction[86] or confined to conspicuously isolated chapters of edited volumes.[87] The relatively rare peace-building or rule of law reconstruction scholars who devote serious attention to transitional justice adopt an explicitly agnostic position on the prospects for positive spill-over effect from transitional justice to domestic rule of law.[88] Rule of law reconstructors must balance a holistic approach with the imperative of prioritizing that which is fundamental over that which is desirable. Transitional states are not faced with an oversimplified dilemma of 'no rule of law without transitional justice', but instead must cope with smaller , more discrete and complex choices about whether and how the often exceptionalist, ad hoc and localized/internationalized bodies of transitional justice can interact with more permanent, sustainable and nationalized processes of reform in the justice sector. In transitional societies with a handful of justice sector personnel, widespread public hostility to the idea of law and rampant crime or disorder , a concern with selectively accounting for the crimes of an already discredited and powerless regime may in rule of law terms seem like treating a nasty knee wound while the patient suffers major organ failure. As a recent study concluded, most policy-makers and rule of law development professionals have scant awareness of international justice issues, and even many of those most aware of its presumed urgency 'question the value of devoting signifi-cant resources to integrating international justice into their work, which is already replete with its own challenges and competing priorities'. [89] Only if scholars and practitioners of transitional justice can cast off their belief in its determinative importance to the rule of law can fruitful interaction begin.

1.3 Reasons for modesty: the transitional context

A further cause for modesty is the context in which rule of law reconstruction and transitional justice take place. The states in question are ranged on a continuum of state effectiveness and performance that extends from the neglect of basic public services such as in Côte d'Ivoire or Bosnia to Somalia- or East Timor-style total collapse of governance. They include states that are best described as fragile or 'low income under stress' (LICUS)[90] and states that have collapsed (lacking any central governmental authority)[91] or are in failure (where the state is unable to perform central functions such as security, welfare or the preservation of civil freedoms).[92] One of the by-products of the state's weak capacity is its inability to establish an effective relationship with all, or a signif cant proportion, of the society it purports to govern. The present failure to govern competently may be exacerbated by recent histories of repression or war, resulting in damaged social relationships between citizen and state in what, without a minimum of external assistance, may amount to essentially unfeasible political communities. Doyle and Sambanis, for example, have noted a complex interaction between residual hostilities, diminished local capacities and modalities of international assistance after war, suggesting that international actors could focus on measures to build local institutions and capabilities where post-war hostilities between factions are low, but might address issues related to hostility through methods such as prosecutions and purges where societal groupings remain highly antagonistic.[93] Regardless of the precise characteristics of the transition, peace-builders will invariably attempt to approximate a Western model of good governance characterized by free political competition in multi-party elections, competent state administration, free markets, human rights and the rule of law. However, transition presents very diff cult environment in which to do this. Krasner describes the typical transitional peace-building ecology as follows:

> States that experience failure or poor governance more generally are beset by many problems. In such states, infrastructure deteriorates; corruption is widespread; borders are unregulated; gross domestic product is declining or stagnant; crime is rampant; and the national currency is not widely accepted. Armed groups operate within the state's boundaries but outside the control of the government. The writ of central government may not extend to the whole country; in some cases, it may not extend beyond the capital.[94]

It is at these times that the need for law, order and stability is greatest. Unfortunately, it is also at these times that the institutions of governance, the administration of justice included, have broken down. It is no exaggeration to say that weak judicial institutions are the invariable companion of fragile, failed or collapsing states on the one hand, or transitioning authoritarian regimes on the other. One must caution against assuming any common set of characteristics of rule of law breakdown, given that the concept exhibits a marked diversity of symptoms that will vary from state to state. For example, Mani presents a three-fold typology of rule of law 'states of disrepair': illegitimate but functional (core legal institutions continue to function but human rights are routinely abused), corrupt and dysfunctional (the legal system exists as a façade but is subservient to military, political or economic elites) and devastated and non-functional (where the legal system collapses after long neglect).[95] Even these loose categories will show infinite individual variation – characteristics like functionality, illegitimacy and corruption exist on a wide spectrum.

In states where the rule of law is severely impaired, the essential conditions for a fair and effective judiciary are rarely present. [96] In particular, where the state is in the developing world or emerging from colonization, institutions of justice may never have been very strong to begin with, though war and repression can have a very deleterious effect on a hitherto high-functioning rule of law system. The most obvious handicaps are of a technical or resource-related quality. The physical infrastructure of the justice system (buildings, reference materials, office space) is usually destroyed, severely impaired or historically under-developed. As O'Neill observed in Haiti in the mid-1990s:

> Haitian justice lacks everything … Courts lack even rudimentary materials necessary to do its work … [A]lthough Haitian law creates elaborate proceedings governing arrests, detentions and prison inspections and monitoring, all these procedures and protections are systematically breached.[97]

However, the greater concern is usually that of human resources. The number of judges, lawyers, prosecutors and administrators will often be very low. This may be a function of the state's poverty – there may never have been any universities or law schools to begin with. Often, the low quantity will be a consequence of the postponement of legal education during the period of war or repression. For example, even before the war in Sierra Leone, the judicial system was deeply dysfunctional. Under the Stevens and Momoh regimes, the legal system became synonymous with corruption, politicization and discrimination.[98] Publication of cases ceased in the 1970s.[99] The war exacerbated these problems. Courtrooms were destroyed, and most judges and lawyers fled after the 1997 coup.[100] By the end of the war, there were only 18 judges and 15 magistrates for a 5 million population. [101] The national Master and Registrar could not recall any judicial training in her memory.[102] The courts only functioned in Freetown. One report concluded that the judiciary 'desperately lacks almost everything a judicial system needs to deliver justice efficiently, independently and impartially'.[103] These exigencies are far from unique. In neighbouring Liberia, only three out of a paltry 130 magistrates were lawyers, while over half the justices of the peace fell short of the professional prerequisite of literacy.[104] In the years before the UN Transitional Administration in

Cambodia (UNTAC) commenced work in 1992, the state had only a dozen judges.[105] Only one-sixth of the DR Congo's courts function and employ only half the number of judges required to administer justice.[106] Authoritarianism generally tends to be less debilitating than long-term war. Though such states will rarely dismantle their justice system, illiberal rule still has a signif cant impact – Bolivia and Guatemala, for example, began their state rebuilding processes with only 90 and 30 prosecutors respectively *in situ*.[107]

Some judicial incapacity is the product of deliberate policy . The UN Transitional Administration in East T imor was presented with a situation where there was no pool of qualif ed East Timorese lawyers or judges to oper- ate the courts. Though the weakness in the justice system can be traced back to Portuguese neglect, greatest damage was done when all Indonesian or pro- autonomy judges, prosecutors, defenders and court administrators f ed the country after the referendum to avoid possible retributive violence. There were no East Timorese professionals untainted by association with the prior regime who could immediately ameliorate the human resources def cit, bar one judge who had served in the Portuguese courts and became the f rst President of the Court of Appeal. While a modest number of East T imorese had law degrees and worked for domestic NGOs or law f rms or legal organ- izations in Indonesia, Timorese lawyers were never allowed to occupy judicial or prosecutorial off ce, with the purpose of resisting their participation in the administration of justice.[108] From 1989 onwards, ethnic Albanians in Kosovo were largely excluded from the Yugoslav judicial system, though they could work as advocates. Serbian law became the law of the land, and Serbian became the off cial language of all legal proceedings and documents. Albanian law students could not get a legal education in their own language from the state and the bar exam was removed from Pristina to Belgrade. As a result of this systemic discrimination, there were only 30 ethnic Albanians out of 756 judges and prosecutors in Kosovo at the end of the conf ict.[109] The result was a mono-ethnic judiciary where those Albanians who had served were widely viewed as illegitimate.

Low capacity in these states is mostly a symptom of social, cultural and historical factors which have served to diminish the legitimacy of the judici- ary and legal professions. The national system of justice may be tainted by association with the former regime, a microcosm of the social and political divisions existent in the previous era of war or repression. This has two main consequences. Firstly, in oppressive regimes, law is subordinated to politics. Justice may have operated as an instrument of the prior rulers in vindicating and upholding persecutory and discriminatory laws, or in failing to prevent them. Emergency law may have justif ed almost all state acts, while many abuses may have occurred with clandestine impunity . Promotion of judges may have depended on subservience, corrupt patronage, complicity in crimes or loyalty to a party or junta. Previously warring groups or those aligned with the political opposition may not accept the decisions of judges who hail from a formerly antagonistic faction.[110] If judges propped up the prior regime, their decisions will have no legitimacy in the eyes of the local population. Where the judiciary operated in the narrow interests of ruling elites rather than the population as a whole, there exists no expectation that justice can be done through the courts. For example, the judiciary in Gaddaf 's Libya was strongly associated with his regime and left a legacy of human rights violations such as arbitrary detention, torture, extrajudicial execution and disappearances.[111] In the DR Congo, a number of powerful V ice-Presidents have systematically attempted 'to keep national courts weak so as to avoid prosecution'.[112] Guatemala's Historical Clarif cation Commission criticized the national judiciary's stance as a 'policy of retreat from the administration of justice'.[113] Even lawyers have legitimacy issues. Like judges, lawyers can be part of the repressive state machine and deprived of independence, while bar associations are sometimes divided on ethnic and political lines. In many states, the prosecutorial function is seen as an adjunct of the previously incumbent political regime, while less commonly the state may exercise tight control on the exercise of the defence function. In Cambodia, prosecutors and investigatory judges are subjected to political interference and physical threats by the security forces.[114]

The second main consequence is that in the aftermath of repressive regimes or war, the public may have little or no conception of what fairly administered justice means, with predictable results for public trust in the judicial system which might be manifested in an unwillingness to resolve disputes through law or to abide by it. As Teitel points out, '[w]hen it is the state that is complicit in persecution, fundamental notions of criminal justice are turned on their head: state complicity, cover-up, and other obstructions affect the very possibility of justice'.[115] In states later subject to rule of law reconstruction, law frequently means little more than discriminatory emer gency decrees or is simply unknown, while justice is the product of political distortion and contrived weakness, aff rming neither substantive human rights norms nor procedural fairness. Ideas of judicial independence are frequently anathema in illiberal rule. East Timorese citizens were unwilling to co-operate with a court system which was used as an instrument of the occupation.[116] In Kosovo, Albanian and Serbian judges mistrusted each other in a microcosm of wider antagonisms.[117] Most Serb judges had left Kosovo and those that remained were too intimidated to serve or refused to do so on nationalistic grounds.[118] In responding to Albanian exclusion, there was a further danger of 'over -correction' – of replacing one mono-ethnic judiciary with another.[119] Similarly, Burundian Hutu are suspicious of the criminal justice system because it is dominated by T utsi and historically prosecuted more Hutu individuals.[120] A cultural commitment to the rule of law may also have been undermined by security disincentives (such as the threat of violent retribution for going to court) and access disincentives (such as cost, distance, gender exclusion etc.).[121] A 2004 survey on attitudes to law and justice give striking examples of the legacy of the Indonesian court system on Timorese citizens.[122] 17 per cent of respondents said they had no association with the term 'rights',[123] while 27 per cent said they did not know what justice meant. [124] The Report found that as a result of the Indonesian administration of justice, 'East Timorese may be unclear on how a fully independent and accountable judiciary should function'.   [125] As Daniels and Trebilcock point out, the policy prescriptions entailed in overcoming these pervasive cultural barriers are nowhere near as obvious as in the case of technical or resource-related impediments.[126]

Though it is clear from the above that in many cases the rule of law has very little on which to be built, the point should not be exaggerated. For every Haiti or DR Congo, there is a Chile, a South Africa or a Hungary where the judicial system may be functioning (even if exclusionary) and credible (even if not fully trusted). The sweeping changes one sees in transitional states in the political, administrative and (less frequently) economic bases are rarely replicated in the judicial system once it retains a threshold credibility . Pointing out the endurance of colonial judicial structures in Africa, socialist legal structures in Eastern Europe and certain persistent legal arrangements in Latin America in times of turbulent political change, Schauer argues that new legal beginnings take place either not at all or much slower than economic, cultural and political change in times of political transition. [127] While courts that are devastated and non-functional present great opportunities for reform, given the technical diff culty and time it takes to train and retrain lawyers in even a quasi-functioning legal system, one should not be overly surprised to see legal systems as comparatively 'stickier' than political, cultural and economic institutions even in some of the less cataclysmic transitions. [128]

In these conditions of weak states and even weaker justice sector legacies, it is hardly surprising that the record of rule of law reconstruction is dismal. As Brinkeroff points out, post-conf ict (and, it might be argued, post-authoritarian) reconstruction faces the same diff culties as development assistance more generally, but in more diff cult circumstances.[129] The record of developing the rule of law in even the more benign conditions of development in stable countries is inauspicious – for example, the era of 'law and development' in the 1960s and 1970s which saw a glut of legal education and law reform in Africa and Latin America is lar gely deemed to have failed. [130] Though lessons have been learned, the results of reform projects disappoint consistently.[131] The Corruptions Perceptions Index has consistently found that the countries most subject to state-building activities rank among the most corrupt in the world. [132] If we take the sharp increase in post-Cold W ar rule of law reform as a base-line, a decade or more after the glut of transitions to democracy in Latin America, only three out of 18 states had positive World Bank rule of law ratings, while in 2002 only six out of 47 African countries had positive rule of law ratings.   [133] Rule of law reformers still struggle to develop effective guidelines and benchmarks for practice, while projects undertaken remain more reactive than pro-active. [134] Plainly, whether one assesses progress a decade or a quarter century after the processes began, the impact of most rule of law reconstruction programmes has been one of soaring ambition met with def ating disappointment. The primary reason for this is the complexity of the task relative to the time and resources (both domestic and international) that are available. Because the social, political and professional interconnections that form functioning legal systems everywhere may not exist in developing countries, national and international actors are attempting to f nd shortcuts in the development of institutions that, at their most developed and functional (i.e. in industrialized democracies), are highly particularized historical products born of centuries of conf ict, contestation and ref nement.[135] Most would accept 'even in the most peaceful, stable societies it is extraordinarily diff cult to translate the rule of law from abstract, idealistic notions into concrete, practical outcomes'.[136] The perspectives of any outside practitioner and scholar, the author included, can only ever have limited effectiveness and validity in environments so radically different from those they ordinarily live in.

One can readily accept, therefore, how much more diff cult rule of law reform is in the types of transitional states examined herein. T o the normal impediments such as economic underdevelopment and lack of qualif ed personnel must be added the challenges of security and governmental legitimacy which are heightened in transition. The problem of political legitimacy is one that is obvious in periods of dramatic and often violent change from one rulership to another, while security will always remain a concern bearing in mind that countries with a recent history of civil violence have a nearly 50 per cent chance of slipping back into violence within f ve years of peace.[137] Of the nearly one hundred states considered transitional in the decade after the fall of the Berlin Wall, less than twenty made a clear conversion to well-functioning democracy.[138] When one considers that the aspiration is for a self-sustaining state capacity that can endure after international support and advice are withdrawn, the diff culties appear prohibitive. Farrall is by no means unduly pessimistic when he acknowledges the task requires peace-builders to navigate between the impossible and the necessary.[139] The administration of justice 'is an area where observers of post-conf ict reforms virtually always see resistance and deeply disappointing results. From Bosnia to Afghanistan, from Palestine to Liberia, the rule of law has proven singularly diff cult to cultivate'.[140]

Nevertheless, the UN, international agencies and transitional governments themselves retain the hope or expectation that signif cant progress can be made. Much of the optimism may derive from the potential absence in liberalizing transition of the 'meagre resources/monumental aspirations' problem identif ed by Bull – the relative abundance of resources that peace-building activities guarantee for training justice system actors, building infrastructure and improving management is a signif cant cause for optimism given that lack of funding is consistently identif ed as a cause of mission failure in normal developmental contexts.[141] In cases where the transitional leadership lack political capital, the presence of international actors is believed highly conducive to progress either because of the perceived legitimacy of international law[142] or their ability to compel co-operation.[143] The potential for these actors to work productively with domestic reform constituencies like NGOs, minority groups and political parties is obvious. Nevertheless, even well-resourced missions tend to disappoint. Rule of law reconstruction in Bosnia was widely considered a failure after a decade of operations, [144] notwithstanding the fact that it enjoyed the combined attentions of the UN, EU, NATO and the OSCE, as well as more funding per capita assistance than the Marshall Aid average for Western Europe.[145] Multi-million pound justice reform efforts in Latin America by international actors consistently failed. [146] Though Kosovo at one stage enjoyed a ratio of one international actor for every 36 Kosovars,[147] its legal system has failed to cope with organized crime, ethnic violence and executive interference with the rule of law .[148] Indeed, Kosovo, together with Cambodia and East Timor have attracted arguably the most rule of law assistance since the end of the Cold War but in each case none 'were able to establish well-functioning institutions that were perceived as just, reliable and accessible', and nor were they 'adopted accordingly by the population as their preferred means of resolving disputes'. [149] The ongoing executive interference in the administration of justice in post-UNTAC Cambodia has become apparent in the travails of the Extraordinary Chambers trials of the Khmer Rouge. [150] East Timor has seen executive interference in criminal proceedings relating to the major civil disturbances in 2006 and the assassination attempts against the President and Prime Minister in 2008, [151] while a 2007 study of citizen attitudes to the legal system (so scathing that its publication was suppressed) found that 95.3 per cent rejected the idea that the justice system functions 'effectively and efficiently'.[152] International assistance may be necessary to develop the rule of law in post-conflict and post-authoritarian societies, but it is never a sufficient factor in achieving success.

The most serious impediment to rule of law reconstruction is hostility of powerful, obstructive groups in the transitional society . Projects can be de-railed either by the ongoing impact of social hostility *towards* the government which complicates the process of building peace, or it can be thwarted by the hostility *of* the government to the process. To begin with the former, it is clear that insecurity can damn the process of rule of law reconstruction to failure regardless of how much international or governmental support it enjoys.[153] There is rarely a categorical delineation between a state of conflict and a state of post-conflict. The conflict may not be fully transferred from the military to the political arena and instead continues at lower levels of intensity because the bitterness that precede transition endures, because the society may lack natural conflict dampeners to resolve disputes or because the state lacks the governmental institutions to manage the competitive pathologies of liberalization.[154] As noted above, countries with a recent history of civil violence have a nearly 50 per cent chance of slipping back into violence within five years of peace.[155]

If one looks at the travails of Iraq, Afghanistan and Libya, the conventional wisdom that the maximum chance for successful reconstruction occurs where no parties are actively attempting to topple the emerging political *modus vivendi* through force appears sound.[156] The failure to demobilize, disarm and canton the four factions in the war undermined efforts to establish law and order in Cambodia, while the crisis-driven nature of the United Nations Interim Administration Mission in Kosovo's rule of law work (i.e. persistent ethnic riots) precluded careful weighing of resources and energy.[157] Surveying the key relationship between rule of law and conf ict management, Hurwitz and Studdard ar gue the primary objective in the immediate aftermath of conf ict must be to re-establish security as a fundamental prerequisite for the successful implementation of any longer -term development strategies.[158] If the transition is chimerical, or the transitional settlement is not supported, or if DDR has not taken place amongst unreconciled military forces in the territory, the rule of law will struggle to take hold. Even if it does temporar - ily take hold, the fact that potential spoilers are not reconciled or contained can pave the way for the cycles of conf ict and intervention that have blighted attempts to (re)construct the rule of law in Haiti, East T imor, Sierra Leone and Côte d'Ivoire. Peace-building activities like rule of law reconstruction advanced far in the likes of Namibia and Croatia relative to similarly placed states because major belligerents effectively withdrew from the territory at conf ict's end,[159] while peace under -pinned by counter-productive stalemate (e.g. Mozambique) or the strong emer gence of a victor in conf ict (e.g. Sierra Leone) are both conducive to constructive work.[160] Security may be as much a matter of the mind as the body. Like all peace-building efforts, where there is no agreement on what the ultimate outcome for the polity must be, the temptation to appeal to parochial constituencies through rejection of the courts is ever present. For example, Kosovo's unresolved f nal status 'provoked local political agendas that ran counter to rule of law objectives', as did the failure in Cambodia to implement the peace settlement in the Paris Agreements.[161] When examining the impact of security, it is worth remem- bering that rule of law reconstruction is typically conceived of as a tripod of the judiciary, police and prisons, and any aspirations for progress require simultaneous reform across the institutions. Progress in the f rst element of this tripod (the only one with which this book is concerned) will be fatally undermined if the police cannot guarantee public safety or if serious criminals can routinely escape from prison. As T ondini puts it, in the absence of a secure environment, efforts to establish a functioning justice system 'are probably doomed to fail'.[162] It should be noted that peace-keeping and secu- rity sector reform usually precede rule of law reconstruction as a matter of practice.

If rule of law reconstruction is best served by security, then it follows that transition to a highly-functioning government is conducive to developing the justice sector. However, even if society as a whole is better off with good institutions, all new institutional arrangements produce people who will benef t and some whose positions of wealth, power and security will suffer . The latter can generally be depended on to assume an antagonistic position to reform.[163] The less rule of law is articulated in technical terms, the more the highly political nature of the projects becomes unmasked – it is not neutral and technocratic, but instead tends to redistribute power and may accentuate cleavages between the people exercising power and those they exercise it over. While that balance of power might change in transition from what Smiley calls a regime whose norms are bad to one whose norms are good, state institutions may not be fully insulated from social conf ict.[164] Resistance to reforms will predictably come from those who fear being made accountable for crimes committed in the past and those who fear the consolidating effect of the rule of law for the new regime in the future. Opposition may also come from those who derive benefts from corruption, cronyism, and favouritism in existing legal processes.[165] Pulver points out that while the benef ts of a functional rule of law are spread widely among the population at large, most citizens have a relatively weak personal incentive to seek improvements in the system, in contradistinction to the few powerful individuals who may have a strong incentive to oppose it.[166]

This issue of winners and losers is one that raises much concern in the literature.[167] As the euphoria that initially greeted the Orange, Rose and Cedar revolutions or the Arab spring illustrates, the ordinary intuition is that the consolidation of a liberal and democratic social order is the natural endpoint of convulsive political transition from repressive rule. However, not all democratizing transitions are led by f gures committed to the norms of liberal democracy. Transitions may be catalysed by victorious armies, external interventions, rigged elections or elections where illiberal groups win or form part of a coalition, meaning one cannot be too presumptuous about their views of principles like democracy, rule of law or human rights. Carothers, pointing out that the nearly 80 per cent of third-wave transitions neither achieved nor deepened a functioning majority, argues that most transitions are to a political 'gray zone' between liberal democracy and authoritarianism. While these 'qualif ed democracies' maintain attributes of democratic life like elections, civil society and constitutions, those elections are frequently dubious and mark the sum total of the public' s political participation, while the government disregards the law.[168] The two main manifestations of qualif ed democracy are 'dominant-power politics' (where there is genuine opposition but one political grouping dominates the system in such a way that there appears little prospect of power transfer) and 'feckless pluralism' (where politics is widely seen as a stale, corrupt, elite-dominated domain that delivers little good to the country, and remains persistently weak in the face of social and economic problems).[169] Lines between the rulership and state institutions tends to be blurry in both instances, particularly in the more common 'dominant power politics' systems which are particularly prevalent in Africa. Others note how democracy can serve as a veneer masking the use of violence to preserve one-party and one-man rule.[170] As Carothers contends, democracy promoters

> should start by assuming that what is often thought of as an uneasy,
> precarious middle ground between full-f edged democracy and outright

dictatorship is actually the most common political condition today of countries in the developing world and the postcommunist world. [171]

Opposition to reform might therefore be found in the nominally democratic executive and legislative branches of government. In strengthening the state, the rule of law inevitably imposes constraints on the personalized exercise of executive authority, which may not suit all incoming regimes ostensibly committed to democracy. The history of rule of law reconstruction is pock-marked by instances of leaderships who are rhetorically committed to the rule of law only to resile from that position when this abstract ideal takes a concrete judicial form that may curtail the executive power they longed for in opposition.[172] For example, Kleinfeld Belton suggests new executive may see a political interest in appointing unqualifed judges lacking in independence as it would reduce their potential to form an alternative power centre separate from government patronage. [173] Given that state legal institutions have a vital role in guarding against majoritarianism, a judiciary that cannot invalidate illegitimate elections or repeal unconstitutional laws may prove tempting to any government who wants 'to get things done'. For example, in ethnically-divided Bosnia, a signif cant proportion of the Government preferred a weak federal judiciary to a strong one. [174] Relatively progressive transitional governments in the likes of El Salvador and East T imor have undermined rule of law reform to protect policies like the existing economic settlements and bilateral peace processes. [175] In particular, predatory new democracies might prefer disorder and uncertainty to order and stability because a distribution of wealth based on personal connections is more conducive to corruption than bureaucratic regulation. [176] Indeed, the International Development Bank has concluded that resistance to reform is often more common than co-operation.[177] If, as Chapter 2 goes on to ar gue in far more detail, establishing a rule of law culture is fundamentally a matter of trans-forming the norms of behaviour between executive and judiciary, then where the ruling group is not amenable to respecting the autonomy of the judiciary the whole enterprise may be entirely prof tless. After a survey of rule of law assistance in Latin American and Asian states where there was no political will to pursue reform, Blair and Hansen ar gue that 'constituencies and coalitions may be so fragmented and fractious, and the political environment so inimical to judicial reform (perhaps even to the notion of ROL [rule of law]) as to eliminate any effective program activity'. [178] They advise rule of law reformers to steer clear of such ecologies and to concentrate on more propitious developing countries. Mani presents a four -fold typology of possible government attitudes to rule of law reconstruction: willing and able, willing but not able, able but not willing, and not able and not willing. [179] The f rst category presents little diff culty and international action can supply the want of ability in the second category . However, in the third and fourth categories (where the political leadership is fundamentally opposed to a functioning rule of law that can constrain its action, such as Aristide's Haiti,

Hun Sen's Cambodia, Kabila's DR Congo), the international community has consistently failed to ground the rule of law . As Chopra notes, the shallow resolve and disinterest of international or   ganizations can rarely hope to succeed against determined local opposition.[180]

1.4 Reasons for optimism: the transitional opportunity

Even if international support and resources are forthcoming, the prospects for rule of law reconstruction after conf   ict or democratization are far from healthy, especially in the grey zones of 'no peace, no war' or merely nominal democratic government. This is the reason why the ar   guments this work makes are most applicable to the relatively benign 'paradigmatic' transitions from war or peace to democratic, peaceful, rights-respecting polities that formed the basis for the f rst discussions on transitional justice. [181] Though there is a recent tendency to stretch the application of transitional justice to non-transitional contexts like ongoing war, mature democracies and authoritarian states to such an extent that its f   elds of application are potentially limitless,[182] this work accepts Schauer's warning that 'by def ning the problem [of transition] so broadly, we lose a crisp sense of what the problem is and where it has its most signif cant bite'.[183] The paradigmatic transition is where transitional justice has most bite in justice sector reform terms. There is general optimism in the literature that the time of paradigmatic transition is most conducive to successful rule of law reconstruction, in spite of the weaknesses in terms of security and governance. Observers speak of transition as the 'moment of maximum inf uence'[184] or suggest the 'best time to work is immediately after conf ict',[185] repeating the usual state-building mantra about interveners enjoying brief windows of opportunity .[186] Some of this ref ects the oft-stated belief that conditions of crisis can catalyse reform in a way that the inertia of stability cannot:

> Rule of law initiatives in societies that have   *not* gone through major conf icts or interventions inevitably proceed in piecemeal fashion, because it is hardly feasible or desirable to wholly dismantle state and civic institutions to start from scratch with 'better ones'. But in post-intervention societies, the very degree of breakdown creates unique opportunities for renewal and change ... the 'old institutions' have often collapsed, and local stakeholders may be willing, even eager, to make an entirely new start.[187]

These local stakeholders are key , but the most important of them are the incoming political leadership who enjoy suff   cient power to disrupt or develop rule of law reform. As the previous sections have ar   gued, the surrounding security and political environment is ultimately what will deter mine the success or failure of rule of law reconstruction. If, as most practitioners and writers accept, political will and a degree of receptivity to change of those in power are the fundamental prerequisites for building the rule of law, then transition to a government committed to human rights and accountability is highly propitious for rule of law reformers. [188] Most instances of rule of law reconstruction must grapple with situations where domestic demand for the rule is outweighed by opposition, a problem that exacerbates the obvious difficulty in most walks of public life that it is easier to obstruct than create. In a genuinely liberalizing transition from authoritarianism or war (what Teitel calls 'the move from less to more democratic regimes'), [189] a commitment to the rule of law does not need to be created *ab initio* because socio-political alliances committed to the creation, development and prioritization of the rule of law are predominant (if not hegemonic). The lack of reform constituencies or 'change agents' that has bedevilled so many operations in the past is greatly diminished as a salient impediment, while potential spoilers are at their weakest. [190] The institutional inertia of a judiciary with high social authority resisting change to its inherited power or influence which typically blights rule of law reconstruction will in all likelihood be greatly diminished if it is associated with a discredited prior leadership. The political economy-based impediments to implementing the rule of law are sharply limited when the *ancien régime* figures who can destabilize society and undermine public confidence in the rule of law are eclipsed by more supportive figures who may reflect a broadly representative range of domestic constituencies that define themselves by their commitment to the rule of law. While it is more than arguable that the competitiveness of democracy can be ruinous in politically developing societies, it is a more fertile ground for rule of law reconstruction than states where war, authoritarianism or the 'grey zone' between democracy and authoritarianism are dominant:

> Why do people with power accept limits to that power? ... [W]hy do politicians sometime hand over power to judges? ... Society may approximate the rule of law if they consist of a large number of power-wielding groups, comprising a majority of the population, and if none of them becomes so strong as to be able to dominate the others. [191]

This confluence of circumstances explains the book's focus on state-level institutions at a time when transitional scholarship increasingly emphasizes bottom-up projects. As Daniels and Trebilcock note, the top-down, state-centric reform strategies which so frequently fail are more likely to succeed in 'Type 1' states with broad political and popular support for rule of law reform or 'Type 2 states' with a generally reform-minded leadership who endure a less secure political base and more effective opposition from vested interests. [192] This is not to say that bottom-up rule of law activities are unwelcome in these contexts, but they should only ever constitute the *primary* aspect of rule of law reform in those 'Type 3' states run by corrupt political leadership with strong incentives for maintaining a weak rule of law.[193] These states, still wracked by authoritarianism, conflict and misrule, are not the focus of this book.

Of course, one can argue that the selection of states that f t the teleological paradigm of transitional justice as the most propitious circumstances for productive interaction between the rule of law development and transitional justice communities is self-serving and that more politically precarious states are more deserving of attention. However, the experience of the last 20 years demonstrates that without a base-line of security and political will, neither rule of law reconstruction nor transitional justice will leave much of a legacy individually, let alone together. Focusing on states where these fundamental preconditions are met avoids the mutual negative reinforcement of insecurity and illegitimate governance already canvassed. At best, domestic political good will coupled with international resources offer the possibility for radical reform as the rule of law and government mutually reinforce one another   . While the UN is content to spend millions on rule of law programmes in states it categorizes as 'major conf ict' such as Somalia, Sudan, DR Congo and Afghanistan or in constitutional dictatorships like Rwanda,[194] even the most precious gains in these areas (such as representing the illegally detained or building access to justice) are precarious, reversible and subject to the whim of leaders who can undo the work with impunity. To the extent that external actors help develop the institutions of justice in these states, it may merely serve to consolidate and legitimize unaccountable and irresponsible rule or re-open conf ict. For example, in Rwanda it is ar gued that due to the enduring politicization of the judiciary, 'it is not at all clear that investing more in the Rwandan justice system would have promoted the rule of law and encour aged reconciliation'.[195] Though Chesterman suggests it might be enough to create the space for local actors to 'start a conversation that will def   ne and redef ne their polity', a combination of a secure environment and a moderate amount of political will should allow for greater ambition to accelerate a generational shift in cultural attitudes towards justice. [196] More sustainable legacies can be achieved in a prosecutorial process which encapsulates the fair trial norms the new government wishes to inculcate, in a truth commission that not only speaks truth *to* power but which speaks truth *with* that power or in customary/traditional justice mechanisms that assertively share jurisdiction with the state rather than jealously guard it. Only where the opportunity for progress coincides with domestic will and stability can policy-makers be conf dent they may seek effective humanitarian ends without sustaining an unjust legal order. Concededly, it is hard to identify genuinely liberal democratic transitions – at various points, it has appeared that the likes of Laurent Gbagbo, Mohamed Morsi and Boris Y eltsin were helming governments ostensibly committed to these principles. Pin-pointing neatly on a timetable the stage when genuinely rule of law-based government is consolidated is often a fool's errand.

These contexts, though relatively rare, are hardly idealized. As V   illa-Vicencio puts it, 'a transitional society is by def   nition located between an illegitimate past and a future shaped by a set of ideals to which it aspires – without all such aspirations necessarily being immediately realizable'. [197]

Behaviour can only change over time. It is wise therefore not to adopt too panacean a view of what peace-builders can achieve – transition alone does not guarantee rule of law reform will be a priority and projects in the f eld will be hostage to many fortunes (most notably those of available resources) and may not be able to respond to the multiple demands made of it. Unintended consequences should be expected amidst the interplay of the contingent and the unforeseen, while positive consequences are reversible. Ultimately, the legacy may be less the creation of the perfect rule of law than merely avoiding anarchy or minimizing conf ict in society. It should of course be pointed out that even the most successful interaction of rule of law reconstruction with transitional justice will be overshadowed by successful constitutional reform that respects rights, guarantees remedies for breach of the law, empowers an independent judiciary, def nes the powers of the executive and outlaws discrimination. However , even a constitution may only afford paper-thin protection if a government is f rmly intent on disregarding it. A good constitution on paper is not the equivalent of a constitutional order . The strongest normative regimes are those backed up with legitimate, functioning institutions. Any progress in terms of the rule of law can be undone if measures are not taken to address socio-economic questions – education, food and health will have a bigger impact on the success of transition than judicial reform. The sectoral isolation of the rule of law from the range of development projects and reform projects should be avoided. Finally , it should be remembered that successful rule of law reconstruction is measured incrementally in decades or generations.[198]

1.5 Organization of the book

Of course, understanding transitional justice' s modest place in rule of law reconstruction as a prelude to mutually-reinforcing practice does not take us far into understanding how an improved practice can be realized. Because of the aforementioned failure to study the implications of transitional justice for the wider process of rule of law reconstruction, the full potential of accountability proceedings to ground cultural, normative and institutional reform in the administration of justice has not been met. As Stromseth, W ippman and Brooks argue,

> [W]e are relatively early in the process of understanding the longer-term impacts of accountability processes – such as criminal prosecutions, truth commissions, reconciliation proceedings, vetting – in different postconf ict societies … more systematic thinking and empirical research on the impact of accountability proceedings in specifc post-conf ict societies is a critical need.[199]

This book can be understood as a contribution to the empirical research vacuum. It argues that a wide gap has emer ged between how actors in both

transitional justice and rule of law construction view the rule of law , which
has had a regrettable impact on practice. The book does not favour the
perspective of one sector over the other , but rather tries to identify the
strengths and weaknesses of both approaches. The purpose is to explain how
theorists and policy-makers can use insights from both felds to assess existing
practice and to propose solutions for better integration of the two perspectives, preferring to identify what is achievable with available resources in an
allotted time frame than seeking perfect solutions. Though pragmatic, the
book's contribution is nevertheless more theoretical than operational – given
the marked diversity of transitional states along the lines of development,
the nature of the prior conf ict, human resources, stability and politico-
historical background, one must caution against the search for uniformly
applicable answers one sees in some of the 'how-to' books in the literature.
It attempts to couple analytical insight with sober pragmatism in introducing, synopsizing and contextualizing the key issues in the nexus between
transitional justice and rule of law reconstruction. There is no claim here that
this book submits anything like a complete prescriptive agenda, but it does
represent an initial attempt to propose a tentative framework for approaching
reform or resolving conf icts of interest. At a time when increased profession-
alization of transitional justice risks templatization and convergence of available models,[200] there is much to be gained from drawing attention to one of
the biggest blind-spots in the f eld.

Finally it is necessary to outline two caveats, the f rst pragmatic and the
second philosophical. As to the f rst, the book is organized thematically rather
than through specif c country case-studies, but it integrates lessons and experience from states like East T imor, Cambodia, Sierra Leone, Kosovo, Haiti,
Bosnia, Liberia, the DR Congo, El Salvador, Libya, Kenya and Rwanda which
have effectively served as laboratories for the simultaneous interaction of rule
of law reconstruction and transitional justice. Chapter 2 examines the indeteɛ
minate nature of the rule of law and how this frequently leads to the conf ation
of it with values such as human rights, democracy and justice. It demonstrates
how the concept of the rule of law has developed in peace-building discourse
as a programme of institutions, culture and norms, and sketches obvious areas
of convergence and clash with transitional justice. In contrast to this programmatic understanding of the rule of law in peace-building, Chapter 3 illustrates
how a distinctly transitional rule of law is presented as a progressist narrative
in transitional justice discourse which serves to legitimize departures from the
institutions, values and norms that underpin the reconstructing justice sector.
Rejecting the existence of a contingent transitional rule of law and ar guing
that the potential benef ts of transitional justice are exaggerated, it ur ges a
rebalancing of transitional justice mechanisms against the demands of rule of
law reconstruction and recommends that a more clear-eyed vision of costs and
benef ts, risks and opportunities in this regard is required. Chapter 4 examines
how the profound objectives of transitional trial (retribution, deterrence,
reconciliation, political expressivism) have operated to turn transitional trial

into an imbalanced, punitive model that eschews exemplary due process. Questioning whether these aspirations can ever be achieved in the radically imperfect conditions of transition, it ar gues for a more pragmatic approach that elevates judicial process over political product. Chapter 5 examines the consistent failure of international criminal justice to catalyse, interact with or promote domestic justice sector reform, laying the blame at the feet of a preoccupation with achieving a global rule of law instead of the more mundane task of fostering it domestically . Chapter 6 examines how the valorization of traditional justice mechanisms as inherently restorative, bottom-up sites of resistance to the state in transitional justice conf icts with the emphasis of rule of law reconstructors on employing customary law to plug rule of law gaps, facilitating state oversight and integrating these subnational structures with the formal justice system. It concludes with a brief chapter summarizing the lessons learned.

Given that this book is primarily concerned with one of transitional justice's blind-spots, it is as well to begin by acknowledging the author' s own. Because depth is preferred to breadth, space necessarily precludes all but the most cursory examination of a number of salient issues such as the needs of victims, gender issues and the panoply of legislative, policing and custodial programmes required to ground the wider rule of law in post-confict/authoritarian environments. Because the book deals with states where transitional justice has occurred extensively, the issue of political calculation in limiting punishment is not examined. Prosecutorial selectivity , which above all else blurs the line between the rule of law and political judgment, is not examined. The issue of judicial lustration is highly relevant to the books' focus, but notwithstanding numerous casual references in the literature to judicial reform as a form of transitional justice (itself indicative of the sort of conceptual conf ation of the two this book explores), [201] it has occurred too infrequently to yield generalizable lessons. T ruth commissions are the one area where practical questions of rule of law reconstruction have been well-aired, most notably in relation to amnesty and the circumvention of the courts. As the literature is voluminous in this regard, an editorial decision has been made to forgo an exploration of this area in the interests of more fully developing more neglected subjects. One gets the sense in much of the recent transitional justice literature that any research in the f eld that is not primarily focused on the everyday , the restorative or the community-level is irredeemably f awed, but rule of law reconstruction is generally an elite-driven, state-level phenomenon – cognisance is taken, however, of attempts to relate its programmes to ordinary lives, especially in Chapter 6 which examines traditional justice and the 'from-below' perspective. T ransitional justice has commendably expanded beyond the legal aspects of past violations in specif c cases to look at the underlying social and economic root causes that underlie them and actively promote systemic social change. This book is less holistic – development and redistribution are not specif c foci of the work, though it does f nd highly compelling the arguments of Alexander and de Greiff to the effect that improving levels of access to justice and rebuilding civic trust in its institutions can serve as an effective means of improving the prospects for socio-economic rights as justified claims.[202] The role of civil society groups as transitional activists and rule of law reform partners is under-explored. Similarly, the obvious paradox that those involved in transitional justice and rule of law promotion frequently operate unaccountably outside the national legal system itself is examined only parenthetically.[203] Finally, considerations of space preclude addressing the generic organizational failings of rule of law reconstruction missions such as the need for mission coherence, exit strategies, pursuit of identifable deliverables, consultation, partnership, accountability, identifying the best local interlocutors etc. Solutions to these issues outlined in the literature, most notably in the UN Secretary-General's *Rule of Law and Transitional Justice Report*, are endorsed, even if frequently they are so general and obvious as to be meaningless.

As to the more philosophical caveats, it is necessary to engage briefy with two criticisms frequently levelled at transitional justice that may with some validity apply to this work, namely that it is legalist (defned by Judith Shklar as 'the ethical attitude that holds moral conduct to be a matter of rule following, and moral relationships to consist of duties and rights determined by rules')[204] and statist (the theory or practice of concentrating political power in the state, resulting in a weak position for the individual or community with respect to the government). To begin with the former, the allure of legalism lies in the faith that the government of the social world of human interaction by the mechanical and zealous application of law is inherently superior to 'the sordid squabbles of political and social intercourse'.[205] Global liberalism privileges the growing legalization of international and domestic relations, as evidenced by the elevation of legal over political solutions in international criminal tribunals, soft law on domestic accountability and positivist trends in transitional justice scholarship. This legalism has been increasingly criticized in the literature[206] in terms with which this book is in broad agreement, i.e. that the liberal-legalist paradigm has prioritized violations of civil and political rights over issues of socio-economic inequality, the insistence that trials *must* always take place jeopardizes peace, the emphasis on formalist legalist responses misrepresents war or authoritarianism as the acts of a handful of individuals, attenuates the complexities of life in these societies, and marginalizes useful restorative and bottom-up approaches. It is hard to quibble with McEvoy's position that legalism generally forecloses questions from other complementary disciplines and perspectives,[207] though it should be pointed out these charges carry less weight in this 'do everything, engage everyone' era.

Where this book departs from McEvoy's argument is in relation to the domestic rule of law. While he suggests that the growth of rule of law promotion in transitional state criminal justice systems exemplifes the dominance of legalism, it is in fact a victim of it.[208] Domestic rule of law reconstruction is one of those complementary disciplines ignored in transitional justice.

The latter is above all def ned by its lar gely ad hoc, temporary , non-state innovations like truth commissions and international criminal tribunals, which are often treated as synonymous with transitional justice.[209] Institutions like domestic courts, where opportunities for innovation or participation by international actors are limited, are overlooked and neglected in the literature. Some surveys of the performance of contemporary transitional justice mechanisms ignore national trial processes completely.[210] A good example of this trend is Rwanda' s experience of transitional justice, which is usually presented as a dichotomized choice between local   *gacaca* and the global ICTR.[211] The domestic criminal trial process for genocide offences were of central importance to the development of the national rule of law, but analysis was drowned out completely by the inf nitely larger literatures on the more glamorous innovations in Arusha and at village level.   [212] Ethiopia's purely domestic Red Terror trials are the most vigorous example of criminal accountability for past atrocity in action since transitional justice was mainstreamed, but has attracted a paltry literature.[213] That these trials were highly politicized and departed radically from rule of law standards should make study of them more imperative, not less. Chapters 5 and 6 examine how the dominant modes of analysis in international criminal justice (from above) and traditional/customary justice ('from below') exist in splendid isolation from ongoing processes of justice sector reconstruction. Even where domestic criminal processes are examined, Chapter 4 demonstrates that the particularly ambitious variant of legalism one sees in transitional criminal trial that pursues political-utilitarian goals like modifying behaviour, political signalling and improving social equilibrium often does so at the expense of the types of exemplary criminal process rule of law reformers would hope to inculcate. While this book agrees with McEvoy on the need for an honest acknowledgment of the limits of legal thinking, it also highlights how limited (or superf cial) this legal thinking tends to be in transitional justice discourse – perhaps paradoxically , if transitional justice needs to become thicker than its current legalist emphasis, perspectives from justice sector reform should form an integral part of the project. [214]

The statist critique of transitional justice is one that f ows from legalism, i.e. that it conduces to an understanding of transitional justice that is too institutionalized, state-centric or 'top-down', resulting in the needs of the state trumping those of individuals or communities. [215] There is some merit in this critique – state-level trials and truth commissions generally fail to engage with messy, on-the-ground realities that f ow from the state's overall social structure for the reasons described above in relation to legalism. At times, they instrumentalize the pain of victims and even re-traumatize them. Others argue that discourse in the area serves to substitute an emancipatory politics founded on active citizenship for a statist politics of passive disempowerment reliant on state delivery.[216] This stance may f ow from the role of NGOs, who often def ne themselves in opposition to the state, while the international human rights community has historically seen the sovereign

state as its enemy .[217] Some suggest the disjunction that has developed
between transitional justice and the various forms of development like the
rule of law have emer ged because the latter employ massive and anonymous
policies directed at the whole population, while the institutions transitional
justice deploys have a narrower focus on identif able individuals or communities.[218] Nevertheless, a book that examines rule of law reconstruction must,
by def nition, focus on state-level processes. Rule of law reconstruction adopts
a 'lack' perspective, in that the state lacks proper laws and institutions and
therefore requires state institutions and normative frameworks to restrain the
exercise of government power, to def ne and enforce the criminal law and to
make the state more effective in providing public goods. [219] Gray argues that
'[t]he rules in the rule of law are the minimum standards necessary to achieve
an ordered society',[220] but there is also a more facilitative dimension to law in
that it enables people to co-operate by embodying collective goals in a corpus
of rules, principles and policies. [221] This work concurs with Ignatieff that
looking forward to an era beyond state sovereignty is unhelpfully utopian and
that a state whose power is restrained by the rule of law remains the best
guarantee of human rights. [222] Transitional justice concentrates on systemic
violations and therefore requires systemic solutions, even if one should not
'see like the state' exclusively. It will have its widest benef t where it complements simultaneous processes of nation-building. The state is no less impor -
tant a stakeholder in transitional justice than victims and perpetrators.
However, in transitional justice discourse the domain of state institutions is
'normally consigned to the wish-list of potential outcomes (via truth commission recommendations, for example) rather than being seen as a necessary
enabling environment'.[223] None of this is to argue transitional justice should
be unidirectional, that the legal culture of the state will not ref ect certain
elite values, that a market economy should follow from state reconstruction
or that non-state justice mechanisms do not have an important role to play .

Notes

1 In some of the states examined in this book, it may be more accurate to say that a
  national rule of law is being constructed *ab initio*, as opposed to being re-constructed.
  However, 'rule of law reconstruction' or 'rule of law reform' are employed in the
  literature in both eventualities, and this is the terminology adopted here.
2 Z. Miller, 'Effects of Invisibility: The Search of the "Economic" in T ransitional
  Justice' (2008) 2 *International Journal of Transitional Justice* 226, 271.
3 N. Kritz, 'Policy Implications of Empirical Research on Transitional Justice' in H.
  van der Merwe, V. Baxter and A. Chapman (eds.), *Assessing the Impact of Transitional
  Justice: Challenges for Empirical Research* (Washington, D.C.: USIP Press, 2009), 13
  at 14.
4 B. Oomen, 'Donor-Driven Justice and its Discontents' (2005) 36 *Development and
  Change* 887.
  5 J. Subotic, 'The Transformation of International Transitional Justice Advocacy'
  (2012)6 *International Journal of Transitional Justice* 106, 110.

6 J. Boli and G. Thomas, 'INGOs and the Oganization of World Culture' in J. Boli and G. Thomas (eds.), *Constructing World Culture: International Nongovernmental Organizations Since 1875* (Stanford: Stanford University Press, 1999), 13.

7 Subotic, supra n5, 112.

8 W Lambourne, 'Transitional Justice and Peace-building After Mass Violence' (2009)3 *International Journal of Transitional Justice* 28, 35.

9 K. McEvoy, 'Beyond Legalism: Towards a Thicker Understanding of Transitional Justice' (2007) 34 *Journal of Law and Society* 411, 433.

10 P. Arthur, 'How "Transitions" Reshaped Human Rights: A Conceptual History of Transitional Justice' (2009) 31 *Human Rights Quarterly* 321.

11 On the role of conferences, see generally Arthur , ibid., and D. Orentlicher , '"Settling Accounts" Revisited: Reconciling Global Norms with Local Agency' (2007) 1 *International Journal of Transitional Justice* 10, 12.

12 E. Lutz and K. Sikkink, 'The Justice Cascade: The Evolution and Impact of Foreign Human Rights Trials in Latin America' (2001) 2 *Chicago Journal of International Law* 1 and K. Sikkink and C. Booth W alling, 'The Impact of Human Rights Trials in Latin America' (2007) 44 *Journal of Peace Research* 427.

13 Lutz and Sikkink, ibid., 4.

14 K. Sikkink, *The Justice Cascade: How Human Rights Prosecutions are Changing World Politics* (New York: W.W. Norton & Co., 2011), 96–128.

15 T Olsen, L. Payne and A. Reiter, *Transitional Justice in Balance: Comparing Processes, Weighing Efficacy* (Washington, D.C.: U.S. Institute of Peace, 2010), 99–104.

16 Ibid, 99–104.

17 L. Mallinder, *Amnesty, Human Rights and Political Transitions: Bridging the Peace and Justice Divide* (London: Hart Publishing, 2008), 26 and 27.

18 Olsen, Payne and Reiter, supra n15, 54–55 and 117.

19 R. Wilson, 'Justice and Legitimacy in the South African T ransition' in A.B. de Brito, C. González-Enríquez and P . Aguilar (eds.), *The Politics of Memory: Transitional Justice in Democratizing Societies* (Oxford, New York: Oxford University Press, 2001), 190 at 198.

20 Y Beigbeder, *Judging War Criminals: The Politics of International Justice* (New York: St Martin's Press, 2000), 171.

21 Wilson, supra n19, 216.

22 Miller, supra n2, 271–272.

23 A.B. de Brito et al., 'Conclusions' in de Brito et al. (eds.), supra n19, 303 at 308.

24 P Gready, 'Reconceptualising Transitional Justice: Embedded and Distanced Justice' (2005) 5 *Conflict, Security and Development* 3, 7.

25 K. McEvoy and A. Eriksson, 'Restorative Justice in T ransition: Ownership, Leadership, and "Bottom-Up" Human Rights' in D. Sullivan and L. T ifft (eds.), *Handbook of Restorative Justice: A Global Perspective* (London, New York: Routledge, 2006), 321.

26 Off ce of the United Nations High Commissioner for Human Rights, 'Rule of Law T ools for Post-Conf ict States: T ruth Commissions' (2008) HR/PUB/ 06/1.

27 D. Gray, 'An Excuse-Centred Approach to Transitional Justice' (2005 –06) 74 *Fordham Law Review* 2621, 2688 and N. Roht-Arriaza, 'The New Landscape of Transitional Justice' in N. Roht-Arriaza and J. Mariezcurrena (eds.), *Transitional Justice in the Twenty-First Century: Beyond Truth Versus Justice* (New York: Cambridge University Press, 2006), 1 at 3.

28 UNSecretary-General, *The Rule of Law and Transitional Justice in Conflict and Post-Conflict Societies* (2004) UN Doc. S/2004/616.

29   Mostnotably the *Basic Principles and Guidelines on the Right to a Remedy and Reparation for Victims of Gross Violations of International Human Rights Law and Serious Violations of International Humanitarian Law* UN Doc. A/RES/60/147 (2005) and the *Updated Set of Principles for the Protection and Promotion of Human Rights Through Action to Combat Impunity*, UN Doc. E/CN.4/2005/102/Add.1, 8 February 2005.

30   E. Mobekk, *Transitional Justice and Security Sector Reform: Enabling Sustainable Peace* (Geneva: Geneva Centre for the Democratic Control of Armed Forces, 2006), 6. See generally A. Cutter, P. de Greiff and L. Waldorf (eds.), *Disarming the Past: Transitional Justice and Ex-Combatants* (New York: Social Science Research Council, 2009).

31 Seegenerally S. Buckley-Zistel and R. Stanley (eds.), *Gender in Transitional Justice* (London: Palgrave Macmillan, 2011), F Ní Aoláin, 'Political Violence and Gender in Times of Transition' (2006) 15 *Columbia Journal of Gender and Law* 829 and the special issue on gender and transitional justice in (2007) 1 *International Journal of Transitional Justice* 315.

32 P. de Greiff, 'Theorizing T ransitional Justice' in M. W illiams, R. Nagy and J. Elster (eds.), *Transitional Justice* (New York: New York University Press, 2012), 31 at 53.

33 M. Ndulo and R. Duthie, 'The Role of Judicial Reform in Development and Transitional Justice', in P. de Greiff and R. Duthie (eds.), *Transitional Justice and Development: Making Connections* (New York: Social Science Research Council, 2009), 250 at 263.

34 International Center for Transitional Justice, 'Meeting Summary of the Retreat on "Complementarity after Kampala: The Way Forward"' (2010), available < http://ictj.org/sites/default/files/ICTJ-Global-Complementarity-Greentree-2010-English.pdf>, 1.

35 A. de Brito et al., 'Introduction' in de Brito, González-Enríquez and Aguilar (eds.), supra n19, 1 at 32.

36 T. Abdulhak, 'Building Sustainable Capacities – From an International T ribunal to a Domestic W ar Crimes Chamber for Bosnia and Herzegovina' (2010) 9 *International Criminal Law Review* 333.

37 E. Witte, *International Crimes, Local Justice: A Handbook for Rule-of-Law Policymakers, Donors and Implementers* (New York: Open Society Justice Initiative, 2011), 29.

38 Kritz, supra n3, 16.

39 Witte, supra n37, 21.

40 C. Bjork and J. Goebertus, 'Complementarity in Action: The Role of Civil Society and the ICC in Rule of Law Strengthening in Kenya' (2011) 14 *Yale Human Rights and Development Law Journal* 205, 218.

41 C.L. Sriram, O. Martin-Ortega and J. Herman , 'Just Peace? Lessons Learned and Policy Insights' in C.L. Sriram, O. Martin-Ortega and J. Herman (eds.), *Peacebuilding and Rule of Law in Africa* (Oxford: Routledge, 2011), 197 at 198.

42 W.W. Burke-White, 'The Domestic Inf uence of International Criminal Tribunals: The International Criminal Tribunal for the Former Yugoslavia and the Creation of the State Court of Bosnia & Herzegovina' (2008) 46 *Columbia Journal of Transnational Law* 279, 281, Ndulo and Duthie, supra n33, 265.

43 R. Kerr and E. Mobekk, *Peace & Justice: Seeking Accountability After War* (Cambridge: Polity Press, 2007), 124.

44Mobekk,supra n30, 29.

45 Ndulo and Duthie, supra n33, 265. They counsel caution over this f   gure in footnote 71.

46 C. Call, 'Introduction: What W e Know and Don' t Know about Postconf ict Justice and Security Reform' in C. Call (ed.), *Constructing Justice and Security After War* (Washington, D.C.: United States Institute of Peace, 2007), 3 at 3–4.

47E.Posner and A. Vermeule, 'Transitional Justice as Ordinary Justice' (2004) 117 *Harvard Law Review* 762, 801.

48Ibid.

49 P. van Zyl, 'Dilemmas of T   ransitional Justice: The Case of South Africa'   s Truth and Reconciliation Commission' (1999) 52 *Journal of International Affairs* 647, 652.

50J.Stromseth, M. Wippman and R. Brooks, *Can Might Make Rights? Building the Rule of Law After Military Interventions* (Cambridge: Cambridge University Press, 2006), 253.

51Ibid.

52Call,supra n46, 13–14.

53R. Wilson, 'The *Sizwe* Will Not Go A way: The T ruth and Reconciliation Commission, Human Rights, and Nation-Building in South Africa' (1996) 55 *African Studies* 14, 20.

54P van Zyl, 'Promoting Transitional Justice in Post-Conf ict Societies' in A. Bryden and H. Hanggi (eds.), *Security Governance in Post-Conflict Peacebuilding* (Geneva: Centre for the Democratic Control of Armed Forces, 2005), 209 at 210 and Lambourne, supra n8, 29.

55Kritz,supra n3, 16.

56 W. Channell, 'Lessons Not Learned About Legal Reform' in T . Carothers (ed.), *Promoting the Rule of Law Abroad: In Search of Knowledge* (Washington, D.C.: Carnegie Endowment for International Peace, 2006), 137 at 138 and 143, UN Secretary-General, supra n28, para. 58.

57 R. Pulver, 'Rule of Law, Peacekeeping and the United Nations' in Sriram, Martin-Ortega and Herman (eds.), supra n41, 60 at 72.

58A.Potter, *The Rule of Law as the Measure of Peace? Responsive Policy for Reconstructing Justice and the Rule of Law in Post Conflict and Transitional Environments* (Geneva: Centre for Humanitarian Dialogue, 2004), 15.

59The Conflict, Security and Development Group, *A Review of Peace Operations: A Case for Change* (London: Kings College, 2003), 12 and 36.

60R. Sannerholm, *Rule of Law after War and Crisis: Ideologies, Norms and Methods* (Cambridge: Intersentia, 2012), 3–4.

61Witte, supra n37, 30 and 35.

62 ICTJ, UNDP, Ministries of Foreign Affairs of Denmark and South Africa, 'Supporting Complementarity at the National Level: An Integrated Approach to Rule of Law' (2011), available <   http://www.ictj.org/sites/default/f les/ICTJ-Global-Greentree-Two-Synthesis-Report-2011.pdf>, 3. They note there were more interactions between them over time.

63UNSecretary-General, *Uniting Our Strengths: Enhancing UN Support for the Rule of Law*, UN Doc. A/61/636-S/2006/980 of 14 December 2006, paragraph 38 et seq.

64 Among the more positive assessments of transitional justice in this regard are R. Teitel, *Transitional Justice* (Oxford: Oxford University Press, 2001), Roht-Arriaza and Mariezcurrena (eds.), supra n27, M. Aukerman, 'Extraordinary Evil,

Ordinary Crimes: A Framework for Understanding T ransitional Justice' (2002) 15 *Harvard Human Rights Journal* 39, R. Lipscomb, 'Restructuring the ICC Framework to Advance T ransitional Justice: A Search for a Permanent Solution in Sudan' (2006) 106 *Columbia Law Review* 182, J. Malamud-Goti, 'Transitional Government in the Breach: Why Punish State Criminals?' (1990) 12   *Human Rights Quarterly* 1.

65 Sannerholm, supra n60, 47.

66 Subotic, supra n5, 118.

67 UN Secretary-General, supra n28 and *The Rule of Law and Transitional Justice in Conflict and Post-Conflict Societies* (2011) UN Doc. S/2011/634 of 12 October 2011.

68 In 2003, the Off ce of the High Commissioner for Human Rights, as the United Nations focal point for coordinating system-wide attention for human rights, democracy and the rule of law, began to develop rule-of-law tools (policy documents) so as to ensure sustainable, long-term institutional capacity within UN missions to respond to these demands. The tools outline the rule of law implications for a number of transitional justice initiatives.

69 Supran50, esp. 178–347.

70 C. Call, 'Conclusion: Constructing Justice and Security After W ar' in Call (ed.), supra n46, 375 at 398.

71 Kerr and Mobekk, supra n43, 108 and 173.

72 M.C. Bassiouni, 'Perspectives on International Criminal Justice' (2010) 50 *Virginia Journal of International Law* 269, 275.

73 R. Post and C. Hesse, 'Introduction' in R. Post and C. Hesse (eds.), *Human Rights in Political Transitions: Gettysburg to Bosnia* (New York: Zone Books, 1999), 13 at 18.

74 Exceptions include E. Bayliss, *'Reassessing the Role of International Criminal Law: Rebuilding National Courts Through Transnational Networks'* (2009) 50 *Boston College Law Review* 1, J. Stromseth, 'Pursuing Accountability for Atrocities After Confct: What Impact on Building the Rule of Law?' (2007) 38   *Georgetown* Journal of International Law 251, P. McAuliffe, 'Transitional Justice and the Rule of Law: The Perfect Couple or Awkward Bedfellows?' (2010) *2 Hague Journal on the Rule of Law* 110.

75 E.g. L. Kgalema and P. Gready, *Transformation of the Magistracy: Balancing Independence and Accountability in the New Democratic Order* (Johannesburg: Centre for the Study of V iolence and Reconciliation, 2000) and Human Rights Center UC Berkeley & Centre for Human Rights, University of Sarajevo, 'Justice, Accountability and Social Reconstruction: An Interview Study of Bosnian Judges and Prosecutors' (2000) 18 *Berkeley Journal of International Law* 102.

76 Stromseth, supra n74, 256.

77 L. Fletcher and H. W einstein, 'Violence and Social Repair: Rethinking the Contribution of Justice to Reconciliation' (2002) 24 *Human Rights Quarterly* 573, 601.

78 J. Matthews, 'Foreword' in Carothers (ed.), supra n56, vii at vii.

79 D. Brinkerhoff, 'Rebuilding Governance in Failed States and Post-Confict Societies: Core Concepts and Cross-Cutting Themes' (2005) 25   *Public Administration and Development* 3, 9.

80 J. Bush, 'Nuremberg: The Modern Law of W ar and Its Limitations' (1993) 93 *Columbia Law Review* 2022, 2070.

81 G. Thallinger, 'The UN Peacebuilding Commission and Transitional Justice' (2007) 8 *German Law Journal* 682, 695.

82 E.g. J. Hamre and G. Sullivan, 'Toward Post-Conf ict Reconstruction' (2002) 25 *Washington Quarterly* 85, 91, C. Bull, *No Entry Without Strategy: Building the Rule of Law Under UN Transitional Administration* (New York: United Nations University Press, 2008), 69.

83 J. Farrall, 'Impossible Expectations? The UN Security Council's Promotion of the Rule of Law after Conf ict' in B. Bowden, H. Charlesworth and J. Farrall (eds.), *The Role of International Law in Rebuilding Societies after Conflict: Great Expectations* (New York: Cambridge University Press, 2009), 134 at 144–145.

84 The metaphor is taken from a fragment of a poem by the ancient Greek poet Archilochus. In the poem, Archilochus implies (a) that the hedgehog' s trick is superior to the fox's many tricks, and (b) that the hedgehog' s trick may actually defeat the fox. This book makes no claim as to which approach is superior.

85 A.J. McAdams (ed.), *Transitional Justice and the Rule of Law in New Democracies* (Notre Dame, London: University of Notre Dame Press, 1997), Teitel, supra n64, M. Minow, *Between Vengeance and Forgiveness: Facing History After Genocide and Mass Violence* (Boston: Beacon Press, 1998).

86 M. Trebilcock and R. Daniels, *Rule of Law Reform and Development: Charting the Fragile Path of Progress* (Cheltenham: Edward Elgar, 2008), Carothers (ed.), supra n56, D. Isser (ed.), *Customary Justice and the Rule of Law in War-Torn Societies* (Washington, D.C.: USIP, 2011), Sannerholm, supra n60.

87 E.g. A. Boraine, 'T ransitional Justice' in S. Chesterman, M. Ignatieff, and R. Thakur (eds.), *Making States Work: State Failure and the Crisis of Governance* (New York: United Nations University Press, 2005), 318 or P. Clark, 'Grappling in the Great Lakes: The Challenges of International Justice in Rwanda, the Democratic Republic of Congo and Uganda' in Bowden, Charlesworth and Farrall (eds.), supra n83, 244.

88 Stromseth, Wippman and Brooks, supra n50, especially at 253 and Call (ed.), supra n46, throughout.

89 Witte, supra n37, 21.

90 S. Hameiri, 'Failed State or a Failed Paradigm? State Capacity and the Limits of Institutionalism' (2007) 10 *Journal of International Relations and Development* 122, 127.

91 A. Yannis, 'State Collapse and its Implications for Peace-building and Reconstruction' (2002) 33 *Development and Change* 817, 821–822.

92 R. Gordon, 'Saving Failed States: Sometimes a Neocolonialist Notion' (1997) 12 *American University Journal of International Law and Policy* 903 has criticized the notion of the failed state for its essentialist use of language, the dichotomy it establishes between 'successful' and 'failed' states and the way it condemns people for the failings of their own elites. Nonetheless, for want of a better phrase, it is used here.

93 M. Doyle and N. Sambanis, *Making War and Building Peace: United Nations Peace Operations* (Princeton: Princeton University Press, 2006).

94 S. Krasner, 'Sharing Sovereignty: New Institutions for Collapsed and Failing States' (2004) 29 *International Security* 85, 91–92.

95 R. Mani, *Beyond Retribution – Seeking Justice in the Shadows of War* (Cambridge: Polity Press, 2002), 72–73.

96 Any number of def nitions or lists of what are necessary can be drawn up, but Ratner and Abrams' summary is concise and thorough. The conditions necessary are '[A] workable legal framework through well-crafted statutes of criminal law and procedure; a trained cadre of judges, prosecutors, defenders, and investigators; adequate infrastructure, such as courtroom facilities, investigative offces, record-keeping capabilities, and detention and prison facilities; and, most important, a culture of respect for the fairness and impartiality of the process and the rights of the accused.' S. Ratner and J. Abrams, *Accountability for Human Rights Atrocities in Human Rights Law: Beyond the Nuremberg Legacy* (New York: Oxford University Press, 1997), 22–23.

97 W O'Neill, *No Greater Priority: Judicial Reform in Haiti* (New York: National Coalition for Human Rights, 1995), 1 and 4.

98 N. Thompson, 'In Pursuit of Justice: A Report on the Judiciary in Sierra Leone' (2002) Commonwealth Human Rights Initiative and Sierra Leone Bar Association, available <http://www.humanrightsinitiative.org/publications/ffm/sierra_leone_report.pdf>, 5.

99 N. Fritz and A. Smith, 'Current Apathy for Coming Anarchy: Building the Special Court for Sierra Leone' (2001) 25 *Fordham International Law Journal* 391, 410.

100 L. Juma, 'The Human Rights Approach to Peace in Sierra Leone: The Analysis of the Peace Process and Human Rights Enforcement in a Civil W ar Situation' (2002) 30 *Denver Journal of International Law and Policy* 325, 346.

101 Z.Bangura, *Sierra Leone: Ordinary Courts and the Special Court* (New York: Open Society Justice Initiative, 2004), 55.

102 Thompson,supra n98, 13.

103 International Commission of Jurists, 'Attacks on Justice – 11th edition' available <http://www.icj.org/IMG/pdf/sierraleone.pdf>, 324.

104 International Crisis Group, 'Liberia: Resurrecting the Justice System' (2006), available <http://www.crisisgroup.org/ /media/Files/africa/west-africa/liberia/Liberia%20Resurrecting%20the%20Justice%20System.pdf>, 1.

105 Bull,supra n82, 74.

106 M. Tondini, *Statebuilding and Justice Reform: Post-Conflict Reconstruction in Afghanistan* (London: Routledge, 2010), 28.

107 L. Bhansali and C. Biebesheimer , 'Measuring the Impact of Criminal Justice Reform in Latin America' in Carothers (ed.), supra n56, 301 at 317.

108 W. Hayde, 'Ideals and Realities of the Rule of Law and Administration of Justice in Post-conf ict East Timor', UNITAR Programme of Correspondence Instruction Thesis, available <http://www.unitarpoci.org/theses/hayde.pdf>, 10.

109 H. Strohmeyer, 'Collapse and Reconstruction of a Judicial System: The United Nations Missions in Kosovo and East T imor' (2001) 95 *American Journal of International Law* 46, 50.

110 D. Tolbert and A. Solomon, 'United Nations Reform and Supporting the Rule of Law in Post-Conf ict Societies' (2006) 19 *Harvard Human Rights Law Journal* 29, 82.

111 UNSecretary-General, supra n28, paras. 19 and 27.

112 W.W. Burke-White, 'Complementarity in Practice: The International Criminal Court as Part of a System of Multi-Level Global Governance in the Democratic Republic of Congo' (2005) 18 *Leiden Journal of International Law* 557, 569.

113 Comisión para el Esclarecimiento Histórico, *Guatemala: Memoria del Silencio, Vol. I* (Guatemala City, CEH, 1999), para. 426.

114 *Report of the Group of Experts for Cambodia established pursuant to General Assembly Resolution 52/135*, UNGAOR, Annex, UN Doc A/53/850-S/1999/231 (1999), paras. 166–167.

115 Eitel, supra n64, 33.

116 C. Reiger and M. Wierda, *The Serious Crimes Process in Timor-Leste: In Retrospect* (New York: International Center for Transitional Justice, 2006), 11.

117 Kosovo Judicial Assessment Mission, 'Kosovo Judicial Assessment Mission Report' (2000), available <http://pdf.usaid.gov/pdf_docs/PCAAB112.pdf>, 10.

118 M. Hartmann, *International Judges and Prosecutors in Kosovo: A New Model for Post-Conflict Peacekeeping* (Washington, D.C.: United States Institute of Peace Special Report, 2003), 5.

119 L. Dickinson, 'The Relationship Between Hybrid Courts and International Courts: The Case of Kosovo' (2003) 37 *New England Law Review* 1059, 1066.

120 R. Schweiger, 'Late Justice for Burundi' (2006) 56 *Journal of International and Comparative Law* 653, 659.

121 Bull, supra n82, 258.

122 P Pigou, *Law and Justice in East Timor – A Survey of Citizen Awareness and Attitudes Regarding Law and Justice in East Timor* (Dili: Asia Foundation, 2004).

123 Ibid., 29.

124 Ibid., 31.

125 Ibid., 9.

126 R. Daniels and M. Trebilcock, 'The Political Economy of Rule of Law Reform in Developing Countries' (2004) 26 *Michigan Journal of International Law* 99, 108.

127 F. Schauer, 'Legal Development and the Problem of Systemic Transition' (2003) John F Kennedy School of Government Harvard University Faculty Research Working Papers Series, available <web.hks.harvard.edu/publications/getFile.aspx?Id=85>, 13–16.

128 Ibid., 20.

129 Brinkeroff, supra n79, 9.

130 D. Trubeck and M. Galanter, 'Scholars in Self-Estrangement: Some Ref ections on the Crisis in Law and Development' (1974) 4 *Wisconsin Law Review* 1062.

131 Bull, supra n82, 5–6.

132 Endini, supra n106, 26.

133 Daniels and Trebilcock, supra n126, 118.

134 Sannerholm, supra n60, 242–243.

135 N. Bhuta, 'Democratisation, State-Building and Politics as Technology' in Bowden, Charlesworth and Farrall (eds.), supra n83, 38 at 60, M. Ottaway, 'Rebuilding State Institutions in Collapsed States' (2002) 33 *Development and Change* 1001, 1004, Call, supra n46, 9.

136 Farrall, supra n83, 135.

137 P Collier et al., *Breaking the Conflict Trap: Civil War and Development* (New York: Oxford University Press, 2003), 83.

138 T. Carothers, 'The End of the Transition Paradigm' (2002) 13 *Journal of Democracy* 5, 9.

139 Farrall, supra n83, 154.

140 C. Call, 'Building States to Build Peace? A Critical Analysis' (2008) 4 *Journal of Peacebuilding and Development* 60, 69.

141 S. Quast, 'Rule of Law in Post-Conf ict Societies: What is the Role of the International Community?' (2004–05) 39 *New England Law Review* 45, 49 and

C. Rausch (ed.), *Combating Serious Crimes in Postconflict Societies: A Handbook for Policymakers and Practitioners* (Washington, D.C.: USIP Press, 2006), 147.

142 Elbert and Solomon, supra n110, 40.

143 Stromseth, Wippman and Brooks, supra n 50, 313.

144 International Crisis Group, 'Courting Disaster: The Misrule of Law in Bosnia and Herzegovina' (2002), available <http://www.ciaonet.org/wps/icg241/icg241.pdf>.

145 S.von Einsiedel, 'Policy Responses to State Failure' in Chesterman, Ignatieff, and Thakur (eds.), supra n87, 13 at 26.

146 L.E. Nagle, 'The Cinderella of Government: Judicial Reform in Latin America' (2000) 30 *California Western International Law Journal* 345.

147 Stromseth, Wippman and Brooks, supra n50, 66.

148 Bull, supra n82, 120–182.

149 Ibid., 250.

150 Associated Press, 'Swiss Judge Resigns from T ribunal Trying Khmer Rouge Leaders, Alleges Interference', *Washington Post*, 19 March 2012.

151 P. McAuliffe, 'UN Peace-Building, Transitional Justice and the Rule of Law in East Timor: The Limits of Institutional Responses to Political Questions' (2011) 58 *Netherlands International Law Review* 103.

152 R.A. Gomes, 'Perceptions on Justice in T imor-Leste: A Report Prepared for UNMIT' (2007), copy on f le with the author, 10.

153 See generally R. Oakley, M. Dziedzic and E. Goldber g (eds.), *Policing the New World Disorder: Peace Operations and Public Security* (Hawaii: University Press of the Pacif c, 2002).

154 R.Paris, *At War's End: Building Peace After Civil Conflict* (New York: Cambridge University Press, 2004), 168.

155 Supran137 and accompanying text.

156 C. Ahlund, 'Major Obstacles to Building the Rule of Law in a Post-Conf ict Environment' (2004) 39 *New England Law Review* 39, 40–44.

157 Bull, supra n82, 72 and 134.

158 A.Hurwitz and K. Studdard, *Rule of Law Programs in Peace Operations* (New York: International Peace Academy, 2005), ii.

159 Paris, supra n154, 153.

160 Ottaway supra n135, 1018–1019.

161 Bull, supra n82, 181 and 262.

162 Endini, supra n106, 16.

163 F Fukuyama, *State Building: Governance and World Order in the Twenty-First Century* (New York: Cornell University Press, 2004), 44.

164 M.Smiley, 'Democratic Justice in Transition' (2001)99 *Michigan Law Review* 1332, 1336.

165 Danielsand Trebilcock, supra n126, 133.

166 Pulver supra n57, 81.

167 Potter, supra n58, 12, Hurwitz and Studdard, supra n158, 4, Call, supra n46, 18.

168 Carothers, supra n138, 9–10.

169 Ibid., 10–12.

170 A.Schedler, 'The Menu of Manipulation' (2002) 13 *Journal of Democracy* 36.

171 Carothers, supra n138, 17–18.

172 E.g. S. Carlson, 'Legal and Judicial Rule of Law W ork in Multi-Dimensional Peacekeeping Operations: Lessons-Learned Study' (2006), UN DPKO Peace-keeping Best Practice Section, available: http://www.peacekeepingbestpractices.

unlb.org/PBPS/Library/ROL%20Lessons%20Learned%20Report%20%20 March%202006%20FINAL.pdf>, 19, noting that 'transitional and democratic governments rarely pursue ROL reform enthusiastically'.

173 R. Kleinfeld Belton, *Competing Definitions of the Rule of Law: Implications for Practitioners* (Washington, D.C.: Carnegie Endowment for International Peace, 2005), 19.

174 Burke-White, supra n42, 318.

175 Mani, supra n95, 79, McAuliffe, supra n151.

176 Krasner, supra n94, 92.

177 C. Biebesheimer and J.M. Payne, *IDB Experience in Justice Reform* (Washington, D.C.: International Development Bank, 2001), ii–iii.

178 H. Blair and G. Hansen, *Weighing In on the Scales of Justice: Strategic Approaches for Donor-Supported Rule of Law Programs* (Washington, D.C.: USAID, 1994), 51. Similarly, Stromseth, Wippman and Brooks argue that '[b]elow some minimum threshold of resources and commitment … peace implementation and rule of law efforts will be wasted' (Stromseth, Wippman and Brooks, supra n50, 370).

179 Mani, supra n95, 70–72.

180 J. Chopra, 'Building State Failure in East T imor' (2002) 33 *Development and Change* 979, 995.

181 F. Ní Aoláin and C. Campbell, 'The Paradox of T ransition in Conf icted Democracies' (2005) 27 *Human Rights Quarterly* 172, 182.

182 P McAuliffe, 'Transitional Justice's Expanding Empire: Reasserting the Value of the Paradigmatic T ransition?' (2011) 2 *Journal of Conflictology* 32, T. Obel Hansen, 'Transitional Justice: Toward a Differentiated Theory' (2011) 13 *Oregon Review of International Law* 1.

183 Schauer, supra n127, 12–13.

184 M. Plunkett, 'Rebuilding the Rule of Law' in W . Maley, C. Sampford, and R. Thakur (eds.), *From Civil Strife to Civil Society: Civil and Military Responsibilities in Disrupted States* (Tokyo, New York: United Nations University Press, 2003), 207 at 223.

185 Carlson, supra n172, 2.

186 S. Chesterman, M. Ignatieff and R. Thakur, 'Introduction: Making States Work' in Chesterman, Ignatieff and Thakur (eds.), supra n87, 1 at 9.

187 Stromseth, Wippman and Brooks, supra n50, 313. Similarly , Call argues that transitions 'represent perhaps the most optimal conditions for efforts to (re) constitute security and justice systems. In all cases, entrenched elite interests that generally resist changes to state institutions and practices have been weakened or ousted by force. We would expect posttransition {sic} settings, and especially post-conf ict societies, to present an opportunity for institutional transformation' (Call, supra n46, 20).

188 USAID Off ce of Democracy and Governance, Guidelines for Promoting Judicial Independence and Impartiality (2002), available < http://www.usaid.gov/our_ work/democracy_and_governance/publications/pdfs/pnacm007.pdf>, 40.

189 Eitel, supra n64, 5.

190 Daniels and T rebilcock, supra n126, 109 and Hurwitz and Studdard, supra n158, 4, ii.

191 S. Holmes, 'Lineages of the Rule of Law' in J.M. Maravall and A. Przeworski (eds.), *Democracy and the Rule of Law* (Cambridge, New Y ork: Cambridge University Press, 2003), 19 at 24 and 50.

192 Trebilcock and Daniels, supra n86, 352–353.
193 Ibid.,354.
194 UNDP, 'Strengthening the Rule of Law in Confict- and Post-Confict Situations: A Global UNDP Programme for Justice and Security 2008–2011', available <http://www.unrol.org/fles/rol_fnal_apr09.pdf>, 5 and 11.
195 A. Des Forges and T. Longman, 'Legal Responses to the Genocide in Rwanda' in E. Stover and H. Weinstein (eds.), *My Neighbor, My Enemy: Justice and Community in the Aftermath of Mass Atrocity* (Cambridge: Cambridge University Press, 2004), 49 at 62.
196 S.Chesterman, *You, the People: The United Nations, Transitional Administration, and State-Building* (Oxford, New York: Oxford University Press, 2004), 31.
197 C.Villa-Vicencio, 'Transitional Justice, Restoration, and Prosecution' in Sullivan and Tifft (eds.), supra n25, 387 at 390.
198 K.Samuels, *Rule of Law Reform in Post-Conflict Countries: Operational Initiatives and Lessons Learnt* (Washington, D.C.: World Bank, 2006), 18, ar guing it is 'increasingly clear that a realistic timeframe for re-creating a working criminal justice system following serious armed confict with formal courts, trained judges and a retrained police force is close to twenty-years'.
199 Stromseth,Wippman and Brooks, supra n50, 253.
200 Subotic,supra n5, 114 and 119.
201 E.g. Olsen, Payne and Reiter, supra n15, 31, Subotic, supra n5, 116, International Center for Transitional Justice, 'What is Transitional Justice?', factsheet available <http://ictj.org/about/transitional-justice>.
202 J.Alexander, *A Scoping Study of Transitional Justice and Poverty Reduction* (London: DFID, 2003) at 47 and P.de Greiff, 'Articulating the Links Between Tansitional Justice and Development: Justice and Social Integration' in de Greiff and Duthie (eds.), supra n33, 28 at 46–58.
203 On this issue, see Sannerholm, supra n60, 211–232.
204 J.Shklar, *Legalism: Law, Morals, and Political Trials* (Cambridge, MA: Harvard University Press, 1964), 1.
205 J. Czarnetzky and R. Rychlak, 'An Empire of Law? Legalism and the International Criminal Court' (2003) 79 *Notre Dame Law Review* 55, 61–62.
206 E.g. Czarnetsky and Rychlak, ibid., McEvoy, supra n9, and Miller, supra n2, 267 and 290, criticizing 'increased legalism' and the 'fetishization of law'.
207 McEvoy ibid., 417.
208 Ibid.,412.
209 J. Webber, 'Forms of Transitional Justice' in Williams, Nagy and Elster (eds.), supra n32, 98 at 118.
210 E.g. J. Ramji-Nogales, 'Designing Bespoke Transitional Justice: A Pluralist Process Approach' (2010) 32 *Michigan Journal of International Law* 1, 24–71 examining the ad hoc tribunals, hybrid courts, the ICC, TRCs and locally-grounded (traditional/customary) justice processes, but not domestic trials.
211 E.g.Webber, supra n209, at 110.
212 Notable exceptions include M. Drumbl, 'Rule of Law Amidst Lawlessness: Counselling the Accused in Rwanda' s Domestic Criminal T rials' (1998) 29 *Columbia Human Rights Law Review* 546, W . Schabas, *Battling Impunity for Genocide in Underdeveloped States: The Crisis in Rwandese Justice* (Occasional Paper, International Centre for Human Rights and Democratic Development, 1996) and Avocats Sans Frontières' volumes of case law on domestic trials.

213 C. Schaefer, G. Alemu Aneme and K. Tronvoll (eds.), *The Ethiopian Red Terror Trials: Transitional Justice Challenged* (London: James Curry, 2009) remains the only treatment of the process in monograph form.

214 K. McEvoy, 'Letting Go of Legalism: Developing a "Thicker" V   ersion of Transitional Justice' in K. McEvoy and L. McGregor (eds.), *Transitional Justice from Below: Grassroots Activism and the Struggle for Change* (Portland: Hart Publishing, 2008), 15 at 44.

215 McEvoy, ibid., 28 and 37, J. Halpern and H. W   einstein, 'Rehumanizing the Other: Empathy and Reconciliation' (2004) 26   *Human Rights Quarterly* 561, 562–563, Ndulo and Duthie, supra n33, 252.

216 T. Madlingozi, 'On T ransitional Justice Entrepreneurs and the Production of Victims' (2010) 2 *Journal of Human Rights Practice* 208, 212–213.

217 F. Mégret, 'The Politics of International Criminal Justice' (2002 *European Journal of International Law* 1261, 1266.

218 R.A. Cobián and F. Réategui, 'Towards Systemic Social T ransformation: Truth Commissions and Development' in P. de Greiff and R. Duthie (eds.), supra n33, 142 at 147.

219 Sannerholm, supra n60, 236.

220 Gray supra n27, 2641.

221 T. Farer, 'Restraining the Barbarians: Can International Criminal Law Help?' (2000) 22 *Human Rights Quarterly* 90, 97.

222 M. Ignatieff (edited and introduced by A. Gutmann), *Human Rights as Politics and Idolatry* (Princeton: Princeton University Press, 2001), 35.

223 P. Gready, 'Telling Truth? The Methodological Challenges of Truth Commissions' in F. Coomans, F. Grunfeld and M. Kamminga (eds.), *Methods of Human Rights Research* (Antwerp: Intersentia, 2009), 159 at 162.

2 Institutions, culture and norms

The elements of rule of law reconstruction

2.1 Introduction: a contested concept

It seems that no examination of any aspect of the rule of law can progress without reference to its essentially prismatic nature, and this book is no exception. Viewed globally, there are as many conceptions of the rule of law as there are people def ning it.[1] A multiplicity of individual def nitions has in turn led to some less than illuminating generalizations about what it is. Finnis describes the rule of law as 'the name commonly given to the state of affairs in which a legal system is legally in good shape'.[2] Similarly, Tamanaha represents it as 'an exceedingly elusive notion' analogous to the notion of the Good insofar as 'everyone is for it, but have contrasting convictions about what it is'.[3] As Peerenboom puts it, rule of law 'means different things to different people and has served a wide variety of political agendas from Hayekian libertarianism to Rawlsian social welfare liberalism, to Lee Kuan Yew's soft authoritarianism to Jiang Zemin' s statist socialism to a Sharia-based Islamic state'.[4] Others note its equal acceptability to the bottom-up, participatory development traditions of the left and the law and order , individual empowerment ethic of the right.[5] The fundamental principle that it is preferable that law should rule instead of any given individual or clique is reconcilable with almost all ethical systems, even if disputes over the substance of what that law should be are inevitable.[6]

The fact that everyone agrees that the rule of law is benef cial may explain its historically unparalleled near -unanimity of endorsement, particularly in the f elds of peace-building and development – like all abstract political ideas, its susceptibility to multiple def nitions and interpretations has bolstered its appeal to governments both cynical and earnest. In practice, this elusiveness has served to becloud the issue of what precisely the rule of law is or does – for many practitioners, and especially those in transitional justice, an intuitive and crude 'I know it when I see it' [7] standard applies to the rule of law which exacerbates the problems of professional balkanization canvassed in Chapter 1. The concept may appear most attractive in post-conf ict and post-authoritarian transitions given that survivor populations have endured prolonged periods where law was suspended, abused or incapable. However , experience has shown that as the rule of law progresses from a nebulous, abstract concept towards concrete, practical projects, the rule of law as a tenet loses much of its moral, political and rhetorical power .[8] To explain the limited eff cacy of many rule of law promotion efforts, Stromseth, W ippman and Brooks convincingly lay much of the blame for this on the 'superf ciality and obtuseness' with which policy-makers understand the concept. [9] Though we generally accept that the rule of law is a bundle of institutional, cultural and normative commitments, the tendency to think of formal institutions as being separate conceptually and methodologically from normative and cultural values is one that has consistently bedevilled all state-building processes.[10] This recurrent blind-spot has left practitioners ill-equipped to deal with the complications and contradictions of the rule of law, resulting in poorly-conceived and internally contradictory programmes. [11] It is worthwhile, therefore, pondering these complexities as they apply with force to transitional justice, where the rule of law exists more as an intuition than a concrete programme.

For all the apparently multifarious support it receives, the rule of law remains an essentially contested concept. Def nitions of the rule of law, almost always considered in the abstract, are generally ranged between either 'thick' (maximalist) or 'thin' (minimalist), even if closer scrutiny reveals that most def nitions of the concept contain elements of both. Thick notions of the rule of law adopt a basic thin conception of the rule of law that all persons within a state, whether public or private, should be bound by and entitled to the benef t of laws publicly and prospectively promulgated, and publicly administered in courts (without which no legal system can function), and then thicken this conception by incorporating the state' s dominant political morality .[12] This political morality encompasses the arrangement of government (for example democratic, autocratic, socialist), economy (free-market, centrally-planned, mixed) and human rights (classically liberal, communitarian, non-existent), but at the core retains a thin or formal rule of law .[13] These thicker conceptions of the rule of law are attractive because they are described in idealistic terms, but in peace-building their utility is questioned because they are abstracted from the inherently non-ideal conditions that obtain in post-conf ict and post-authoritarian states. The thin conception of the rule of law understood as one where all people, citizen and ruler , are ruled by law and obey it, and where the law is such that people may be guided by it, is equally unsatisfying as it does not necessarily incorporate the human rights guarantees deemed necessary to build either a 'sovereign' peace (which requires an end to conf ict, the undivided sovereignty of a Hobbesian Leviathan, no residual violence and no mass-level human rights abuses) or a 'positive'/'participatory' peace (where there is a resolution to end the conf ict which includes a return to a minimum of political openness and properly functioning state institutions) in conf icted or post-conf ict societies.[14] It should of course be pointed out that advocates of formal conceptions of the rule of law in peace-building tend to conceptualize their prescriptions as *thinner*, as opposed to merely thin.

Of course, outside of academic theorizing, most practitioners would accept that attempts to rigidly def ne the rule of law are unhelpful and unnecessary when compared with approaches that examine areas of commonality between competing versions, and avoid the choice of defnitions that ref ect ideological bias or fail to account fully for the concept. Nevertheless, the maximalist/minimalist debate is relevant because it closely tracks the two models of thought about how the rule of law should be developed. One associates maximalist views with those who emphasize the ends that the rule of law is intended to serve within society (such as human rights, law and order, equality), while minimalist approaches tend to be the preserve of those who undeʀ score the institutional attributes believed necessary to actuate the rule of law (such as a competent judiciary, law enforcement apparatus, clear and prospective law).[15] As Kleinfeld Belton notes, those engaged in rule of law reconstruction historically tended to favour the latter approach, while the more ends-driven approach is typically emphasized by legal scholars and philosophers less subject to the demands of time, emer gency and resources.[16]

2.2 The rule of law in peace-building

The initial institution-driven approach was very much a legacy of the circumstances surrounding the mainstreaming of rule of law reform, though an institutional focus had also been dominant in the global wave of bureaucratic reform after World War II and the law and development movement's heyday in the 1960s and 1970s.[17] In UN peace operations before the late 1980s, rule of law reform was dormant for the same reasons the world oɡanization stayed out of all domestic politics – a restrictive understanding of Article 2(7) of the UN Charter prohibiting it from intervening in matters 'essentially within the domestic jurisdiction' of any state, a reluctance to countenance the cost or precedent of intrusive roles for international personnel, and the Cold W   ar stasis which ensured that (a) the US or USSR would intervene in their client states if conf ict broke out in place of any supranational or   ganization, and (b) no thickly prescriptive model of domestic governance could garner widespread normative consensus as a model for peace operations.   [18] When the bipolar world order collapsed, these obstacles to intervention were removed. The early 1990s saw a revival of the concepts of good governance, [19] a rebalancing of the relationship between human rights and sovereignty [20] and reaff rmation of the liberal peace thesis, all which were based on the premise that there was a causal connection between a particular kind of domestic order and peace.[21] The end of the Cold W ar not only allowed for a greater supply of intervention and state-building, it also created demand as a proliferation of failed states and intrastate conf ict resulted as old elites were replaced by new successor regimes 'that could destroy but not replace' state infrastructure. [22] In the early 1990s, 30 per cent of states were in failure,   [23] while throughout the next decade the typical country emerging from civil war had a 44 per cent chance of returning to conf   ict within f ve years as social cleavages, underdevelopment and abundant weapons interacted.[24] As ethnic strife, civil war and resultant humanitarian emer gencies became common in places as diverse as the Solomon Islands, Bosnia, Afghanistan, Liberia and Cambodia, more f exible and responsive understandings of 'threats to peace and security' became the basis for collective security action. The events of September 11, 2001 conf rmed the emerging understanding that the world order was posed a greater menace by failing states than by aggressive ones, and consolidated the broadening of the interpretation of Article 2(7).

In this milieu the traditional blue-helmet role whereby the UN separated antagonists (peace-keeping) gave way to progressively more ambitious attempts to develop a social, economic and political order conducive to establishing a sustainable peace (peace-building). The UN Secretary General' s *Agenda for Peace* (1992) was the f rst attempt to get to grips with the changing challenges of more complex UN peace operations. [25] It identif ed the new concept of 'post-conf ict peace-building' as 'action to identify and support structures which will tend to strengthen and solidify peace in order to avoid a relapse into conf ict'.[26] A progressive accretion of state-building tasks over time was the product of largely ad hoc interventions in over 40 UN missions around the close of the 20th century as the UN stumbled haphazardly into Namibia, Somalia, Bosnia, Haiti and exercised sovereign authority in the East Timorese and Kosovan transitional administrations.[27] Practice generally coalesced around three broad preconditions for successful missions – consolidating internal and external security, promoting economic and social transformation, and strengthening political institutions and good governance. [28]

Of the third precondition, a clear normative preference emer ged for an executive branch created through a liberal democratic electoral system on the presumption that conf ict could best be transformed into peaceful political competition channelled through governmental institutions. [29] The need for judicial development was not readily apparent, though it was soon realized that transitional arrangements for justice would have to be developed at the outset of any operation to conduct arrests for breaches of public order and to deal with issues of property or corruption that could cause destabilizing grievances at a local level. It gradually became evident in states like Liberia, Cambodia and Rwanda that public order and elections alone would not suffce to foster the conditions of a stable and lasting peace as a series of young democracies degenerated into tribalism, war and poverty . The lack of rule of law was acknowledged as both a cause of these renewed conf icts and a by-product. State-level justice systems moved rapidly from the subsidiary to the integral as peace-builders recognized power could be violently abused or resisted without some framework for compelling obedience to the law from below and self-limitation of power from above. As such, democracy could only be reconciled with human rights through the rule of law . However, in these early missions, the neoliberal institutionalist perspective of state-building, which understood the task as primarily a technical one of crafting eff cient institutions, took precedence.[30] Its *modus operandi* of management by targeted performance in semi-autonomous sectors tended to emphasize a technocratic, insular focus on building institutions of justice like laws, courts and police, and accorded scant attention to the cultural and political ecology within which the institutions would have to function. Because no-one knows precisely how states that do not enjoy the rule of law ultimately develop it, rule of law practitioners compensated for the lack of knowledge by reproducing familiar institutional blueprints from their own countries barely modifed for the transitional ecology.[31] Perhaps the most notable example of this is the use of justice packages, i.e. ready-made deployments of legal experts (judges, trainers, police) and applicable norms (model codes of procedure and substantive law) to transitional states.[32] Mid-1990s' missions in Bosnia[33] and Haiti[34] repeated the Cambodian and Somalian problems of handing over power to rulers who did not wish to be ruled and citizens frustrated by the lack of any apparatus to resolve disputes. As the UN Secretary-General put it:

> Our experience in the past decade has demonstrated clearly that the consolidation of peace in the immediate post-conf ict period, as well as the maintenance of peace in the long-term, cannot be achieved unless the population is conf dent that redress for grievances can be obtained through legitimate structures for the peaceful settlement of disputes and the fair administration of justice.[35]

Even beyond these pressing medium-term problems, there was a longer-term imperative to develop the legal system lest the transitional state be left behind in a globalized world of international legal obligations under various treaty regimes and a highly integrated transnational economy.[36]

In 2000 the Secretary-General set up a panel to improve UN peacekeeping both operationally and doctrinally. The resulting *Report of the Panel on UN Peace Operations* (also known as the *Brahimi Report*) conf rmed strengthening the rule of law as a key thematic peace-building goal that deserved greater attention.[37] It spelled out the needs for judicial and penal reform, human rights monitoring, investigation of past abuses and adequately resourced and experienced personnel.[38] Courts were seen as especially essential, and an international expert role in their reconstruction was proposed. [39] The UN would now prioritize sustainable justice system reconstruction to f ll domestic vacuums in the area of law enforcement and the rule of law . There was a learning process at work – the Timorese and Kosovan missions were more comprehensive and participatory than the 'line of least resistance' approach in Cambodia years earlier, but still suffered from a lack of prioritization among more visible competing issues, a lack of clarity regarding the rule of law' s own priorities, disappointing implementation and a lack of suffient expertise and resources.[40] The obvious rule of law shortcomings of the transitional administrations in Bosnia (under control of the Off ce of the High Representative), Kosovo and East Timor particularly called into question this technocratic approach. Experience here and elsewhere showed that the prospects for successful reform might be signif cantly diminished unless due attention was given to matters of norms and cultural commitment to the rule of law at elite and citizen levels. While past missions taught the UN what needed to be done, there was little doctrinal precedent for actually doing it, most notably in building a functioning criminal justice system. [41] For example, a Harvard study of the UN Mission in Kosovo found that the failure to formulate a 'coherent approach to criminal justice reform' was so 'profound that it puts at risk the transition as a whole'. [42] Similarly, a King's College London report on East Timor argued that no coherent or comprehensive strategy for the administration of justice had ever been formulated by its UN transitional administrators, negatively impacting in all areas of rule of law delivery.[43]

In 2002 a taskforce was established to examine specif c issues of justice and the rule of law in peace operations, which ultimately culminated in the UN Secretary-General's *Rule of Law and Transitional Justice Report* (2004). The *Report* went on to outline its interpretation of what post-conf ict rule of law meant, signalling a clear move away from its previous formalist model detached from the socio-political interconnections that form actual legal systems. W e now see a general acceptance that fundamental issues of socio-political (cultural) relationships and norms should take equal or greater precedence to institution-building.[44]

> The 'rule of law' is a concept at the very heart of the Or ganization's mission. It refers to a principle of governance in which all persons, institutions and entities, public and private, including the State itself, are accountable to laws that are publicly promulgated, equally enforced and independently adjudicated, and which are consistent with international human rights norms and standards. It requires, as well, measures to ensure adherence to the principles of supremacy of law , equality before the law, accountability to the law, fairness in the application of the law , separation of powers, participation in decision-making, legal certainty , avoidance of arbitrariness and procedural and legal transparency.[45]

Most of these prescriptions are technical and formal. The core of rule of law reform here is inoffensively technocratic, most obviously in relation to building the capacity of institutions. However , the extent to which cultural matters such as restraining governmental interference and building public access to law are emphasized is highly signif cant. Though the promotion of institutions like courts and civilian police or insistence on separation of executive and judiciary have incurred assertions of ethnocentricity ,[46] these reforms are not necessarily western imports but integral parts of domestic rule of law in functioning states worldwide, even those that systematically breach human rights. [47] Nevertheless, the demand that laws conform to a particular notion of justness in the references to international human rights norms, democratic separation of powers and fairness can be said to have crystallized the world or ganization's gradual equation of the rule of law with good governance, democracy and human rights. [48] Whereas once it could fairly be said that practitioners invariably conceived of the rule of law in institutional terms,[49] since the explicit rejection of pre-packaged solutions in the 2004 *Report*[50] the theory (and often the practice) of rule of law reconstruction missions has been commendably more holistic, adaptive and explicitly premised on 'national assessments, national participation and national needs and aspirations'.[51] In the last decade, cultural and normative issues now attract a hitherto unimaginable inf uence on rule of law policy . One can of course argue this change in emphasis was inevitable given that all of the international bodies most engaged in rule of law reconstruction such as the UN, UN Off ce of the High Commissioner for Human Rights (OHCHR), UNDP, EU, OSCE, national development agencies and INGOs are ideologically committed to liberal, democratic and human rights-based norms.   [52] Both the *Brahimi Report* and the *Rule of Law Report* make consistency with human rights standards a precondition for UN implementation of peace agreements.[53] Bell notes that these agreements typically include some type of self-determination, a collection of human rights institutions and mechanisms to deal with past human rights abuses. [54]

The 2004 Report's def nition has been commended for a breadth and specif city heretofore lacking. [55] It subsequently spawned more consistent strategic and operational planning, most notably in the Secretary-General' s 2006 report *Uniting Our Strengths: Enhancing UN Support for the Rule of Law*[56] and a Rule of Law Coordination and Resource Group to bring together key rule of law actors in the UN system such as the DPKO and UNDP due to the lack of harmonization identif ed in the Report.[57] There have been Security Council resolutions emphasizing the importance of rule of law issues in the context of women, peace and security (Resolutions 1325 and 1820), children in armed conf ict (e.g. Resolution 1612) and the protection of civilians in armed conf ict (e.g. Resolution 1674), while the OHCHR has issued its very useful *Rule of Law Tools for Post-Conflict States* series.[58] The UN Secretary' s 2011 follow-up report to take stock of the progress made in implementing the recommendations contained in the 2004 Report shows that in a short period of time, the UN's comprehension of the rule of law improved dramatically into a nuanced appreciation of its inextricably-linked normative, cultural and institutional properties.[59] Increasingly, even scholars and practitioners advocating self-consciously pragmatic def nitions of the rule of law urge synergistic approaches that focus more on the ends law is to serve than on the institutions that embody it.[60] This has fed into practice in subsequent peace-building missions such as those in Liberia (since 2003), Côte d'Ivoire (since 2004), Haiti (since 2004) and Democratic Republic of the Congo (since 2007) with distinct rule of law or legal and judicial support divisions. For example, in Liberia an explicitly ends-based approach is being adopted, focusing on issues like women's rights, human rights training in the judiciary and the rights of juvenile offenders at the expense of an emphasis on the conf guration and manner of functioning of state institutions. [61] These more nuanced approaches can be contrasted with the very superfcial understanding of the rule of law on the part of transitional justice practitioners that will be examined in Chapter 3.

2.3 Transitional justice, the rule of law and the risk of conflation

Concern has been expressed about how the all-encompassing def   nition outlined in the *Report* may be translated into specif   c f eld activities.[62] In particular, Bull argues that proven causal linkages between the assumedly indivisible values of the rule of law, human rights and democracy are 'noticeably absent' from the Report. [63] While this norm-intensiveness is ar guably a sensible and welcome response to the problems identif   ed in earlier more technocratic approaches to rule of law reconstruction, it has done little to clarify the damagingly intuitive 'I know it when I see it' attitude to the rule of law its nebulousness promotes at the expense of engaging with its complexities and anomalies.[64] If anything, it has worsened the danger – as an increasing number of ends become associated with the rule of law, it becomes more diff cult to def ne in concrete terms what it will take to realize them. [65] Stromseth, Wippman and Brooks note that confusing formalist and substantive of the rule of law concepts can actually harm the reconstruction process as formalist and substantive ideas become conf ated, with a mistaken belief that one automatically f ows from the other:

> Because many decision-makers ignore the question of whether it is best to conceptualize the rule of law in a formal or substantive way, many rule of law programmes simply conf ate two very different facets of rule of law in a simplistic manner, assuming that substance will naturally f ow from form – or that a normative commitment to substantive values (such as respect for individual and minority rights, a commitment to non-violent means of resolving disputes, etc.) will naturally f   ow from structurally independent courts and from newly drafted legislation that highlights those values.[66]

As Chapter 3 goes on to examine in greater detail, transitional justice represents the paradigmatic example of this intuitive approach to the rule of law . Transitional justice is inescapably maximalist in approach to the rule of law , believing that law must be about justice and cannot be separated from morality and substantive norms. Amnesty International's argument that '[t]he only way to make a break from the past, a time when human rights were routinely abused, is to establish the rule of law, with the protection of human rights at its centre'[67] is one that is consistently echoed in the literature and UN policy documents.[68] This is particularly the case with transitional justice. Even though the title of the *Rule of Law and Transitional Justice Report* links the two and various paragraphs take for granted that transitional justice and the rule of law go together,[69] areas of clash mentioned earlier and examined in detail in later chapters, are not acknowledged, let alone explored. As Pulver notes, transitional justice is largely treated as a separate and distinct phenomenon in the Report even though it purports to integrate the two.[70] The rule of law is viewed as a matter of substantive commitments which f ow naturally from whatever institution is created, be it a court, an international tribunal, local restorative processes, a truth commission or any combination of the above. This perhaps explains why so much aid under the rubric of 'rule of law assistance' is dispensed by agencies such as USAID to transitional justice processes in the likes of Ethiopia's Red Terror trials[71] which are marked by fagrant due processes deprivations, political interference and tend, if anything, to manifest an un-rule of law . As Chapters 3 to 6 examine, in modern transitional justice the rule of law is less a def ned programme of institutions, culture and norms but rather a broad narrative of progress from a brutal politics of force to a liberal judicialization of politics. W ithin this narrative, only blanket impunity is intolerable – anything that accounts, acknowledges, condemns or punishes past atrocities inherently aff rms the rule of law and contributes to developing it. This whiggishness is hardly surprising – one of the core ar guments of the advocates of formalist theories is that the thicker the conception of the rule of law becomes, the more likely it is to be swallowed up in lar ger debates or assumptions about the dominant social or political philosophy .[72] It then becomes easy to equate the rule of law with liberal policies such as democratic government[73] or transitional justice.[74]

This brings us to the central theme this book explores – how the rule of law and transitional justice have at various junctures been confated with each other, presumed mutually benef cial or had their clashes downplayed as a matter of incorrect sequencing or inattention to detail, when in fact the rule of law and transitional justice are distinctly different ideas. As such, they are as likely to contradict as to complement each other , and to do so in manners that may be genuinely intractable and unsusceptible to technical tweaking. One of the core ar guments of the book is that the conf ation of transitional justice's response to human rights abuses with the rule of law is an unnecessarily narrow conception of the rule of law' s value (and transitional justice' s potential) by emphasizing its human rights role but ignoring, mar ginalizing and often denying those more formal, 'thinner' values which are essential to both sustainable peace and realizing the dignity of the individual that is at the core of what we understand as human rights. There is little awareness in the literature that transitional trial might benef t (and benef t from) contemporaneous processes of judicial reconstruction or that local restorative justice processes of transitional reconciliation might benef   t (and benef t from) national processes of integrating grass-roots justice processes. The notorious failure to attempt outreach, capacity-building or norm diffusion between the ad hoc tribunals and national courts in the early years of the International Criminal Tribunal for Y ugoslavia (ICTY) and International Criminal Tribunal for Rwanda (ICTR), the much criticized failure to integrate rule of law assistance with hybrid courts in Sierra Leone, Kosovo and East T imor or the promotion of justice from below as sites of resistance to democratizing governments who may in fact be keen to integrate them in a sensibly plural-ist manner, are just some of the examples this book will study.

Of course, the existence of transitional justice in splendid isolation from ongoing projects of rule of law reconstruction is unfortunate but not actively harmful if one assumes, as the 2011 follow-up report to the 2004 *Rule of Law and Transitional Justice Report* does, that separate processes of accounting for the past and rebuilding for the future are inherently mutually benef cial.

> There is currently wider acknowledgement that transitional justice processes and institutional capacity-building are mutually reinforcing. It is recognized, for example, that vetting procedures and national pros-ecutions can assist in dismantling abusive State structures and criminal networks that would otherwise impede efforts to strengthen justice and security institutions. The reports of truth commissions can expose patterns of violations, raise awareness about the rights of victims and offer road maps for reform. T ransitional justice processes can serve to build the capacities of national justice and security actors where these are included in the design and implementation of national prosecution initiatives.[75]

Over time, however, rule of law practitioners have come to realize that push-ing for one goal does not automatically advance any or all of the others. To adopt Packenham's observation on modernization theory's f awed assump-tion that transition to market democracy would be lar gely self-reinforcing once initiated, not all good things go together.[76] As Kleinfeld points out, if any end may be implied when the phrase rule of law is invoked, the differ - ences between those ends are often ignored when in fact success in relation to one end may impair progress in another.[77] Because rule of law reconstructors have long been conscious that no element of the rule of law can or should operate in isolation from other institutional complements or the wider polit-ical environment, these tensions have been internalized by rule of law practi-tioners who must attempt to reach their rule of law ends across multiple institutions.[78] For example, it has long been recognized that bolstering the independence of the judiciary can undermine judicial accountability , that developing pristine due process rights in underdeveloped institutions can clash with community demands for justice against known or ganized crime f gures or that promoting traditional justice processes to alleviate case-loads can clash with constitutional protections of women and minorities. However, because those in the transitional justice f eld maintain a distance from related projects, they appear to be less aware of the danger that their usually ephem-eral and exceptionalist projects might contradict the principles underlying the wider reconstruction effort. One sees a common assumption in transi-tional justice literature that accountability for wrongdoers from the prior regime or conf ict automatically contributes to building the rule of law in formerly lawless or repressive states. [79] For example, the enthusiasm among scholars and practitioners for the internationalizing of transitional trial disregards the risk of undermining the legitimacy of domestic tribunals, the conviction that trials should be used as a means of explicit political signalling can call into question the long-term neutrality of the courts, while many truth commissions operate more to circumvent than complement the judicial structures peace-builders are developing. While peace-builders have long argued that a 'secure environment is the *sine qua non*' that must precede courts and human rights,[80] transitional justice has traditionally been premised on the supposition that states should be willing to run the risk of destabilizing revanchist discontent to ensure accountability .[81] Similar clashes have been noted in peace-building generally between developmental actors who see rule of law as primarily an issue of governance or economic development and human rights actors who prioritize the protection of human rights as a primary goal of justice sector reform. [82]

Despite ample opportunity for clashes between the two f elds, Chapter 3 outlines in greater detail that those active in the f eld of transitional justice operate on the presumption that their activities demonstrate and substantiate a transitional rule of law through any form of accountability ranging from conviction in trial to being named in a report or by a truth commission, regardless of the extent to which that accounting contradicts the principles and institutions of the rule of law being established elsewhere in the state. As such, transitional justice manifests the tendency rule of law reconstruction generally is moving away from, namely treating the rule of law as a single good rather than as a system of goods in tension. While the obvious solution is the generic observation that transitional justice practitioners and rule of law reconstructors can learn from each other, it should be recognized that the latter have gone much further in recognizing the paradoxes and complexities inherent in tackling issues of justice and justice sector reform. This is so not only because they have a necessarily wider and more long-term perspective, but also because they have been forced by experience to engage in much deeper thought about what the rule of law means, even if it is still only manifested in a set of 'best practices'. [83] None of this is to ar gue that rule of law reconstruction is perfect. Signif cant shortcomings remain. For example, f ve years into rule of law reform in Liberia, the UN Secretary-General would criticize the United Nations Mission in Liberia (UNMIL) for having no coherent strategic plan.[84] Justice sector reform still tends to be more reactive than pro-active[85] and the intensive empirical research that would improve practice on the ground is generally eschewed in favour of less rigorous 'assessment' exercises.[86] The UN Secretary-General's aforementioned 2011 follow-up report impliedly acknowledged the lack of coordination between the UN, Member States and national stakeholders in rule of law reform missions. [87] The best that can be said about many rule of law reconstruction programmes is that they are works in progress. However , rule of law reconstruction no longer manifests the tendency to focus directly on institutional means without considering the ultimate ends of those reforms. By contrast, as Chapters 3 and 4 explore, transitional justice tends to do the opposite in recognizing an end (a broadly understood justice for an increasingly broadly understood array of human rights abuses) without giving any thought to how it may impact on national institutions and cultures of justice beyond a vague intuition that all accountability is necessarily useful. Much like the old formalist orthodoxy that '[a]ny work to reform laws, any change to policy is considered rule of law reform'[88] transitional justice scholarship and practice now assumes that pursuit of accountability and/or restoration is a tide that lifts all rule of law boats. While rule of law practitioners are now more likely to consider the desired goals of the rule of law before commencing institutional change, transitional justice commits to ends without pondering its impact on the domestic justice sector. At various junctures, theorists and practitioners have preferred internationalized trials over national ones, explicitly pedagogical and conviction-centred trials over exemplarily neutral justice and localized restorative processes of conditional amnesty and truth over the state-level trials caricatured as 'retributive'. These decisions are often justif   able and frequently unavoidable, but intuitively conceiving of the rule of law primar - ily/exclusively as a matter of substantive commitments means that they are generally arrived at with little consideration for how they might impact on the processes of rebuilding national judicial structures.

Because of this intuitive understanding of the rule of law (explored more fully in Chapter 3), we see two problems that recur in transitional justice. The f rst is the conf ation of means and ends manifested in an assumption that a normative commitment to substantive human rights values will naturally f ow from given institutions like trials, truth commissions and inquiries. The second is the assumption that all programmes of accountability automatically re-enforce the rule of law, that all goods *do* go together. The task of the rest of this book, therefore, is to identify those areas where transitional justice assumes normative commitments f ow from creating transitional justice institutions, the degree to which these activities complement or contradict on-going rule of law reconstruction processes, and the extent to which transitional justice might benef t from concentrating on means as well as ends.

First, however, it is necessary to undertake a preliminary examination of how transitional justice might interact for good or ill with the tripartite institutional, normative and cultural elements of rule of law reconstruction. A word of caution is necessary, because the distinctions between the three are indeterminate. While the distinction between norm-based thick/substantive/ maximalist conceptions and institutional thin/formalistic/minimalist conceptions is relatively clear at their extremes, issues of culture f   ts somewhat awkwardly between the two poles. For example, some consider equality before the law or predictable and eff   cient justice as inherently substantive ends,[89] while others would consider these as indispensable elements of a thin, formalistic account.[90] Herein, what is meant by culture is anything that relates to the commitment, support and adherence of either rulers or ruled to the law. We see clear differences between transitional justice actors and rule of law reformers in terms of norms – for the former, human rights norms are paramount while for the latter the substance of the law is but one building block of the rule of law broadly understood. In terms of institutions, the latter are pre-occupied with the development of permanent national judicial institutions, while the former are more content to use temporary measures or circumvent those institutions by establishing special tribunals, internationalizing the accountability process, or pursuing convictions through processes deliberately tilted against the defendant that are unsustainable in terms of ordinary crime. As noted in the previous chapter, the domain of state institutions is 'normally consigned to the wish-list of potential outcomes (via truth commission recommendations, for example) rather than being seen as a necessary enabling environment'.[91] Scholars such as Bosire, who contends that the development of sustainable state institutions is a fundamental precondition for successful transitional justice, are very much in the minority in the feld.[92] Both f elds are agreed on the need to foster a commitment to the rule of law on the parts of rulers and ruled, but differ subtly in how they view them. While rule of law reconstructors see the need to engage with the national political elite to foster adherence to law in the future, transitional justice has historically been motivated by distrust and often antagonism towards them for their reluctance to address crimes of the past. While rule of law reformers see the ruled as citizens entitled to justice in functioning state institutions, transitional justice increasingly (though not uniformly) views its constituents as victim-survivors to be restored through discrete, localized, exceptionalist programmes beyond state institutions and political elites.

2.4 Institutions and the benefit of a 'thin' rule of law

A thin rule of law has two main facets. The f rst is the establishment of formal rules of behaviour enjoying the force of law. The Fullerian criteria of generality, publicity, non-retroactivity, clarity, non-contradiction, non-impossibility, constancy and congruity stipulate the generally requisite conditions for making what law-makers pass to count as law.[93] Though the *Rule of Law and Transitional Justice Report* observes that these legislative frameworks will show neglect, politicization and discrimination, because the procedures for making and revising laws are primarily vested in the legislature and judiciary, they lie outside the scope of this book.[94] However, the rule of laws is not the same as the rule of law – legislation validly created and enshrined in formally written documents will be nugatory to a large extent unless it is embedded in an institutional structure that favours compliance by all and sanctions disobedience.

This brings us to the second facet, which is the establishment of mechanisms for enforcing and otherwise supporting the law . As noted earlier, the typical rule of law-building framework is that of a 'tripod' of judiciary, police and the correctional system, though space precludes consideration of all but the f rst leg. While international actors can help restore peace by carrying out executive functions like policing and detention, genuine judicial functions such as trials require different skills and greater indigenous inclusion because the role of the judiciary as an institution of governance is heightened in transition, owing to the weakness of the executive and legislative branches.[95] The importance of the judiciary as the central pillar of the rule of law in ordinary times is well understood. As the UN Basic Principles on the Independence of the Judiciary state, judges are 'char ged with the ultimate decision over life, freedoms, rights, duties and property of citizens'. [96] Bull neatly summarizes the ultimate institutional end-goal of rule of law reconstruction as that of a 'state-based enforcement model constituted by publicly promulgated formal rules of behaviour with the force of law and coercive state structures to enforce those laws, namely state judicial, law enforcement and correctional structures',[97] though best practice encourages experiment and innovation in terms of f nding the institutional design that f ts. If law is to be obeyed it must be capable of guiding behaviour – as Daniels and T rebilcock note, 'the social coordinative function of institutions, including legal ones, f ow ... from their ability to create and manage expectations and the conditions of predictability'.[98] At a minimum then, these institutions of enforcement and support must not deprive law of its ability to guide behaviour Rule of law reconstruction attempts to inculcate process values (transparency , predictability, enforceability, stability, competence) in addition to institutional values (independence, accountability) to make this a reality .[99] A typical list of tasks include training national actors (judges, lawyers, defence counsel), establishing training institutes and reforming university curricula, legal system assessment and monitoring, reforming judicial selection, rebuilding physical infrastructure, inaugurating management and administrative systems, developing the national ministries of justice/interior and founding bar associations.

While these reforms in theory apply to the entire judicial system, institutional reform has in practice often been equated with the criminal justice system (for example, in Kosovo and East T imor, UN off cials did not distinguish clearly between the rule of law and the justice).[100] Here in this common sphere of interest may lie the root of the presumption that justice sector reform and transitional justice are inherently simpatico. Given the over - riding concern with punishing criminality , one would assume that justice sector reformers and transitional justice constituencies would sing from the same page. However, the relatively recent normative tendency in rule of law reconstruction has not been accompanied by a revision of the suspicion of formalist approaches to the rule of law one sees traditionally in the human rights community, of which transitional justice scholarship is the most obvious example. Indeed, Rama Mani, as one of the very few writers who have thought deeply about the interaction of rule of law reconstruction and transitional justice, criticizes what she calls the 'programmatic minimalism' of rule of law projects, interpreting the institution-driven rule of law programme 'as a mechanism for establishing order rather than as a vehicle to restore justice within society'.[101] This suspicion complements an observable reluctance in transitional justice' s current emphasis on holistic approaches to embed the 'iconic status' of the courtroom and the jailhouse as the best means of promoting justice after mass violence.[102]

The sources of this suspicion in much of transitional justice discourse are four-fold, namely (i) the origins of institutionalism, (ii) its top-down nature, and its compatibility (iii) with human rights abuses and (iv) predatory capitalism. To begin with, there is a tendency in peace-building to 'pull a standard menu of lowest common denominator reforms off the shelf for the simple reason that it is easier to engage in technical reform like writing laws, train judges, construct buildings and establish legal centres than it is to alter the beliefs of rulers and ruled about the law , particularly when political will is questionable.[103] Indeed, for most state-building ideas to become operationalized in post-conf ict or post-authoritarian environments, there is a pragmatic tendency to conceive them thinly .[104] The immediate need to avoid relapse has tended to favour immediate institutionalization to provide security rather than justice broadly understood as equality or redistribution. [105] As noted in the previous chapter, rule of law reconstruction has therefore been very state-centric and 'top-down' in form, focusing mostly on national-level institutions and working with law , lawyers and political elites. [106] By contrast, those in the human rights and development communities tend to emphasize supposedly more democratic, bottom-up state-building strategies that utilize civil society.[107] Furthermore, there is also a palpable fear that rule of law reform can operate as a T rojan horse for certain deleterious economic policies. For example, Richmond suggests that the rule of law extends the liberal framework of rights, checks and balances required for a neo-liberal architecture of free markets and economic self-help that reduce the state's role in redistributing resources.[108] This danger of course exists, but its realization cannot simply be assumed – if development is conceived, per Sen, as the expansion of human freedoms,[109] the rule of law can equally serve as a channel for social transformation by serving as a venue for excluded sectors of society to litigate for their rights.[110] Though improved performance by the court system generally fosters economic development by facilitating market transactions, [111] the extent to which the institutions of justice alter or perpetuate social and economic inequalities in society will depend far more on the commitments of domestic political leadership than the mere existence of developing rule of law institutions.

However, most criticism of minimalist, technical conceptions of the rule of law instead comes from individuals and agencies concerned with the risk that formal conceptions of the rule of law minimize democracy and human rights[112] and those who believe it may actually facilitate the pursuit of immoral ends.[113] Considering that rule of law has often served to justify abusive rule in states such as Brazil that have received much rule of law aid, this mistrust is defensible.[114] However, post-conf ict and post-authoritarian societies will benef t signif cantly from the formalistic objectives of a government that acts according to rules derived from a legitimate political arena and that empowers the ethic of neutral treatment of disputes by judges. After all, in the types of society to which intensive rule of law missions will deploy 'excessive legality is generally not one of the challenges'. [115]

The clearest and most articulate conception of formal rule of law is that of the positivist Joseph Raz. [116] His account of it has two aspects. The f rst is that all people, citizen or ruler, be ruled by law and obey it. The second is that the law should be such that people will be able to be guided by it. This account has been interpreted as demanding nothing in terms of moral substantive content, merely the presence or absence of observable criteria decided beforehand. [117] It does not pass judgement on the content of the law or make moral decisions as to whether it is good or bad. The main critique of a thin rule of law impliedly commends it. Allan argues, for example, that the formal conception of rule of law is itself based on substantive ideals of respect for the individual and moral autonomy and so is substantial. [118] Even if one accepts that it does not ensure human rights, a formal rule of law respects human dignity by treating humans as persons capable of plotting their future. [119] In the worst case scenario of a formal rule of law , predictable (and hence more avoidable) repression is preferable to unpredictable autocratic caprice. [120] Even if a thin rule of law does not guarantee positive moral good, the rule of law has a non-instrumental value in minimizing the harm law can do. The thinnest rule of law which outlaws legislative retroactivity and arbitrariness with a competent, independent and accessible judiciary can be contrasted with states where rulers refuse to be ruled, who pass executive decrees, emasculate judicial and police independence and deny citizens recourse to them for basic dispute resolution.[121] Though historical exceptions persist, a thin rule of law is more apt to restrain than empower bad government. Hammer gren's assertion that by addressing the more technical and politically manageable issues of the rule of law, practitioners can establish the credibility, progress and experience that will help them to thwart fundamental obstacles to future reform, makes a good deal of practical sense. [122] However, considering the context of liberalizing transition and participation by international agencies unavoidably inf uenced by their experiences from home, few formal conceptions will ultimately be so minimal. A transitioning state which abides by validly enacted law, that guarantees access to justice, which appoints competent judges and lawyers and then allows them to adjudicate and advocate the law independently of political inf uence is apt to facilitate the multiplicity of life choices that a human rights-based state makes possible and tends to reduce the motivation for conf ict. Where citizens can be confdent they will be treated equally before the law and perversions of the law are impermissible, the trust among adversaries necessary for peace is more likely to be fostered in a context where previously the antithesis was the norm.[123] Thinner, more institutional accounts offer great practical advantages in post-conf ict and post-authoritarian societies. Thinner accounts also have a theoretical appeal, both in their ability to generate support from across the political spectrum by mar ginalizing, delaying or eliminating controversial questions over rights [124] and by reducing the risks of a wasteful perfectionism. [125]

All rule of law reconstruction must enhance capacity and change behaviour, and so attempts to establish a competent judiciary which resolves disputes and administers justice in a predictable, eff cient and transparent manner. This is a diff cult task given the adversity of post-conf ict and post-authoritarian contexts and the inherent limitations of peace-building missions. As Farrall warns, it is necessary to avoid idealized and resource-intensive models from the industrialized democracies because they will be unsustainable in the long term. [126] Due regard must be given to the often very limited absorptive potential of a given state. Desirables like the provision of legal aid, victim-support or witness protection might be a generation away. Nevertheless, progress in terms of institution-building is achievable given the relative susceptibility of organizations like the judiciary to a threshold of formalization and transferability across societal and cultural boundaries. [127] Provision of resources allied to the training and vetting of national human resources can make an appreciable impact once a threshold competence is reached and built on. The 2004 *Report* broke new ground in its focus on building national justice structures instead of international substitutes. Domestic actors were to be empowered, consulted and trained in the creation of a sustainable justice system, manifesting a policy preference for 'solidarity, not substitution'.[128]

Three tasks are imperative in rebuilding the judiciary – identifying legal professionals, applying some sort of qualif cation standard (through, for example, UNMIK's Technical Advisory Commission on Judiciary and Prosecution Service or Afghanistan's Judicial Reform Commission) and then training those identif ed and qualif ed.[129] This training can occur both in the classroom and from learning at the side of international judges and lawyers, though workshops and conferences have their place. T raining should be both practical (opinion writing, courtroom management) and procedural (evidentiary rules, protection of defendant rights). Capacity-building must incorporate the training of a bench and bar to provide judges and lawyers with the requisite skills to undertake transitional trials if they should arise and to decide and argue the ordinary cases that come before the courts on issues such as property, family and contracts. As regards the training of judges to fulf l these roles, there exist no detailed international guidelines. The best general guidance available is the UN Basic Principles on the Independence of the Judiciary , which state that 'Persons selected for judicial off ce shall be individuals of integrity and ability and training or qualif cations in law'.[130] This clearly goes beyond a mere law degree or years of service as a lawyer – a suitable judge needs training in specif c judicial skills, on-the-job training and experience. Likewise, there are no extensive guidelines on the qualif cations of lawyers, though the UN Basic Principles on the Role of Lawyers are slightly more elaborative:

> Governments, professional associations of lawyers and educational institutions shall ensure that lawyers have appropriate education and training

and be made aware of ideas and ethical duties of the lawyer and of human rights and fundamental freedoms recognized by national and international law.[131]

A bar association should be developed to regulate the legal profession in the public interest and establish codes of conduct, [132] while prosecutors should also be subject to standards of independence and capability .[133] Again, a degree or diploma alone does not suff ce to prepare a lawyer for his or her onerous role in the administration of justice. Advanced training in research, writing, ar gument, presentation and the f lling-in of gaps in substantive knowledge of law are required. In the longer terms, higher legal education to bring young new lawyers on stream is necessary as is monitoring of performance.[134]

Judicial training programmes tend to be 'remedial', attempting to bring judges up to minimum international standards in substantive areas of law.[135] However, it is essential that an objective assessment of what judges actually do is performed. Some of the tasks performed by judges in transition are complex and quasi-legislative. However , Toope counsels that rule of law reconstruction must be careful not to imagine that all judges are required to perform Herculean intellectual tasks.[136] There is a danger that adherence to international standards for all may be a waste of judicial resources and delay the entrance of much-needed professionals into the justice system to handle the more mundane cases that make up the majority of a legal system's workload. For example, observers warn that states 'may be tempted to seek ICC-inspired high-tech upgrades and complicated solutions where low-tech and simple solutions will suff ce and be more sustainable'. [137] Though it is important to remember that transitional justice actors will often enjoy only a tenuous relationship with many of the actors and processes involved in the legal system reconstruction overall, straining towards a national level of competence raises distinct issues in relation to transitional justice. In the era of the ICC and a vast transnational advocacy network, transitional justice always exists under international scrutiny where pressure is exerted to ensure individual trials reach a standard of competence far beyond that which the national judicial system can consistently attain. One sees in the transitional justice literature a great willingness to prefer foreign experts, foreign models and foreign-conceived solutions to secure convictions for mass atrocity when national capacities are low. Typically, pressure is exerted to allow temporary international augmentation of the national judicial system, international supervision or to remit the case abroad. While in state-building projects capacity-building is the primary objective, the incentives of the transitional justice community are different and emphasize the immediate remedies ('justice delayed is justice denied') that capacity-building is ultimately designed to provide. Much like when outside donors are presented with a choice of providing anti-retroviral drugs through the local country's def cient public health structure or to distribute the drugs directly by themselves, [138] in transitional states the more immediately satisfying process of international transplantation often takes priority over the more perilous and fraught process of leaving responsibility with the state. This does not automatically operate to the detriment of durable improvements and sustainable capacity , but may not help it much. Though 'solidarity , not substitution' are the watchwords of rule of law reconstruction, the reverse may well be the case. As the international tribunals and the problematic experiences of hybrid courts and complementarity demonstrate (see Chapter 5), transitional accountability often illustrates what Ignatieff inelegantly describes as 'capacity sucking out', whereby the international and NGO communities become so abundantly equipped with capabilities that they can exclude or mar ginalize, rather than complement or develop, the institutional capabilities of the targeted state.[139] This risk is exacerbated by the f ight of actors from domestic justice systems to more ad hoc, temporary , international or non-state mechanisms.[140]

Of course, one can argue that external involvement in transitional accountability can catalyse institutional reform at home, but ultimately sustainable benef ts will only f ow from internal change. This is because even though they speak (and are criticized) in the language of institutionalism, all peacebuilders can only ever do is establish *organizations* like judiciaries, state prosecutors or defence counsel . Only when these become signif cant and established, i.e. 'where the relevant actors believe that they provide solutions to real problems' do they actually become *institutions*.[141] To get to this key point where 'most people most of the time' use the courts to resolve their disputes,[142] rule of law practitioners over time have changed from promoting law as a technocratic, procedural ideal to conceive of it as a more broadly understood cultural commitment with substantive, rights-based content. Institutions can no longer remain the sole end of reconstruction – certain norms and cultural commitments must be embodied within them. Courts and buildings and staff nevertheless remain imperative. However, sometimes what the international community considers best practice departs radically from that which the national community believes in or can possibly achieve, imperilling the process of changing the or ganization into an institution.

2.5 A culture of the rule of law: binding citizens to the courts

Rule of law does not exist where either rulers or ruled (or both) feel free to ignore it. These are cultural commitments, radically different from what went before when law was wielded arbitrarily by the former and resented by the latter.

> Without a widely shared cultural commitment to the idea of the rule of law, courts are just buildings, judges are just bureaucrats, and constitutions are just pieces of paper.[143]

The challenge is to co-opt or coerce political elites, on the one hand, and to expand the participation of the public on the other .[144] Building respect for rule by law on the part of both political elites and ordinary citizens is a *potentially* mutually-sustaining process. Because the courts are effectively power - less against forceful executive assault, support from the general population can mitigate or reverse reluctance on the part of leaders to abide by the law . On the other hand, in hierarchical and stratif ed societies, support from the political leadership may be key to securing popular acceptance of law' s validity. A natural corollary of this, however , is the Fullerian position that where governments routinely abuse or violate the law, citizens may no longer feel they have a duty to abide by the law it creates.[145] Both rule of law recon- structors and transitional justice practitioners agree that transitional justice can help develop a rule of law culture at both levels. However , closer inspec- tion reveals different biases and areas of clash.

Tyler, in his seminal work *Why People Obey the Law*, notes throughout that the key to the effectiveness of law is public compliance. [146] Legislation or court judgments mean little if people feel they can be ignored. Instrumental perspectives on the law hold that people shape their behaviours on the basis of incentives and penalties contained within the law, most notably in the area of criminal punishment. This social control model rewards compliance with the law, and punishes violations of it. [147] As argued above, creating the insti- tutions of law is a prerequisite for enforcing it. This enforcement model is essential in the typical post-conf ict/post-authoritarian society because the decrease in the habitual obedience that functioning states enjoy inevitably tracks to a greater or lesser degree the disintegration of state-citizen political relationships in that period of conf ict or repression, which transition at government level itself cannot remedy. As Channell points out, in these peri- ods cultures develop for defending oneself against government institutions, not engaging with them.[148] The state lacks trust from all or a signif cant part of the population – the reciprocal relationship between the state and society wherein (a) the citizenry accepts and complies with the rules of the state and (b) the government responds and adapts to social demand is diminished or destroyed.[149] The typical post-conf ict/post-authoritarian context of high hostility levels, low capacities, mass traumatization, poverty and displace- ment make rule-based interaction extremely diff cult.

Empirically, however, instrumental perspectives are unsatisfying because citizens very frequently obey the law when the probability of punishment for non-compliance is minimal and will break the law when risks of punish- ment are high.[150] A legal system cannot operate solely on the basis of social control as it would consume too many social resources. Though T yler's work is US-centric, the logic of this is even stronger in post-conf ict and developing states where the cost of crime control is as much as 15 per cent of GDP, compared to an average of 5 per cent in the W est.[151] The option of such control is in all likelihood not available given the enormous transaction costs in weak legal systems, [152] while coercive rule of law models may be too reminiscent of pre-transitional illegitimacy.[153] Though some state apparatus is imperative to deal with serious law and order issues and to avoid the ever - present risk of recourse to vigilantism or mass non-compliance, the need for institutions must be put in perspective. Adherence to the law in all societies always depends more on the voluntary consent of citizens than on state sanction mechanisms.[154] While the risk of punishment is always signif cant, voluntary compliance with law may also be a function of 'convenience, or other utilitarian factors, personal morality , ethics, relationships and ... the legitimacy of the source of law itself   '.[155] Because most disputes are resolved outside the law in all societies, recourse to institutions (formal *and* informal) is far less signif cant in ensuring the law is adhered to than the acceptance of law's legitimacy and its internalization into everyday behaviour and expectations.[156] Over time, it has become more and more apparent that technical institutional issues are impediments of second order importance in ensuring compliance with the law relative to those social, cultural and historical issues that impede the transition of law from a phenomenon complicit in repression or ineffective against it to something that claims the allegiance of ruler and ruled alike.[157] The reconstruction of institutions will do less to transform the substance of the citizenry' s action than the emer gence of a social, cultural and political environment that makes obedience to law normal. [158]

In place of instrumental calculations, compliance studies focus on two normative perspectives on the law, both concerned with internalized obligations for which the citizen takes personal responsibility . The f rst is moral, where people follow the law on the basis of a personal sense of whether the law is right or wrong. Because moral intuitions can also lead a citizen to disobey the law , rule of law reconstruction emphasizes the other type of normative commitment. Here, the citizen complies with law because he views the legal authority he is dealing with as legitimate, as one having *'auctorictas'* or 'capacity to engender the belief [it] deserve[s] obedience and respect'.[159] Support for the legitimacy perspective lies in its status as a more stable base for compliance. Legitimacy of law and institutions must be strong enough to guide behaviour as adherence to law often means voluntarily acting against one's self-interest (by prohibiting things we might want to do and mandating things we do not). Courts are special cases in this regard, as they are not derived from electoral process and so do not enjoy the same democratic legitimacy as the legislature or executive. Developing a cultural commitment to the rule of law means reinforcing public acceptance of the courts, even when they adversely affect people' s interests, for example where they imprison people or deliver unfavourable civil decisions. As Farrall puts it, 'no matter how enormous the task of material reconstruction may be, the most important reconstruction lies in the non-material area of reconstructing human relations and governance'. [160] A supply-side approach of providing institutions needs to be matched with a demand-side programme that will create and sustain appeal for law on the part of the population after the interveners depart.[161]

Though the voluntary commitment of citizens to law is of greater impor - tance for habitual law-abidingness than enforcement, enforcement of the law nevertheless tends to reinforce the societal respect for its institutions. [162] Like all institutions, the public must have conf dence in the courts' ability to deliver on the tasks for which they were designed or they will not be trusted.[63] Given that criminal justice operates at the boundary of the state and society , rule of law specialists display a similar conf dence to that of their transitional justice brethren that accountability for past atrocities can help develop the legitimacy of law and the legal system. While fragile phenomena like trust and legitimacy are a product of the unmeasurable and inf nitely variable mysteries of social contracting, most in the f eld who give the matter thought accept transitional justice can amount to a symbolically potent moment or one of those essential 'quick wins' that demonstrate the seriousness and competence of the mission. [164] Legal sociologists have long accepted that legitimacy is a dynamic concept – perceptions of justice institutions can change over time on the basis of how they perform. Most scholars and practitioners accept that resolving the legal issues of utmost important to the population constitutes a critical opportunity to demonstrate the relevance of the rule of law (though transitional justice is often of less immediate importance to the population than many assume).[165] Hurwitz and Studdard, for example, argue that domestic legal institutions can gain greater legitimacy among the population by addressing past human rights abuses, [166] while Call questions whether any post-transition regime could 'credibly establish the rule of law if its very birth rests in granting impunity or amnesty for morally heinous acts'. [167] Though there are states in Africa, Eastern Europe and Latin America that developed the rule of law in the midst of almost total impunity, the record seems to suggest that the failure to pursue transitional accountability can damage perception of the law and its institutions. In East Timor, for example, the failure to secure the convictions of those deemed most responsible for the crimes of the Indonesian occupation 'eroded' support for rule of law initiatives.[168] Similarly, in Rwanda and Bosnia, 'popular perceptions of present-day justice are closely linked to the adjudication of those who committed past human rights abuses'.[169] The self-legitimating effect of trials for the domestic justice system ('output legitimacy') is a theme developed in greater detail in Chapters 4 and 5. Furthermore, there is an expectation that transitional justice can galvanize public awareness of, and demand for , accountability on a national level. [170] Transitional justice can provide valuable links for domestic reform constituencies with international human rights networks and may generate leverage to inf uence public discourse. As Musila ar gues, transitional justice invariably rallies 'reformist forces' who might be expected to support legal reform. [171]

However, transitional justice can also be counterproductive in actively inf uencing citizen attitudes to the courts. Even with impeccable fairness and even-handedness, the political symbolism of transitional justice is a double-edged sword if the law' s long arm reaches out 'against men whose bloody boldness had been welcomed, or to respect sentences that do not treat wartime circumstances as extenuating'.[172] Note for example how the decision to indict and indeed begin the Special Court for Sierra Leone process with the trial of the pro-government Civil Defence Forces (CDF) was initially criticized by many Sierra Leoneans, [173] while Kosovo's f rst conviction of ethnic Albanians for war crimes led to widespread protests and a generally articulated disbelief that Albanians should be treated the same as Serbs in the eyes of the law.[174] Similarly, the inevitable leniency evident where decimated legal systems must engage with overwhelming numbers of criminals across borders tends to undo whatever good work is done by prosecutions by throwing into stark relief the prevalence of impunity. If resources are marshalled into prosecuting the 'big f sh' there is popular dissatisfaction that those who actually commit the crimes evade justice. While Sierra Leone' s decision to try the leaders of each faction was commended internationally for demonstrating that justice must now be 'qualitatively different from "business as usual"', [175] Sriram observed a popular feeling that 'the interpretation of greatest responsibility is incorrect – that it is those direct perpetrators who in fact bear it, not those who "just" gave orders'.[176] When 'small f sh' were the primary focus of prosecution, as occurred in East Timor's Special Panels, citizens and judges alike were dismayed at the message it sent about the law .[177]

While transitional justice can help advance the rule of law , it is only ever a partial response – dissatisfaction with prosecution policy is universal. Predictably, rule of law practitioners are more aware of how mar ginal transitional justice might be to social perspectives on the criminal justice system' s legitimacy, accepting that compliance 'depends most heavily on the perceived fairness and legitimacy of the laws, characteristics that are not established primarily by courts, but by other means, such as the political process'.   [178] Trebilcock and Daniels, for example, criticize the high priority given by the international community to lar ge formalist projects (such as elaborate transitional accountability proceedings), reasoning that experience in areas where citizens have day-to-day interactions with the legal system such as police, prosecutors, specialized law and administrative agencies, informal community-based schemes and alternative dispute resolution (ADR) will yield more visible and material benef ts for the rule of law' s acceptance.[179] Dedicated programmes of public education aimed at creating new expectations of the justice sector are key to building law's legitimacy.[180] The growth of outreach in transitional justice programmes and the emer   ging concern for consultation suggests a belated recognition of the importance of how local understandings of justice are given expression in informal and formal transitional justice mechanisms, though they remain more focused on the eff cacy of the mechanisms themselves than the rule of law overall.   [181] In terms of fostering a social understanding of law among citizens, transitional justice may play a relatively mar ginal role relative to that of media projects on law, support for human rights or ganizations and public relations programmes.[182]

One area where mainstream rule of law initiatives and transitional justice are *ad idem* is in their understanding that after a period of illiberal rule, there may be widespread scepticism about the value of justice institutions and that they do not enjoy the same primacy that they do in W estern societies. They understand that rule of law values cannot therefore be expressed abstractly – they must be relevant to the specif c social, political and cultural life of the nation. Golub's famous criticism of the institution-focused, law-dominated, internationally-driven 'rule of law orthodoxy' as being the product of rule by lawyers, bureaucratic inertia and lack of applied research is probably now the new orthodoxy.[183] The community-driven legal empowerment strategy grounded in grassroots needs which he advocates is echoed in the *Rule of Law and Transitional Justice Report*, which emphasized the need to possess suff cient knowledge of conditions and needs on the ground to tailor generic rule of law solutions (such as transitional justice) to local circumstance. Imperative in this regard is consultation, if rule of law reformers are to respond to or build on indigenous demand. These lessons are apparent in the *Report* which speaks of the need to eschew one-size-f ts-all formulas and the importation of foreign models but instead base support on 'national assessments, national participa-tion and national needs and aspirations'.[184]

The other necessary element in building legitimacy of both rule of law reform and transitional justice is the facilitation of local *participation* in the justice process, a term best def ned as the process through which primary stakeholders inf uence and share control of development initiatives, decisions and resources.[185] A judicial system cannot be imported or imposed – local people must feel a sense that their interests drive the process. Access to justice becomes as signif cant a benchmark as institutional competence. Participation can be cosmetic, co-opting or empowering, though best practice should emphasize the latter.[186] This involves the employment of ordinary citizens driving the process from the ground up, and of integration with national authorities who ultimately exercise oversight from the top down. Unfortunately, in most cases local ownership is fundamental to, but ignored in, judicial reform. Though not named specif cally in the *Rule of Law Report* as 'ownership', the concept is seen as imperative:

> Too often, the emphasis has been on foreign experts, foreign models and foreign-conceived solutions to the detriment of durable improvements and sustainable capacity. Both national and international experts have a vital role to play , to be sure. But we have learned that effective and sustainable approaches begin with a thorough analysis of national needs and capacities, mobilizing to the extent possible expertise resident in the country. Increasingly, the United Nations is looking to nationally led strategies of assessment.[187]

Where the *Report* broke new ground was in its focus on building national justice structures instead of international substitutes. Contrary to practice in the like of Cambodia, Kosovo and East T imor, domestic actors were to be empowered, consulted and trained in the creation of a sustainable justice system. Thus we see the aforementioned move to 'solidarity, not substitution'.[188]

However, though rule of law practitioners and transitional justice actors would both agree that participation and ownership are imperative, this belief will be manifested in different ways. Transitional justice projects increasingly urge consultation, involvement and localization. Similarly   , justice sector reformers commit to 'facilitate the processes through which various stakeholders debate and outline the elements of their country's plan to address the injustices of the past and secure sustainable justice for the future[189] However, this can only go so far – though the people can be consulted and involved in drawing up plans for the justice system, ultimately the legal system is state-based and to some extent unavoidably top-down and elitist. Nevertheless, rule of law reconstructors seem more committed to binding the national population to the legal system than transitional justice scholars. Despite commendable progress in mainstreaming consultations with affected populations by prosecutors and outreach programmes from formal justice institutions, Chapter 6 examines the increasing tendency of transitional justice scholars and policy-makers to stigmatize formal, criminal justice system programmes as too remote, too elitist and too irrelevant to the population at large. Much of the energy and resources that might go into binding the local population to state-based criminal prosecutions is instead diverted to subnational, localized processes of reconciliation, truth and healing which are deemed inherently more restorative and participatory . This is not to ar gue that local processes are not benef cial. The other element of Golub' s rule of law orthodoxy critique is that its top-down, government-centred approach focuses too much on law, lawyers and state institutions and gives insuff cient attention to the legal needs of the disadvantaged[190] is one that has been taken to heart by rule of law reformers and transitional justice activists. Golub contends that the dominant institution-based paradigm is frequently inapplicable and that the legal priorities of citizens are elsewhere. He instead argues for the legal empowerment alternative – 'the use of legal services and related development activities to increase disadvantaged populations control over their lives' – on the basis that civil society and indigenous justice mechanisms can yield more sustainable outcomes. [191] One statistic in particular is worth noting – 90 per cent or more of the law-orientated problems involving the poor are handled outside the courts in much of the developing world. [192] Botswana, Africa's best performer on indices of judicial eff ciency for the past 40 years, still resolves most disputes through customary law .[193] However, as Chapter 6 illustrates, there is a disparity between how justice sector reformers and transitional justice practitioners view these mechanisms. As regards the former, scholar-practitioners such as Faundez, [194] Wojkowska,[195] and Isser[196] argue that rule of law reformers must note the division of labour between formal courts and traditional ones and trust the latter to f ll inevitable vacuums after transition. By contrast, though transitional justice has responded with great alacrity to the need to design processes that reach the poor   , the rural, and the disaffected, many localized transitional justice schemes are explicitly valorized as sites of resistance to the state on the part of the disempowered.

2.6 A culture of the rule of law: restraining rulers

Of course all work to bind people to the courts will ultimately prove fruitless if a perception exists that there is no equality before the law, i.e. if rulers and the ruled are treated differently in the courts and that the latter are not subject to the same law as the former. Social commitment to the rule of law depends not only on mass commitment to the rule of law and the courts, therefore, but also on elite obligation to respect the law at all times at the expense of arbitrary action or wilful disobedience. In the conditions that pertain pre-transition, rulers govern in neopatrimonialist fashion, claiming to rule for the common good but considering themselves *de legibus solitus*.[197] The use of law for purely instrumental purposes before transition can condition attitudes towards it afterwards, a phenomenon recognized in the f rst *Rule of Law Report*, which noted that '[i]n some cases, state authorities have been more concerned with the consolidation of power than with strengthening the rule of law, with the latter often perceived as a threat to the former'. [198] The test after transition therefore is whether judges (and indeed prosecutors and lawyers) can exercise truly independent judgement or whether they will serve as tools of the new elite. In the long-term, the rule of law and peace will be threatened where governmental actors enjoy wide discretionary authority because this tends to encourage less principled and predictable decision-making. Where accountability of rulers is weak, so too is the rule of law. As Madison once argued, '[i]n framing a government ... the great diff culty lies in this: you must f rst enable the government to control the governed; and in the next place oblige it to control itself '.[199] Such restraint may very well f t with the declared aspirations of the new liberalizing government, though this should not be assumed. If the state was mistrusted as oppressive (or incompetent in the face of violence) then building trust in the idea of the state requires transformation in the way the state is perceived.

Given the Western leadership of UN peace operations generally and the turbulent nature of many transitions, most such UN activity will attempt to build or assist in building some form of representative democracy. In this system, rulers are subject to vertical accountability where the electorate can enforce standards of good conduct by government at the polls. However, studies of the defects of third wave democracies have shown that elections alone are insuff cient to curb the power of executives who frequently return to the corruption, abuses and plebiscitary practices of prior illiberal rule. [200] Binding rulers to the law by other agencies such as the courts can prove a more effective check on political power than the vagaries of elections, where other interests can cloud the issue. This checking process is known as 'horizontal accountability', a concept outlined by Guillermo O'Donnell [201] and

Richard Sklar.[202] Here, the courts uphold the rule of law by checking the validity of all enacted norms. Though usually associated with inter -branch separation of powers in democracies with an executive, legislature and judiciary, Sklar reminds us that it is also compatible with structuralist conceptions of constitutions imbued with little spiritual content based on more diverse (or indeed more illiberal) philosophical principles than democracy.[203] Horizontal accountability literally connotes a degree of equality in as much as we deem the judiciary, executive and legislature as equally worthy of respect. However, Schedler points out that if accountability is to succeed, the accounting party cannot stand on an equal footing with the accountable one – in its sphere of competence, the courts must be more powerful than the executive.[204] This is the 'paradox of accountability' – where a specialized agency holds accountable actors who are immeasurably more powerful than it except in the narrow sphere of competence of the former.[205] The key to horizontal accountability then is not equality but independence, or , more correctly, autonomy. If this does not exist, the courts cannot succeed in either making rulers answerable or enforcing their judgments.[206] The boundaries of the courts must be respected. Encroachment through control of appointment, force, bribery etc violates the autonomy necessary for effective horizontal accountability, as does interference in criminal or constitutional cases. None of this is to say that absolute independence is necessary – there is also value in reciprocal monitoring and oversight by the executive and legislative branches as occurs in all functioning rule of law systems. Indeed, one of the primary rule of law objections to internationalized tribunals or the administration of justice by the UN is that the judges appointed are often independent of democratic accountability. The objective of any separation of powers principle is to achieve an optimum rather than maximum degree of institutional independence.[207]

The autonomy of the courts is largely a constitutional issue. In transition, either a new constitution is written or effect is given to the old, with or without amendment where necessary . Formal requirements for respecting the courts' autonomy will be laid out or implied therein, and the courts for the most part lack the capacity to enforce their autonomy without executive acquiescence. Increasingly, international standards have come to infuence the design of the institutional setting on which the independence of the justice sector is reliant. Any attempts to secure the autonomy of judges, prosecutors and lawyers should incorporate the *Basic Principles on the Independence of the Judiciary*[208] and the *Basic Principles on the Role of Lawyers* which express the international community's admittedly non-binding view of how their autonomy is secured.[209] Merit-based appointment, f xed tenure, high professional competency, judicial councils with transparent discipline procedures and safeguards for the right to fair trial can help preserve judicial autonomy .

Genuine autonomy requires more than reform of institutions, however . As Domingo points out:

> It would appear that the problem of judicial independence and constitutional control goes well beyond constitutional and legal prescriptions

and ref ects a deep-rooted lack of rule observance and law-abidingness – and long-established habits of impunity and disrespect for the law.[210]

It requires rulers to act against their immediate self-interest and entrenched concerns. As such, autonomy is primarily a matter for executive self-restraint and constitutional sensitivity. Because of its inherent politicization and the diff culties that may f ow from inevitably contentious decisions to investigate, prosecute and convict, transitional accountability can serve as an overt example of executive deference to the judicial system, and in so doing set a strong precedent for future interaction. If governments are trying to widen the 'radius of trust' to build co-operation between antagonistic groups,[211] the choice to apply the law equally to friend and foe is a very dramatic signal that a substantially new type of executive-judiciary relationship is commencing. As history shows, even the most democratizing of transitional governments might have a strong wish to retain control of accountability because it wishes to keep the peace stable, to keep any criminality it may have been involved in secret or because of a pre-transitional experience of opposing the judiciary it now has to work with. Judicial autonomy may prove diff cult to respect at various points, but if actually secured in these conditions can do much to signal a new era where a government is willing to enforce law against its own interests (or even its own leaders):

> Some states in periods of crisis may draw on the crisis itself to generate legitimacy. Precisely those conditions that threaten the viability of the state may present opportunities to demonstrate its relevance to the population.[212]

What any transitional bench must do is assert its autonomy wherever it is called into question, and insulate itself from cultural or social inf uences that can impair the detachment of judges or prosecutors. This is a diff cult task in divided societies with very obvious social cleavages. The courts are often impotent in the face of executive or legislative interference if this is what the latter really want. As a result, autonomy may only be secured by the courage of individual judges or prosecutors in resisting pressure, in what Schedler dubs 'the mystery of human agency'.[213] Transitional accountability is an obvious means of exemplifying resistance. For example, Collins ar gues that progress since 1998 on the part of a reforming Chilean judiciary on accountability for Pinochet-era human rights abuses 'hav[e] less to do with the particular issue at hand than with a desire to assert autonomy vis-à-vis other branches of government or the "political class" as a whole' and to end a long-term trend from pre-transitional times for judicial glosses to be given to essentially political decisions.[214] Securing accountability for heinous crimes by being demonstrably impartial and effective, creating alliances with national and international NGOs and outlining a rights-based jurisprudence can furthermore help create a supportive constituency among the public that can preserve the judiciary from executive interference. As the Tanzanian Chief Justice Nyalali puts it:

> The ultimate safeguard is really public opinion. Judges cannot force the military back to the barracks. They can' t run for seats in parliament in order to inf uence the legislature. The people have to value an independent judiciary and be willing to defend it.[215]

By demonstrably elevating the public interest over that of the government in the highest-prof le legal proceedings, transitional justice may give them a strong reason to do so.

The task of the rule of law reconstruction is to help develop this autonomy through monitoring, education and support. However, given that transitional justice has progressively been internationalized 'to rescue the possibility of universal justice from the revenge frenzies, political compromises, and local partialities of national justice',[216] and localized to evermore microscopic subnational processes, transitional justice policy seems willing to opt out of (or prematurely admit defeat in) addressing the government' s incentive structures for respecting judicial autonomy , preferring instead exceptionalist, temporary solutions when faced with executive reluctance to pursue immediate prosecutions. The complementarity regime, with its in-built system of monitoring national justice systems, would appear to offer a useful possibility of solidifying judicial autonomy from executive interference by acting as a form of conditional punishment or reward that has worked well in other contexts. However, the experiences of the hybrid courts and international tribunals tend to suggest that where transitional justice practitioners have a choice between buttressing domestic participation and judicial autonomy, on the one hand, or hiving accountability off from the process of domestic reform by internationalizing it to a greater degree, the latter will be preferred. As Chesterman puts it, 'if accountability depends on the massive international presence that may follow a crisis then it may be seen as the exception rather than the norm. Episodic prosecutions when outside political will and resources available may do little to establish sustainable institutions.'[217] This issue is addressed in greater detail in Chapter 5.

2.7 The diffusion of fair trial norms

In retrospect, the diver gence of interest and opinion between rule of law reconstructors and transitional justice practitioners over institutions and issues of culture should come as no surprise. T ransitional justice is so ends-based (justice, accountability, human rights) that its essential ambivalence about means (national courts, international courts, alternative institutions) is in some ways predictable. The almost messianic zeal transitional justice advocates demonstrate for pressing ends such as peace, reconciliation and justice explain its urgent willingness to by-pass engaging the government in long-term behavioural change that would ground a more sustainable rule of law culture. The focus on those who have suffered most and longest that has made transitional justice so commendably victim/survivor-centred has tended to relegate the wider , more everyday relationships of citizens with their criminal justice system as a priority . One would assume that the normative aspects of the rule of law, i.e. those relating to human rights, would provide greater opportunity for convergence of interest and opinion. The modern feld of rule of law reconstruction was born out of a desire to f rmly ground liberal democracy and human rights in Latin America and Eastern Europe,[218] encapsulating 'an increasing demand for law, or, more specif cally, for the treatment of human rights as justiciable claims rather than mere aspirations, and for legal institutions that are able to enforce these claims'.   [219] The new or reformed constitutions of most transitional countries guarantee civil rights, including fair trial rights. Strong correlations have been found between the rule of law and social, economic and bodily integrity rights.[220] The normative primacy the UN and various international NGOs afford to human rights clearly informed the *Rule of Law and Transitional Justice Report*, which evinces a desire to go far beyond formal institutions and habitual law-abidingness by incorporating consistency with international human rights norms as the *sin qua non* of the rule of law. Transitional accountability for crimes of mass atrocity and human rights abuses is clearly envisaged as being at the heart of this normative vision, something practitioners and scholars in either f eld would hardly quibble with.

However, if we look at the practice of transitional justice and rule of law reconstruction in detail, once more we see a divergence in opinion and interest. While for the transitional justice practitioner   , trial is a means of condemning abuses of the right to life, torture, false imprisonment and aff rming a political order based on democracy and human rights, as far as rule of law practitioners are concerned, the over-riding human rights imperative is a more limited one of ensuring a standard of fair trial is guaranteed. Earlier Berlin's hedgehog-fox metaphor was employed to describe how transitional justice practitioners and scholars tend to view the rule of law through the lens of a single def ning idea (an almost exclusive focus on legal responses to human rights, albeit broadly understood), while rule of law practitioners are foxes who, of necessity, must know many things like the need for institutions, hierarchies within those institutions, public legitimacy   , executive restraint in the face of the judiciary , popular commitment to legal institutions, etc. In human rights terms, the emphasis is reversed. T   ransitional justice advocates are the far-ranging generalist foxes, employing transitional justice to aff rm humanitarian law, personal integrity rights and, increasingly, socio-economic rights. Rule of law practitioners, on the other hand, emer ge as concentrated specialist hedgehogs. While certainly not hostile to humanitarian law or the wide panoply of human rights concerns in transition (no more than transitional scholars should be considered hostile to national judicial institutions or cultural commitments to the rule of law), their over-riding normative concern in accountability processes is not whether and how it aff rms *ius cogens* norms, the democratic settlement, equality or personal integrity, but rather whether the process abides by fair trial rights such as due process, habeas corpus and non-retroactivity.

> [T]rials for atrocity crimes should demonstrate and reassure people that justice can be fair – procedurally fair in terms of due process and the rights of the accused, and substantively fair in terms of evenhanded treatment of comparable actions regardless of who committed them … procedurally fair and impartial trials underscore the importance of respect for all persons, including defendants accused of severe atrocities, providing a concrete example of fair justice to domestic populations that may have little conf dence in justice institutions based on prior experience.[221]

Such assessments are made by analysing a given process with regard to international standards as found in codes such as, *inter alia*, the International Covenant on Civil and Political Rights (ICCPR), International Covenant on Economic, Social and Cultural Rights (ICESCR), UN Basic Principles on the Independence of the Judiciary , the UN Basic Principles on the Role of Lawyers and the Body of Principles for the Protection of All Persons under Any Form of Detention and Imprisonment. Probably the most important of these is the ICCPR.[222] The Convention contains, among other things, the principles of equality before the law,[223] the presumption of innocence,[224] the right to a fair and public hearing by a competent, independent and impartial jury,[225] and the right to be tried without delay .[226] A recognizably fair trial cannot be decided against a party until he has had the opportunity to be heard and he should be adequately informed of what is said against him. If a defendant's interest at trial cannot be adequately protected without the benef t of legal counsel, the state should provide such assistance. The accused should have adequate time and facilities to prepare his defence to char   ges against him, the accuser or prosecutor should make available any and all material helpful or exculpatory, and above all he should be presumed innocent until guilt is proved. If such standards were absent before, their necessity in future may not be immediately accepted by the populace and the content of such rights remains to be delineated. Only when the population observing these *rules* 'tak[e] a normative, evaluative attitude' to their application and endow them with the authority to regulate their behaviour can they be recognized as *norms*.[227] Transitional trials probably offer the most high-prof le opportunity to publicly reinforce the norms' validity and content.

Few transitional justice advocates would disagree with the desirability of these standards. One sees in the literature a general commitment to due process, while any unfairness of trial has often proven a potent source of criticism for many types of accountability . However, it would not be inaccurate to say that traditionally many in the transitional justice f eld have not attached the same paramountcy to fair trial as their counterparts in justice sector reform. Indeed, in many of the formative debates on transitional justice, the fairness of trial was treated as a far more open question than those rebuilding the justice system would wish. As Chapters 3 and 4 go on to show both realist and idealist ideas theories of transitional justice have been content to jettison aspects of due process and fair trial in pursuit of ill-defined but greatly desired human rights dividends. The history of transitional justice's attempts to redefne the social order is pock-marked with breaches of defendants' rights, politicization and retroactivity which are generally incompatible with fair trial rights. Though content where the judicial process coincidentally serves important instrumental functions, rule of law reconstruction emphasizes the intrinsic value of trial independent of its effect for good or ill on transitional society. Rule of law reconstruction has long had to grapple with the problem that improved due process rights can erode public support for the rule of law because the resultant acquittals can undermine law and order, but nevertheless stresses the longer -term interest in abiding by procedural rules.[228] Systems of training and monitoring in rule of law reconstruction stress enforcement of legal safeguards against illegal state action as essential to a norm-based rule of law – a court that pursues human rights breaches from the past by denying defendants' rights in the present is less likely to have the legitimacy or will to protect human rights in the future than one which respects the autonomy and worth of the individual even where the benef ts of speedy trial, selective prosecution or mass convictions seem self-evident. This is not to ar gue that rule of law reconstructors always succeed – for example, the UN T ransitional Administration in East T imor's Human Rights Unit documented frequent violations of due process not only in the Special Panels trials but in the ordinary judicial system, including unlawful detention, inequality of arms and departure from the transitional rules of criminal procedure.[229] However, while peace-builders are self-critical of these failings, deviations from the fair trial one sees in domestic attempts at transitional justice and, to a much lesser extent, internationally, have been justif ed as part of a distinctly transitional rule of law . While justice sector reformers emphasize the intrinsic value of fair trial, all too often more retributive or utilitarian transitional justice concerns trump a more scrupulous concern for the integrity of the trial process. It is to this that attention now turns in Chapters 3 and 4.

Notes

1 See generally F. Neate (ed.), *The Rule of Law: Perspectives From Around the Globe* (London: LexisNexis, 2009).

2 J.Finnis, *Natural Law and Natural Rights* (Oxford: Clarendon Press, 1980), 270.

3 B.Tamanaha, *On the Rule of Law: History, Politics, Theory* (Cambridge, New York: Cambridge University Press, 2004), 3.

4 R. Peerenboom, 'Human Rights and the Rule of Law: What' s the Relationship?' (2005) 36 *Georgetown Journal of International Law* 809, 826.

5 T. Carothers, 'Steps Towards Knowledge' in T. Carothers (ed.), *Promoting the Rule of Law Abroad: In Search of Knowledge* (Washington, D.C.: Carnegie Endowment for International Peace, 2006), 327 at 328.

6 G.Casper, *Rule of Law? Whose Law?* (Stanford: Center on DemocracyDevelopment, and the Rule of Law, 2004), 13–14.

7 J.Stromseth, M. Wippman and R. Brooks, *Can Might Make Rights? Building the Rule of Law After Military Interventions* (Cambridge: Cambridge University Press, 2006), 57.

8 J. Farrall, 'Impossible Expectations? The UN Security Council's Promotion of the Rule of Law after Conf ict' in B. Bowden, H. Charlesworth and J. Farrall (eds.), *The Role of International Law in Rebuilding Societies after Conflict: Great Expectations* (New York: Cambridge University Press, 2009), 134 at 135. Peerenboom makes a similar point (Peerenboom, supra n4, 817).

9 Stromseth,Wippman and Brooks, supra n7, 69.

10 F Fukuyama, *State Building: Governance and World Order in the Twenty-First Century* (New York: Cornell University Press, 2004), 39.

11 Stromseth,Wippman and Brooks, supra n7, 57 and 73.

12 Peerenboom,supra n4, 827–828.

13 Ibid.

14 M.Doyle and N. Sambanis, *Making War and Building Peace: United Nations Peace Operations* (Princeton: Princeton University Press, 2006), 17–19 and 73.

15 R. Kleinfeld Belton, *Competing Definitions of the Rule of Law: Implications for Practitioners* (Washington, D.C.: Carnegie Endowment for International Peace, 2005), 3.

16 Ibid.

17 E. Jensen, 'The Rule of Law and Judicial Reform: The Political Economy of Diverse Institutional Patterns and Reformer' s Responses' in E. Jensen and T. Heller (eds.), *Beyond Common Knowledge: Empirical Approaches to the Rule of Law* (Stanford: Stanford Law and Politics, 2003), 336 at 345–346.

18 R.Paris, *At War's End: Building Peace After Civil Conflict* (New York: Cambridge University Press, 2004), 15.

19 J. Demmers, A. Fernández Jilberto and B. Hogenboom, 'Good Governance and Democracy is a W orld of Neoliberal Regimes' in J. Demmers, A. Fernández Jilberto and B. Hogenboom (eds.), *Good Governance in the Era of Global Liberalism: Conflict and Depoliticisation in Latin America, Eastern Europe, Asia and Africa* (London: Routledge, 2004), 1 at 4.

20 Fukuyama,supra n10, 131.

21 N. Bhuta, 'Democratisation, State-Building and Politics as Technology' in Bowden, Charlesworth and Farrall (eds.), supra n8, 38 at 45.

22 W. Zartman, 'Introduction: Posing the Problem of State Collapse' in W. Zartman (ed.), *Collapsed State: The Disintegration and Restoration of Legitimate Authority* (Boulder: Lynne Rienner, 1995), 6.

23 S. Krasner, 'Sharing Sovereignty: New Institutions for Collapsed and Failing States' (2004) 29 *International Security* 85, 91.

24 PCollier et al., *Breaking the Conflict Trap: Civil War and Development Policy* (Washington, D.C., New York: World Bank and Oxford University Press, 2003), 83.

25 UNSecretary General, *An Agenda for Peace: Preventive Diplomacy, Peacemaking and Peace-Keeping: Report of the Secretary-General*, UN SCOR, 47th Session, UN Doc A/47/277 – S/24111, of 17 June 1992.

26Ibid.,para. 21.

27 For a useful history of the progressive intensity of UN peace missions, see R. Wilde, *International Territorial Administration – How Trusteeship and the Civilizing Mission Never Went Away* (Oxford: Oxford University Press, 2007).

28UNSecretary-General, *No exit without strategy: Security Council decision-making and the closure or transition of United Nations peacekeeping operations*, UN Doc. S/2001/394 (2001), of 20 April 2001.

29Paris,supra n18, 79.

30 S. Hameiri, 'Failed State or a Failed Paradigm? State Capacity and the Limits of Institutionalism' (2007) 10 *Journal of International Relations and Development* 122.

31KleinfeldBelton, supra n15, 18.

32Panelon UN Peace Operations, *Report of the Panel on United Nations Peace Operations* UN Doc. A/55/305-S/2000/809, 21 August 2000, paras. 81–83.

33 International Crisis Group, 'Courting Disaster: The Misrule of Law in Bosnia and Herzegovina' (2002), available <http://www.ciaonet.org/wps/icg241/icg241.pdf>, 6–7.

34 See generally S. Beidas, C. Granderson and R. Neild, 'Justice and Security Reform after Intervention: Haiti' in C. Call (ed.), *Constructing Justice and Security After War* (Washington, D.C.: United States Institute of Peace, 2007), 69.

35UNSecretary-General, *The Rule of Law and Transitional Justice in Conflict and Post-Conflict Societies* (2004) UN Doc. S/2004/616, para. 2.

36Stromseth,Wippman and Brooks, supra n7, 312.

37 Panel on UN Peace Operations, supra n 32, paras. 39–40.

38Ibid.,para. 13.

39Ibid.,para. 39.

40C.Bull, *No Entry Without Strategy: Building the Rule of Law Under UN Transitional Administration* (New York: United Nations University Press, 2008), 250.

41Ibid.,45.

42 D. Marshall and S. Inglis, 'The Development of Human Rights-Based Justice in the UN Mission in Kosovo' (2003) 16 *Harvard Human Rights Journal* 95, 95.

43The Conflict, Security and Development Group, *A Review of Peace Operations: A Case for Change* (London: Kings College, 2003).

44UNSecretary-General, supra n35, para. 16.

45UNSecretary-General, supra n35, para. 6.

46 E.g. P. Uvin, 'Diffcult Choices in the New Post-Confct Agenda: The International Community in Rwanda after the Genocide' (2001) 22 *Third World Quarterly* 177 and G. Knaus and F Martin, '"Travails of the European Raj": Lessons from Bosnia-Herzegovina' (2003) 14(3) *Journal of Democracy* 60.

47 R. Daniels and M. Trebilcock, 'The Political Economy of Rule of Law Reform in Developing Countries' (2004) 26 *Michigan Journal of International Law* 99, 108, Peerenboom, supra n4, 825.

48 A. Boulokos and B. Dakin, 'T oward a Universal Declaration of the Rule of Law: Implications for Criminal Justice and Sustainable Development' (2001) *International Journal of Comparative Sociology* 143, 149.

49T Carothers, supra n5, 330.

50UNSecretary-General, supra n35, para. 16.

51Ibid.,Preamble. See also paras. 15 and 17.

52Paris,supra n18, 22–32.

53 Panel on UN Peace Operations, supra n32, para. 58 and UN Secretary-General, supra n35, para. 10.

54 C.Bell, *Peace Agreements and Human Rights* (Oxford, New York: Oxford University Press, 2000), 6.

55 S. Carlson, 'Legal and Judicial Rule of Law W   ork in Multi-Dimensional Peacekeeping Operations: Lessons-Learned Study'(2006), UN DPKO Peacekeeping Best Practice Section, available: < http://www.peacekeepingbestpractices.unlb. org/PBPS/Library/ROL%20Lessons%20Learned%20Report%20%20March%20 2006%20FINAL.pdf>, 2–3.

56 UNDoc. A/61/636-S/2006/980 of 14 December 2006.

57 Ibid.,para. 36.

58 Fora list see <http://www.ohchr.org/EN/PUBLICATIONSRESOURCES/Pages/ SpecialIssues.aspx>.

59 UNSecretary-General, *The Rule of Law and Transitional Justice in Conflict and Post-Conflict Societies* (2011) UN Doc. S/2011/634 of 12 October 2011.

60 Stromseth, Wippman and Brooks, supra n7, 328, C. Call, 'Introduction: What We Know and Don' t Know about Postconf ict Justice and Security Reform' in C. Call (ed.), supra n34, C.L. Sriram, O. Martin-Ortega and J. Herman (eds.), *Peacebuilding and Rule of Law in Africa* (Oxford: Routledge, 2011).

61 R. Sannerholm, 'Legal, Judicial and Administrative Reforms in Post-Conf ict Societies: Beyond the Rule of Law T emplate' (2007) 12 *Journal of Conflict and Security Law* 65, 87.

62 A.Hurwitz and K. Studdard, *Rule of Law Programs in Peace Operations* (New York: International Peace Academy, 2005), i and 2.

63 Bull,supra n40, 48.

64 Stromseth,Wippman and Brooks, supra n7, 57.

65 R. Sannerholm, *Rule of Law after War and Crisis: Ideologies, Norms and Methods* (Cambridge: Intersentia, 2012), 90.

66 Stromseth,Wippman and Brooks, supra n7, 73.

67 AmnestyInternational, 'Afghanistan: Police Reconstruction Essential for Human Rights' (2003) Amnesty International, available < http://www.amnesty.org/en/ library/info/ASA11/003/2003>, 1.

68 For example, the Preambles of UN Security Council Resolutions 1580 and 1545 on the situations in Guinea-Bissau and Burundi explicitly linked the rule of law with ending impunity for violations of international criminal law.

69 E.g.UN Secretary-General, supra n35, paras. 23–26.

70 R. Pulver, 'Rule of Law, Peacekeeping and the United Nations' in Sriram, Martin-Ortega and Herman (eds.), supra n60, 60 at 71.

71 M.Trebilcock and R. Daniels, *Rule of Law Reform and Development: Charting the Fragile Path of Progress* (Cheltenham: Edward Elgar, 2008), 92.

72 R. Summers, 'A Formal Theory of the Rule of Law' (1993) 6 *Ratio Juris* 127 and J. Raz, 'The Rule of Law and its Virtue' (1977) 93 *Law Quarterly Review* 195.

73 C. Rose, 'The "New" Law and Development Movement in the Post-Cold War Era: A Vietnam Case-Study' (1998) 32 *Law and Society Review* 93.

74 P. McAuliffe, 'Transitional Justice and the Rule of Law: The Perfect Couple or Awkward Bedfellows?' (2010) 2 *Hague Journal on the Rule of Law* 110.

75 UNSecretary-General, supra n59, para. 20.

76 R.Packenham, *Liberal America in the Third World* (Princeton: Princeton University Press, 1973), cited in C. Call and S. Cook, 'On Democratization and Peacebuilding' (2003) 9 *Global Governance* 233, 236.

77 KleinfeldBelton, supra n15, 6.

78 Febilcock and Daniels, supra n71, 336.

79 For a bibliographical list of the more positive assessments of transitional justice, see Chapter 1, n64 and surrounding text.

80 Doyleand Sambanis, supra n14, 338.

81 D. Orentlicher, 'Settling Accounts: The Duty to Prosecute Human Rights Violations of a Prior Legal Regime' (1991) 100 *Yale Law Journal* 2537, 2548–2549.

82 Pulver supra n70, 71.

83 One OSCE survey concluded that many rule of law practitioners lack a comprehensive understanding of what the rule of law promotion means (FEvers, *OSCE Efforts to Promote the Rule of Law: History, Structures, Survey* (Hamburg: Centre for OSCE Research, 2010), 9–10.

84 UNSecretary-General, *Seventeenth Progress Report on the United Nations Mission in Liberia* UN Doc. S/2008/553 of 28 August 2008, para. 39.

85 Sannerholm,supra n65, 243.

86 D. Isser, 'Understanding and Engaging Customary Justice Systems' in D. Isser (ed.), *Customary Justice and the Rule of Law in War-Torn Societies* (Washington, D.C.: USIP, 2011), 325 at 343.

87 UNSecretary-General, supra n59, para. 15.

88 KleinfeldBelton, supra n15, 23.

89 Carothers, supra n5, 330, Stromseth, Wippman and Brooks, supra n7, 75.

90 E.g.Peerenboom, supra n4.

91 P. Gready, 'Telling Truth? The Methodological Challenges of Tuth Commissions' in F. Coomans, F. Grunfeld and M. Kamminga (eds.), *Methods of Human Rights Research* (Antwerp: Intersentia, 2009), 159 at 162.

92 L. Bosire, *Overpromised, Underdelivered: Transitional Justice in Sub-Saharan Africa* (New York: ICTJ, 2006).

93 L.Fuller, *The Morality of Law* (New Haven: Yale University Press, 1969), 39 and 46–90.

94 UNSecretary-General, supra n35, para. 27.

95 See generally D. T olbert and A. Solomon, 'United Nations Reform and Supporting the Rule of Law in Post-Confict Societies' (2006) 19 *Harvard Human Rights Law Journal* 29, 45–51.

96 The UN Basic Principles on the Independence of the Judiciary, endorsed by the UN General Assembly Resolution 40/32, UN Doc. A/RES/40/32 (1985) of 29 November 1985, Preamble.

97 Bull,supra n40, 11.

98 Febilcock and Daniels, supra n71, 28–29.

99 Ibid,332.

100 Bull,supra n40, 53.

101 R.Mani, *Beyond Retribution – Seeking Justice in the Shadows of War* (Cambridge: Polity Press, 2002), 76.

102 M. Drumbl, 'Policy Through Complementarity: The Atrocity Trial as Justice' in C. Stahn and M. El Zeidy (eds.), *The International Criminal Court and Complementarity: From Theory to Practice* (Vol. I) (Cambridge: Cambridge University Press, 2011), 197 at 197.

103 Peerenboom,supra n4, 911.

104 O. Korhonen, 'The "State-Building Enterprise": Legal Doctrine, Progress Narratives and Managerial Governance' in Bowden, Charlesworth and Farrall (eds.), supra n8, 15 at 16.

105 Mani, supra n101, 77.

106 S. Golub, 'A House Without Foundation' in Carothers (ed.), supra n5, 105 at 105.

107 S. von Einsiedel, 'Policy Responses to State Failure' in S. Chesterman, M. Ignatieff, and R. Thakur (eds.), *Making States Work: State Failure and the Crisis of Governance* (New York: United Nations University Press, 2005), 13 at 25–26.

108 O. Richmond, 'The Rule of Law in Liberal Peace-Building' in Sriram, Ortega-Martin and Hermans (eds.), supra n60, 44 at 45.

109 A. Sen, *Development as Freedom* (Oxford: Oxford University Press, 2001).

110 R. Gargarella, P. Domingo and T. Roux (eds.), *Courts and Social Transformation in New Democracies – An Institutional Voice for the Poor?* (Aldershot: Ashgate, 2006).

111 R. Islam, 'Institutional Reform and the Judiciary: Which Way Forward?' (2003) World Bank Policy Research Working Paper, available: < http://www-wds. worldbank.org/external/default/WDSContentServer/WDSP/IB/2003/10/06/0001 60016_20031006120937/additional/112512322_20041117165029.pdf>, 6–9.

112 Sannerholm, n61, 75.

113 D. Dyzenhaus, *Hard Cases in Wicked Legal Systems: Pathologies of Legality* (New York: University of Oxford, 2010).

114 J. Gardner, *Legal Imperialism: American Lawyers and Foreign Aid in Latin America* (Madison: University of Wisconsin Press, 1980), 122.

115 Sannerholm, supra n65, 86.

116 Raz, 'The Rule of Law and its Virtue', supra n72.

117 Daniels and Trebilcock, supra n47, 105.

118 T.R.S. Allan, *Law, Liberty and Justice, The Legal Foundations of British Constitutionalism* (New York: Oxford University Press, 1993).

119 J. Raz, *Authority of Law* (Oxford: Clarendon Press, 1979), 221.

120 Ibid., 23 and F. Neumann, *The Rule of Law: Political Theory and the Legal System in Modern Society* (Leamington Spa: Berg, 1986), 32.

121 Peerenboom, supra n4, at 944–945.

122 L. Hammergren, *Rule of Law: Approaches to Justice Reform and What We Have Learned: A Summary of Four Papers* (Washington, D.C.: USAID, 1998).

123 C. Murphy, *A Moral Theory of Political Reconciliation* (Cambridge: Cambridge University Press, 2010), 99.

124 Summers, supra n72, 135.

125 Trebilcock and Daniels, supra n71, 42.

126 Farrall, supra n8, 156.

127 Fukuyama, supra n10, 58.

128 UN Secretary-General, supra n35, para. 17.

129 Sannerholm, supra n65, 168–169.

130 Supra n96, para. 10.

131 *The UN Basic Principles on the Role of Lawyers*, endorsed by the UN General Assembly in UN General Assembly Resolution 45/166, P 15 UN Doc. A/RES/45/166 (December 18, 1990), para. 9.

132 M. Ellis, 'Developing a Global Program for Enhancing Accountability: Key Ethical Tenets for the Legal Profession in the 21st Century' (2003) 54   *South Carolina Law Review* 1011.

133 Guidelines on the Role of Prosecutors, Eighth U.N. Congress on the Prevention of Crime and the Treatment of Offenders, Havana, Aug. 27–Sept. 7, 1990, UN Doc. A/CONF. 144/28/Rev.1 at 189.

134 Off ce of the United Nations High Commissioner for Human Rights, 'Rule of Law Tools for Post-Conf ict States: Monitoring Legal Systems' (2008) HR/PUB/06/3.

135 S. Toope, 'Legal and Judicial Reform through Development Assistance: Some Lessons' (2003) *McGill Law Journal* 357, 400.

136 Ibid.

137 E. Witte, *International Crimes, Local Justice: A Handbook for Rule-of-Law Policymakers, Donors and Implementers* (New York: Open Society Justice Initiative, 2011), 13.

138 Fukuyama, supra n10, 54–55.

139 M Ignatieff, *Empire Lite: Nation-Building in Bosnia, Kosovo and Afghanistan* (London: Vintage, 2003), 98–101. Similarly, the R2P report warns against the tendency of international actors to conf scate or monopolize political responsibility on the ground (International Commission on Intervention and State Sovereignty, *The Responsibility to Protect* (Ottawa: International Development Research Centre, 2001, 45).

140 For example, many national rule of law actors enjoyed training and skills development at the Special Court for Sierra Leone, but subsequently sought employment in international oganizations and tribunals (ICTJ, UNDP, Ministries of Foreign Affairs of Denmark and South Africa, 'Supporting Complementarity at the National Level: An Integrated Approach to Rule of Law' (2011), available <http://www.ictj.org/sites/default/f les/ICTJ-Global-Greentree-Two-Synthesis-Report-2011.pdf>, 3).

141 M. Ottaway, 'Rebuilding State Institutions in Collapsed States' (2002) 33 *Development and Change* 1001, 1004.

142 Stromseth, Wippman and Brooks, supra n7, 78.

143 Ibid.,76.

144 S. Eizenstat, J.E. Porter and J. W einstein, 'Rebuilding Weak States' (2005) 84 *Foreign Affairs* 134, 138.

145 Fuller, supra n93, 39–40.

146 T Tyler, *Why People Obey the Law* (Princeton: Princeton University Press, 2006).

147 Ibid.,20–21.

148 W. Channell, 'Lessons Not Learned About Legal Reform' in Carothers (ed.), supra n5, 137 at 146.

149 J. Migdal, 'Why Do So Many States Stay Intact?' in P . Dauvergne (ed.), *Weak and Strong States in Asia-Pacific Societies* (Sydney: Allen and Unwin, 1998), 11 at 22–23 and Murphy, supra n123, 41.

150 Tyler, supra n146, 32.

151 Department for International Development, 'Justice and Poverty Reduction: Safety, Security and Access to Justice for All' (2000), available < http://www.gsdrc.org/docs/open/SSAJ35.pdf>, 3.

152 Douglass North, *Institutions, Institutional Change and Economic Performance* (Cambridge: Cambridge University Press, 2001), 54.

153 W. Maley, 'Institutional Design and the Building of T rust' in W . Maley, C. Sampford and R. Thakur (eds.), *From Civil Strife to Civil Society: Civil and Military Responsibilities in Disrupted States* (Tokyo, New York: United Nations University Press, 2003), 163 at 170.

154 Bull, supra n40, 10.

155 M. Plunkett, 'Rebuilding the Rule of Law' in Maley , Sampford and Thakur (eds.), supra n153, 207 at 212.

156 R.Ellickson, *Order Without Law: How Neighbours Settle Disputes* (Cambridge, MA: Harvard University Press, 1991).

157 Danielsand Trebilcock, supra n47, 127–128.

158 A.Przeworski, *Sustainable Democracy* (Cambridge: Cambridge University Press, 1995), 51.

159 J.J. Toharia, 'Evaluating Systems of Justice Through Public Opinion: Why   , What, Who, How, and What For?' in Jensen and Heller (eds.), supra n17, 21 at 24. See also Tyler, supra n146, especially 19–39 and 170–178.

160 Farrall,supra n8, 154.

161 Though Kleinfeld Belton quite reasonably points out that institutional reform can be a 'lever of change' that pushes culture and politics in the right direction (Kleinfeld Belton, supra n15, 22), while Schedler notes supportive habits and attitudes can be stimulated through the establishment of new structures (A. Schedler, 'Measuring Democratic Consolidation' (2001) 36   *Studies in Comparative International Development* 66, 81).

162 G. Shabbir Cheema, *Building Democratic Institutions: Governance Reform in Developing Countries* (West Hartford, CT: Kumarian Press, 2005), 187.

163 C. Offe, 'Designing Institutions in East European Tansitions' in R. Goodin (ed.), *The Theory of Institutional Design* (Cambridge: Press Syndicate of the University of Cambridge, 1996), 199 at 200–201.

164 On'quick wins', see Carlson, supra n55, 12.

165 See Chapter 3, Section 3.7, on the relative lack of priority attached to transitional justice in population surveys of transitional states.

166 Hurwitzand Studdard, supra n62, ii.

167 Call,supra n60, 14.

168 Bull,supra n40, 189.

169 C. Call, 'Conclusion: Constructing Justice and Security After War' in Call (ed.), supra n34, 375 at 399.

170 J. Stromseth, 'The International Criminal Court and Justice on the Ground' (2011) 43 *Arizona State Law Journal* 427, 444.

171 G. Musila, 'Accountability Debate in Kenya in Near Policy Vacuum and Ethnic Tension' in P. Clark (ed.), *Oxford Transitional Justice Research: Debating International Justice in Africa* (Oxford: FLJS, 2010), 104 at 105.

172 J. Widner, 'Courts and Democracy in Post-Confct Transitions: A Social Scientists Perspective on the African Case' (2001) 95 *American Journal of International Law* 64, 65.

173 C.L. Sriram, 'Wrong-Sizing International Justice? The Hybrid Tribunal in Sierra Leone' (2006) 29 *Fordham International Law Journal* 472, 490.

174 International Crisis Group, 'Finding the Balance: The Scales of Justice in Kosovo' (2002), available <http://www.crisisgroup.org/home/index.cfm?id=1609&l=1>, 21.

175 E. Keppler, *Bringing Justice: The Special Court for Sierra Leone: Accomplishments, Shortcomings and Needed Support* (New York, Freetown: Human Rights W atch, 2004), 19.

176 Sriram,supra n173, 493.

177 D.Cohen, *Seeking Justice on the Cheap: Is East Timor Really a Model for the Future?* (Honolulu: East-West Center, 2002), 3.

178 T. Carothers, 'Promoting the Rule of Law Abroad: The Problem of Knowledge' in Carothers (ed.), supra n5, 15 at 20–21.

179 Trebilcock and Daniels, supra n71, 335.

180 Call,supra n169, 375 at 403.

181 See e.g. the *International Journal of Transitional Justice*'s special issue entitled 'Whose Justice? Global and Local Approaches to T ransitional Justice' (2009) 2 *International Journal of Transitional Justice* 295.

182 Carlson,supra n55, 17.

183 S. Golub, 'Beyond Rule of Law Orthodoxy: The Legal Empowerment Alternative' (2003) 25 Carnegie Endowment for International Peace Paper No. 41 (Rule of Law Series) available <http://www.carnegieendowment.org/f les/wp41.pdf>.

184 UNSecretary-General, supra n35, Summary, 1.

185 J. Blackburn, R. Chambers and J. Gaventa, *Mainstreaming Participation in Development* (Washington, D.C.: OECD, 2000), 1.

186 N. Nelson and S. W right, 'Participation and Power' in N. Nelson and S. Wright (eds.), *Power and Participatory Development: Theory and Practice* (London: Intermediate Technology Publications, 1995), 1.

187 UNSecretary-General, supra n35, para. 15.

188 Ibid.,para. 17.

189 Ibid.

190 Golub,supra n183, 3.

191 Ibid.,3.

192 Ibid.,16.

193 T. Ringer, 'Development, Reform and the Rule of Law: Some Prescriptions for a Common Understanding of the "Rule of Law" and its Place in Development Theory and Practice' (2007) 10 *Yale Human Rights and Development Law Journal* 178, 183.

194 J. Faundez, 'Legal Pluralism and International Development Agencies: State Building or Legal Reform?' (2011) 3 *Hague Journal on the Rule of Law* 18.

195 E.Wojkowska, *Doing Justice: How Informal Systems Can Contribute* (Oslo: UNDP Oslo Governance Centre, 2006).

196 Asser, supra n86.

197 G. O'Donnell, 'Horizontal Accountability in New Democracies' in A. Schedler, L. Diamond and M. Plattner (eds.), *The Self-Restraining State: Power and Accountability in New Democracies* (Boulder: L ynne Rienner Publishers, 1999), 29 at 37 and J.J. Linz, *Totalitarian and Authoritarian Regimes* (Boulder: Lynne Rienner Publications, 2000).

198 UNSecretary-General, supra n35, para. 19.

199 J.Madison, *The Federalist Papers/The Federalist*, No. 51.

200 L. Diamond, M. Plattner and A. Schedler, 'Introduction' in Schedler, Diamond and Plattner (eds.), supra n197, 1 at 1.

201 See generally J. Méndez, G. O'Donnell, and P.S. Pinheiro (eds.), *The Un(Rule) of Law and the Underprivileged in Latin America* (Notre Dame: University of Notre Dame, 1999).

202 R.Sklar, 'Developmental Democracy' (1987) 29 *Comparative Studies in Society and History* 686.

203 R. Sklar, 'Comments on O'Donnell: Democracy and Constitutionalism' in Schedler, Diamond and Plattner (eds.), supra n197, 53 at 57.

204 A.Schedler, 'Conceptualizing Accountability' in Schedler, Diamond and Plattner (eds.), supra n197, 13 at 23.

205 Ibid.,24.

206 O'Donnell,supra n197, 39.
207 P. Domingo, 'Judicial Independence and Judicial Reform in Latin America' in A. Schedler, L. Diamond and M. Plattner (eds.), supra n197, 151 at 154.
208 The UN Basic Principles on the Independence of the Judiciary, supra n96.
209 The UN Basic Principles on the Role of Lawyers, supra n131.
210 Domingo,supra n207, 162.
211 Bull,supra n40, 38.
212 S. Chesterman, M. Ignatieff and R. Thakur , 'Conclusion: The Future of State-Building' in Chesterman, Ignatieff and Thakur (eds.), supra n107, 359 at 363.
213 A. Schedler, 'Restraining the State: Conf icts and Agencies of Accountability' in Schedler, Diamond and Plattner (eds.), supra n197, 333 at 347.
214 C.Collins, *Post-Transitional Justice: Human Rights Trials in Chile and El Salvador* (University Park: Pennsylvania University Press, 2010), 145 and 146.
215 J. Widner, 'Building Judicial Independence in Common Law Africa' in Schedler, Diamond and Plattner (eds.), supra n197, 177 at 187.
216 M.Ignatieff, 'We're So Exceptional', 59(9) *New York Review of Books*, 26 March 2012.
217 S. Chesterman, 'An International Rule of Law?' (2008) 56 *American Journal of Comparative Law* 331, 343.
218 Kleinfeld-Belton,supra n15, 14.
219 O.Fiss, 'The Autonomy of Law' (2001) 26 *Yale Journal of International Law* 517, 521.
220 C. Apodaca, 'The Rule of Law and Human Rights' (2004) 87 *Judicature* 292, 297–298.
221 Stromseth,supra n170, 433.
222 International Covenant on Civil and Political Rights, General Assembly Resolution 2200, at 52, UN GAOR, 21st Session, Supp. No. 16, UN Doc. A/6316 (Dec. 16, 1966).
223 Article14(1).
224 Article14(2).
225 Article14(1).
226 Article14(3)(c).
227 P. de Greiff, 'Articulating the Links Between T   ransitional Justice and Development: Justice and Social Integration' in P de Greiff and R. Duthie (eds.), *Transitional Justice and Development: Making Connections* (New York: Social Science Research Council, 2009), 28 at 60.
228 KleinfeldBelton, supra n15, 25.
229 Judicial System Monitoring Project, 'JSMP background paper on the justice sector' (2003), copy on f le with author.

3 The rule of law in transitional justice discourse

A narrative, not a programme

> Judicial reform is a long-term process ... which can be contrary to the immediate demands for justice arising within a post-conf ict setting.[1]

> Thus the question we need to consider is the ultimate goal of these trials: are we focused upon the success of each immediate trial or the development and reconstruction of the judicial system? If we look to immediate outcomes, there is a tension between these two goals.[2]

3.1 Introduction: does judicialization of politics equal rule of law?

The previous chapter argued that while in justice sector reform, the rule of law is conceived of as a loosely-def ned programme of institutions, culture and norms, in transitional justice it is instead understood as a broad narrative of progress from the dominance of force to the judicialization of politics, primarily viewed through the lens of a single def ning idea, namely an almost exclusive focus on legal and non-legal responses to human rights broadly understood. Consequently, theorists and practitioners in the feld of transitional justice have conf ated the rule of law and mechanisms to facilitate transition to a liberal polity, viewing them in some cases as virtually synonymous when in reality they are two very different concepts. The confation of the rule of law with liberal democratic rule, or the elements thereof, is a risk that most liberalizing projects historically have run.[3] Because transitional justice generally occurs in states transitioning to W estern-style rule of law democracies, or purporting to do so, this risk is exacerbated. As one scholar describes it:

> Transitional justice is about situations in which a society is moving from a state of injustice to justice, from oppressive government to government that respects the rule of law, from authoritarianism to democracy.[4]

Treatment of the interaction between rule of law and transitional justice is generally unsophisticated and based on simple teleological narratives of a path from a degraded conf ict/authoritarian rule of law to one redeemed and def ned by processes of accountability or restoration, even if they are severely limited or merely symbolic. National truth commission reports read as tragic accounts that end on a redemptive note where the burgeoning self-knowledge of victimization buttresses the liberalizing polity against reoccurrence. [5] For example, the report of Argentina's National Commission on the Disappeared was called *Nunca Mas* ('Never Again') and argued that 'great catastrophes are always instructive ... The tragedy which began with the military dictator - ship in March 1976, the most terrible our nation has ever suffered, will undoubtedly serve to help us understand that it is only democracy that can save a people from horror on this scale.' As Chapter 4 examines, the expressivist role of trial presents criminal justice as the culmination of a redemptive chronicle. In this schema, democracy, justice, rights and the rule of law are inextricably linked.

As Kennedy argues, humanitarians are 'quick to conclude that emancipation means progress forward from the natural passions of politics into the civilized reason of law'.[6] The tendency he notes of human rights practitioners to present their policies as the grand story of the progress of law against power and reason against ideology is more pronounced in transitional justice than in most analogous felds.[7] Transitional justice advocacy is often presented in heroic terms, speaking truth to power on behalf of disenfranchised masses, self essly enduring rocky relationships with the state[8] and reacting against the cynicism and betrayal of values inherent in the sovereign control of international affairs[9] to 'goad' states into creating justice mechanisms and making them effective.[10] Teitel's presentation of transitional justice as 'a depoliticized legalist language of right and wrongs, duties and obligations, [that] is supplanting the dominant political language based on state interests, deliberation and consensus'[11] is a seductive one. There is a sense in the literature, which this chapter examines in depth, that the judicialization of politics in place of the previous subordination of law to duress in and of itself amounts to the substantive content of the rule of law. This is both a cause and a consequence of the failure of scholars and practitioners to engage suff ciently with rule of law theory generally or the distinct dilemmas of its (re)construction in post-conf ict states. This confusion over the parameters of the rule of law and transitional justice is hardly unique – other observers of the f eld have noted a tendency in transitional justice literature to conf ate analytically distinct concepts like peace and democracy or peace and reconciliation.[12] As Kennedy reminds us, there is well-intentioned propensity in international humanitar - ian policy-making to treat certain tools (like transitional justice) as surrogates for outcomes (like the rule of law). [13] The task of this chapter is to substantiate this claim of conf ation and explain its origins.

Though concededly polysemic concepts, the answer may lie in unpacking both 'transitional' and 'justice' as applied in the f eld's paradigmatic transitions of conf ict or authoritarianism to democratic peace. Once this is done, the chapter will vindicate the claim made in Chapter 2 that the treatment of the rule of law in transitional justice is superf cial by examining the main debates on the issue in the f eld, before turning to the thorny question of whether there is a distinctly transitional rule of law. Arguing that there is no transitional rule of law, merely departures from it that are justif able or not justif able, the chapter contends that because the claims about the potential of transitional justice to effect positive change in transition which have justi-f ed deviation from the rule of law are over -stated, renewed attention should be paid to more prosaic issues of justice sector reform. First, however , it is necessary to examine how a narrative understanding of the rule of law as a journey from a repressive, rights-denying polity to one of a liberal, rights-aff rming one, has obscured a programmatic view of the rule of law as a combination of institutions and culture as well as norms.

3.2 The 'transition' paradigm

To the extent that any primary objective of a transitional justice policy can be identif ed, it is to end the culture of impunity and establish a human rights culture in a context of democratic governance in the transitional state. However, there is an inevitable tension in the use of transitional justice' s mechanisms between a short-term role of mediation between one regime type and a more liberal alternative (which is primarily normative) [14] and the more long-term process of using that mechanism to exemplify, catalyse and estab-lish rule of law institutions guided by rule of law development principles (which are institutional and cultural as much as normative). The initial conceptualization of transitional justice was presented as a problem def ned by, and contingent on, political dilemmas that were short-term in nature and revolved around f nding the right transitional mechanism to account for the past in a bounded interregnum between one regime and another. Within this interregnum, there may be a degree of instability , but the very notion of transition implies that some commitment to peace and/or democratization already exists. To the extent that transitional justice attempts to re-order the relationship between the state and the individual or promote human rights, it is very often pushing at an open door , facilitating a process of change that is already underway. As DuBois and Czarnota put it, frequently law in transi-tion merely closes off certain issues from conf ict, operating as a centre which blocks destructive possibilities to enable politics:

> Transitional politics requires only a 'thin community' among the signif -cant adversaries, only just enough to ensure that the society is question is not SLORC's [State Law and Order Restoration Council] Burma, Bosnia, Chile after Allende or apartheid South Africa. It requires no more than that the parties recognize suff cient commonality to allow politics to take place. It does not require a 'thick' community. [15]

Consequently, what transitional justice is required to do to help consolidate peace in the short-term interregnal period is not the same as what long-term

socio-political and economic reform requires. It mediates a process of political change that is happening independently of it – it does not attempt to recreate society anew. As a result, though transitional justice is ostensibly both backward-looking (punishing wrongdoers, revealing truth, returning property) and forward-looking (establishing the bounds of political morality , containing the inf uence of revanchist forces, normalizing accountability), its institutions have traditionally adopted a historical view of justice rather than conceiving of it as a broader structural reform project. [16] Debates about transitional justice were generally framed by the normative proposition that various legal responses should be evaluated on their prospects for mediating the immediate transition to democracy,[17] and not on the basis of how they established the more long-term preconditions for a fully functioning society   .
As Arthur puts it:

> [W]hy were these changes understood as 'transitions' to democracy? Why were these phenomena not seen, for example, as merely the beginning of a long, open-ended process of establishing the social preconditions for democratic institutions – including a shift in socioeconomic structures, behavioral habits, and the structural conditions that would allow for a thriving public sphere? [18]

While rule of law reform is typically an incremental, long-term process that may take decades, the contrasting transformational conception of the paradigmatic transition as one of a negotiated deal to end repressive rule or war followed by reform of the constitution and the institutions of governance makes transitional justice a 'f nite and contained affair'.[19] Simply put, because transitional justice and rule of law reconstruction have different emphases, they consequently have different time-scales, which may have the effect of removing any compulsion to reconcile the two. The focus on immediate political outcomes has operated to the detriment of or ganizing transitional justice responses with a view to long-term development of society, including the judicial system. Trials, reparations and truth commissions are initiated to assist or catalyse the sorts of changes in ideas and beliefs that might inoculate against challenges to the new political order, but consideration is rarely given to whether or how such initiatives could be sustained or institutionalized permanently (similar arguments are made with greater frequency about the exclusion in transitional justice of future-oriented socio-economic reform). [20] The potential for high-prof le transitional proceedings to catalyse judicial reconstruction was mooted in the previous chapter , but Kerr and Mobekk point out that it is questionable whether rule of law and capacity-building are realistic objectives for transitional justice given that the available mechanisms are inevitably stretched by the complexities and diff culties of dealing with past abuses.[21]

It has become commonplace to accept there are two competing ideas on the relationship between law and democratic development. [22] The f rst is the realist argument that justice in transition is epiphenomenal, where transitional responses are the product of political or institutional constraints. The second is the idealist argument that legal responses to the crimes of the past are necessary for liberalizing change, a much broader political mission than simply restoring the institutions of justice and a culture of obedience to law. Lost among the urgent antinomies of peace versus justice, truth versus justice and idealism versus realism is the possibility that both idealist and realist impulses alike contain dangers for the development in the long-term rule of law, which are developed in greater detail here and in subsequent chapters. The realist dangers are perhaps the most apparent, and have been exhaustively canvassed in the peace versus justice literature of the f rst decade of transitional justice. Characterized as this cautious, consequence-driven approach is by blanket, conditional or de facto amnesty, extreme selectivity or pardon in contravention of national and/or international law, it is accepted that the short-term compromises that stability requires are in inevitable tension with the long-term aspiration to create a state where accountability and equality before the law are the norm.

> One important reason for the neglect of judicial reform is the primacy of order among the priorities of the international community ... Peace seems to offer easier, more immediate, and more prized benefts to powerful countries than the diff cult provision of justice in divided societies.[23]

The dangers to the rule of law from transitional justice processes which are relatively untrammelled by political compromise have received less attention, but inhere in the inevitably politicized ends to which a trial, truth commission or vetting process is directed. Because transitional justice is focused more on re-aff rming human rights norms than developing rule of law institutions, it has 'tilt[ed] towards international approbation and inf uence rather than on-the-ground domestic impact in the concerned states'.[24] Transitional justice's discourse of perpetrators and victims and their interests in terms of reconciliation, revenge, social pedagogy and deterrence has often proven too urgent and narrow to incorporate a consideration of how the institutions chosen and the approach taken might affect the attitudes of the vast numbers of citizens who do not fall into these dichotomized roles. When one looks at the desirability of the goals commonly associated with transitional justice (reconciliation, rehabilitation, truth, healing), it is not surprising that more thought is given to the legacy of a given mechanism than to its process, notwithstanding increased doubts about whether any mechanism can deliver any or all of the dividends promised. Scrupulously, exemplarily fair and apolitical trial is slow, expensive and uncertain when the transitional moment appears to demand speed, economy, and authoritative clarity.

> In many contexts it is illusory to think one could vindicate fully all of the traditional values associated with the rule of law, such as general

applicability, procedural due process, as well as more substantive values of fairness or analogous sources of legitimacy.[25]

Perhaps one reason why transitional justice theory is far more comfortable postulating effects on individuals like deterrence and reconciliation than effects on institutions like courts is that they have analogies with normal trials, investigations or reparations in ordinary domestic contexts. By contrast, as Burke-White posits, domestic judicial development from scratch has not been subject of signifcant enquiry because it lacks pertinent domestic analogies on which such enquiry could draw .[26] As a result, the focus on the relatively few victims and even fewer perpetrators who will come before a court, truth commission or reparations tribunal obscures lar ger rule of law issues which might have a greater impact on the reconstructing polity While much of the literature concentrates on how to make the immediate mecha- nisms better in terms of victim support or outreach or comprehensiveness, far less attention is devoted to questions of legacy or continuity of benef ts for the justice sector. For example

> Criminal trials single out intellectual authors and actual perpetrators of atrocities while leaving to broader initiatives in rule of law, humanitarian assistance, democracy building, and economic development the task of resuscitating a 'sick society' ... such an approach that does not integrate trials with these other capacity-building measures is insuff cient to attend to social repair.[27]

Rule of law reconstruction is but one small part of this social repair .

3.3 Justice or the rule of law?

As Lutz notes, since its inception, the transitional justice movement has oper ated under the presumption that its methods and goals 'are by def nition a good thing'.[28] Within the wider human rights community, it has long been recognized that a belief in the inherent humanitarian potency of a given policy tool may come at the cost of a detailed analysis of its substantive costs.[29] The failure to engage with rule of law theory generally or the distinct dilemmas of its construction or reconstruction in post-conf ict states is perhaps most apparent in the common presumption in the literature that a substantive, Western model of the rule of law is of automatic application. For example, Fletcher, Weinstein and Rowen's analysis of the rule of law in pre- conf ict states is explicitly based on W estern liberal theory,[30] while Affa'a- Mindzie argues that democracy and good governance are encompassed in the notion of the rule of law .[31] Kritz requires representative government, adop- tion of legislation by public procedure and detailed guarantees in the area of criminal procedure to form core elements of the rule of law .[32] Because of the historic links between human rights and the rule of law in W estern history and the functional interdependence we see between guarantees such as the right to life, fair trial or habeas corpus and rule of law institutions like the courts and police, many assume that 'in practice, the rule of law and human rights tend to overlap and the theoretical boundaries between the two become unclear'.[33] Chesterman notes transitional justice and the rule of law are often synonymized, and where they are the former typically attracts the most attention and resources.[34] Rule of law reform and human rights programmes are often usefully linked, but the pragmatic justice sector reformer must delineate the boundaries between the two. None of this is to ar gue that Western models of the rule of law are inappropriate – in Chapter 1 the book accepts the UN position that the rule of law enjoys the greatest potential and is most likely to endure in democratic, rights-respecting states. However, it is symptomatic of a wider confusion in transitional justice between the rule of law on one hand, and measures to create a human rights-based socio-political environment where it can thrive, on the other. It is submitted that this is a product of transitional justice' s emphasis on the normative (i.e. rights and democracy), which has served to obscure consideration of institutional and cultural elements of the rule of law. The emphasis is more on reconstructing the substance of the law rather than on rehabilitating its structures. The latter cannot be presumed to f ow as a matter of course from the former.

As noted at the end of Chapter 1, the liberal-legalist paradigm is increasingly questioned. Scholarship increasingly questions whether transitional justice can accomplish any or all of the goals associated with it such as:

- Endingviolence
- Promoting reconciliation across a divided society
- Restoring dignity to victims and promoting psychosocial healing
- Creating a common history of the pre-transition era
- Educating the public about politics and human rights
- Legitimizingthe new regime.

As Section 3.7 of this chapter later examines, the historical record of transitional justice in delivering these goals is very limited. Far from fostering circumspection about the f eld, however, the common response to the failure of transitional justice to live up to its diverse assumed potentials has been to urge 'broader'[35] and 'thicker'[36] conceptions of transitional justice to make it more responsive to the needs of victims, to create a wider historical consensus, to catalyse socio-economic reform or to open political space to the mar ginalized (the aforementioned 'do everything, engage everyone' hypothesis).[37] Few would countenance reining in these ambitions to concentrate on more mundane issues of rule of law reconstruction, even though the relationship between a functioning justice sector and future peace is far more direct and the legacy is more plausible than many of the aforementioned goals. Instead, many of the justif cations for transitional justice have gradually become divorced almost entirely from law. From legalistic origins transitional justice has, in its

own legitimating language, 'transcended' law as a mechanism of justice.   [38]
Whereas once transitional justice was ref ected in primarily legal responses to
the wrongdoing of repressive predecessor regimes, Roht-Arriaza' s expansive
and widely-cited def nition of transitional justice as that 'set of practices,
mechanisms and concerns that arise following a period of conf ict, civil strife
or repression, and that are aimed directly at confronting and dealing with past
violations of human rights and humanitarian law' better captures the ever -
expanding parameters of the f eld.[39] The changing def nitions illustrate how
formal legal structures have gradually conceded their always-precarious
centrality in transitional justice debates. This may benef t transition – after all,
law limits its purview to rules, accountability and punishment and so cannot
reach all corners of human activity [40] – but does little to facilitate a constructive consideration of how transitional justice affects the rule of law .

  The conf ation of the rule of law and successful transition to a liberal polity
is made easier by the inextricable linkage between the concept of justice and
the rule of law. A good example of this is Dyzenhaus, who rejects the privileging of Western liberal democracy as the telos of transition but nevertheless
outlines a highly normative vision of the rule of law   , which he def nes as
'government in accordance with the laws of nature'.   [41] He ar gues that the
South African Truth and Reconciliation Commission (SATRC) supported the
restoration of the rule of law simply because it drew attention to and
condemned the evils of apartheid and off cially sanctioned transgressions of
the rule of law.[42] Drawing on Allen' s argument that the SA TRC should be
understood in terms of justice as recognition (an education in what goes
wrong when legality or the rule of law are not respected) and justice as ethos
(an education in the claim that justice transcends the ideology of the particular group that happens to be in power), [43] he argues that any form of justice
served in any process that serves the transformation of an unjust society into
a just one is 'the justice of the rule of law'. [44] Aside from the obvious danger
that equating justice (or, indeed, merely an education about justice) with the
rule of law may deny both justice and the rule of law any independent functions, this position highlights the dangers of looking at the rule of law in
terms of a narrative from bad law to good law instead of a programme of
institutions, culture and norms. In effect, Dyzenhaus is ar   guing that the
deliberations of an ad hoc body established by political compromise to in
effect by-pass the criminal law (to the extent the crimes under apartheid
broke either domestic or *ius cogens* norms of international law) or the institutions of criminal justice actually substantiates the rule of law purely because
it educates us about justice. In short, the institutional basis of the rule of law
understood as settled law and legal institutions is sacrif ced for a primarily
normative understanding of the rule of law that exists in isolation from this
institutional setting. Arguably, his thesis is as much about rule of law culture
as it is about norms, given that he emphasizes the importance of civic education in the rule of law .[45] In these terms, the SA TRC commendably demonstrated that the rule of law means certain types of laws should not be passed,

but it also less commendably illustrated that the judiciary can be circumvented through political bargaining. Elsewhere in the same piece, Dyzenhaus argues that a sovereign commandment that judges f nd in favour of a party that pays the biggest bribe would be contrary to the rule of law because it 'subverts the off ce of Judicature' and that the problem of men obeying the law out of fear instead of an acceptance of the law's legitimacy is exacerbated when 'the sovereign has not put in place the institutional mechanisms that permit recourse to a higher authority' to resolve rule of law predicaments. [46] However, it is highly arguable that truth commissions subvert the judiciary no less than this when their fact-f nding does not lead to the full rigour of established law and undermine it when its procedures can be abandoned by even the most well-meaning of executive f ats. As Posner argues in response, 'the TRC was a compromise between the desire to achieve substantive justice for the victims of apartheid and the exigencies of power-sharing. It had little to do with legality ... The TRC abandoned legal form.' [47] The compromise was arguably a wise one and the lessons the SATRC taught about legality were undoubtedly valuable, but these complexities in the rule of law are obscured when narrative conceptions of the rule of law predominate to the exclusion of more programmatic understandings.

While scholars accept almost unanimously the centrality and utility of transitional justice in the re-establishment of the rule of law[48] and some, like Dyzenhaus, argue that the debate about transitional justice should 'be boiled down to one about how to achieve the rule of law', [49] the danger is that the normative notions of justice which transitional justice of necessity adopts become confused with, or ignore, the more programmatic demands of the rule of law. Rule of law reconstructors need to separate justice conceptually from the rule of law if the latter is to be pursued with the greatest degree of clarity possible. Justice is an essentially contested concept, i.e. one driven by substantive disagreements over a range of different, entirely reasonable interpretations of a mutually-agreed-upon archetypical notion. [50] It is an ideal whose meaning varies epistemologically according to different collective and individual beliefs about human nature, fundamental principles of social co-operation and control, and the context in which it is applied, such as political transition. For example, V illa-Vicencio identif es f ve diverging concepts of justice – deterrent justice seeking to dissuade potential violators by punishing past crime; compensatory justice, requiring restitution by those who have benef ted from past inequities; rehabilitative justice, which recognizes the needs of both victims and perpetrators need to be addressed in the interests of social harmony; justice as the aff rmation of human dignity which recognizes the equal dignity of all in the aftermath of mass criminality directed at certain collectivities; and justice as exoneration which attempts to exculpate those falsely accused or convicted in the past. [51] Mani, on the other hand, outlines a three-pronged conception of justice, based on legal justice (which she synonymizes with the rule of law) which addresses legal injustice, rectif catory justice arising from the need to address injustices inf icted on people such as gross human rights abuses, war crimes and crimes against humanity, and distributive justice which attempts to address structural and systemic injustices that underlie conf   ict.[52] Andriu distinguishes legal, restorative and social justice.[53]

At f rst glance, nothing could be more in keeping with the rule of law than a 'legal' conception of justice in transition, given that mass political criminality with which it is primarily concerned is for the most part constituted by ordinary crimes prohibited in national legislation like murder disappearances and rapes, or *ius cogens* crimes prohibited under international criminal law such as crimes against humanity, war crimes, genocide or torture to which an obligation *erga omnes* to prosecute attaches. Stripped of any additional utilitarian functions and upholding the rule of law as a value in itself, individual accountability for breaches of the law uphold the regularity   , stability, and adherence to settled law the rule of law requires, while failure of enforcement vitiates its authority[54] and adversely affects the prospects for habitual lawfulness.[55] This nexus between rule of law and punishment becomes all the more apparent when crimes are committed on a massive scale or by political leaders for whom accountability is a fundamental tenet of the rule of law   . As Landsman puts it, holding violators accountable for their misdeeds makes clear to 'all members of society that law's authority is superior to that of individuals' and that no prerogatives attach to individuals merely because of status or position.[56] In contrast with the arbitrary, politicized law of the prior regime, judgment is neither political nor moral, but legal.

However, the opportunities for the paradigmatic legalist response are rare, and may not in any case respond to the diverse injustices that require remedy in transition after war or authoritarianism. The diver   ging laundry lists of justice noted above recognize f rstly that 'justice' cannot be reduced merely to a juridical def nition, and secondly that a juridical def nition alone would respond badly to the vagaries of transitional states. For these reasons, fexible, differentiated and context-specif c understandings of justice are advantageous in post-conf ict states. From the turn of the century there has been an observable willingness to consider the goals and mechanisms of transitional justice as complementary and mutually-reinforcing, with an increased eagerness to consider an adaptable continuum of strategies over the previous binary choice of truth or justice.[57] Just over two-thirds of states under going transitional justice now employ more than one mechanism,[58] while combinations of trials with amnesties and truth commissions tend to correspond with positive outcomes for democracy and governance.[59] As a result, within the literature, justice is as likely to refer to restorative and non-prosecutorial mechanisms like reparations, truth commissions and lustration as it is to trial. This is of course entirely reasonable – different institutional structures are appropriate for different types of justice. However, in reviewing the scholarship and practice of transitional justice, it becomes apparent that this commendable f exibility and nuance in the conception of justice is being extended to the rule of law, whereby any legal or non-legal measure which accords with a conception of justice, or any measure which can help guarantee the stability on which the rule of law may develop, is deemed to be in accordance with an exceptionalist rule of law or to actually constitute it. The growth of non-legal approaches has led some to question 'whether any threshold remained regarding what constitutes the predicate transitional rule of law'. [60] The divorce of transitional justice from primarily legal accountability has worried some on the basis that it makes distinguishing between legitimate and illegitimate ends of transitional justice more diff cult.[61] Justice, understood in its dictionary sense as that quality of being just or as righteousness, equitableness, or moral rightness may be an expression of commitment to the rule of law and a means to strengthen it. However, it does not of itself constitute the rule of law, and may in certain instances contradict it. In some cases, a conception of justice in transition or the institutions created (or , more pertinently, circumvented) to deliver it may conduce to transitional justice's teleological impulse towards justice and democracy, but nevertheless undermine the cultural commitments and institutional integrity the rule of law demands. As any positivist will acknowledge, morals and legality are not necessarily linked.

3.4 Deeper examinations of the rule of law in transitional justice discourse

There have been exceptions to this simplistic, linear, progressist narrative in which justice automatically helps secure the rule of law . In three situations in particular, the rule of law dilemmas inherent in transitional justice have been given a thorough airing, namely (a) the Nurember g tribunals, (b) the post-Communist transitions, and (c) the f rst major truth commissions. In these examples, the tension between transitional justice's tendency to maximize its normative potential in advancing democratization, aff rming universal rights and pursuing justice, on the one hand, and the more technical and cultural concerns of (re)establishing the rule of law, on the other, were explored. These debates are ostensibly quite deep, but closer inspection suggests that the conclusions drawn tend towards the superf cial, and are of limited application to the dilemmas of rule of law reconstruction in developing states.

3.4.1 *The Nuremberg debate*[62]

The 1958 Fuller–Hart debate, 'one of the great jurisprudential exchanges of our time'[63] remains a touchstone of most contemporary discussions of transitional justice and the rule of law, and still dominates debates on the degree of legal exceptionalism tolerable in transitional justice in the leading works.[64] Given the weary familiarity of the debate in the literature, a summary will suff ce. On the positivist side of the argument, f delity to the rule of law amounts simply to regular compliance with clear , general and validly enacted rules – when the rules have a pernicious content, then adher ence to the rule of law amounts to enforcing those rules. In contrast is the natural law understanding which reiterates that the rule of law requires the same regular compliance but implies a moral content that transcends positively enacted rules – mere compliance with positive rules when the rules have violated that moral content may later be judged illegal. The positivist Hart argued that adherence to the rule of law meant Nazi laws must be accepted as valid until repudiated by subsequent legislation – the procedural regularity this continuity implied would be central to restoring belief in legality.[65] Fuller, taking a natural law position, countered that the rule of law required disregard for Nazi law and contended that such lawless laws could not constitute a valid legal regime.[66] Though Shklar justif ed Nuremberg as a great legal drama that would reinforce the dormant legal consciousness of the German people,[67] the dilemma of criminalizing actions which no prior law had made illegal in a forum which did not previously exist was not, and never has been, satisfactorily resolved. While the lawyers strained to ground their indictments positivistically by relying on earlier treaties condemning wars of aggression to justify charges of crimes against peace and by restricting the novel concept of crimes against humanity to those committed as part of a war of aggression,[68] even Counsel for the Prosecution Telford Taylor later admitted the 'creative' indictments and convictions pursued were entirely indefensible and inconsistent with fundamental principles of legality.[69]

3.4.2 *The post-Communist transitions*

Similar concerns over retroactivity recur in the widely cited processes of transitional accountability in Hungary and East Germany after the Cold W ar.[70] In Hungary, legislation lifted the 30-year statute of limitations for offences of treason, voluntary manslaughter and fatal injury committed between 21 December 1944 and 2 May 1990, with the intention of making possible the prosecution of those involved in the suppression of the 1956 uprising. The Court recognized the 'paradox of the revolution of the rule of law', as it faced a Solomonic choice between the principle of predictability outlawing retroactive law on the one hand, and substantive justice on the other ,[71] before rescinding the law on eight counts of unconstitutionality The Court expressly stated that the rule of law required continuity in the law between the Communist era and the present. Halmai and Scheppele commended the court for explicitly adhering to a 'strict application of the principle of human rights for all – even ... for those who did not respect the rights of others'. [72] By contrast, in the 'extreme case' of the East German Berlin W all guards, the courts of the German Federal Republic rejected any defence based on East German law on the basis that formal validity was not substantive right, enunciating the principle that 'when the contradiction between positive law and justice has reached ... an unbearable degree ... the law must yield to justice'.[73] McAdams has criticized the *ex post facto* invalidation of the German Democratic Republic (GDR) legal system, ar guing it deprived those living under the system fair notice of what actions could later be regarded as criminal.[74] Instead, he commended the later judicial method of convicting the border guards based on East German law, though Blankenburg criticizes the Court for reinterpreting this legislation 'like it had never been practiced in its history' and for creating their own 'ideal' GDR law.[75] Notwithstanding the Berlin court's stringency, almost all border guards received suspended sentences.[76]

Teitel justifies the diverging approaches in East Germany and Hungary on the basis of their expressive potential given their distinctive historical and political legacies of crimes against humanity in the Nazi past and routine deviation from the rule of law under Communist rule respectively:

> For the Berlin court, the controlling rule-of-law value was what was 'morally' right, whereas for the Hungarian court, the controlling rule-of-law value was the protection of pre-existing 'legal' rights. [77]

Both states, like the post-World War II trial states, arguably reached an appropriate balance between strict legality and substantive justice most suitable to their cultural, historical and political realities. In differing transitional ecologies, strict legality may be affirmed as a critical response to past eschewal of the rule of law, or may be renounced as a critical affirmation of legally violated human rights norms. Where these dilemmas have emerged elsewhere, they have rarely been as stark, more finessed than resolved along a middle ground between both positions. [78] The concern, however, is not that inevitably contextual responses will predominate in such dilemmas, but rather the weight the *nullum crimen, nulla poena sine lege* dilemma carries in transitional justice and how it has affected debates over strict legality versus substantive justice. While Andriu posits that 'one of the main concerns of TJ [transitional justice] is the issue of retroactivity' [79] and Teitel describes it as the 'core dilemma',[80] the risk of abrogating today's legality to punish yesterday's crimes has declined rapidly in relevance to contemporary transitional justice debates. The precedent of Nuremberg and the flurry of human rights instruments that followed decreased the retroactivity dilemma:

> Paradoxically, Nuremberg's weaknesses, not its strengths, have proven most enduring. Even Nuremberg's most vociferous supporters admit that the prosecutions had only the shakiest foundations in existing law; prosecutors at the International Military Tribunal and in later U.S. tribunals in Nuremberg and ... Tokyo improvised as they went along. But Nuremberg's principles have now been codified and accepted by most nations of the world and form the basis for much of current international and human rights law.[81]

Indeed, the Hungarian Constitutional Court later upheld a new statute allowing the statute of limitations to be lifted for offences constituting crimes against humanity or war crimes under international law[82] while in the border guards cases the Court held that the legislation concerned infringed international human rights law.[83] By the time the ICTY was established, old debates on positivist law versus natural became futile – as Gray puts it, the 'fuzzy presumptions of universal right' were replaced with solid claims of international law.[84] As Chapter 5 goes on to examine, the reliance on international criminal justice in a putative international rule of law creates dilemmas for domestic rule of law reconstruction. In effect, one dilemma has been replaced by another.

3.4.3 *The first major truth commissions*

The establishment of the f rst major truth commissions in South America (Chile and Argentina) and in South Africa raised signif cant rule of law issues regarding the subordination of existing legal obligations of domestic law or international human rights law to (conditional) amnesty and the subordination of the prosecutorial services and judiciary to ad hoc, non-punitive institutions. Though disputes in these areas clearly revolved around the retrospective demands and future prospects of the rule of law they were rarely phrased in these terms. The f rst debates in South America tended to emphasize deeply realist concerns over the destabilizing potential of trials, while the later debates in South Africa were polarized between security concerns and an idealistic belief in the healing, restorative power of truth commissions. In all cases, the debate boiled down to the merits of legal obligation and courts, on the one hand, and alternatives on the other, but it tended to focus on immediate transitional political or social outcomes, as opposed to a concern with what the employment of temporary, ad hoc bodies to circumvent the demands of law would have on long-term prospects for the rule of law. Those advocating truth commissions in situations where trial would imperil transition willingly conceded that justice (in the sense of legal accountability) was explicitly being traded for truth.[85] It was argued that truth commissions were a principled compromise reconciling the ethical with the political [86] or expressed a preference for the politically possible over the morally ideal. [87] Those justifying truth commissions outside of the security calculus ar gued that truth was a different form of restorative justice that was equal or superior to 'retributive' justice.[88] Relatively few addressed the rule of law issue – even those opposed to truth commissions usually did so in political or moral terms, arguing that the dignity of victims required punishment[89] or that they risked amounting to 'a sop aimed at masking moral defeat'. [90]

However, there was a signif cant debate among a minority of observers on whether truth commissions accorded with the rule of law , even if most participants were talking past one another. Many advocates and practitioners of truth commissions see no clash between their activities and the rule of law. As de Greiff notes, 'virtually all truth commissions to date have used the concept both in an explanatory role – lack of respect for the principles of the rule of law is one of the factors leading to the violations – and as one of the objects of their work – their recommendations are intended to strengthen the rule of law'.[91] Others go further and argue that truth commissions effectively substantiate the rule of law . For example, some ar gue that they develop morally rich practices that provide a model for rule of law procedures in future,[92] that they promote the functioning of law as a form of protection for people,[93] or that society can 'imput[e] the administration of the transitional response with the legality traditionally associated with judicial proceedings'.[94] Certainly, truth commissions mimic much of what is expected from criminal justice – most truth commissions have a legal foundation (for some, this brings it within the scope of 'legal justice'), [95] combat impunity and may achieve some punishment-related purposes like accountability , punishment, shaming and rehabilitation. However, while truth commissions substantiate a humane quasi-judicialization of politics (as Minow argues, they may be a form better suited to meet the goals pertinent to transitional politics),[96] they do not substantiate the rule of law in action. The attribution of moral responsibility , though welcome and of assistance in clarifying whether the law was breached, is not the same as establishing legal guilt. As Orentlicher put it:

> Whatever salutary effects it can produce, an off cial truthtelling {sic} process is no substitute for enforcement of criminal law through prosecutions. Indeed, to the extent that such an undertaking purports to replace criminal punishment (rather than to promote distinct goals that punishment cannot serve), it diminishes the authority of the legal process; it implicitly concedes that the machinery of justice is powerless to punish even those crimes that any civilized society views as most pernicious. [97]

The obvious retort is that the record generated by truth commissions can pave the way for prosecutions, but the historical record in this regard offers scant support for this.[98] If anything, outlining the truth of violations reveals the egregiousness of forgoing the prosecution law demands[99] and broadcasts the weakness of the new leadership to enforce the law .[100] Even if truth commissions are genuinely designed to promote goals prosecutions cannot serve, the lack of due process protections, [101] the naming of perpetrators through untested allegations [102] and disproportionately lenient punishments[103] risk publically undermining the norms of the rule of law under a veneer of legality. While the preference for truth and reconciliation over trial may be justif ed in restorative terms, from a rule of law perspective survivors are more appropriately conceived of as citizens entitled to legal justice than victim-patients entitled to truth/healing.

In the last decade, this interesting debate on whether truth commissions accord with the rule of law has faded into obsolescence. Over time, a bespoke jurisprudence outside law began to develop around truth commissions, drawing on normative discourse from the felds of ethics, medicine and theology.[104]

Arguments rejecting the legality of TRCs became far less acceptable and less common due to the almost-hegemonic language of reconciliation. [105] The debate in the late 1980s and early 1990s where the rule of law trade-offs, tensions and dilemmas that arose between truth and justice were given an airing gave way from the turn of the century to a general willingness to consider the goals and mechanisms of transitional justice as complementary and mutually-reinforcing.[106] There emerged a tendency with non-judicial mechanisms to focus more on best practice than their rule of law implications – for example, infnitely more attention was given to the modalities of the Sierra Leone TRC's interaction with Special Court than how creation of an alternative, temporary forum for justice affected local perceptions of the legitimacy of court institutions. [107] A rule of law-oriented assessment would ask the very pertinent question of whether the non-judicial mechanism is commendably complementary to the formal justice system (like normal public inquiries) or an undermining alternative. If, as is often the case, truth commissions are favoured because the national courts are weak,[108] is it in the long-term interests of the rule of law to divert energies and resources from rebuilding to a transient process? If criminal law is ordinarily conceptualized as a unitary practice incorporating the establishment and punishment of wrongdoing, what is the effect of a state-sponsored process of sundering the two? These questions are rarely asked anymore given the focus on complementary approaches and truth commissions' potential to clarify and acknowledge abuses, promote reconciliation, outline institutional responsibility and recommend reforms. The use of truth commissions refects a commendable willingness to no longer confate justice with trial. However, in so doing it instead risks confating one conception of justice with the rule of law.

3.4.4 Irrelevant precedents?

Given that subsequent progress in international law has rendered much of the earlier agonizing nugatory, why then has the Nuremberg precedent occupied so much of the debate over transitional justice's relation to the rule of law? One might with justice point to Kennedy's theory of the humanitarian brain in which there is a map of the world that infuences the decisions and policies adopted in humanitarian projects but is 'marked by the exaggerated size of well-known political and historical hotspots'. [109] In terms of transitional justice and the rule of law, the often-repetitive literature suggests that Nuremberg, Tokyo, Hungary, East Germany and South Africa constitute such hotspots. It is necessary to question the applicability of these precedents to debates surrounding conscious departures from the rule of law in post-confict states in the developing world. Deviations from the rule of law in a highly-developed state where a *Rechtsstaat* was long developed (Germany) or a highly-educated and modern state in a Mitteleuropean neighbourhood where EU membership became inevitable (Hungary) is radically different to the context of post-colonial, post-authoritarian and post-confict states where legal exceptionalism, emergency decree or complete legal vacuum have historically been the norm. As Bosire argues, the issue of the 'vacuous state', namely one which had little in the way of institutional strength, was not really in issue in the European and Latin American transitions which formed the basis for the general understanding of the transition paradigm. [110] States like this may not have rich legal histories to draw on as an example of the correct path that must eventually be returned to. Departures from the ordinary values and already-weak institutions of the rule of law may not be understood as the *sui generis* epiphenomenon they are in countries with a long history of legality or one found in a supportive rule of law 'good neighbour-hood' like Europe. The solutions accepted in the retroactivity dilemma between an exceptional natural law-based conception of the rule of law or a more conventional positivistic one is unrepresentative and far from the most pertinent in states that are trying to reconstruct the institutions, culture and norms of the rule of law from scratch from a degraded level while simultaneously pursuing some form of transitional accountability. General principles on the relationship between transitional justice and the rule of law extracted from debates on merely one variant of legal exceptionalism of declining contemporary purchase in relatively prosperous and stable European states surrounded by established democracies with a long rule of law pedigree may be of limited guidance to the dilemmas that face a Burundi or a Côte d'Ivoire trying to build the institutions of justice and cultural commitment to legality from scratch. Nevertheless, principles extrapolated from this debate inform the dominant conception of how the rule of law in 'ordinary' times interacts with transitional justice, most notably in the work of Ruti Teitel.

3.5 Does transitional justice imply a 'transitional rule of law'?

There are two main ways of viewing justice in transition. One is to view it as ordinary justice where the basic, conventional rules of justice apply in all circumstances, regardless of how extraordinary the political context is. Writers like Posner and Vermeule or Dyzenhaus argue that the issues that arise in transitional justice situations such as retroactivity, suspension of rules of evidence or selectivity are 'at most overblown versions of ordinary legal problems' [111] or merely 'more dramatic manifestations of problems faced by all societies'. [112] Essentially, the differences between law in transition and law in ordinary time are differences of degree, and not of kind. On this view, though implementation of the law may be difficult given the exigencies of transition, law in transition does not call into question the basic foundations of justice. They argue that the view of transitional justice as distinctive (as 'backward-looking and forward-looking, between retrospective and prospective, between the individual and the collective' in a bounded period spanning two regimes, per Teitel[113]) is based on a misguided stereotype of justice in stable states as inherently ulterior, effective and settled.[114] They contend that justice in transition differs from the quotidian problems of consolidated states only in scale, and merely requires f nding appropriate institutional arrangements to achieve peace.[115]

While proponents of this view are correct in arguing the portrayal of ordinary justice in the transitional justice literature elides its deceptively complex nature,[116] the analogies drawn by Posner and V ermeule between the typical dilemmas of mass criminality in transition and the non-transitional quandaries of the Gore-Bush election, economic shock or court congestion are overly-simplistic.[117] In stability terms, even the most inept or controversial resolution of extraordinary dilemmas in 'ordinary' justice will rarely call the security or viability of the polity into question. In prospective terms, the analogies cited do not replicate the intensif ed symbolic, pedagogical or restorative purposes realized or merely claimed by transitional justice processes – values of reconciliation, political pedagogy or tolerance ordinarily considered of second-order importance to the application of law are conspicuously relevant. There is no mere 'justice in transition' where non-transitional modes can be applied uncritically – law has a distinctive nature and function in times of regime f ux, a modif ed form, and it was Teitel who explained it.

In her seminal *Transitional Justice*, Teitel outlines a dialectical theory of justice in transition, and then identif es the key dilemma inherent in it – how to reconcile normative change with adherence to conventional legality.[118] She recognized that universal norms derived from stable states were inapplicable in transition. In some transitions, because of the instability , the scale of past criminality and the parlous state of the justice system, the ideals of justice must be bargained or sacrif ced in the interests of securing peace.[119] Equally, law can be more dynamic and transformative by symbolically drawing lines in the sand between regimes or rendering certain political acts outside the realms of legitimate choice. Transitional justice may be an element of stability or change, constituted by and constitutive of, transition. As such, 'justice in periods of political change is extraordinary', maintaining order while enabling transformation.[120] It follows that the conception of justice that emerges is contextualized and partial.[121] As seen with the border guards and Hungary, the particular approach taken should be tailored to respond to the particular legacy of past repression or war such as its political traditions, its legal culture and past injustice.[122]

Even the most cursory glance at the assortment of compromises, omissions and vigorous accountability that characterize the universe of transitional justice supports the contention that *justice* must of necessity be contingent, contextual and partial in the period spanning liberalizing change while conventional understandings of law as regular, stable, prospective and adherent to standing legislation may be of greater or lesser applicability The stakes after all are quite high – given the perceived need to rebuild a broken community or to prevent its further destruction, the ordinary dictates of the rule of law may be supplemented by novel rules or revised temporarily   . Notwithstanding a greater degree of human rights qualif cations being attached to amnesty ,[123] there is frequently a conscious trade-off between peace and accountability – 'the imperative of normative discontinuity often trumps the protection of other values in the hope that whatever depar - tures from conventional legality this will entail will pay off in democratic consolidation'.[124] The paradigmatic examples are the abstention from trial in the decades following the wave of transitions in Latin America and Eastern Europe in the late 1980s and early 1990s. In more propitious circumstances for accountability that are more susceptible to implementing idealist theo- ries, the need to politically stigmatize the old regime, to incapacitate certain revanchist f gures or to speedily draw political lines in the sand may mean that a recalibration of evidentiary standards is necessary to enable law's trans- formative role.[125] As Aukerman notes

> Trials conducted before impartial courts that scrupulously observe due process requirements may showcase the benef ts of the rule of law … Yet when those same due process protections free those who are perceived to be guilty, fair trials may well inspire contempt for the rule of law .[126]

The paradigmatic examples here are the *Pinochet* case, where both the UK House of Lords and the Chilean appeals court suspended his prosecution on the grounds that he was unf t for trial,[127] and the original *Barayagwiza* deci- sion, where the ICTR Appeals Chamber dismissed the case against a media leader indicted for inciting genocidal violence on the grounds that his funda- mental rights had been violated by prolonged detention without trial. [128] In both cases, prolonged public outcry forced the authorities in Chile and The Hague to f nd alternative routes to secure conviction. Acquittals on technical grounds, so normal in ordinary times, can considerably undermine support for a trial process and the willingness of states to fund them. [129]

Where this work departs from T eitel is in the understanding of how the rule of law interacts with justice. There is no single appropriate response to past political criminality – f exible, differentiated and context-specif c under- standings of justice are often necessary in mediating transition. However , it does not necessarily follow that there should be f exible, differentiated and context-specif c understandings of the rule of law in post-conf ict states. In attempting to untangle the Gordian knot tying context-specif c ideas of justice with the less mutable demands of the rule of law , Teitel at times appears to conf ate the two issues. Because transitional justice cannot meet all the traditional values associated with the rule of law, she conceives an extraor- dinary 'transitional rule of law' where '[t]ranscendent notions of rule-of-law in transition are highly contingent, depending, in part on the states' distinc- tive political and legal legacies'. [130] Building on Nuremberg, Hungary, the border guards and South African examples, she juxtaposes the value of settled law versus law as transformative – by advancing the normative shift between regimes, departures from conventional notions of legality may be justif ed as 'critical undoings' of the predicates justifying the ancien régime. [131] The compatibility of breaches of what citizens should ordinarily expect from judicial institutions is assessed on the basis of whether it enables liberal democratic transition, and not on whether it serves as a model for future interaction of the state or individual with the national institutions of justice.

Where this becomes contentious is her conclusion that these compromises in transition are 'constructive of transition, condemnatory of wrongs – even as it renders them past – *while affirming the rule of law*' [emphasis added]. [132] Though de Greiff goes too far in asserting T eitel's analysis tends towards 'a type of casuistry',[133] her explanation of justice in transition gets tied in knots once it departs from the concept of justice and incorporates the rule of law. To conceive of amnesties, selective prosecutions, truth commissions designed intentionally or otherwise to circumvent the courts and systematically unfair trials as aff rming the rule of law requires degrees of mental legerdemain that conceptualize the rule of law so elastically as to deny it any value. Adherence by ruler and ruled alike to law is damaged when individuals can avoid criminal accountability by virtue of their military might or number. Forbearance from accountability may be conducive to creating an environment where the rule of law thrives, but cannot in and of itself aff rm it. The strength of judicial institutions is compromised when they are geared predominantly towards conviction. Existing legislative or constitutional rights are denied in the courts when retroactivity, selectivity, presumptions of guilt and coercive plea-bar gaining are employed. Once more, these acts may help advance the transition to a democratic, rights-respecting polity, but at a temporary cost of denying the integrity of the law. One needs to guard against the inherently self-excusatory nature of transitional justice – even the limited, liminal nature of the phrase *transitional* justice can itself serve to legitimize its practices. [134] Deviations from strict legality may ultimately amount to a price worth paying in diffcult circumstances, but a more rigid conception of the rule of law reminds us of what is lost. Though transitional justice is posited as the solution to the lack of rule of law, it may merely deliver a less virulent form of the problem.

The conclusion T eitel ultimately reached, that even when the normal predicates of legality do not apply , we are still left with an admittedly 'symbolic rule of law' [135] that can square away our concerns, is too neat. Policy-makers need to ask what is being symbolized and whether it actually constitutes a critical undoing of the prior regimes (when it may in fact mimic its practices for more benign purposes), and if so, whether it can still be justif ed as such. An elastic conception of the rule of law derived from the unavoidable incongruities of justice in transition can risk questionable conclusions, most notably T eitel's contention that 'the previous politicized nature of law and adjudication partially justif es non-adherence during the transition',[136] when most observers in the area of post-conf ict reconstruction and transitional justice would ar gue precisely the opposite – the past politicization makes it imperative that successor justice moves as far away from power politics as possible. Similarly, the argument that 'when the institutions and processes of criminal justice lack the legitimacy ordinarily associated with the rule of law, the partial (i.e., compromised) criminal form nonetheless shows that attributes of the rule of law are still working' is contentious; if anything, it represents the (perhaps unavoidable) sacrif ce of the rule of law to political exigencies. [137] The equalization of punishment' s waiver with punishment similarly highlights an unsatisfying elasticity , leading to the worrying conclusion that almost any response can be understood as advancing the rule of law so long as it simultaneously advances transition. Once the rule of law becomes def ned as symbolic, the problem of its inf nite malleability sets in, justif ed by present exigencies at the cost of future coherence.

3.6 Getting realistic about the rule of law in transition

None of the above is to suggest that the ordinary predicates of rule of law should be employed as 'trumps' in a debate over the wisdom of any transitional justice mechanism. I readily accept the argument that if the rule of law and justice/reconciliation are in tension, the balance between them is best judged according to criteria of what most effectively creates peace and stability in a divided community , though the choice of course will rarely be so stark.[138] Deviations from the rule of law might better be characterized as trade-offs, given that some of the elements that contradict the rule of law (lack of due process, systematic stacking of the deck in favour of the prosecution, employment of unaccountable actors) may facilitate other rule of law goals like accountability and non-violent conf ict resolution. Often, of course, it will be a choice between two different breaches of the rule of law – the prohibition of retrospectivity versus *erga omnes* human rights obligations, selective prosecution of the few versus permanent incarceration of the many . Transitional justice, like peace-building, is ultimately a hyperpoliticized question. It is here submitted that the better way to conceive of the compromises of justice in transition is that they are necessary and sometimes unavoidable departures from the rule of law . One can then reconcile the understandable unease these practices occasion with the socio-political progress they facilitate by adopting Raz's theory of the rule of law as just one value competing amidst a number of others. As he ar gues:

> Since the rule of law is just one of the virtues the law should possess, it is to be expected that it possesses no more than prima facie force. It always has to be balanced against competing claims and other values ... A lesser degree of conformity is often to be preferred precisely because it helps realisation of other goals. [139]

The best outcome may need compromise with what the rule of law demands having due regard for transitional political constraints or opportunities. Along a similar line, Ohlin put the choice thus:

> The f rst, naïve version, as I shall call it, simply says that the principle of legality was violated and that the needs of transitional justice justif ed it

as an exception to the general rule. This suggests a broader implication, i.e., that the rules of justice are up for grabs in times of transitional justice. As I have said before, this is precisely the kind of poor argument that must be avoided. The second version of the argument – the nuanced version, as I shall call it – rejects this calculus and appeals instead to Realpolitik. The basic rules of justice are not subject to revision based on the demands of transitional justice. All we can do is attempt to comply with as many of the universal rules of justice as possible. And to the extent that circumstances prevent our total compliance with the basic rules – including the principle of legality – we should make note of it and move on.[140]

Such an approach acknowledges that the defning features of transitions have normative signifcance while at the same time reaffrms the relevance of stable-state intuitions about the rule of law. This is something those involved in rule of law reconstruction have long accepted – emergency situations might require limited, temporary suspension of the rule of law and projects like development, security and democratization might on occasion be imperilled by strict legality, which is merely one of many social values and only one element of a comprehensive political philosophy.[141] Any departures from the institutions, culture or norms of the rule of law are noted, however, and cannot be wished away.

This point is not merely academic – it goes to the core of the dilemma in the use of transitional justice mechanisms to develop the rule of law. Theoretical claims that all measures of transitional justice amount automatically to an expression of a commitment to the rule of law and a means to strengthen it look simplistic compared to, for example, Trebilcock and Daniels' developmental perspective on the rule of law which emphasizes process values (predictability, enforceability, transparency), institutional values (independence and accountability) and legitimacy values that sit uncomfortably with elastic conceptions of the rule of law.[142] Reliance on international tribunals and the prevalence of alternative mechanisms, limited criminal sanctions or trials lacking due process may do little to help the reform of judicial institutions so necessary if peace is to be sustainable.[143] As such, it is submitted that Teitel is wrong to argue that 'the rule of law is not an ideal source of norms'[144] – policy-makers need to retain a keen sense of the disjunction between the institutional, cultural and normative commitments to the rule of law peace-builders try to inculcate and the different conceptions of justice and political desirability inherent in transitional justice. Ideal (or, as some would argue, ordinary) rule of law should be retained as the yardstick by which to judge transitional justice, even if internal contradictions are unavoidable.

When she argues that 'transitional rule of law is, above all, limited and symbolic – a secular rite of political passage', it appears at times that Teitel confuses justifcation, practicality and political legitimacy with the rule of law.[145] Dilemmas of transition do not make the rule of law contingent, merely the wisdom of adhering to it. Justice, in its ordinary or transitional form, is not synonymous with the rule of law – it is merely a virtue of it, which may not always be present. While it is tempting to ar   gue that the complexities of transition should encourage us towards 'more complex under standings' of law,[146] there may be more to be gained from a more prosaic approach, comparing what appears necessary or desirable in transition with what the ordinary rule of law demands, and assess the choice with reference to what is in the best long-term interests of the rule of law   . A fact-based assessment of how transitional justice impacts on the institutions of justice, affects the legitimacy of the judicial institutions it either employs or circumvents or promotes the norms of fair trial needs to replace faith-based belief in transitional justice as an inherent rule of law-aff rming ritual. It constitutes a more useful guide for the future than choosing transitional options on the basis of how critically they respond to the prior regime.

This circumspection is supported by comparative studies in the peace-building community that f nd little empirical basis for many of the stronger claims made by theorists that transitional justice in and of itself contributes signif cantly to rebuilding the rule of law. As noted in Chapter 1, Stromseth, Wippman and Brook's analysis of the impact of transitional trial processes on domestic rule of law found the effects to be mixed and unclear   , while Call f nds no clear link between justice for past abuses and the quality and accessibility of justice in the future. This may just be one more example of the general tendency Leebaw observes to assume the goals of transitional justice are mutually reinforcing and complementary at the expense of identifying problematic assumptions and unacknowledged trade-offs. [147] That the links between transitional justice and the rule of law have proven more complex (or illusory) than predicted over time should alert us to potential trade-offs that transitional justice may demand vis-à-vis long-term rule of law development – for example, that truth commissions may encourage suspicion about the rule of law (as in South Africa), [148] that political interference tolerated in transitional trial processes can endure in politically signif cant trials in ordinary time (as in East Timor),[149] that delegation of responsibility for administering transitional trials to unaccountable international actors undermines the professional identity and credibility of national judicial institutions (as in Bosnia).[150]

In some states, heavily compromised transitional justice may be the only widely acceptable means of mediating the transition from war or illiberal rule to the new regime, and these compromises can be accepted as worthwhile trade-offs for a better future, even where they play fast and loose with conventional understandings of the rule of law that must one day be restored. However, in other transitional societies where domestic conceptions of legality lay in tatters, it is prudent to be more circumspect about departures from the rule of law . It may well be the case that the post-conf ict societal balance is such that retribution, pedagogy or pacif cation are so necessary that departure from strict legality is justif able if so needed. However, it may also be the case that society is better served by strict adherence to the rule of law's ordinary understanding in the long-term interests of the state, notwithstanding the risk of injustice or short-term instability , though it will rarely be a simple binary choice. All transitional justice is at some level a balancing exercise – justice against peace, accountability versus accommodation, reconciliation versus retribution. The means by which one weighs these factors in the balance will differ, depending on whether one' s supreme value is social harmony, negative peace or historical consensus, though the sharp divisions that characterized the earliest debates have given way to more holistic understandings. What this book does is highlight one balancing exercise that hitherto has rarely been undertaken outside of the Nurember   g, Eastern European and early truth commissions examples examined earlier   , namely one weighing the pragmatic rule of law as it is understood in the process of justice system reconstruction against the narrative, norm-driven vision in transitional justice. Whether absolute steadfastness in adherence to the former is justif ed or whether it should be tempered by political goals will depend very much on the post-conf ict peace-building ecology in the transitional state. It is important, however, to recognize deviations from the rule of law for what they are. While transitional compromises may advance transition, they may have a long-term cost which should not be underestimated or misconstrued in an overly-elastic conception of the rule of law . The greatest danger with this approach is that transitions may have obvious beginnings but seldom have def nable ends, and transitional imperatives can be used to justify non-adherence to the law long after violence or repression has ended. As Bell warns:

> Transitional justice discourses have a contemporary purchase well beyond transitions from violent conf ict. Exceptionalism in the name of the diff - culties of transition could lead to broad exceptionalism as more and more situations are def ned as transitional.[151]

Though the concern expressed here refers more to a fear of a post-9/11 appropriation of transitional justice's language to remove legal restraints on hegemonic power on a global level, the same danger exists domestically in even greater form in weak, emergent polities. Indeed, one of the main reasons why it is important to have a time-limited conception of what transition is because the moral obligations and sacrif ces transition demands are too inconsistent with the standard of justice that will be demanded in ordinary times but may nevertheless become 'hardwired' into the new institutional order[152] Transitional justice has a cost in terms of domestic understandings of legality and the credibility of judicial institutions that cannot be wished away by theoretical legerdemain. The cost may be worth paying given the exigencies of transition by contributing to the development of conditions where the rule of law can prosper, but liberalizing societies are better served by understanding these deviations from what we understand as full legality *as* deviations, and not as manifestations of a f uid and contingent transitional rule of law.

3.7 Transitional justice: claiming too much?

Implicit in the above analysis is the need to acknowledge that rule of law reform and transitional justice are not synonymous and that all goods do not necessarily go together. However, it is not enough to re-examine the relationship between the rule of law and transitional justice alone. If a rebalancing must occur, it is necessary to question the weight attached to transitional justice itself. As Andriu points out, the goals attributed to transitional justice of accountability, healing, socio-economic regeneration, settling history etc. are startlingly ambitious – 'nothing less than the transformation, or the regeneration, of a whole society'.[153] The growing acceptance that transitional justice 'claims too much' should encourage a healthy scepticism about mechanisms and practices endorsed on paper but with complex consequences in the f eld that are still not fully understood. [154] One sees in the literature and reports an emotional commitment to transitional justice that generally eschews doubts about its overall effcacy even where isolated shortcomings are accepted.[155] Policy has hitherto proceeded less from analysis to conclusions than from commitments to action – the benef ts of certain mechanisms are assumed instead of being treated as empirical propositions to be proven rigor ously.[156] Others fear that the consequent 'overselling' of transitional justice can encourage unrealizable public expectations of what it can achieve, ultimately causing unduly prejudiced assessments that the mechanisms employed have failed.[157] As Olsen, Payne and Reiter ar gue:

> Governments, societies, and international actors have high expectations for transitional justice – so high, in fact, that it seems to be overloaded with goals ... Regardless of how comprehensive its programs, transitional justice could not possibly fulf l all these goals.[158]

As a fear developed among practitioners and theorists about the damage to transitional justice's credibility from wild, unsubstantiated claims, there has emerged in recent years a commendable attempt to clarify the causal relationships (if any) between individual mechanisms and general ends. By employing social science methodologies and hard data, a tentative literature has emerged on how to assess transitional justices impact. The expectation is that this scholarship can chip away at falsity and overly ambitious claims. [159] One theme this book will pursue throughout its remainder is that the potential impact of transitional justice is exaggerated, a position that needs to be borne in mind when we weigh the eff cacy of a transitional justice process against the damage it may do to the institutions, culture and norms of the rule of law

Transitional justice is routinely described as being as essential to peacebuilding as demobilization, disarmament or elections, [160] as 'the centre-piece

of social repair'[161] and as 'the f rst real test for democratic statehood'. [162]
While some form of accounting may be desirable and indeed legally required,
transitional justice will rarely prove necessary in bridging the gap between
authoritarianism or war and a more liberal future. Far from constituting the
'centerpiece of democratic transition'[163] or 'constructing the relevant political
difference' between old regime and new,[164] transitional justice will usually be
of secondary or even tertiary importance in mediating change and building
peace in comparison to peace agreements, elections, incorporation of soldiers
into civilian life, re-invigoration of the economy, new constitutional arrangements, resettlement of refugees or the panoply of peace-building activities
undertaken by the UN or regional or ganizations like the OSCE. Though
most surveys of survivor populations note support for the notion of transitional justice,[165] it is rarely the core consideration in transition. For example,
in a survey of 2,585 adults in Uganda in 2005, less than 1 per cent believed
justice was the most pressing priority after conf ict, a f gure dwarfed by the
need for food (33 per cent), education (5 per cent) and health (6 per cent). [166]
Similarly, Corkalo et al. found that all communities in Bosnia found economic
reconstruction and social justice more imperative than accountability   .[167]
Transitional justice is but one of many rites of passage in democratization,
and often occurs after others such as elections or demobilization. As such,
even the liminality of transitional justice may be exaggerated – many transitional justice mechanisms begin not in the interregnum between regimes,
but early or even relatively late in the consolidation stage of liberal rule. Most
of the dilemmas it raises will rarely be of existential signif cance for the transition, except insofar as a given accountability policy runs a serious risk of
reversing democratization or peace, such as in Ar gentina or Uganda.

Given that in transition, formerly opposed sides will have committed to
some mutually acceptable means of allocating power in society   , the truth,
accountability or reconciliation a given mechanism may yield will only in
very exceptional circumstances prove causally signifcant in terms of the long-
term viability of the new polity. The modalities of accountability will generally be set by the terms of peace settlements and not the other way around.
As political scientists studying genuine transitions have long acknowledged,
the question 'is not how a democratic system comes into existence. Rather, it
is how a democracy, assumed to be already in existence, can best preserve or
enhance its health and stability .'[168] It is therefore worthwhile reconsidering
the relative value of transitional justice among the competing concerns at
play in transition. Justice may not be a supreme virtue in all contexts – the
importance and priority attached to it will depend on the specif c context. As
Scharf and Williams put it: 'The norm of justice must … compete for inf u-
ence with other highly relevant and practicable approaches such as accommodation, economic inducement, and the use of force, which are based on
equally compelling principles, and which have a longer history of use by
peace builders.'[169]

Even where it appears that transitional justice can make a signif   cant
impact on the nature and sustainability of the process of political change, to

pursue accountability or restoration is to pursue 'impossible solutions to impossible problems'.[170] Transitional justice typically occurs in what de Greiff labels 'very imperfect worlds'. By this, he means a society characterized not just by the massive and systematic violation of norms, but by the fact that there are enormous disadvantages implicated in any attempt to enforce compliance.[171] These costs might predictably include the overthrow of the polity when it tries to enforce these norms. T o pursue transitional justice is to entertain impossibility and paradox. Perhaps the most obvious example is the fact that the crimes that typify transitional justice such as genocide, torture, persecution and war crimes require the most severe legal response, but no punishment can adequately communicate the appropriate scale of outrage. As Arendt famously puts it in relation to Nazi atrocities, such crimes 'transcend the domain of humane affairs'[172] and 'explode the limits of law … [f]or these crimes, no punishment is severe enough'. [173] Dissatisfaction with such limits is palpable, most famously in Rwanda where senior off   cials convicted by the ICTR receive more lenient punishments than the death penalty their subordinates at one stage received domestically[174] The prisoners receive better healthcare and nutrition than many of their victims. The exigencies of security might demand that perpetrators of human rights abuses receive monies from DDR programmes while their victims get nothing, as in Sierra Leone.[175] While trial punishments are designed to communicate society's condemnation of the crimes inficted, the plea-bargaining that commonly attaches to mass criminality in order to prosecute the volume of crimes will result in dismayingly emollient sentencing. As Drumbl writes, an 'enemy of all mankind' may be punished as leniently than a car thief. [176]

Even if a punishment commensurate with the crimes was possible, it is impossible to be comprehensive at the same time given the vast numbers of those involved in atrocity. The most extreme example is the imprisonment of 130,000 in Rwanda, [177] but such diff culties are equally the case in less dramatic contexts, such as the 391 indicted in East T   imor[178] or Bosnia's National War Crimes Prosecution Strategy stating that around 8,000 people remain under investigation.[179] Retributive intuitions must be tempered by the reality that 'it is politically and economically impossible to subject all who bear some level of responsibility for past violations to the strictest proce-dures and the maximum penalties'. [180] Sloan ar gues convincingly that the intuitive-moralistic answers we grasp for in response to the scale and context of mass criminality seem 'pejoratively academic'. [181] This dilemma, so appar-ent at Nurember g and T okyo, is exacerbated by the considerable parallel evolution of, and emphasis on, the rights of both victims and of the accused to ensure their protection during criminal prosecution, most notably the rights to be heard and to a fair and public hearing. Both insensitivity to victims or breaches of the rights of the accused when using criminal prosecu-tion as a measure of transitional justice undermine the justice process, but the twin impulses to rectify these shortcomings may place intolerable strains on the process in even the most developed legal systems, let alone those greatly weakened in the conditions that gave rise to transition. Even before these developments, Shklar was by no means unduly despondent when she posited that '[i]t is indeed doubtful that legal provisions can be devised for events of this sort. There are no civilized responses that are f tting, and certainly no legal norms can cope.'[182]

Such intractable diff culties do not admit of facile resolution. As de Greiff puts it:

> In fact, there is no transitional country that can legitimately claim great successes in this f eld. That is, there is no country that has under gone a transition that has prosecuted each and every perpetrator of human rights violations (let alone has punished them in proportion to the gravity of the harms they caused); that has implemented a truth-seeking strategy leading to the disclosure of the fate of each and every victim, or to an absolutely thorough disclosure of the structures that made the violations possible; that has established a reparations program making each and every victim whole (providing them with benef ts proportional to the harm they suffered); or that, particularly in the short run, has reformed each and every institution that was either involved in or made possible the violations in question.[183]

To the suffering of individuals and the destruction of a wider society , transitional justice can only approximate a response, an illusory closure. In the current, more sceptical climate in which transitional justice is assessed, scholars are beginning to prefer a 'prudential attention to what is possible under the specif c limitations of the circumstances' over the vaulting moral ends that previously characterized the area.[184] Consequently, this book takes seriously McAdams' injunction to admit the possibility of failure in transitional justice under the goal-oriented terms it sets for itself – even in the best case scenarios, due to the 'ineffable qualities of the human mind' we can never know whether goals like reconciliation, healing or deterrence have ever been achieved, and we can never know whether an ostensibly successful justice mechanism will translate into a better overall society .[185] What he suggests is that it is more prof table to think of transitional justice as 'a process in which the outcome is uncertain but the undertaking is valued in itself ' as opposed to the predominant conception of it being a means to an end.[186] Even if justice cannot be attained in any satisfactory sense, the sheer fact of transitional justice is inherently benef cial as a positive exercise in civic affairs demonstrating to the aggrieved party that competing claims can be treated within the framework of a democratic polity .[187] McAdams provides a better standard for judging transitional justice than the unfounded, goal-oriented utopianism that has (a) operated to vindicate an 'end justif es the means' approach to transitional justice and (b) formed a potent framework for criticizing transitional prosecutions and truth commissions.   [188] However, McAdams still does not distinguish the concept of justice from the rule of law, arguing that the mere fact that a legal process replaces arbitrary or capricious standards represents suff cient progress.[189]

The remainder of this book agrees that the process should take precedence over product in transitional justice, but sets a higher standard than non-arbitrariness, fairness or even justice. Process should be measured by how it contributes to, or detracts from, a sustainable standard of domestic rule of law. If the process involves national trials which are systematically weighted against defendants, or institutions of justice which are circumvented in favour of restorative or international solutions, or mechanisms of justice 'from below' which are hermetically sealed from state supervision to achieve an illusory closure, then these process choices should be weighted in future more carefully against the goals of justice sector reformers already in situ than they have been in the past. Invoking the rule of law should not be the end of the debate, but rather the beginning of a discussion of how the imperative towards justice in transition can be reconciled with the promotion or sustainability of legal institutions, cultures and norms. This may indirectly have the effect of making these goals more, not less, likely in the long term given how path-dependent justice outcomes are on surrounding socio-political conditions. In Africa, in particular, it is clear that much of the promise of transitional justice has gone unmet because state institutions are too weak to capitalize on the normative change its assorted mechanisms attempt to catalyse.[190] As Bayliss suggests, ref ecting on the very obvious shortcomings of national court reconstruction and transitional accountability in the Democratic Republic of the Congo, future policy should be guided both by belief in the importance of rule of law reform and a certain degree of scepticism about the prospect of achieving goals such as reconciliation, deterrence and truth.[191]

3.8 Conclusion: pragmatism and paradox

This chapter has examined how superf cial or rose-tinted the prevailing understandings of the rule of law' s relation to transitional justice are. It argued that the short-termism inherent in transition' s foreshortened time horizons has precluded assessment of how justice mechanisms employed in this period can be integrated with the more long-term process of rule of law reconstruction, before examining how the literature has conf ated justice and the rule of law. What this chapter proposes, and what the remainder of this book elaborates, is a need to reconsider the wisdom and utility of certain modes of transitional justice in light of sometimes competing, sometimes complementary, but always wider process of rule of law reconstruction.

Abandoning the prevailing consensus that there is a linear connection between transitional justice and the rule of law, it proposes that trials or truth commissions or local justice processes should be assessed in terms of how they will impact upon the institutions, culture and norms of the rule of law that are in the process of reconstruction. *Pace* Kennedy, the book urges a pragmatism of consequences when policy-makers consider transitional justice institutions, focusing attention on outcomes for the rule of law rather than the good intentions which have characterised theory and practice thus far .[192] If transitional justice mechanisms must be balanced against the demands of rule of law reconstruction, a more clear-eyed vision of costs and benefts, risks and opportunities, is required. Of course, such an approach is open to the same empirical criticisms examined earlier in relation to transitional justice generally. The rule of law , like justice, is ill-suited to measurements of improvement in the way that an economy or levels of public health are. Furthermore, in periods of political tumult so many conditions change simultaneously that it is diffcult to draw valid conclusions about the impact of any one policy. Rule of law reconstruction and transitional justice are becoming so complex in their modalities and hostage to so many inter   -dependent fortunes that even when we succeed in verifying that a certain change for good or ill has resulted, it may be impossible to know what variable was instrumental in producing the effect. There is no single solution to how transitional justice and rule of law reform should interact as the relationship will depend on an intricate web of inter-related factors like the starting conditions in the state, the presence or otherwise of a peace-building mission, the strength of that mission, the impact of constitutional reform and pre-existing public attitudes towards the judiciary. Measures of accountability are a relatively small piece of a much larger puzzle. As one study put it:

> The defciencies of justice under new post-conf   ict regimes varied greatly ... but they seemed rooted in institutional choices, political decisions, and the context of war termination more than in the decision about how to deal with perpetrators of past atrocities. [193]

While this work will examine creative opportunities for transitional justice to help rectify defciencies in justice, equal emphasis will be given to the potentially destructive capacities of accountability measures to inhibit rule of law reform. Because states' circumstances will differ in crucial aspects, it is neither possible nor desirable to outline a generic, cross-cultural schema – Bosnia is not Guatemala which in turn is not Cambodia. On the other hand, it is imperative not to get lost in the infnite uniqueness of every transition, and an attempt will be made to suggest some over-arching principles that in certain situations will be of greater or lesser general applicability Because the area has remained under-analysed and comparative analysis has lagged, analysis must operate more on the basis of justifed belief than empirical certainty.

One of the contentions of this book is that the potential of transitional justice to interact usefully with rule of law reconstruction is greater than hitherto realized, by catalysing justice system reconstruction, by developing a culture of the rule of law through fostering trust among the populace and by exemplifying sustainable minimum standards of due process. Even then, however, the anomalies of transitional justice will apply. Prime among them are what de Brito, González-Enríquez and Aguilar call 'the paradox of the probable and the unnecessary' – transitional justice is most likely to be effective in states with relatively strong social structures like courts and a favourable balance of power , but it is these societies that need transitional justice least. By contrast, it is in weak states where violence and political criminality were the norm and not the exception that the need for the rule of law is most acute, but where the starting conditions for it are least available.[194] A further paradox is that weakness of the respect at the level of ruler and ruled for the rule of law in states whose modern history is def ned by war or authoritarianism (that is, the states of most interest to this book' s inquiry) may mean public demand for accountability is relatively muted. By contrast, where accountability before the law was a generally accepted norm interrupted by an anomalous period of war or repression, the demand for justice is higher and attaches greater expectations:

> The more democratic a country' s past and the less violent its social co-existence, the more likely it is that truth and justice will gain a hear - ing. And it is those that most need an accounting for the past – those with the most violent traumatic histories – that often achieve less in the realm of justice.[195]

This paradox is not always present – one recent study notes forbearance in societies like Northern Ireland and South Africa with relatively developed judiciaries, but notes that selected states with weak judiciaries such as Cambodia, East Timor and Sierra Leone established vigorous programmes to prosecute crimes of the past.[196] A f nal paradox is that the political conditions created by impunity may be more conducive to the long-term development of the conditions in which the rule of law can thrive than accountability before the law.[197] Often, it is only by employing transition-sensitive responses or striking political bargains can the political conditions be created on which rule of law institutions become feasible.[198]

   To conclude, those tasked with transitional justice might benef t from a view of the rule of law that is more programmatic in focus and less based on the liberalizing narratives that have hitherto dominated. This chapter advocates the equal, integrated treatment of rule of law reconstruction and transitional justice in empirical research and policy   , a praxis cognisant that judicial reforms can be undermined by transitional justice, but equally the gains of an accountability process can be nullifed if institutional and cultural rule of law issues remain unaddressed. Bearing this in mind, the next three chapters are both descriptive (i.e. explaining why certain biases and blindspots have emerged in practice and their impacts) and normative (evaluating alternative solutions prescriptively and suggesting what ought to be done according to the interests of rule of law reform). It proposes means by which this can be done, though decisions reached on this basis will invariably be context-specif c. As such, the work explores unacknowledged tensions more so than unrealized outcomes. Even with an approach more sensitive to long-term rule of law reconstruction, transitional justice will remain, as Asmal put it in the South African context, a 'poisoned chalice'.   [199] Problems may be reduced, not eliminated. In view of the inevitable 'hollowness' inherent in transitional justice that follows from the overchar ging of existing mechanisms and unrealistic public expectations, [200] it is best to accept the radical imperfectability and the irreconcilable goals of the context, to seek alternative approaches where they would be better and to move on when they do not exist, to match realism to innovation. There are opportunities to improve on current practice, even if many of the suggestions herein are acts of mitigation – the general question is what mix of principle and exception is optimal.

Notes

1 EMobekk, *Transitional Justice and Security Sector Reform: Enabling Sustainable Peace* (Geneva: Geneva Centre for the Democratic Control of Armed Forces, 2006), 15.

2 E. Bayliss, 'Reassessing the Role of International Criminal Law: Rebuilding National Courts Through Transnational Networks' (2009) 50 *Boston College Law Review* 1, 79.

3 R. Peerenboom, 'Human Rights and the Rule of Law: What's the Relationship?' (2005) 36 *Georgetown Journal of International Law* 809, 834.

4 J. Webber, 'Forms of Transitional Justice' in M. Williams, R. Nagy and J. Elster (eds.), *Transitional Justice* (New York: New York University Press, 2012), 98 at 98.

5 R. Teitel, 'Transitional Rule of Law' in A. Czarnota, M. Krygier, and W. Sadurski (eds.), *Rethinking the Rule of Law after Communism* (Budapest: CEU Press, 2005), 279 at 289.

6 D. Kennedy, *The Dark Sides of Virtue: Reassessing International Humanitarianism* (Princeton: Princeton University Press, 2004), 19.

7 Ibid.,141.

8 E. Brahm, 'Transitional Justice, Civil Society, and the Development of the Rule of Law in Post-Conf ict Societies' (2007) 9 *International Journal of Not-For-Profit Law* 1, 1.

9 P. Akhavan, 'The International Criminal Court in Context: Mediating the Global and Local in the Age of Accountability' (2003) 97 *American Journal of International Law* 712, 721.

10 N. Roht-Arriaza, 'Institutions of International Justice' (1999) 52 *Journal of International Affairs* 473, 491.

11 R. Teitel, 'Humanity's Law: Rule of Law for the New Global Politics' (2002) 35 *Cornell International Law Journal* 355, 372.

12 D. Mendeloff, 'Truth-Seeking, Truth-Telling and Postconf ict Peacebuilding: Curb the Enthusiasm?' (2004) 6 *International Studies Review* 355, 362.

13 Kennedy supra n6, 116.

14 As de Greiff puts it, 'to the extent that [transitional justice] achieves any of its goals, it does so in virtue of its potential to aff rm general but basic norms' (P. de Greiff, 'Transitional Justice, Security and Development: Security and Justice Thematic Paper' (2010) W orld Development Report 2011, available < http://wdr2011.worldbank.org/transitional%20justice>, 2).

15 F. DuBois and A. Czarnota, 'The Transitional Rule of Law' (1999) 24 *Alternative Law Journal* 9, 11.

16 R. Teitel, 'Theoretical and International Framework: T ransitional Justice in a New Era' (2003) 26 *Fordham International Law Journal* 893, 900–901.

17 R.Teitel, *Transitional Justice* (Oxford: Oxford University Press, 2001), 3.

18 P. Arthur, 'How "Transitions" Reshaped Human Rights: A Conceptual History of Transitional Justice' (2009) 31 *Human Rights Quarterly* 321, 337.

19 F. Ní Aoláin and C. Campbell, 'The Paradox of T   ransition in Conf icted Democracies' (2005) 27 *Human Rights Quarterly* 172, 182.

20 P. de Greiff, 'Articulating the Links Between T   ransitional Justice and Development: Justice and Social Integration' in P. de Greiff and R. Duthie (eds.), *Transitional Justice and Development: Making Connections* (New York: Social Science Research Council, 2009), 28.

21 R. Kerr and E. Mobekk, *Peace & Justice: Seeking Accountability After War* (Cambridge: Polity Press, 2007), 177.

22 Teitel, supra n17, 3–4.

23 C. Call, 'Conclusion: Constructing Justice and Security After W   ar' in C. Call (ed.), *Constructing Justice and Security After War* (Washington, D.C.: United States Institute of Peace, 2007), 375 at 396.

24 Bayliss, supra n2, 2.

25 R. Teitel, *Global Transitional Justice* (Washington, D.C.: Centre for Global Studies, 2010), 4.

26 W.W. Burke-White, 'The Domestic Inf uence of International Criminal Tribunals: The International Criminal Tribunal for the Former Yugoslavia and the Creation of the State Court of Bosnia & Herzegovina' (2008) 46 *Columbia Journal of Transnational Law* 279, 283–284.

27 L. Fletcher and H. W   einstein, 'Violence and Social Repair: Rethinking the Contribution of Justice to Reconciliation' (2002) 24 *Human Rights Quarterly* 573, 580.

28 E. Lutz, 'Transitional Justice: Lessons Learned and the Road Ahead' in N. Roht-Arriaza and J. Mariezcurrena (eds.), *Transitional Justice in the Twenty-First Century: Beyond Truth Versus Justice* (New York: Cambridge University Press, 2006), 325 at 339.

29 Kennedy supra n6, 116–119.

30 L. Fletcher, H. Weinstein and J. Rowen, 'Context, Timing and the Dynamics of Transitional Justice: A Historical Perspective' (2009) 31 *Human Rights Quarterly* 163, 190.

31 M. Affa'a-Mindzie, 'Transitional Justice, Democratisation and the Rule of Law' in C.L. Sriram and S. Pillay (eds.), *Peace Versus Justice?: The Dilemma of Transitional Justice in Africa* (Woodbridge: James Currey, 2010), 113 at 119.

32 N. Kritz, 'The Rule of Law in the Post-Conf   ict Phase' in C. Crocker and F. Hamson (eds.), *Managing Global Chaos* (Washington, D.C.: USIP, 2006), 587 at 590.

33 Rama Mani, *Beyond Retribution: Seeking Justice in the Shadows of War* (Cambridge: Polity Press, 2002), 30.

34 S. Chesterman, 'An International Rule of Law?' (2008) 56 *American Journal of Comparative Law* 331, 343.

35 R. Mani, 'Does Power Trump Morality? Reconciliation and Transitional Justice' in W. Schabas, E. Hughes and R. Thakur (eds.), *Atrocities and International Accountability: Beyond Transitional Justice* (New York: United Nations University Press, 2007), 23 at 39.

36 K. McEvoy, 'Beyond Legalism: Towards a Thicker Understanding of Transitional Justice' (2007) 34 *Journal of Law and Society* 411.

37 P. Gready, 'Reconceptualising Transitional Justice: Embedded and Distanced Justice' (2005) 5 *Conflict, Security and Development* 3, 7.
38 E.g. Ruben Carranza, 'Plunder and Pain: Should Transitional Justice Engage with Corruption and Economic Crimes?' (2008) 2 *International Journal of Transitional Justice* 310, 323.
39 N. Roht-Arriaza, 'The New Landscape of T ransitional Justice' in Roht-Arriaza and Mariezcurrena (eds.), supra n28, 1 at 2.
40 J. Shklar, *Legalism: Law, Morals, and Political Trials* (Cambridge, MA: Harvard University Press, 1964), 1–28.
41 D. Dyzenhaus, '*Leviathan* as a Theory of Transitional Justice' in Williams, Nagy and Elster (eds.), supra n4, 180 at 187 (equation) and 211 (def nition).
42 Ibid.,201.
43 J. Allen, 'Balancing Justice and Social Unity: Political Theory and the Idea of a Truth and Reconciliation Commission' (1999) 49 *Toronto Law Journal* 315, 328–332 and 335–338, cited ibid., at 201 and 202.
44 Ibid.,202.
45 Ibid.,187.
46 Ibid.,205 and 207.
47 E. Posner, 'Transitional Prudence: A Comment on David Dyzenhaus, "*Leviathan* as a Theory of Transitional Justice"' in Williams, Nagy and Elster (eds.), supra n4, 218 at 229–230.
48 P. de Greiff, 'Theorizing Transitional Justice' in Williams, Nagy and Elster (eds.), supra n4, 31 at 53.
49 Dyzenhaus,supra n41, 202.
50 WB. Gallie, 'Essentially Contested Concepts' (1956) 56 *Proceedings of the Aristotelian Society* 167, 168.
51 C. Villa-Vicencio, 'Why Perpetrators Should Not Always Be Prosecuted: Where the International Criminal Court and Truth Commissions Meet' (2000) 49 *Emory Law Journal* 205, 215.
52 Mani,supra n33, 5–6.
53 K. Andriu, 'Transitional Justice: A New Discipline in Human Rights' (2010) Online Encyclopedia of Mass V iolence available: < http://www.massviolence.org/IMG/article_PDF/Transitional-Justice-A-New-Discipline-in-Human-Rights.pdf>, 4.
54 D. Orentlicher, 'Settling Accounts: The Duty to Prosecute Human Rights Violations of a Prior Legal Regime' (1991) 100 *Yale Law Journal* 2537, 2542.
55 H. Packer, *The Limits of Criminal Sanction* (Stanford: Stanford University Press, 1968), 287.
56 S. Landsman, 'Alternative Responses to Serious Human Rights Abuses: Of Prosecutions and Truth Commissions' (1996) 59 *Law and Contemporary Problems* 81, 83.
57 B.A.Leebaw, 'The Irreconcilable Goals of Transitional Justice' (2008)30 *Human Rights Quarterly* 95, 98.
58 T Olsen, L. Payne and A. Reiter, *Transitional Justice in Balance: Comparing Processes, Weighing Efficacy* (Washington, D.C.: U.S. Institute of Peace, 2010), 53.
59 Ibid, at 6–7.
60 R. Teitel, 'Transitional Justice Genealogy' (2003) 16 *Harvard Human Rights Journal* 69, 89.
61 C. Bell, 'Transitional Justice, Interdisciplinarity and the State of the "Field" or "Non-Field"' (2009) 3 *International Journal of Transitional Justice* 5, 27.

62 Ofourse the debate was wider than Nuremberg – similar retroactivity questions arose in the Netherlands, France, Denmark, Belgium and Norway (P . Novick, *The Resistance versus Vichy: The Purge of Collaborators in Liberated France* (New York: Columbia University Press, 1968), 209).

63 J. Dugard, 'Retrospective Justice: International Law and the South African Model' in A.J. McAdams (ed.), *Transitional Justice and the Rule of Law in New Democracies* (Notre Dame: University of Notre Dame Press, 1997), 269 at 285.

64 See e.g. Andriu, supra n53, 8–9, M. Minow, *Between Vengeance and Forgiveness: Facing History After Genocide and Mass Violence* (Boston: Beacon Press, 1998), 30–38, E. Posner and A. V ermeule, 'Transitional Justice as Ordinary Justice' (2004) 117 *Harvard Law Review* 762, 791–800, Teitel, supra n17, 12–21.

65 H.L.A. Hart, 'Positivism and the Separation of Law and Morals' (1958) 7 *Harvard Law Review* 593.

66 L. Fuller, 'Positivism and Fidelity to the Rule of Law' (1958) 71 *Harvard Law Review* 630. Teitel reminds us that Fuller' s position was not a straightforward adoption of a substantive idea of the rule of law in contradistinction to a procedural one – Fuller instead proposed a procedural view of substantive justice (T eitel, supra n17, 13).

67 Shklar, supra n40, 156.

68 N.Eiskovits, 'Transitional Justice' in E. Zalta et al. (eds.), *Stanford Encyclopaedia of Philosophy* (Stanford: 2009), available: < http://plato.stanford.edu/entries/justice-transitional/>, Section 1.2.1 and J.D. Ohlin, 'On the V ery Idea of T ransitional Justice' (2007) 8 *Whitehead Journal of Diplomacy and International Relations* 51, 59.

69 T Taylor, *The Anatomy of the Nuremberg Trial: A Personal Memoir* (New Y ork: Knopf, 1992), 635.

70 Teitel, supra n17, 15–21.

71 ConstitutionalCourt Judgment of 3 March 1992 MK No. 11/1992, translated in (1994) 1 *Journal of Constitutional Law in Eastern & Central Europe* 129, paras. 138 and 141.

72 G. Halmai and K. Lane Scheppele, 'Living W ell is the Best Revenge: The Hungarian Approach to Judging the Past' in McAdams (ed.), supra n63, 155 at 156.

73 'Germany: Trial of Border Guards, Ruling of the Berlin State Court, 20 January 1992' in N. Kritz (ed.), *Transitional Justice: How Emerging Democracies Reckon with Former Regimes: Laws, Rulings and Reports, Volume 3* (Washington, D.C.: USIP, 1995), 576 at 579.

74 A.J. McAdams, 'Communism on T rial: The East German Past and the German Future' in McAdams (ed.), supra n63, 239 at 244.

75 E. Blankenburg, 'The Purge of Lawyers after the Breakdown of the East German Communist Regime' (1995) 20 *Law & Social Inquiry* 223, 229.

76 J.Elster, *Closing the Books: Transitional Justice in Historical Perspective* (New York: Cambridge University Press, 2004), 136.

77 Teitel, supra n17, 17.

78 Posnerand Vermeule, supra n64, 792–793.

79 Andriu,supra n53, 8.

80 Teitel, supra n17, 30.

81 T. Rosenberg, 'Tipping the Scales of Justice' (1995) 12 *World Policy Journal* 55, 55.

82 *Resolution of the Hungarian Constitutional Court of 12 October 1993 on the Justice Law* (Case 53/1993).

83 *Border Guards Prosecution Cases* (FRG Bundesgeriichthof, translated in *International Law Reports* 100 (1995) 380–382.

84 D. Gray, 'An Excuse-Centred Approach to Transitional Justice' (2005 –06) 74 *Fordham Law Review* 2621, 2659.

85 J. Torpey, 'Introduction: Politics and the Past' in J. Torpey (ed.), *Politics and the Past: On Repairing Historical Injustices* (Lanham: Rowman & Littlef eld, 2003), 1 at 9–10, K. Asmal, 'T ruth, Reconciliation and Justice: The South African Experience in Perspective' (2000) 63 *Modern Law Review* 1, 12–13.

86 L. Huyse, 'Justice after T ransition: On the Choices Successor Elites Make in Dealing with the Past' (1995) 20 *Law and Social Inquiry* 51, 65.

87 Mani, supra n33, 108.

88 Minow supra n64, 127.

89 Eiskovits, supra n68, 17.

90 S. Dwyer, 'Reconciliation for Realists' (1999) 13 *Ethics & International Affairs* 81, 89.

91 DeGreiff, supra n48, 53.

92 Gray supra n84, 2688.

93 R.A. Cobián and F. Réategui, 'Towards Systemic Social T ransformation: Truth Commissions and Development' in de Greiff and Duthie (eds.), supra n20, 142 at 163.

94 Eitel, supra n60, 89.

95 Fletcher Weinstein and Rowen, supra n30, 208–209.

96 Minow supra n64, 88.

97 Orentlicher supra n54, 2546 at note 32.

98 K. Bohl, 'Breaking the Rules of T ransitional Justice' (2006) 24 *Wisconsin International Law Journal* 558, 574, though noting exceptions in Guatemala, Argentina and Chile.

99 J. Mendez, 'In Defense of Transitional Justice' in McAdams (ed.), supra n63, 1 at 15–16.

100 M. Osiel, 'Why Prosecute? Critics of Punishment for Mass Atrocity' (2000) 22 *Human Rights Quarterly* 118 at 134.

101 S. Levinson, 'Trials, Commissions, and Investigating Committees: The Elusive Search for Norms of Due Process' in R. Rotberg and D. Thompson (eds.), *Truth v. Justice: The Morality of Truth Commissions* (Princeton: Princeton University Press, 2000), 211.

102 Andriu, supra n53, 13.

103 Landsman, supra n56, 88.

104 Eitel, supra n60, 81–82.

105 R. Wilson, *The Politics of Truth and Reconciliation in South Africa: Legitimizing the Post-Apartheid State* (Cambridge: Cambridge University Press, 2001), 171.

106 Leebaw supra n57, 98.

107 Seee.g. W. Schabas and S. Darcy (eds.), *Truth Commissions and Courts: The Tension Between Criminal Justice and the Search for Truth* (Dordrecht: Kluwer Academic, 2004).

108 L. Laplante, 'Outlawing Amnesty: The Return of Criminal Justice in Tansitional Justice Schemes' (2008–09) 49 *Virginia Journal of International Law* 915, 927.

109 Kennedy supra n6, 130 and 131.

110 L. Bosire, *Overpromised, Underdelivered: Transitional Justice in Sub-Saharan Africa* (New York: ICTJ, 2006), 8 at footnote 32, citing T. Carothers, 'The End of the Transition Paradigm' (2002) 13 *Journal of Democracy* 5, 9.

111 Posnerand Vermeule, supra n64, 769.
112 D. Dyzenhaus, 'Judicial Independence, Transitional Justice and the Rule of Law' (2003)10 *Otago Law Review* 345, 346.
113 Eitel, supra n17, 6.
114 Posnerand Vermeule, supra n64, 764.
115 Ohlin,supra n68, 52.
116 It should be pointed out that T eitel later adds that transitional justice bears 'aff nities to law in non-transitional circumstances' and that 'one might think of transitional jurisprudence as exaggerated instantiations that vivify conf icts and compromises otherwise latent in the law' (Teitel, supra n17, 228).
117 Posnerand Vermeule, supra n64, 763,764, 801–802.
118 Eitel, supra n17, 66.
119 Ibid.,51.
120 Ibid.,6.
121 Ibid.,9.
122 Ibid.,219.
123 N. Roht-Arriaza and L. Gibson, 'The Developing Jurisprudence on Amnesty' (1998) 20 *Human Rights Quarterly* 843, 884.
124 Eitel, supra n17, 224.
125 Ibid.,222.
126 M. Aukerman, 'Extraordinary Evil, Ordinary Crimes: A Framework for Understanding Transitional Justice' (2002) 15 *Harvard Human Rights Journal* 39, 75.
127 HumanRights Watch (2001), 'Pinochet Decisions Lamented', available: <http://hrw.org/english/docs/2001/07/09/chile79.htm>.
128 *Prosecutor* v. *Jean-Bosco Barayagwiza*, Case No. ICTR-97-19-AR72, Decision of the Appeals Chamber, 2 November 1999 and *Prosecutor* v. *Barayagwiza*, Case No. ICTR-97-19-AR72, Decision on Prosecutor' s Request for Review or Reconsideration.
129 Peerenboom,supra n3, 894.
130 Eitel, supra n17, 25, 17–18.
131 Ibid.,221.
132 Ibid.,66–67.
133 DeGreiff, supra n48, 60.
134 Arthur supra n18, 329.
135 Eitel, supra n17, 213.
136 Ibid.,21.
137 Ibid.,51.
138 As argued, for example, in C. V illa-Vicencio, 'Inclusive Justice: The Limitations of Trial Justice and Truth Commissions' in Sriram and Pillay (eds.), supra n31, 44.
139 Raz, 'The Rule of Law and its Virtue' (197793) *Law Quarterly Review 195, 210*.
140 Ohlin,supra n68, 60.
141 R. Kleinfeld Belton, *Competing Definitions of the Rule of Law: Implications for Practitioners* (Washington, D.C.: Carnegie Endowment for International Peace, 2005), 24 and Peerenboom, supra n3, 837–838.
142 M.Trebilcock and R. Daniels, *Rule of Law Reform and Development: Charting the Fragile Path of Progress* (Cheltenham: Edward Elgar, 2008).
143 M. Ndulo and R. Duthie, 'The Role of Judicial Reform in Development and Transitional Justice', in de Greiff and Duthie (eds.), supra n20, 250 at 250–282.

Transitional justice and rule of law reconstruction

144 Teitel, supra n17, 7.
145 Teitel, supra n5, 286.
146 Ibid.,283.
147 Leebaw supra n57.
148 J. Gibson, 'Truth, Reconciliation and the Creation of a Human Rights Culture in South Africa' (2004) 38 *Law & Society Review* 5.
149 P. McAuliffe, 'UN Peace-Building, T ransitional Justice and the Rule of Law in East T imor: The Limits of Institutional Responses to Political Questions' (2011) 58 *Netherlands International Law Review* 103.
150 Human Rights Center UC Berkeley & Centre for Human Rights, University of Sarajevo, 'Justice, Accountability and Social Reconstruction: An Interview Study of Bosnian Judges and Prosecutors' (2000) 18 *Berkeley Journal of International Law* 102.
151 Christine Bell, 'The "New Law" of T ransitional Justice' in K. Ambos, J. Lar ge and M. Wierda (eds.), *Building a Future on Peace and Justice: Studies on Transitional Justice, Peace and Development* (Berlin: Springer, 2009), 105 at 123.
152 M. Williams and R. Nagy, 'Introduction' in W illiams, Nagy and Elster (eds.), supra n4, 1 at 21.
153 Andriu,supra n53, 3.
154 Fletcherand Weinstein, supra n27, 601.
155 Jon Elster, 'Emotions and Transitional Justice', symposium 'Emotions that matter', University of Tennessee, March 6–7, 2003.
156 L. Vinjamuri and J. Snyder , 'Advocacy and Scholarship in the Study of International War Crimes Tribunals and Transitional Justice' (2004) 7 *Annual Review of Political Science* 345, 359.
157 McEvoy, supra n36, 426, Kerr and Mobekk, supra n21, 181.
158 Olsen,Payne and Reiter, supra n58, 131.
159 E.g. H. van der Merwe, V . Baxter and A. Chapman (eds.), *Assessing the Impact of Transitional Justice: Challenges for Empirical Research* (Washington, D.C.: USIP Press, 2009), O. Thoms, J. Ron and R. Paris, 'State-Level Effects of Transitional Justice: What Do We Know?' (2010) 4 *International Journal of Transitional Justice* 1.
160 Mendeloff,supra n12, 355–356.
161 Fletcherand Weinstein, supra n27, 577.
162 Bohl,supra n98, 559.
163 D.Orentlicher, '"Settling Accounts" Revisited: Reconciling Global Norms with Local Agency' (2007) 1 *International Journal of Transitional Justice* 10, 15.
164 Teitel, supra n17, 221.
165 E.g. V. Espinoza Cuevas, M.L. Ortiz Rojas and P. Rojas Baeza, *Truth Commissions: An Uncertain Path? Comparative Study of Truth Commissions in Argentina, Chile, El Salvador, Guatemala and South Africa From the Perspectives of Victims, Their Relatives, Human Rights Organizations and Experts* (Santiago and Geneva: Codepu and Association for the Prevention of T orture, 2002), Chapter 3 and E. Stover , 'Witnesses and the Promise of Justice in The Hague' in E. Stover and H. Weinstein (eds.), *My Neighbor, My Enemy: Justice and Community in the Aftermath of Mass Atrocity* (Cambridge: Cambridge University Press, 2004), 104 at 105–106.
166 P Pham et al., *Forgotten Voices: A Population-Based Survey of Attitudes about Peace and Justice in Northern Uganda* (Berkeley: ICTJ & Human Rights Center , 2005) at 25.
167 D. Corkalo et al., 'Neighbors Again? Intercommunity Relations after Ethnic Cleansing' in Stover and W einstein (eds.), supra n165, 143. See also Berkeley/

Sarajevo Study, supra n150, especially at 126, and W. Lambourne, 'Transitional Justice and Peace-building After Mass Violence' (2009) 3 *International Journal of Transitional Justice* 28, 41–44.

168 D. Rustow, 'Transitions to Democracy: Toward a Dynamic Model' (1970) 2 *Comparative Politics* 337, 339.

169 M. Scharf and P. Williams, 'The Function of Justice and Anti-Justice in the Peace-Building Process' (2003) 35 *Case Western Reserve Journal of International Law* 161, 179.

170 W Schabas, 'Justice, Democracy and Impunity in Post-Genocide Rwanda: Searching for Solutions to Impossible Problems' (1996) 7 *Criminal Law Forum* 523.

171 DeGreiff, supra n48, 35.

172 Hannah Arendt, *The Human Condition* (Chicago: Chicago University Press, 1958), 307.

173 L.Kohler and H. Saner (eds.), *Hannah Arendt – Karl Jaspers Correspondence 1926–69* (New York: Harcourt Brace, 1992), 5.

174 ICTY Rules of Procedure and Evidence 101(A) and Rome Statute of the ICC, Article 77(1).

175 R. Shaw, 'Linking Justice with Reintegration? Ex-combatants and the Sierra Leone Experiment' in R. Shaw, L. Waldorf and P. Hazan (eds.), *Localizing Transitional Justice: Interventions and Priorities after Mass Violence* (Stanford: Stanford University Press, 2010), 111 at 113.

176 M.Drumbl, 'Collective Violence and Individual Punishment: The Criminality of Mass Atrocity' (2005) *Northwestern University Law Review* 539, 542.

177 Gready supra n37, 10.

178 UN Secretary-General, Letter dated 24 June 2005 from the Secretary General addressed the President of the Security Council, UN Doc. S/2005/458, Annex II, *Report to Secretary-General of the Commission of Experts to Review the Prosecution of Serious Violations of Human Rights in Timor-Leste (then East Timor) in 1999*, of 25 May 2005, para. 48.

179 M.Bergsmo et al., *The Backlog of Core International Crimes Case Files in Bosnia and Herzegovina* (Oslo: International Peace Research Institute, 2009) Annex 2, at 183.

180 P. Van Zyl and M. Freeman, 'Conference Report' in A. Henkin (ed.),*The Legacy of Abuse: Confronting the Past, Facing the Future* (Washington, D.C.: Aspen Institute, 2002), 3 at 4.

181 R. Sloan, 'The Expressive Capacity of International Punishment: The Limits of the National Law Analogy and the Potential of International Criminal Law' (2007) 43 *Stanford Journal of International Law* 39, 39.

182 Shklar, supra n40, 167.

183 DeGreiff, supra n48, 35.

184 Williams and Nagy, supra n152, 11.

185 A.J. McAdams, 'Transitional Justice: The Issue That Won't Go Away' (2011) 5 *International Journal of Transitional Justice* 304, 311–312.

186 Ibid.,312.

187 Ibid.

188 For example, the 'creeping utopianism' in claims for the benefts of truth commissions is noted in C. Campbell and C. Turner, 'Utopia and the Doubters: Truth, Transition and the Law' (2008) 28 *Legal Studies* 374, 375.

189 'As long as both [proponents and opponents of using Stasi fles in administrative proceedings] have been treated carefully and with careful concern for their interests, they will have been exposed to a notably different set of legal processes than the arbitrary and capricious standards of the East German police state. In itself, this experience is a lesson in democracy.' McAdams, supra n185, 312.

190 Bosire, supra n110, 2, 3 and 30, ar   guing there is a minimum institutional strength necessary for transitional justice measures to be successful.

191 Bayliss,supra n2, 8.

192 Kennedy supra n6, xx.

193 Call,supra n23, 398.

194 A.B. de Brito et al., 'Conclusions' in A.B. de Brito, C. González-Enríquez and P. Aguilar (eds.), *The Politics of Memory: Transitional Justice in Democratizing Societies* (Oxford, New York: Oxford University Press, 2001), 303 at 314.

195 Ibid.,311–312.

196 Fletcher Weinstein and Rowen, supra n30, 212.

197 S. Cohen, 'State Crimes of Previous Regimes: Knowledge, Accountability , and Policing the Past' (1995) 20 *Law and Social Inquiry* 7, 34.

198 J. Snyder and L. V injamuri, 'Trials and Errors: Principle and Pragmatism in Strategies on International Justice' (2003–04) 28 *International Security* 5, 6.

199 Asmal,supra n85, 6.

200 R. Mani, 'Editorial: Dilemmas of Expanding Transitional Justice, or Forging the Nexus Between Transitional Justice and Development' (2008) 2 *International Journal of Transitional Justice* 253, 255.

4 Process over product

Towards a revised retributivism and utilitarianism in transitional trial

> Conventional accounts of transitional justice frequently depict the enterprise in goal-oriented terms. In this view, the measure of success is the completion of a fervently held objective: one indicts a war criminal, extracts a confession from an abusive policeman or pays compensation to the families of the afflicted. Yet, this approach has limitations of its own. First, there is the possibility of failure ... Second, even the attainment of these goals is unlikely to bring us lasting satisfaction, either as individuals or as members of a collectivity. It tells us nothing about the progress we are making toward the establishment of a post-dictatorial society.[1]

> [T]he maximum that can possibly be done within the constraints of the rule of law and non-retroactivity is way below the minimum that would have to be done in order to reconcile the small but vocal groups of those who have suffered most under the old regime.[2]

4.1 Introduction

The previous chapter argued that because those involved in advocating, designing and implementing transitional justice conceive the rule of law as a progressist narrative as opposed to a programme of institutions and culture as well as norms, due attention to institutional and cultural factors has not been given in the academy or in practice. Though it argued that the value of the rule of law as understood in ordinary times is not the supreme value, the potential of a given mechanism or approach to impact positively or adversely the institutions, culture and norms of the rule of law should be given greater weight in the balance when designing policy, especially if the socio-political legacy of transitional justice is exaggerated. As such, it argued that an approach that elevates questions of process over product would be more apt to generate a positive legacy, at least in relation to the impact of a given process on the rule of law. This chapter examines the difficulty in doing so in criminal trial, illustrating how transitional justice's concern with product not only marginalizes process values, but can actively undermine them. It studies the dangers to rule of law reconstruction of retributivist and utilitarian approaches to transitional justice and proposes a more programmatic, rule of law reconstruction-based course more applicable in transition than the unconvincing domestic criminological analogies that are currently employed to justify punishment. The presumption in retributive and utilitarian justifcations that punishment builds a safer society has dangers, and more than anything else elevates transitional accountability to the level of epiphenomal special justice where the regular requirements of the rule of law may be supplanted or circumvented by novel rules. As Ohlin argues, the imperative of rebuilding broken communities is seen as so critical for morality and law (and, it might be added, peace) that the basic principles of justice are subject to revision. [3] Avowedly benign macro-aspirations for peace, democracy and human rights thought to f ow from trial may detract from the law' s main business of weighing evidence, rendering judgment and meting out due punishment. [4] The intuition that, as Osiel puts it 'the majesty of the law at such tumultuous times consists not in vainly maintaining a facade of apolitical neutrality , but in openly serving a decent, worthy politics' is seductive but runs contrary to the goal of divorcing *as far as possible* law's application from moral or political exigencies of the day.[5]

   In the current era of globalized justice, hybrid tribunals, the ICC complementarity regime and the UN Secretary-General' s 2004 *Report* all implicitly accept a role for the international community in assisting, running or sharing responsibility for the operation of domestic transitional trial and reconstructing the justice sector . This opens up the possibility/necessity of mutually benefcial international and NGO involvement, but the view of trial in transitional justice is somewhat distinct from that of those entrusted with justice sector reform. In a reconstructing justice sector, a fair trial in and of itself represents the fundamental rule of law values of the emerging polity, but historically transitional trial has instrumentalized criminal justice, with a greater ambivalence about the necessity for due process. The chapter begins by tracing the rise of utilitarian perspectives in transitional justice and then examines how the categorization of trial as retributive has obscured the value of the criminal process in transition. It then goes on to study how the product- or goal-oriented values of transitional justice may compel the politicization of trial with a 'conviction at all costs' mentality diametrically opposed to the type of neutral, apolitical criminal justice rule of law reconstructors attempt to cultivate (however optimistically). T aking cognisance of these departures from the values of the rule of law and ar guing that the goals pursued cannot be achieved in the radically imperfect conditions of transition, it ar gues for a more modest utilitarianism less concerned with achieving a positive moral good than it is with avoiding even temporary degradation of the criminal justice system, and looks at how the prevailing utilitarian goals of social reconciliation, social pedagogy/expressiv-ism and deterrence can be conceived in this way . It concludes by advocating a 'fair enough' standard of trial as one both justice sector reformers and transitional justice practitioners can work towards.

4.2 The rise of utilitarianism

Transitional justice, like most forms of liberal policy-making, rests on both principled and causal beliefs. The former are those which constitute 'normative ideas that specify criteria for distinguishing right from wrong and just from unjust', while the latter are those beliefs concerning 'cause-effect relationships which derive authority from the shared consensus of recognized elites'.[6] This distinction is one that legal theorists are readily familiar with in justifying punishment in trial. Most theories of criminal punishment can loosely be characterized as either retributive or utilitarian, backward-looking or forward-looking.[7] Retributive justice theory considers that punishment, if proportionate, is a morally acceptable response to crime. While other goals of prosecution like deterrence, rehabilitation or incapacitation have obvious forward-looking social benefts, retribution is a backwards-looking, duty-based approach infuenced by Kantian philosophy that punishes wrongful acts for no greater reason than the fact that they deserve punishment, with punishment as an end in itself as opposed to a means to some wider societal purpose.[8] In transition, it is always assumed that justice must be pursued. The argument is usually posed as a counterfactual – what if there is no justice? Where the crimes concerned are as reprehensible as crimes against humanity, they must be prosecuted. Though no punishment can be equal to the crime itself, only the sentencing power of prosecution can guarantee a penalty of suffcient severity. Serious crime is perpetrated against society as a whole and so that society must ascertain the perpetrators' guilt and assign a proportionate punishment. The non-utilitarian case for retribution rests on the moral necessity of punishment for transgression, regardless of any deterrent or pedagogical effect.

As time has gone on, however, retributive theories of transitional justice have given way to more utilitarian rationales, where the moral value of an act is based on its socially useful consequences.[9] For example, while the jurisprudence of the Nuremberg and Tokyo trials betrayed a palpable retributive impulse, the ad hoc tribunals and ICC are consciously designed and implemented in instrumental ways as forms of peace-building.[10] One can argue that international criminal justice is inherently utilitarian – the Security Council would have no Chapter VII authority to unilaterally set up the ad hoc tribunals but for the presence of the larger geopolitical need of restoring collective peace and security.[11]

The reasons for this shift from a retributive application to the individual perpetrator(s) towards an approach more corrective to the wider society are easily ascertained. The inescapably collective nature of the crimes to which trial would respond is probably the primary reason for the switch. The exclusive focus of retributivism on victims and perpetrators could not incorporate the full spectrum of relevant transitional actors, not only wrongdoers and their casualties, but also other agents with varying degrees of culpability for the crimes of the past such as neutrals, resisters and benef ciaries from wrongdoing. As the need for social reconstruction became more apparent with a commensurate focus on peace-building, there was an increased emphasis on the collective and structural:

> Generally, the more deeply rooted the causes of atrocities, the more pressures accountability processes will face to be not only the arbiter of justice in specif c cases, but also to become an agent for achieving more systemic social change.[12]

Transitional justice moved away from a primary concern with assigning moral meaning to past violence and instead would attempt to reduce it by becoming an active instrument of social reconstruction. Indeed, it was this addition of causal beliefs about facilitating transition that made the f eld of transitional justice distinct from human rights generally with its more retributive emphasis.[13] A second reason is a palpable discomfort with retributive rationales – Tallgren argues that even the most utopian of beliefs in utilitarian goals retain an unjustif ed currency because the alternative basis in retribution comes close to being mere satisfaction of instincts of revenge.[14] Others posit that the retributivist discourse of 'just deserts' is too imbued with Judaeo-Christian notions of moral order and divine punishment. [15] Indeed, nowadays retribution is routinely euphemized as 'combating impunity'. The fact that the demand for retribution is highly variable accord-ing to the nature of the crimes, passage of time, spread of responsibility and relationships of victims and perpetrators, may make it an uncomfortable basis for policy.[16] Many of those who embrace utilitarianism do so on the basis of a conscious and explicit break from retributivism. [17] A third explanation might be that because no punishment can adequately respond to mass atrocities like genocide, torture or persecution, bigger consequentialist claims needed to be made about transitional justice to justify it. Finally , retributive justif cations may have been eclipsed for the simple reason that no political philosophy like Kantian deontology can or should separate questions of justice from political conceptions of the common good in a particular community, which utilitarian perspectives ar guably are better placed to consider.[18] Utilitarian theories are consistently applied to transitional justice mechanisms because they can lend support to normative claims associated with policy choices.[19] The *Rule of Law and Transitional Justice Report* explicitly accepts the potential for criminal trial to de-legitimize extremists, restore civility and deter, in addition to the more pedestrian provision of direct accountability.[20]

4.3 Reconceiving retributivism

One of the main reasons for the discomfort with retributivist approaches to transitional justice is the frequent equation of criminal punishment with vindictiveness.[21] The prime example is Desmond T utu's argument against retribution, which identif es trial-based punishment with vengeance and prefers instead the reconciliationist South African TRC model.[22] The increasing currency of this belief has frustrated the integration of transitional criminal accountability and rule of law reconstruction. The OHCHR's Rule of Law Tools project rejects this equation with unusual opprobrium for its 'suggest[ion] that the pursuit of justice is a matter of vengeance and somehow a morally dubious pursuit. This concept ... distorts the very essence of criminal justice, which is to avoid lawless vengeance and maintain the rule of law.'[23] Certainly, the vengeful attitude of 'catch the bastards and hang them' among both victims and policy-makers is among the most prevalent responses to past atrocities.[24] It is also among the most understandable – revenge is a legitimate moral desire to keep faith with the dead, a ritual form of respect in honour of their memory.[25] However, retribution differs signif cantly from vengeance and can be justif ed without reference to it on the basis that the conduct objectively merits punishment on a 'just deserts' basis. Crocker outlines a number of ways in which they can be distinguished from one another but two in particular stand out. Firstly, retribution is constrained by an upper limit of severity of punishment while revenge has no such fetters, and secondly the agent of retribution need have no special or personal tie to the victim of the wrong while revenge is motivated by personal animus.[26] Minow puts it best in her familiar distinction between the two, arguing that '[r]etribution can be understood as vengeance curbed by outside intervention and the principles of proportionality and individual rights'.[27]

Other, less sensationalist, objections to a retributive approach can be grouped in three. The f rst is the common argument that retributive justice may still shade into vengeance, even if it does not equate to it. History is replete with examples of even the most rule of law-based legal systems stringently attempting to approximate a talionic response to past atrocity , from Lloyd Geor ge's electoral pledge to 'Hang the Kaiser', Churchill' s willingness to summarily execute the Nazi leadership at the Quebec Conference, the renewed appeals for the death penalty at the Rome Conference for the ICC and Guantanamo Bay. States where the rule of law is less established have had greater diff culty in drawing the line between legitimate retribution and untrammelled vengeance even where trial is preferred to summary execution or vigilantism. Ethiopia and Rwanda have been the most uncompromising in their intent to try as many perpetrators as possible. Here the rights of the accused have been systematically curtailed, most notably by prolonged detention and lack of defence, as a result of the fact that the small number of criminal justice actors is inversely proportional to the enormous will to punish.[28] The Kosovar Albanian trials of Serbs were so biased that they necessitated mass international intervention.[29]

The second objection is the utilitarian ar gument that retributivism' s inherently retrospective focus contributes nothing to the reconstruction of society by implicitly rejecting any appeal to consequences and even contemplating adverse ones ('Let there be justice, though the world perish').

Indeed, the retributivist prides herself on the trial' s lack of utility, positing
Kant's hypothetical dissolving island society where one unpunished murderer
yet remains – though the dissolution of society removes all instrumental
motive to punish, if the facts suggests the murder deserves punishment then
he should be penalized.[30] The rejection of other motives inherent in retributivism has frustrated theorists and activists in the f eld who wish to exploit
the perceived latent potential of high-prof le criminal processes to catalyse
positive socio-political change. For example, Malamud-Goti in rejecting
retributivism instead argued that reformation of institutions responsible for
past crimes and restoration of victim dignity should inform prosecution
policy.[31] The third objection is the restorative justice-based argument that an
approach which focuses on the needs of the victims and the offenders, as well
as the involved community, instead of satisfying abstract legal principles or
punishing the offender, would be better. This latter objection is explored in
Chapter 6.

These generalized objections to retributivism have tended to undermine
trial as a policy option either because it pursues its mandate too vigorously
(the argument from history) or because its mandate does not go far enough
towards ameliorating the conditions precedent to its formation (the utilitar -
ian critiques). Both critiques are ultimately more concerned about the
product of trial than the process, making it easier to de-legitimize the
concept of trial by inveighing against 'the absolutism of retributive justice'.[32]
When application of the criminal law is portrayed simply as retributivist,
trial can be discredited by playing upon fears of bias, victor' s justice and
destabilization as natural by-products of court-based processes. This misplaced
equation of trial with retributivism [33] has served to obscure the value of
positivist justif cations for trial that respond as much to institutional and
cultural concerns as to past violations of human rights norms. Advocates of
transitional trial rarely justify trial purely on the basis that the pre-existing
law derived from established criminal and constitutional principles demands
it, because more intuitively appealing moral and consequentialist justif cations are available that better f nesse the limitations of the perpetrator/victim
dichotomy at the root of trial. This is understandable given the preoccupation
of transitional justice scholars with morality and wider social reconstruction.

However, a positivist justif cation of trial divorced from all considerations
bar the demands of the law remains the least assailable rationale for prosecutorial initiatives. Such an approach justif es trial not only in backward-
looking moral terms like retributivism does, but also as a reassertion by the
state of the executive's duty to enforce the law and the courts' constitutional
role adjudicating it, as much an aff rmation of the everyday responsibilities of
the state as a critical, corrective response to what went before. A salient
example is President Fox of Mexico' s declarations that appointment of a
special prosecutor to investigate federal crimes committed by public servants
against members of social and political movements in its transition from near
hegemonic Institutional Revolutionary Party rule was designed to restore the

legitimacy of state institutions and conf dence in the rule of law.[34] Similarly, when in 2007 Serbia's War Crimes Court issued its f rst convictions of four Serbs for the Srebrenica massacres, Judge Bozilovic-Petrovic ar gued that it conf rmed beyond doubt that the national judiciary were heading in the right direction.[35] Such an approach justif es punishment at least in part on the basis of its future consequences and clearly departs from full-blooded retributivism which rarely appeals to any considerations of social usefulness. This approach of positivism simpliciter as a mid-point between retributivism and utilitarianism appeals more to the ongoing, continuing relevance of norms than their past abrogation. However, it f ts awkwardly with utilitarianism, which rests more on the wider consequences of trial than the mere fact that enforcing the law is a good thing.

Three inter-related benef ts to the reconstruction of the rule of law that fow from the very process of trial as an end in itself can be sketched. They are

(a) restoring the authority of the law
(b) reviving public confidence in the law
(c) establishing equality before the law.

4.3.1 *Restoring the authority of the law*

In authoritarianism or war, the collective experience of criminality is shaped by one or both of two phenomena. The f rst is selective application of the law, manifested in both laxity of enforcement and the use of secret or emer gency laws to justify violations of individuals and collectivities, while the second is the use of force or relationships based on force in place of the institutions of the law. In the early days of transitional justice it was ar gued that retrospective justice is one of the most important tests of the viability of the new democracy[36] and that it highlights the nature of the new regime, [37] but this is to overstate the case – as observers of the Iraqi, Sudanese or Egyptian trials of past abuses can testify , pursuit of accountability alone is a poor guide to the democratic or human rights bona f des of the new regime. What trials do, however, is demonstrate that the gap between the law as written and the law as enforced, so wide in war or repressive rule, is being reduced in good faith.

> Another justif cation for criminal prosecutions of perpetrators of mass atrocities is that trials serve as powerful symbols of the new governments' intent to 'break with the past' ... Through the judicial process, a new regime is understood to re-establish the orderly function of the civil state ... Trials also represent a substantive claim about the legal character of a new regime.[38]

The harder the cases that are taken, the more numerous they are or the higher the competence and fairness with which they are conducted, the more they aff rm the credibility and independence of the justice system. Lutz and

Sikkink's argument that no Latin American country wishes to foster the perception that its courts lack the competence, capacity and independence to effectively try its own nationals is also true of other states [39] – witness for example the vigour of diverse new rulerships in the likes of Cambodia, Rwanda, Libya etc. in maintaining control of their trial processes. While Chile at the turn of the century was in a stronger position than most societies engaged in justice sector reconstruction, the people's sentiments are of general application in this regard:

> The consensus [that Pinochet's trial should take place in Chile] was founded on both ideological and practical concerns. Although temporarily weakened during dictatorship, Chileans have a long history of pride in their judicial system, which has a reputation for impartiality, fairness and effective administration of justice. They also have a high level of national pride and confidence in their capacity to solve domestic problems without external interference.[40]

The enforcement of criminal justice is one of the special prerogatives of sovereignty in the reconstructing state and serves as a *marque* of where true sovereignty resides.[41] For this reason, most states maintain restrictions on outside involvement in the provision of legal services domestically.[42] The intuition that domestic trials resound more in a domestic setting is sound.[43] However, debates on transitional justice and its internationalization tend to overlook issues of democratic deficit[44] and the need to foster national judicial self-reliance. These issues are examined in Chapter 5.

4.3.2 *Reviving public confidence in the law*

In Chapter 2, the centrality of public confidence to the rule of law was discussed. State criminality on a wide scale or failure by the state to punish private armies and groups operating nationwide corrodes public trust in the law. The social conviction that transgressions bring sanctions becomes greatly weakened – 'learned disloyalty' to the state's legal institutional framework frequently results.[45] While formal, trial-based approaches to transitional justice have been criticized for the state's assumption of the individual's experience, both the victim and the wider public may welcome the state's renewed or nascent commitment to upholding the law that should on paper protect them. It has been assumed since the earliest days of transitional justice that trial can redress the demoralization of systematic injustice by diluting any suspicion of continuity with past impunity or incapacity and by restoring confidence in the mechanisms of justice.[46] Trial may even go further – in contending that prosecution can chip away at public pessimism about the possibility of meaningful accountability, Stromseth argues that increased public confidence in the courts will lead to increased public demand for functioning institutions of justice, pointing out the precedent of Sierra Leone.[47]

4.3.3 Establishing equality before the law

It is something of a commonplace in transitional justice that undoing past impunity implies a signif cant change in adjudicatory rules and practice – by taking high-prof le cases when once the courts supported impunity , a compromised judiciary can transform itself into something more credible. [48] Though inevitably *ex post facto*, the fact that a transitional trial does not exempt those who wield power or who previously wielded power or those who can destabilize the current exercise of power can substantiate the gener- ality of law and the equality of all (or at least a highly symbolic 'some') before the law, demonstrating that might is no longer right. Though in light of the scale of criminality , trial must be extremely selective and therefore may generate valid criticisms of arbitrariness or unrepresentativeness, as long as transparent and even-handed criteria are applied to the selection of indictees, trials may establish or further equality under the law.[49]

However, these more process-based justif cations for trial have been superseded by more ambitious claims about what trials can do and the ends to which they should be directed. Though a utilitarian approach to criminal justice is not necessarily incompatible with an emphasis on exemplarily fair and competent trial, the temptation to compromise standards of due process and justify them by the exigencies of transition is one that historically has proven hard to resist.

4.4 Transitional trial: the defendant as a means to an end?

In utilitarian philosophy, the moral value of an act is based upon the social advantage of its consequences – the proper course of action is the one that maximizes the overall 'good' of the society . Utilitarian approaches assume that law, by its nature, should concern itself primarily with effect, and not merely with moral culpability.[50] In transition, the desirability of an effect beyond mere punishment increases given society's parlous state and the depth of its pathologies, while questions of moral culpability become clouded due to the collective nature of crime. As noted in the previous chapter , debates about transitional justice are usually framed by the normative proposition that various legal responses should be evaluated on their prospects for mediating the immediate transition to democracy.[51] Sieff and Vinjamuri, for example, argue that war crime trials need clear policy goals beyond mere accountability and should centre on their prospective contribution to peace, democracy and the rule of law .[52] Four main utilitarian justif cations for punishment are typically advanced in the transitional justice literature, though the boundaries between them are somewhat indeterminate deterrence, social pedagogy/expressivism, reconciliation, and containment/incapacita- tion.[53] These justif cations are applied in an inconsistent, haphazard and overlapping manner. The clearest example of the uncertainty is in the generally sophisticated jurisprudence of the international criminal tribunals where the philosophical justifcations for sentencing have never been rationalized, presenting a muddled picture of putative transitional penology .[54] In *Todorovic* and *Nikolic*, the ICTY affrmed retributivism as the most relevant paradigm, though conceded utilitarian purposes could also justify punishment generally.[55] Other judgments emphasize more consequentialist goals. For example, in *Furundzija* the ICTY Trial Chamber asserted that punishment was a dependable vehicle for the achievement of stigmatization and deterrence.[56] Indeed, in *Delalic* deterrence has emerged as 'probably the most important factor in the assessment of appropriate sentences'.[57] Though it has been argued that rehabilitation and reconciliation are marginal concerns in international sentencing,[58] one can point to the ICTR and ICTY Trial Chambers in *Ruggiu* and *Erdemovic* respectively referring to the aims of truth and reconciliation as their key purposes.[59]

The preference for deterrence over impunity, truth over obscurity or reconciliation over embitterment are unobjectionable, but that what contributes to peace and democracy may not contribute to developing the institutions, culture and norms of the rule of law. A recurrent problem arises when pursuit of utilitarian goals involves a modifcation of the trial which runs contrary to the principles and practices rule of law reformers would wish to inculcate. If on the utilitarian or consequentialist view a trial process (and by extension a trial verdict) is justifed by its promotion of the greater good, this moral duty may exist independent of individual rights that might impede the effcient realization of that good. The danger is greatest in transitional justice because its concern with collective victimhood and culpability increases the risk that the interests of the individual defendant will be marginalized.[60] When transitional justice is understood instrumentally , the imperative of the fair trial may diminish as more immediately appealing transitional goals take precedence.

> Trials conducted before impartial courts that scrupulously observe due process requirements may showcase the benefts of the rule of law ... Yet when those same due process protections free those who are perceived to be guilty, fair trials may well inspire contempt for the rule of law .[61]

A case in point is Robert Jackson's fnal report to President Truman where he argued that the Nuremberg trials should not be measured in terms of the personal fate of the defendants, but rather to 'support the peaceful and humanitarian principles that the UN was to promote'. [62] Transitional justice may contradict liberal societies' usual rejection of utilitarian calculations in ordinary justice when they confict with fundamental rights.[63]

Though there is an appreciable diversity among legal systems (for example, non-Western societies may not insist on individual culpability for crimes, prohibit trial *in absentia*, make judicial proceedings open etc.), there is nevertheless a degree of consensus visible in national constitutions as well as

international and regional human rights instruments on the basic set of fair
trial rights such as the right to an impartial tribunal, the right to present
evidence in one's defence, the right to counsel etc. [64] As noted in Chapter 2,
Article 14 ICCPR establishing the right to fair trial as a human right outlines
a general framework of basic best practice and has been incorporated in the
statutes of the ad hoc tribunals and ICC to varying degrees. [65] Nevertheless,
the idea of insisting on, and rigidly adhering to, fundamental trial rights is
problematic in the context of transitional justice when applied domestically.
Perhaps more than any other type of civil or political right, the rights of fair
trial and due process presuppose the apparatus and interests of a democra-
tized, centralized, bureaucratized, liberal polity. The necessity of excluding
illegally-obtained evidence or hiring qualifed translators or cross-examination
may seem of limited utility, feasibility or relevance in states with underdeveloped legal systems, especially when the crude transitional political calculus
predicts benef ts accruing from conviction. Procedural protection presupposes
functioning procedures – the average Bosnian, Ethiopian or Ugandan who
might welcome criminal accountability may well wonder why such elaborate
protections which were rarely applied in the past should apply to defendants
whose guilt will rarely be in question. In transitional criminal accountability
painstaking processes of fairness may in such circumstances seem like
imposed, artif cial and even counter -productive Western affectations
developed in non-transitional societies materially better able to indulge such
norms. This intuition is both understandable and natural given the glaring
proportional inadequacy of law as a response to mass political criminality.

However, transitional trial does not happen in a vacuum. Initiating a
process of transitional criminal accountability in the type of paradigmatic
trial described in Chapter 1 presupposes an existing, bur geoning or at least
minimal commitment to trial processes and at least a minimal level of
centralized, bureaucratized, democratic liberalism. The discrepancy between
the norms central to W estern legalism and the traditions of the national
formal criminal justice system is one that peace-builders and national reform
constituencies generally wish to address. That due process norms may have
seemed irrelevant in the past diminishes in relevance as an objection to the
necessity of fair trial once a decision has been made at state level to rebuild
the institutions of justice – only with these procedural protections can the
re-emerging criminal justice system be considered rule of law-based because
without them the system would appear arbitrary and capricious. [66] Past
unfamiliarity makes the example of procedural protections more, not less,
imperative. Transitional trial cannot be hermetically sealed from this wider ,
contemporaneous process of reviving or founding the institutional, normative
and cultural aspects of administering criminal justice. Theory and practice in
transitional trial, though generally supportive of the idea of fair trial rights,
rarely consider the possible impact of transitional trial on the future conduct
of ordinary criminal justice. This may be explained by the fact that though
most transitional trials are domestic, most coverage and practice occurs in the

f eld of internationalized justice, where domestic impact is of secondary or tertiary importance, to the extent it is considered at all.

4.4.1 Transitional justice: setting the standard of fairness low

While there is an observable belief that trial should tend towards fairness, this represents more the desire to avoid gross or overt politicization that would call into question the symbolic messaging of the trial than the intention that trial should operate as a foundational example for the future. Transitional justice draws a distinction between political and legal trial without engaging deeply with the grey zone in between in which post-conf ict or post-authoritarian states inevitably dwell. Elster , for example, argues that in transition, pure legal justice has four characteristics.[67] First, the law applied must be as unambiguous as possible to reduce the scope for judicial discretion. Secondly , the judiciary must be independent of the inf uence of other branches of government. Thirdly , judges (and jurors, if applicable) should be unbiased in interpreting the law in a given case. Fourthly, legal justice adheres strictly to the principle of due process – adversarial and public hearings, the right to choose one's legal representation, the right to appeal, non-retroactivity , respect for statutes of limitation, individual guilt, the presumption of innocence, the right to due deliberation and the right to a speedy hearing. These principles are enshrined most notably in Article 14 ICCPR, though even before transition they may be articulated in national constitutions even if they are not yet vindicated in practice. These characteristics closely map the standards justice sector reformers wish to develop. Pure political justice, by contrast, is where the successor government 'unilaterally and without the possibility of appeal designates the wrongdoers and decides what shall be done with them'. [68] Show trials, with what Kirchheimer calls their 'mechanical certainty', are the most obvious example of pure political justice. [69] This is a sensible and, in the context of transition, very relevant distinction. Elster is quick to point out that lack of one or part of any of the characteristics of legal justice does not amount to political justice.[70] However, he goes on to point out that these requirements of legal justice are 'routinely violated' out of transitional necessity.

> As we shall see, violations may be unavoidable and on occasion even desirable, and even when they are neither , they may be understandable and perhaps forgivable. When many violations accumulate or where core criteria are violated, there comes a point, however , when legal justice is replaced by political justice.[71]

Elster correctly identif es the quotidian slippage between acknowledged or merely aspirational norms and actual practice in transitional justice. He notes elsewhere the familiar use of exceptional measures such as retroactive legislation, lack of appeal, biased selection of judges, collective guilt and de facto or de jure presumptions of guilt at various junctures. [72] What is problematic is the means by which he assesses the validity of trial. There is a tendency to assess the deviations from established national or international standards of trial not by the precedent they set for the ordinary administration of criminal justice, but by whether they cross the threshold into political trial. To the extent they do not, the routine violations he identif es are justif ed because of the way in which they respond to transitional necessity or advance political transitional goals.

Without doubt, predetermined outcomes in trial taint the credibility of the entire criminal justice system, making it imperative that this be avoided.[73] However, what this standard of assessment neglects is that the gap between the standard of trial peace-builders and domestic authorities hope to inculcate (which will strain towards something resembling pure legal justice, settling on something akin to a 'fair enough' standard, examined in Section 4.5 of this chapter) and a transitional trial that falls short of political justice is quite large and may permit and even commend many practices that f atly contradict or undermine the standards of justice peace-builders are attempting to establish. As Posner and V ermeule argue, '[o]n a spectrum with the show trial at one end and the conventional domestic criminal or civil trial on the other, trials conducted for the purpose of achieving transitional justice usually lie somewhere in between'.[74] While transitional justice practitioners are keen to avoid prosecuting past lawlessness through lawless practices, the mere avoidance of show trial is not a suff ciently exacting standard for transitional trial. The very fact of trial embodies a core liberalism, but a reconstructing justice sector requires something more by way of example than the mere renunciation of a kangaroo court. High quality trial may be an unattainable ideal, but the success of a criminal justice process should be judged to a signif cant degree by how closely it is approximated.

Though some contend that it is illogical to expect that a criminal process initiated to help bring peace to a country could operate without fair trial standards,[75] the experience of transitional justice in countless post-conf ict states that successfully mediated the passage from repression to peace has often been partly (and sometimes paradigmatically) contradictory to the standards justice sector reformers would seek to inculcate in a transitional polity, but are rarely criticized because they fall short of outright political justice. Elster is correct in suggesting that the main operational indicator of legal justice is the requirement that the outcome of trial be shrouded in uncertainty,[76] but too often this is not the case – there remains a great reluctance to relinquish control of the outcome solely to rules and lawyers, or if doing so to stack the deck in favour of conviction through inequality of arms or altering rules of evidence. In one sense, all criminal justice systems are used as a tool of social control and therefore one may see the moral merits of individual cases becoming somewhat compromised to achieve systemic aims.[77] Because of the prevalence of group-level considerations in transitional accountability that warrant special exceptions to international aronstitutional principles of legality, the interests of individual defendants are mar ginalized far more than would be tolerated in the ordinary administration of justice. [78] It has become commonplace to accept that the 'explicit politicization of criminal law in these periods challenges ideal understandings of justice' or that the transitional paradigm may require 'levelling of evidentiary standards'.[79]

4.4.2 *The difficulty of securing convictions*

Ordinarily, most criminal justice systems can meet due process requirements like credible or verif able testimony, the presumption of innocence and the right to defend oneself. However, when coupled with the well-known eviden-tiary diff culties of mass criminality, the arduousness of making the case in transitional trial often becomes almost directly proportional to the heinous-ness of the offence. Guilt cannot simply be inferred from the existence of well-known pattern of abuses and well-known civilian, military or rebel leaders. For example, crimes against humanity require not only proof of indi-vidual acts like rape or murder, but also evidence that they were committed as part of a widespread or systematic attack directed against a civilian popula-tion. Establishing a criminal defendant' s genocidal *mens rea* or kleptocratic practices by inference from the surrounding factual circumstances has proven extremely diff cult in many circumstances. As a result, it is not enough for investigators and prosecutors to explore the results of the criminality alone, but to explore an entire system in which those crimes were manifested. As with most types of or ganized crime, system crimes are diff   cult to prove because the division of labour between those who plan and those who execute the plans is organized in such a way as to make the connections between the two levels diff cult to establish.[80] While there may be a clearer paper trail for low-level offenders as well as greater physical evidence and more witness testimony, evidentiary requirements make it far more diff   cult to secure convictions of civilian leaders or those higher in the military hierarchy who ordered the crimes but have no actual blood on their hands.   [81] Variegated command structures make criminal responsibility diff   cult to identify, in particular when paramilitaries, secret groups or   *nacht und nebel* tactics are employed on the basis of nods and winks. Both sporadic and lar   ge-scale crimes may be unplanned and undocumented.

Of course one can point to the ad hoc tribunals and the SCSL as examples of tribunals which have overcome such diff   culties by using doctrines like joint criminal enterprise and command responsibility , but these are extraor -dinarily well-resourced and are not typical of the conditions faced in even the most developed transitional societies. Few national police or prosecution services will have developed the necessary competences and techniques to unearth and present persuasive evidence of the practices of military or bureau-cratic organizations, the general socio-historical context of the alleged crimes, the local context and dynamics of violence, to undertake comprehensive analysis of public and restricted documentation or to secure the protection of witnesses and victims.[82]

4.4.3 Presumptions of guilt?

The quality of enforcement and trial varies with the attributes of different criminal justice systems in different countries or different internationalized tribunals. Of course, it is possible to show international trials such as those at the ICC and domestic trials such as those in Greece which overcame such difficulties to secure convictions and acquittals in demonstrably fair ways. Nevertheless, on the occasions when defendants perceived as guilty are acquitted for lack of evidence or have their cases dismissed on procedural grounds, there has been great outcry. The everyday bureaucratic 'presumption of guilt' that Packer identifies as falling on those whose cases are proceeded with in ordinary domestic law becomes magnified in transitional accountability where the courts attempt to establish the guilt of public figures that 'everybody knows' to be culpable.   [83]   The very process of establishing a dedicated, reactive trial process is suggestive of a guilt that need only be allotted and confirmed.[84] Maintaining a presumption of innocence 'will test the judges when the defendants are those wanted for the most serious crimes against international law, whose alleged deeds and whose identities will be well-known'.[85] The paradigmatic example (and one referred to in an earlier chapter) is perhaps the ICTR's initial *Barayagwiza* decision in 1999 where the Appeals Chamber dismissed the case against a media leader indicted for inciting genocidal violence on the grounds that the indictment had not been served in time, because the Trial Chamber did not rule on a writ of *habeas corpus*, because the prosecution had not acted with due diligence and because of the delay between indictment and first appearance.[86] Indeed, in what is perhaps the best example the subversion of the autonomy of even the most independent judiciary from political pressure to punish known or reputed malefactors, the Rwandan Government threatened it would cease all cooperation with the ICTR after the initial decision. The Appeals Chamber reversed its own decision, citing new evidence,[87] but 'the impression remains that it did this to safeguard Kigali's renewed co-operation'.[88] Rwandan citizens have criticized the ICTR for its 'excessive emphasis on respect for the rights of the accused'.[89] Similarly, in the ICC's *Lubanga* case, it was held that failure by the Prosecutor to disclose exculpatory evidence 'ruptured' proceedings 'to such a degree that it ... [was] impossible to piece together the constituent elements of a fair trial', thus warranting staying the case and the accused's release.[90] It was argued that his release would provoke outrage on the part of victims and civil society.[91] The Appeals Chamber agreed to keep him in custody while the Prosecutor appealed. After the Prosecutor had agreed to make all the confidential information available to the court, the Trial Chamber lifted the stay and ordered that the trial could go ahead. Observers criticize the decision for setting a threshold where a violation of the rights of the accused can only be remedied by a permanent stay of proceedings that is so high as to make it impossible to meet.[92]

If this pressure affects one of the best resourced and most monitored courts in the world, it should come as no surprise that the same compulsion for conviction to trump procedural guarantees occurs in domestic transitional trials. Similar outrage greeted the application of due process in the suspension by the Chilean courts of proceedings against Pinochet on the grounds that he was not mentally f t to stand trial,[93] the acquittal on the char ge of murdering 200 students in South Korea of former dictator Chun Doo Hwan for lack of evidence,[94] the exculpatory decisions by the Polish courts in the mid-1990s[95] and the acquittal of Magnus Malan and Wouter Basson in South Africa in the 1990s.[96] Indeed, the fate of individuals who have been acquitted by transitional criminal tribunals on returning to their communities has been consistently grim.[97]

We are familiar with states of emergency where procedural protections are suspended in periods of radical social violence and replaced by novel institutions and standards because the standard rules appear too 'burdensome'.[98] A notable feature of international transitional trial which is no less apparent domestically is what Schabas observes as a shift in human rights law from a defence-based to a prosecution-based perspective, from a culture of acquittal to a culture of conviction.[99] The wariness of criminal law as a potential agent of repression appears to have been dispensed with in favour of 'a playing f eld that tilts in one direction'.[100] Ryngaert argues that 'while concentrating on the perpetrator, the [ad hoc] tribunals may have overemphasized the need to bring the perpetrator to justice at all costs ... As a result, they have paid insuff cient attention to the duties which they have vis-à-vis the perpetrator (as opposed to an international community intent on breaking the cycle of violence and impunity), and the corresponding human rights of the perpetrator.'[101] Perhaps the best exemplar of this is the persistent inequality of arms that attends transitional criminal justice given that a degree of parity between defence and prosecution is a core element of due process whose absence can distort the nature of trial.[102] The systematic diversion of the vast preponderance of resources to the prosecutorial functions has been apparent at internationalized level[103] (as Chapter 5 explores, the hybrid tribunals for East Timor, Sierra Leone and Kosovo had signif cant shortcomings in this regard), while domestically priority is given to police and prosecutors over legal aid to defendants when addressing serious crimes.[104] Equality of arms means relative parity as opposed to exact parity. The ICTY has held that 'a principle of basic proportionality, rather than a strict principle of mathematical equality' generally governs issues of equality of arms.[105] Normally, the task of the prosecution in a criminal trial is more diff cult than that of the defence, given that   it must outline the entire narrative of a crime and prove every element of it beyond reasonable doubt, while the defence is concerned with 'poking specif cally targeted holes' in the prosecution case, and so the preponderance of resources should be directed to the former   .[106]

However, even in supposedly exemplary international tribunals the prosecution tends to be an or gan of the court while defence is not (ensuring less funding, lobbying power and continuity), enjoys greater immunities and privileges and has higher staff ng,[107] in contrast to 'emaciated' defence teams that struggle with lack of time and facilities for defence. [108]

Even the Inter -American Court of Human Rights has so changed the balance between defence and accusation in cases of state political violence (for example in *Bulacio* requiring the Argentine domestic court to limit a defendant's constitutional right to be tried within a reasonable time) that it is now suggested that as a result of its burgeoning duty to punish doctrine a 'criminal law of the enemy' might emerge there.[109] While the Iraqi Special Tribunal was established to restore the rule of law in Iraq with the help of third-party states ostensibly committed to its principles, in the rush to punish issues of due process, provision of adequate defence and transparency persisted,   [110] while procedural guarantees for defendants were lowered over time.[111] Others have referred to an 'impartiality def   cit' where demands for justice and fairness attach more to victims than alleged perpetrators, impairing the status, respect and resources of the defence function. [112]

While it is arguable that the best justice is slow, expensive and uncertain, torpidity, cost and the chance of acquittal are inimical to, or politically unthinkable in, certain transitions. If, as both retributivist and utilitarians argue, transitional accountability is best employed in the earliest period of transition, it would appear natural to prefer the 'diminished legalism' in the year-long trial of 22 suspects at Nuremberg over painstaking legal exactitude seen in the decade it took the ICTR to reach that f   gure.[113] Similarly, it is clear to see how properly-defended, long trials could jeopardize peace in the short-term as the population grows frustrated with delays. Elster notes that revenge killings in transition are often the result of 'frustration at the slowness of off cial justice'.[114] Sentencing perceived as lenient, even if justif ed by precedent and the gravity of crimes, can enf ame public opinion and provoke violent reaction.[115] Furthermore, the technical and tedious nature of trial may appear to trivialize the atrocities being prosecuted,   [116] while the laws of evidence and the procedural rights of trial severely curtail the trial's potential as a site of historical production. If trials are defended competently and the defendant is given the opportunity to assert his account of events, falsehoods can be uttered publicly and the truth of events challenged. Victim testimony can be dismissed as hearsay , and evidence which would clarify the wider context of the crime can be challenged as irrelevant. The adversarial nature of a vigorously contested trial can undermine potential for reconciliation.   [117] Trials that uphold due process may limit the pedagogical potential of such trials in relation to the conf ict and repression that society is emerging from. A properly contested trial, which in itself would have immense educational effect in a less dramatic manner, might force the prosecution to seek a conviction for the individual rather than to use it as a means of expressing popular consensus on past violence. [118] Where a historically signif cant transgression is def ned in the public imagination as an individual crime by an individual person, the opportunity for kick-starting a public discussion about the legitimacy of political violence or discrimination is weakened. Osiel notes that the dramatic imperatives of legal storytelling may interfere with the due process rights of defendants.[119]

4.4.4 *Tilting the balance against the defendant:*
a historical perspective

Non-democratic successor regimes are better equipped psychologically and philosophically to administer more comprehensive accountability policies due to limited or non-existent concern for due process.   [120] Space precludes examination of anything more than a few pertinent examples. Perhaps the most extreme example of the compromises of domestic trial in such countries is Rwanda, where the Kagame government' s oft-expressed frustration with the pace, cost and legalism of the ICTR was manifested in a national criminal process diametrically opposed to the comparatively scrupulous Arusha proceedings. Aside from the obvious failure to punish crimes committed by Tutsi militants, the unfairness of the trial process is illustrated by lack of legal representation for defendants, ethnically-skewed judiciaries, lengthy detentions of many years without judicial review , threats against defence witnesses, effective presumptions of guilt and re-arrests after release.   [121] Similar conditions applied in the less documented examples of Burundi and Ethiopia.[122] All three are open to the criticism of attempting to prosecute too many given the inf rm nature of the national judiciaries and prosecution services (for example, at the start of the trials Rwanda had only 16 defence lawyers for over 100,000 potential defendants).[123] Persistent and lengthy trial delays are the most obvious consequence of such limitations, though the record of the ad hoc tribunals and ICC suggest that this is a universal feature of transitional accountability in even the best-resourced trial processes.

It might be ar gued that because these transitions to a modif ed authoritarianism are not the type this book is concerned with, they are not germane to the overall argument. However, they are relevant insofar as they highlight a tendency to gear trial towards conviction in a manner that would not be tolerated under normal conditions, a trend which also extends to stronger rule of law traditions. The western European democracies that emerged from World War II had long histories of rule of law institutions and norms which proved to have surprisingly little restraining effect in the years following 1945. The Netherlands, Italy and Norway saw extrajudicial executions, purges, summary trials, curtailment of the right to defence, revival of the death penalty and mass jailing, where 'severity and speed were prized over adherence to the rule of law'.[124] Though there were some acquittals, postwar French trials displayed judicial and juror bias, most notably the Laval trial.[125] Belgium's historic commitment to legality did not serve to restrain partisan trial and unchecked vengeance.[126] Denmark abandoned the principle of *nulla poena sine lege* and restored the death penalty in response to popular demand.[27] In all states, presumptions of guilt, lack of appeal, retroactivity and shortening statutes of limitation were commonplace.[128] One can of course argue that these decisions could not be reached in the modern era of global and regional human rights instruments and that modern transitions to democracy occur in a radically different normative environment, but there are recent examples of democratic transitions in post-conf ict ecologies where the judiciary has had neither the will nor the autonomy to resist grossly punitive transitional trial processes, most notably Kosovo and Bosnia. In both territories, prosecutions were viewed as a means of continuing conf   ict through ethnically-biased prosecutions. As noted above, the impetus for what became known as the internationalized Regulation 64 Panels came from the bias evident in the initial trials of Serb suspects by the Kosovar Albanian judiciary.[129] Similarly, in Bosnia, fears over the loss of skilled judges since the war   , bias, unfair arrests, and ethnic prosecutions motivated the internationalization of domestic processes of accountability.[130] The Inter-American Court of Human Rights' possible 'criminal law of the enemy' was noted above, which is not without analogue in international criminal justice. A Trial Chamber judge in *Tadic* stated that human rights rulings of the European Court of Human Rights were meant to apply in 'ordinary' criminal jurisdiction, whereas the ICTY was 'in certain respects, comparable to a military tribunal, which often has limited rights of due process and more lenient rules of evidence'. [131] As Schabas notes, this statement is thankfully rather isolated, but it belies a general concern for the possibility of acquittal in trial. [132] The exceptionalist legal regimes insisted upon by the Bush and Obama administrations in the exercise of the war on terror can be seen as a modern example of the undermining of fair trial rights in the face of political violence.

As Osiel notes, 'in the few instances where conviction has been obtained for large-scale, state-sponsored massacres, it has been secured only at the apparent price of departure from settled law and principles'.[133] In the history of transitional criminal justice, it is ar guable that only the ad hoc tribunals and ICC have consistently met the challenge of full legal justice in a post-conf ict context, and even these trials are dogged by selectivity and delays. The ad hoc tribunals are to be commended for their stringent Rule 11 *bis* requirement on both courts to ensure an accused will receive a fair trial (and no death penalty) if he is to be transferred to the national jurisdiction.   [134] Given that these tribunals enjoy primacy and are UN bodies, nothing less than this standard could be expected lest the UN be brought into disrepute. Though international criminal tribunals dominate the discussion on transitional criminal justice, the ICC's complementarity regime in Article 17 assumes that most trials of human rights abuses will occur domestically (of course, this was already the case before 1998). The complementarity regime, by contrast to the ad hoc tribunals, is far more tolerant of unfair or biased domestic proceedings lacking in due process as long as they meet the transitional imperative of prosecuting and convicting. Though scholars point to Article 17's reference to 'due process' as a guide to interpreting the meaning of unwillingness and inability (i.e. contending that a state that cannot provide a fair trial is either unable or unwilling under the terms of the admissibility requirements) and Article 21(3)'s mandate to the Court to interpret and apply the law consistently with international human rights, [135] a number of scholars accept Heller's rejection of this 'due process' thesis on the basis that the plain wording of Article 17 and the surrounding punitive context of the admissibility regime only make domestic proceedings qualify as unwilling or unable if they make a defendant *more* difficult to convict. [136] Any shortcomings must lead the Court to believe proceedings are being conducted in a manner not consistent with securing accountability, while defects in the quality of justice are irrelevant provided the attempt to secure accountability is genuine. [137] As Jurdi points out, the complementarity rules are designed to limit the Court's freedom to determine a state's willingness or inability, not to extend it. [138] Procedural fairness as a ground for defining complementarity was explicitly rejected at the Rome Conference [139] and the Kampala proceedings evinced no desire to make the unfairness of domestic victor's justice a cause for removing jurisdiction to The Hague. The Office of the Prosecutor's 2003 Informal Expert Paper has rejected lack of international trial standards domestically as a ground for finding inability or unwillingness. [140] In its considerations of admissibility thus far, the Court has treated fairness as a relative, as opposed to absolute, standard. [141] As Heller points out, this toleration for unfair proceedings in the interests of conviction undermines any standard-setting function the Court might wish to set for domestic post-conflict criminal proceedings, a problem examined in greater detail in Chapter 5. [142]

4.5 A revised utilitarianism

The persistent history of politicization and deviation from due process in criminal trials reflects a widely, but not unanimously, held belief that questionable judicial means may be justified by noble ends or the exigencies of transition as part of a special transitional rule of law. However, given the widespread disenchantment with the legacy of transitional justice generally (noted in the previous chapter) and transitional trial particularly, it is worth considering whether the purported trial goals of deterrence, social pedagogy, reconciliation and so forth are in any way realizable given that the steady-state theories they are extrapolated from are themselves criticized for the shallow psychological and sociological models of rational choices with gains and losses they employ. Transitional justice scholars increasingly acknowledge the reality accepted by contemporary philosophers and penal reformers that the criminological rationales for punishment practised in both consolidated democracies and transitional societies today are deeply unsatisfactory. [143] This point is worth remembering given the persistent difficulties outlined in Chapters 1 and 3 in drawing causal relationships between transitional justice, its various overarching aspirations (peace, democracy , human rights, rule of law) and the micro-goals which contribute to them (retribution, deterrence, reconciliation, social pedagogy).

The problem with the plethora of utilitarian justif cations for transitional accountability is their tendency to expropriate stable-state municipal criminological theories without regard to the def ning natural variation and individuality of transitional societies. The lack of a transitional or international criminal penology has created a need to 'hungrily – yet arbitrarily' shoehorn domestic punishment rationales into policy justif cation.[144] Utilitarian and retributive theories as well as other invariably W estern-derived theses of criminology and sociology of crime were developed in functioning industrialized democracies and never applied to crimes of state or war in transitioning societies. [145] Nevertheless, in relation to international criminal law 'it is generally seems to be taken for granted that whatever justif cations work – or are supposed to work – on the national level should also, without any extra effort, cover the decisions and actions taken by states in concert'.[146] Given the idealism that characterizes so much of transitional justice literature, it comes as no surprise that transitional justice's utilitarians are apt to 'gloss over the complexities of conf icts by creating an idyllic meta-political sphere within which justice is done'.[147] Sloan suggests three reasons why the mechanical transfer of municipal punishment theory to international criminal law is ill-advised, and the rationale may be extended to transitional justice more broadly.[148] First, both international criminal law and transitional justice serve multiple communities, both literal (the victimized individuals or group) and f gurative (the international community or transitional society), whereas the communal interests are less diverse in national criminal law Secondly, the national law analogy obscures the collective scale and nature of state criminality – the collective victimhood may both aggravate the perpetrator's culpability (murder simpliciter being less offensive than genocide or unlawful killing as a crime against humanity) and mitigate it (collective perpetration may diffuse moral responsibility). Thirdly , building on the mitigation point, is the reality that the normative universe in which state crime and war crime occurs differs dramatically from the settled, peaceful society where intuitions about state control are most applicable. Simply put, in stable societies criminal acts are exceptional and normatively recognized as such, while in the state of war or authoritarianism, abuse is both normal and/or state-sanctioned. [149] If, as some suggest, the potential of transitional trial to deliver hypothesized goals from truthful history to rehabilitation has been oversold or encourages unrealizable public expectations, the misplaced domestic law analogy might be the root cause. [150]

Even if transitional punishment could realize the ambitions theorists set for it and justify in political and moral terms the departures from legality they may require, other methods may achieve the same results without impugning the integrity of the criminal justice system. In terms of retribution, the fact of transition itself and the rejection of prior rule it implies may be a more satisfactory collective recompense than even the most comprehensive series of trials. Many policy-makers and theorists in the f eld would concede that vetting may be better than trial in terms of containing (or ostracizing) offenders from the prior regime in public life or communicating a political message about the intolerability of certain human rights abuses and public policy standards.[151] It has long been ar gued that truth commissions are preferable to trials in terms of generating a public record and social pedagogy. It is diff cult to imagine how trials can do more to establish the legitimacy of a successor regime than the elections that gave rise to it. Similarly, while trials may serve to maintain difference between groups rather than reconcile them, a well-tailored amnesty may do more to appease and conciliate diametrically opposed groups to each other than the inevitably adversarial prosecutorial process.[152]

If, as Tallgren suggests, 'everybody knows' that utilitarian theories like deterrence do not work [153] or if the cases for retributive and utilitarian approaches to transitional trial are exaggerated, duplicative or obsolete in light of other ongoing process and risk signif cant departure from the rule of law, it is worth considering whether policymakers would be better off (a) trusting those other methods to achieve retributive and utilitarian goals, and (b) modifying retributive and utilitarian goals to something less ambitious but more conducive to rule of law reconstruction. Along these lines de Greiff argues that because the implementation of transitional justice mechanisms will inevitably fall short of expectations, it is semantically diff cult to give such initiatives the meaning of *justice* which he (in a rare rule of law-centred def nition of the concept) understands as promoting the possibility of a more direct relationship between effort to enforce compliance with the law and success in achieving that conformity.[154] Something more than a mere modif cation of existing justif cations for punishment is required.

A useful starting point might be to turn on its head the vaguely but conf dently articulated presumption in the literature that deterrence, reconciliation, retribution etc. help develop the rule of law and realize the causal relationship may turn in the opposite direction. In place of the quixotic pursuit of deterrence, healing or truth, policy-makers at the state and international level may reap the greatest dividend by conceiving of the various retributive or utilitarian goals of transitional justice in rule of law terms. Instead of conceiving of trial punishment as retribution which can easily pursue unpalatable directions, it may be better to reiterate the positivist justif cation of prosecution and conviction by reference to existing law . Perhaps the political expressivist/pedagogical role of transitional trial is best directed not at changing mindsets with regard to oneself and the other (after all, there are a plethora of institutions and events which can do this better in qualitative and quantitative terms), but rather at changing mindsets in relation to the institutions of state, most relevantly the courts. As Orentlicher argues, 'the expressive function of prosecutions will surely be undermined in the absence of public measures that institutionalize a government' s commitment to fundamental rights'.[155] On the same lines, reconciliation may be better served by the demonstration that judicial institutions will scrupulously treat formerly competing groups equally than by pursuing interper - sonal restoration and rehabilitation of perpetrators and victims through trial. If, as Koh suggests, 'the most effective form of law enforcement is not the imposition of external sanction, but the inculcation of internal obedience',[156] perhaps the best form of deterrence is not a self-contained process of investigation, prosecution or tough sentencing in a series of trials but rather the demonstration that the state has the will and capacity to undertake fair and credible prosecutions. Ultimately, the strongest utilitarian justif cation for trials may not be containment of revanchists, establishment of the historical record or stigmatization of certain political beliefs and strategies, but rather the re-establishment of the institutions, culture and normative commitments of the rule of law.

If the analogy with domestic criminological rationales is misplaced and if the pursuit of utilitarian ends is undertaken through means which contradict the normative and cultural commitments justice sector reformers simultaneously attempt to inculcate, does utilitarianism have any utility? The obvious answer is to instead rest on a retributive rationale (punishment as just deserts) or positivism (punishment because the law says so) as goods in themselves and leave it at that. However, progress towards mutually-benef cial harmonization of transitional justice and rule of law reconstruction might benef t from revisiting the fundamental bases of utilitarian criminology . While the transitional justice literature is replete with reference to the originators of utilitarian penology Cesare Beccaria and Jeremy Bentham, [157] the literature, policy documents and jurisprudence on transitional trial have not really engaged to a signif cant degree with utilitarian theory generally . Instead, scholars in the f eld have superf cially identif ed particular utilitarian ends, neglecting the complexity of the conception of public welfare in utilitarianism which developed historically from a concern to limit the severity of punishment in a monarchical age rather than to maximize its social potential in democratization. The utilitarian presumption in transitional justice discourse that the principles of due process can or should be modif ed or even rejected if it interferes with the eff cient achievement of socially-benef cial ends is misplaced.[158]

Bentham considered punishment not as a behaviour or ethical criterion, but as an institution which should therefore be evaluated from the position of political legitimacy rather than morality.[159] Because the pleasure and pain on which utilitarianism is premised is based as much on anticipation as actual experience (i.e. the expectation of pleasure or pain), his political (as opposed to moral) conception of utilitarianism focuses not so much on reactively achieving the experience of happiness from a given situation, but rather proactively creating the conditions where the expectation of happiness is secure. Because this general security (the freedom from fear or anxiety) trumped satisfaction of even the most laudable immediate desires, Binder maintains that Bentham 'was less interested in advocating particular policies as utility-maximizing than he was in advocating a policy process that would guarantee to the public that policy would systematically serve public utility'.[160] It required a state both powerful enough to preserve the commonweal but too rule-bound to jeopardize it. The public welfare obliges punishment to be justif ed on the basis of the legitimacy of the institution promulgating, enforcing or adjudicating the norm rather than on the basis of its immediate practical outcome. As Binder contends, utilitarianism is not an evaluative principle employed by every actor making every decision as it relates to every end, but is rather a theory about how to design complex institutional processes so as to secure the procedural conditions for making, adjudicating and implementing policy in the interest of public welfare. [161]

> This revised understanding of utilitarianism ... does not by itself imply very def nite prescriptions with regard to criminal justice. But it does imply that, contrary to prevailing perceptions, utilitarian criminal justice will be highly formalistic, consistent, transparent, and procedur - ally scrupulous.[162]

The following consideration of utilitarianism in transitional trial adopts this institutional and cultural perspective. It ar gues that transitional trial can most usefully and most realistically serve the process of transition by redef n- ing the surrounding debates on deterrence or pedagogy or reconciliation around the institutions and culture of the rule of law that justice sector reformers focus on, as opposed to moral or political questions about the conduct of off cials, criminals and victims that transitional justice scholars hitherto have addressed predominantly. How the state tries perpetrators in transitional accountability will have a much greater bearing on the future prospects for the rule of law than the verdict in the trial will have on the prospects for peace and democracy.

4.5.1 Social pedagogy/expressivism

Successful transition to a generally accepted state-wide political community requires a change of mindsets within groups if the violence which character - ized the past is not to recur.[163] Notwithstanding the long history of societies in conf ict externally or subject to repression, colonialism or dictatorship internally, the supposition in transitional justice and peace-buildingliterature is that the context for mass human rights abuses or political violence is some- how not typical of that state or that people. It is common to speak of how 'an aberrant context of inverted morality' was created through indoctrination and misinformation from leaders on high [164] or how the existence of an 'extreme conceptual divergence' led those who committed abuses to believe they were acting in society's best interest.[165] To the extent that serious crime is always committed by a machinery of state or armed forces based on institutions, beliefs, allegiances and complicities, the redeemability of a manipulated, unrepresentative pre-existing public morality may amount to something of a necessary f ction. If we accept that the context of mass atrocity or repression is one where norms are inverted, it is necessary to challenge the collective mythologies of ethnicity, nationality, race, religion or politics that catalyse and permit such criminality. To the extent that the organizers of mass atrocity and persecution justify their crimes ideologically , the paradigm that has developed is one of prosecuting senior leaders in the expectation that condemnation in trial can reverse the earlier 'normalizing the unthinkable', in which ugly, degrading, murderous, and unspeakable acts were routinely accepted as 'the way things are done'. [166] It is now ar gued that given the limitations of law, politics and resources, as well as the diff culties in proving the causal connections between criminal justice and other utilitarian ends, this expressive or social pedagogical role of trial best captures its realistic potential to make a difference in transition, while its dependence on long-term normative values strains the domestic law analogy least. [167] It is when evil becomes banal in the Arendtian sense, where criminal acts are executed not only or predominantly by fanatics or sociopaths, but rather by ordinary people who accepted the dogma of their authorities and therefore participated with the view that their actions were imperative or normal, that the need to stigmatize it is greatest.[168]

Most post-conf ict states embrace new constitutions, charters and laws, but their prospective and self-contained properties only imply institutional disapproval and discontinuity. With its retrospective character and authority, punishment can go further . If, as W alker suggests, a moral community is def ned not only by *whom* but also by *what* it marks as beyond the pale, criminal punishment is probably the clearest way in which to demonstrate institutional disapproval of behaviour that runs contrary to the mores of that community.[169] As Cassel argues, 'there is no more powerful social condemna-tion of evil than to label it a serious crime, for which serious punishment might be imposed'.[170] In Durkheimian terms, punishment expresses moral condemnation and in so doing strengthens social solidarity by reinforcing the norms of social life. [171] However, Durkheimian theory is premised on the existence of a core of pre-existing, widely shared principles about liberal soci-ety on which criminal proceedings draw to reaff rm their validity and to condemn shameful actions. In times of transition this criminology does not suff ciently confront the moral complexity inherent in much of the criminal-ity.[172] Mass atrocity presupposes deep-rooted or merely manipulated mass antagonism. While Durkheim saw solidarity arising out of the shared indig-nation of the innocent many towards the guilty few , this premise is less applicable when many thousands bear some culpability for the harm.   [173] There exists little or no consensus which can infuse a single shared interpreta-tion of the pre-transitional period or a general accord on the propriety of any given transitional justice measure. After repression and particularly after war, there may be no consensus even on what the national community is. [174]

Transitional justice has become concerned with how such a consensus might be created, modifying the Durkheimian notion of trial to the exigencies of transition to posit a series of related arguments about how the criminal justice process might affect or catalyse it. In transition, this more assertive role is invariably assumed by the criminal justice process – it is used as a tool to transform and shape society in accordance with a particular view of it. In the period of f ux between one political order and another , criminal law cannot embody assumptions about the political community as it ordinarily does. The ordinarily posited ability of punishment to communicate meaning 'about power, authority, legitimacy, normality, morality, personhood, social relations, and a host of other tangential matters' matters more than ever .[175] There is, furthermore, a hope that transitional conditions are more conducive to effecting norm change via criminal justice than ordinary trial is. At the core of the expressivist justif cation for transitional trial is the usual counterfactual ar gument – just as impunity in ordinary times denies the validity of law or human rights standards that were previously proclaimed to be normatively and morally imperative, de facto or de jure immunity from punishment in transition can appear to publicly and politically legitimize their violation. In such a context, the very fact of initiating criminal proceedings is highly educative about public power. On the most basic level, trials emphasize the very fact of transition by demonstrating that the ancien régime is too weak to prevent proceedings.[176] Support for transitional criminal accountability on the part of the UN is based on the assumption that that trial can build support for state institutions by drawing the distinction between what is condoned and what is not and what the state will punish and what it will not. [177]

If criminal accountability does take place, it is expected that transitional trial should serve as 'a great occasion for social deliberation and collective examination of the moral values underlying public institutions'. [178] Though indictment alone may suff ce to discredit certain individuals, trials inevitably stimulate debate about the morality of the defendant' s actions in the most public forum available. Because criminal judgments authoritatively establish or reinforce the norms under which society operates, it is widely believed in the literature that they lend force to anyone, most notably liberalizing forces, who can persuasively invoke them in the lar ger forum of political debate. [179] As such, trial can condemn not only the individual human rights abuses that come before the courts, but also other crimes and criminals that do not for political, jurisdictional or resource reasons. T rial can also censure the social attitudes that foster crime. For example, Orentlicher ar gues that by 'laying bare the truth about violations of the past and condemning them, prosecutions can deter potential law breakers and inoculate the public against future temptation to be complicit in state-sponsored violence'. [180] The message conveyed is expected to be both subliminal and explicitly conscious; certain acts, policies, and attitudes are publicly rendered outside the realm of possible choice for both the state [181] and individuals.[182] People as well as violence can be stigmatized – indictment or prosecution can undermine infuence, inhibit political rehabilitation and even inculcate pariah status. Indeed, Bell argues that '[c]ontrol of the transitional justice mechanism can enable victory in the metaconfict – the confict about what the confict is about'.[183] At the Nuremberg trials, indictees were condemned not as individuals alone, but as 'living symbols' of the 'racial hatreds ... fierce nationalisms ... and ... the arrogance and cruelty of power' that underpinned prior rule.[184] The denial through trial of military ideologies of national security and the resulting claims that abuses were merely excesses rather than systematic, mandatory undertakings was at the core of the project of reaffrming civilian rule in Latin America.[185] The trial in South Korea of former dictators Chun Doo Hwan and Roh Tae Woo for mutiny and treason arising from their military coup was intended to cut the country off from a history ofegitimized coups and dictatorships by redefning the student protestors they killed as a democratic movement and condemning their suppression.[186]

The record of trials' successes in terms of social pedagogy is questionable, however. If, as Tajfel and Turner suggest, in-group favouritism and out-group exclusion increase vulnerability to inter-group conflict, it may be that trials of identifable perpetrators are too blunt an instrument to elucidate a new political morality.[187] Trials are generally most possible in a case where one party has been completely defeated – where the balance of forces in a society is precarious, amnesty or truth commissions remain more common.[188] While victor's justice has certain (often justifed) pejorative connotations, trials are usually imposed by a clearly ascendant group in society against a vanquished opposition. The clarity of the political messages trial expresses may be complicated by this political background. The attitudes of the Rwandan and former Yugoslav publics to the ad hoc tribunals, which remain the best polled and researched, suggest that internationalized trials are unsuited to domestic expressivism. The ICTY, for example, was widely considered an illegitimate exercise in victor's justice,[189] which made it much easier for populist appeals to reverse the predicted fow of moral propaganda. No matter how much outreach is engaged upon it is likely that the lens of interpretation will be shaped by local leaders.[190] For example, Mladic and Karadzic enjoyed soaring levels of local public popularity after they were indicted, while political fgures who facilitated accountability suffered commensurately.[191] Far from generating consensus, cooperation with the ICTY became the key dividing line in Bosnian Serb and Croatian domestic politics.[192] Klarin contends that the popularity of the ICTY (and hence its expressive effect) is inversely proportional to the number of accused that come from the various communities.[193] A much-cited study of Bosnian judges and prosecutors found that even those most educated and aware of what law demanded used war crimes trials to reaffrm the victimization of their own group.[194] Far from drawing a clear line between repressive politics of ethnicity and the new Balkan democracies, the ICTY has only muddied the distinction.[195]

While it is easier to criticize (or pillory) international criminal justice as inevitably external and hegemonic, purely domestic processes have similarly failed to foster the predicted consensus. Where society manifests pre-transitional divisions, trial and conviction have rarely suffced to render certain people or policies outside the realm of what is deemed politically acceptable by the public. Even after international and domestic criminal proceedings were mounted against General Pinochet for crimes against humanity and embezzlement, as well as against over forty military personnel for abuses committed during his rule, by 2007 two people who had served at a high level in his administration served as the heads of the two main opposition parties.[196] Widespread naming and shaming in Guatemala did little to prevent Efrain Rios Montt, a general who was in char ge of the country at the height of the repression in the 1980s, from remaining a prominent politician two decades later.[197] Public support for draconian anti-crime measures reminiscent of those so roundly condemned by the El Salvador truth commission was widespread in that country – some interpret this as suggesting that transitional justice' s discernible effects are limited to politically motivated abuses, but this may be too neat a distinction. [198] Likewise, condemnation by the South African TRC of security force brutality did little to inculcate public disapproval of widespread police abuse of criminal suspects and illegal immigrants. [199]

Given the diff culties of using trial as a form of moral propaganda, it is worth considering whether this is a worthwhile mission for transitional trial. In any society moral inf uence is exercised through other forms of socialization – punishment as a means of expressing social disapproval can only ever supplement the moral inf uence acquired through education and other processes outside the law.[200] Furthermore, it is important to remember that in most liberal transitions, there has *already* been at some level a signif cant rejection of the old order that is manifested in military defeat, overthrow , resignation, referendum, protest, democratic coup, external intervention or endogenous reform, or any combination thereof. T utsis did not need to try Hutus to remind themselves of the wrongness of the genocide, the trial of those overthrown in the Arab spring can only gild the lily of an already very public rejection of their rule, and in light of the alacrity with which it was pulled down it is questionable whether the Berlin W all or the system that built it needed to be put on trial to indict the GDR system. It is not enough to condemn – there remains a place for acts and processes that legitimize the new polity, but insofar as this is necessary or desirable, trial is probably less signif cant to transition than hitherto imagined and may even be redundant in light of other concurrent expressive phenomena. The trial' s potential contribution to establishing the legitimacy of the successor regime will in all likelihood be outweighed by the defeat of the ancien régime' s party at the polls as a more equivocal and explicit domestic rejection of its policies than any trial could be. What Sunstein calls the 'self-consciously countermanding constitution', one designed to counteract particular tendencies in a nation' s political culture, not only operates to thwart the deepest risks to transition but may also best demonstrate the new norms that serve as a critical and ameliorative response to the prior regime. [201]

Nevertheless, the presumption remains in scholarship and practice that trials are an appropriate venue for moral propaganda. [202] However, there is a danger that so ostentatiously civic a purpose can make the trial explicitly political, with obvious attendant dangers. As Bell warns, the desire to control the meta-narrative of conf ict may tempt the victor 'to tilt all transitional mechanisms towards an end point for transition that approximates to the victor's battlef eld goals'.[203] Even before trial, the selection of defendants for their communicative value over their culpability tends towards the discrimination and arbitrariness of enforcement that rule-bound, consistent and legitimate legality abhors. While selectivity is inevitable in transitional justice, the 'tokenism' that arises from conceiving the obligation to prosecute as a symbolic gesture or rite of transition should be avoided as far as possible.[204]

> [T]o the extent that ICT investigations are used selectively to vindicate the political objectives of the ruling regime, such investigations will likely undermine rather than promote the dual goals of promoting transitional justice and facilitating institutional reform. [205]

As Osiel argues, 'what makes for a good ' 'morality play" tends not to make for a fair trial', largely due to criminal justice's unsuitability to the simplif cations of melodrama.[206] While transitional trial is commended for its commitment to individualizing guilt, this impulse towards legalism is undermined when that defendant becomes a conduit for wider lessons. It is all too easy for a politically signif cant defendant to 'rather swiftly became peripheral to his own trial'.[207] Some argue that a trial which focuses not so much on whether an accused has broken the law but on whether his conduct comports with generalized socio-political standards is the antithesis of the rule of law .[208] Though Nino suggests that the drama of trial is conducive to stimulating public attention and deliberation,[209] the potential for trial to serve as a means of societal self-examination is trammelled by the dry , formalistic rigours of the ordinary trial. Arendt's observation that professionally scrupulous lawyers are likely to come off as 'plodding dullards' distracted by doctrinal trivia from the signif cant historical issues before them will be readily appreciated by anyone who sat through or monitored the banausic procedures of the European Nazi trials of the last twenty years, the ad hoc tribunals or even the slightly sprightlier hybrid tribunals and domestic trials in the likes of Rwanda, Ethiopia and Latin America. If trials are 'technical, long and tedious',[210] the tendency may be to alter procedure. If, as research suggests, even judges look to transitional criminal accountability as a means to reaffrm their own victimization, is it not more important than ever that f delity to procedural standards is adhered to? [211] 'Self-conscious dramaturgy'[212] can be indulged when a defendant engages upon it – it is a different matter entirely in a state that aspires towards the rule of law when its prosecutors and judges use the public process of trial in this manner. As Malamud-Goti observed in Argentina:

There is an inevitable air of artif ciality in establishing the boundaries of responsibility in a terror-ridden society. By pinning blame on a limited sector of society, human rights trials re-invent history ... far from being seen to administer justice, the judiciary was widely perceived to have merely adjusted to the political convenience of the executive. Accordingly instead of reinforcing whatever authority the judiciary may have enjoyed, the trials had the opposite effect. Instead of turning the judiciary into a democratic authority that would decisively contribute to bridging a fragmented society's multiple versions of reality, the courts generated the belief that the trials were a ploy to draw consensus from a compromised account of reality.[213]

While transitional justice has attempted to build upon a democracy and human rights-based consensus that is already presumed to exist, the vagaries of transition are such that dissensus is inevitable given pre-existing social divisions and the ease with which politicized trials can be stigmatized as victor's justice or as unrepresentative exercises in scapegoating. Though the political pedagogical worth of prosecution and conviction is questionable, the trial process itself can develop social solidarity in a less ambitious way which does not require manipulation of court processes for effect. Osiel ar gues that this Durkheimian view of trial as the interpreter of collective sentiments is inapplicable in the context of transition – while trial can symbolically reassert commitment to norms already shared, in times of great division legal proceedings should instead aspire to a different kind of 'discursive' solidarity that acknowledges this dissensus but stimulates discussion over what those norms should be. The solidarity he envisages is not one that involves declarative, def nitive judgments about political morality , but rather f ows from the civil engagement in disagreement that inheres in trial. [214] Though the political divisions which emer ged before and during transition persist, the sheer fact of trial permits a creative f ction (though, it might be ar gued, no more creative than the idea that a series of trials can capture the complexity of conf ict) that the legal process embodies norms and values all claim to share in a manner that can 'limit the scope and intensity of controversy within mutually tolerable bounds'.[215] As he puts it:

The law remains essential to [the developing attachments of antagonists to each other] not by codifying a consensus on fundamental morality, but simply by providing a key symbolic code through which complexity is reduced, agreements reached, and attachments formed.[216]

It is from this basic discursive engagement, the simple acknowledgement of law and the courts as the appropriate forum for civility and mutual respect in the management of disagreements, that is more likely to establish a realistic and sustainable political solidarity between antagonists, even while elections, vetting, truth commissions etc. engage in more overt and considerably more ambitious processes to draw the moral-political lines between regimes. This is important because transition arises when the state abused power, lost it or never actually developed it suff ciently to provide security for its citizens – changing mindsets in society, especially the mindsets of the weak vis-à-vis the strong, requires not only the ability to relate to each other or to trust the other's peaceful intentions, 'but also to (re)build conf dence in the institutions that have not been able or willing to prevent the violence and abuse in the f rst place'.[217]

Osiel probably goes too far when he suggests that trial 'might make full use of the public spotlight trained upon them at such times to stimulate democratic deliberation about the merits and meaning of liberaþrinciples'.[218] Such a process risks artif ciality and raises the spectre of using trial to create a premature political consensus. He is on safer ground in the ar gument that the trial process itself can create consensus. This relatively unambitious but attainable goal is akin to that advanced by de Greiff when he ar gues that transitional justice measures should aim to promote civic trust, which he def nes as 'the sort of disposition that can develop among citizens who are strangers to one another, and who are members of the same community only in the sense in which they are fellow members of the same *political* community'.[219] Here, he ar gues that a transitional justice mechanism such as trial can be employed to foster a 'mutual normative reciprocity' between groups in society – former antagonists can trust each other by mutually relying on a reasonable expectation of a certain pattern of behaviour on the basis that among their reasons for action is a commitment to shared norms and values.[220] Certain institutions, like courts, are guarantors of that trust and manifest those norms and values. T rials are most politically expressive not through their product, but via their process as a communication that basic norms, once massively and systematically violated, now enjoy currency in an institution committed to their equal protection for all. In so doing, he draws a distinction between civic trust as mediate end (it is reasonable to think the measure's implementation may further achievement of a given end, but just as reasonable to think the intervention of a number of different measures will also be required) and the democratic rule of law as a f nal end (whose attainment is causally even more distant, and therefore whose realization is dependent on the contribution of a lar ger multitude of factors).[221] He contends that the dividing line transitional trial should draw is not one between regimes or between conceptions of political morality but rather between institutions which were once untrustworthy and which now are not, citing Offe thus:

> '[T]rusting institutions' means something entirely different from 'trusting my neighbor': it means *knowing* and recognizing as valid the values and the form of life incorporated in an institution and deriving from this recognition the assumption that this idea makes suff cient sense to a suff cient number of people to motivate their ongoing active support for the institution and the compliance with its rules. Successful institutions generate a negative feedback loop: they make sense to actors so that

actors will support them and comply with what the institutionally def ned order prescribes.[222]

Mistrust, on the other hand, arises because the people suspect that the values embodied by those institutions do not 'make suff cient sense to a suff cient number of people to motivate their ongoing active support for these institutions and the compliance with [their] rules'. [223] Trials that are intentionally and overtly politically expressive may not make 'sense' or indeed offend many of those whose support trials hope to inculcate. As Milner Ball ar gued in the domestic context:

> Insofar as it is made a platform or a forum for educating, a trial is not a trial. Trials may indeed have an educative effect, but they have this effect when, instead of deliberately undertaking to teach, they treat the parties as individuals.[224]

4.5.2 Reconciliation

While the pursuit of retribution, deterrence, social pedagogy and containment have forced transitional trial into inadvisable compromises and deviations from sustainable due process standards, reconciliation-based approaches def ned themselves by their explicit lack of retributive motive, while the ends to which they were directed demanded greater levels of moderation and f delity to procedural norms in trial than the aforementioned consequentialist justif cations. There is a regrettable irony, therefore, in the fact that trial has become marginalized (some might say anathemized) in the literature on reconciliation in transitional justice. Probably the main reason for this is the assumed superiority of the truth commission as a reconciliatory mechanism for its ability to explore wider victimization beyond an exclusively criminal remit, because it can deal with greater numbers of perpetrators and because it is less threatening to those who can most imperil the national reconciliation process. Though the reconciliatory claims for TRCs are exaggerated, [225] this work does not quibble with the widespread assumption that TRCs are a better signal of willingness to reconcile and a superior means to achieve it than through trial. The merits of truth versus justice for reconciliation have been examined in great depth in earlier debates and nowadays ver ge on the redundant – it is now widely assumed that both truth and justice are different points on a holistic spectrum of available options. Implicit in this holistic approach is the assumption that trials are good for some purposes (like retribution or deterrence) but less appropriate for others, such as reconciliation. Over time a polarity between criminal justice and reconciliation has emerged as more micro-level, restorative and 'thick' conceptions of reconciliation replaced earlier views of macro-level, political, 'thin' conceptions.

As noted in Chapter 2, because violent political or military conf icts nowadays largely occur within states, they pitch both local and national communities against each other. Negative peace (i.e. the absence of violence) is rarely deemed a suff cient end-point for peace-builders given the ever - present danger that unmet grievances might degenerate into reawakened violence. Reconciliation is often posited as the most appropriate response. However, it is worth noting that the language of *reconciliation* implies a pre-existing community. In some societies, this may be an inappropriate paradigm because there was no pre-existing conciliation in the sense of a shared society that has compatibly overcome hostility or distrust.   [226] Nevertheless, there is a perceived necessity for reconciliation among victims and perpetrators and the community at lar ge if peace is to be sustainable. However, the concept of reconciliation is multi-vocal. It can mean all things to all men, depending not only on the relationship or community to which it refers (interpersonal, local, national) but also to the provenance of the various conceptions. For example, Mendonca ar gues that there are four distinct dimensions to reconciliation: psychological, theological, cultural and political,[227] while Lederach identif es four concepts of truth, mercy, peace and justice that stand in paradoxical tension with each other to create in their midst a space called 'reconciliation'.[228] These laundry lists have done little to clarify this most indeterminate of abstractions.

There are two major disagreements: (a) whether reconciliation needs to be thick or thin,[229] and (b) whether it is needed at national, community or interpersonal level. To begin with the former disagreement, at the minimalist end of the scale is 'non-lethal co-existence' where former enemies no longer kill one another or violate each other' s basic rights.[230] Almost akin to the peace-keeping status quo of separating antagonistic communities, it eschews attempts to create social harmony or proactive tolerance. At the more maximalist end of the scale are def nitions of reconciliation that require forgiveness between antagonists,[231] a changed psychological orientation toward the other[232] or even 'social and moral reconstruction' requiring collaboration between groups, unifying memories and a search for common identif cations.[233] The distinction between thick and thin conceptions of reconciliation maps loosely on to emphases on reconciliation at community and individual (social) levels on the one hand, and at national (political) level on the other.[234] National (political) reconciliation, primarily a political process, involves consensus or interaction between political parties or leaders which is manifested in peace-building exercises like power -sharing, constitutionalism and national transitional justice schemes like trials, TRCs and vetting. This is a very different process to personal or community reconciliation, which attempts to ensure that citizens can conduct their lives in a similar manner to that enjoyed prior to the conf ict without fear or hate.[235]

It is possible to achieve individual or community reconciliation without national reconciliation, while it is equally possible to achieve national reconciliation among political leaders which is not refected at village or town level. Ideally, a substantive process of conciliation or reconciliation would occur in parallel at both levels. However, they require very different processes and approaches – reconciliation between leaders may require simply a *modus vivendi*, a willingness to mutually scapegoat, sideline or selectively punish the most egregious offenders or even purely symbolic exercises, while the ordinary citizen or villager must live day to day with the former ethnic or political antagonist. National-level initiatives will rarely trickle down to local level given the scale of mass atrocity . Nevertheless, a thin reconciliation that lightly blankets the state may sustain peace more than isolated pockets of thick reconciliation.

It is clear, therefore, that political settlement can thrive or struggle in splendid isolation from processes on the ground. Though this has always been acknowledged, over time it has been argued that national reconciliation may run counter to local or inter -personal reconciliation (the reverse is rarely argued).[236] While national reconciliation may initially (and possibly permanently) be a relatively superf cial process, at the personal level it is an individual act that represents a choice made on the basis of one' s ability to forgive and/or forget.[237] Because so personal a process cannot be accommodated within the artif cial timeline of top-down national proceedings, nation-building discourses on reconciliation invariably subordinate individual needs. Transitional justice discourse began to place national and individual/ community processes in opposition; soon it was argued that '[t]o be effective, reconciliation must arguably begin at the level of the individual – neighbor to neighbor, then house to house, and f nally, community to community'.[238] Ever since, national-level processes have been viewed with something akin to suspicion – their success or otherwise in advancing political integration has diminished a salient factor when it comes time to evaluate the success of a given transitional justice mechanism, while their ability to incorporate disparate views and link up with local processes is increasingly what they have been judged on. There is no doubt that the victims and perpetrators of war-time or authoritarian violence and brutality suffer long-lasting emotional and physical damage and that attempting to repair it is a laudable aim. What is relevant is the impact these views of reconciliation have had on transitional trial. Increasingly it is ar gued that when a national or international transitional criminal process fails to reconf gure itself to promote better inter - personal relations, it can contribute little to reconciliation.

As the 1990s progressed and transitional justice grew from infancy to adolescence, it became apparent that the ad hoc tribunals were doing little to reconcile Serb with Croat or Hutu with T utsi. Selective accountability and the establishment of the historical record of atrocities did little to accommodate or appease former antagonists. The observation by one NGO that what made reconciliation so diff cult in Yugoslavia was the presence of 'an intense resistance by many in the region to the reality that their own ethnic kin committed atrocities' is one that could be applied to a greater or lesser extent to domestic and internationalized tribunals in Ethiopia, Rwanda, East Timor, Indonesia, Kosovo and Sierra Leone in later years.[239] Acknowledgement of the need for, and improvement of, outreach programmes over time did little to improve matters. This lack of faith in trial coincided with the growing sensitivity to the need in peace-building to address questions of victims' requirements and psychosocial healing at a micro-level that macro-level state reconciliatory processes like peace agreements, consociational arrangements or trials neglected. The new emphasis catalysed a move in transitional justice from a trial-based focus (as noted earlier, now unfairly but widely caricatured as 'retributive') to a more restorative focus, concerned less with punishment of perpetrators by the state or its international proxy than with relationships at the level of everyday society, with the express goal of 'healing' victims and communities. A biomedical model of trauma treatment was applied with renewed vigour to victims and their communities to visualize the process of social recovery in a post-conf ict or post-repression society . Therapeutic language of 'coming to terms' and 'closure' began to edge out justice as a reconciliatory paradigm.[240]

Soon, it became a commonplace that not only could trial not develop reconciliation, it was also actively harmful towards it. Because meaningful reconciliation must involve past antagonists, it was argued that the structures and strictures of the prosecution–defence paradigm elided the complexity and dissensus central to meaningful processes of reconciliation. [241] Five arguments were employed to argue that trial and reconciliation were inherently at odds. The f rst dwelt on the victim–perpetrator dichotomy, arguing that the tendency of criminal law to draw a bright line between parties, labelling one the victim and the other the offender, was antithetical to creating the sort of balanced narrative where both communities could accept blame as well as suffering. A second criticism was that this victim–perpetrator dichotomy treated the relevant parties too atomistically. By excluding an expansive 'grey zone' of resistance and complicity that surrounds abuses, trials could not incorporate the wider experience of the entire community or its constituent communities, even if their inclusion and participation would greatly contribute to the advance of social regeneration. The third argument was that while the trial could valuably acknowledge harms, its unyielding call for punishment veered too far from the forgiveness reconciliation required. Fourthly, far from bringing about catharsis, it was feared that the adversarial nature of trial would re-traumatize victims. Finally, it was argued that because trials took place in the sterile (and often foreign) environment of the courtroom, they were 'too far removed – mentally and spatially – from the local population affected by the crime' to foster social harmony.[242] Trials might be legally and morally necessary, but reconciliation would generally only succeed in spite of them. The interests of law and the interests of reconciliation were deemed to have drifted. It became conventional to speak of the tension between justice and reconciliation [243] or how they 'pull in different directions'.[244]

It is no surprise, therefore, that reconciliation over time was abandoned as a justif cation or goal of transitional trial. However , the baby appears to have been thrown out with the bathwater . Criminal justice can advance the process of reconciliation in a more modest, grounded way less dependent on psychosociology and therapeutic language by serving this thinner   , but perhaps more viable and realistic, form of it. The lost amidst the reparative jagon of how trials could heal, repair, restore or record an agreed history were more modest arguments about how the very process of trial could contribute to reconciling victims with the state. The purpose here was not to reconcile identif able victims with perpetrators or def   ned communities with their antagonists, but rather to exemplify how complex conf   icts could be channelled non-violently. The conception of trial as unconducive to reconciliation appears to spring from a belief that conf ict must be eliminated rather than f nessed, that individual healing must take priority over   employing impersonal national institutions to channel strife. The stigmatization of trial processes that express rather than repress discord can have an injurious effect on the rule of law reconstruction. As Campbell and Turner argue, '[a] notion of reconciliation insisting on simplistic concepts of social togetherness (or at-one-ment) may have diff culty in incorporating such agonism, casting law as the enemy of reconciliation'.[245]

While more reconciliation is undoubtedly more useful than less, and harmony better than tolerance, it is questionable whether these more expansive conceptions of reconciliation are either (i) necessary to sustain peace, or (ii) achievable. T o set moral reconstruction as the litmus test for reconciliation may be to confuse the desirable and the necessary . There are many functioning societies which cannot be said to be reconciled – non-xenophobic, pluralistic forms of nationalism compatible with liberal values of freedom, tolerance, equality, and individual rights rarely blossom in the aftermath of inter -communal repression or war , but are relatively exceptional even in more peaceful milieus. The time and effort required to build a shared moral understanding may not accord with the temporal pressures of transition – an agreement to disagree, even over important principles, may be needed to grease the wheels of socio-political progress. [246] The pursuit of for giveness, love or even tolerance may expect too much and make society function little better than with thin conceptions. As Bloomf eld puts it:

> At its simplest, [reconciliation] means f nding a way to live alongside former enemies – not necessarily to love them, or forgive them, or forget the past in any way, but to coexist with them, to develop the degree of cooperation necessary to share our society with them, so that we all have better lives together than we have had separately.[247]

A general distinction between the thinner and thicker conceptions of reconciliation is that advocates of the former are more comfortable conceiving of reconciliation relatively unambitiously as a process, whereas for the latter reconciliation is a more like product, an aspirational goal.   [248] While in peace-building discourse generally a balance is usually struck between the two, in transitional justice, over time, conceptions of reconciliation as a goal to be attained have won out over those who are more limited in their ambitions. Somewhere between the poles, but tending towards a process-oriented vision of reconciliation, is a moderate conception of reconciliation that seeks to achieve something approximating a political community based on consent and shared norms.[249] It would fall short of a thick conception incorporating harmony and moral understanding by accepting that former antagonists might still disagree fundamentally . However, it requires that antagonists should respect each other. The prime example is what Gutman and Thompson call 'democratic reciprocity'.[250] It incorporates, *inter alia*, respect between one-time adversaries, a willingness to engage in mutual deliberation about policy and to forge principled compromises over divisive issues. Democratic reciprocity, like mutual co-existence, requires neither apology nor for giveness. It is premised on a clear -eyed acceptance that some form of conf ict is inevitable in any society and that the most realistic aspiration for a national community may be to move from violent conf ict to non-violent conf ict.[251] Politics in democratic societies requires the channelling of conf ict through peaceful practices and institutions like elections, parliaments and courts, rather than eliminating it.[252] This type of co-existence would imply , and be made impossible without, a mutual respect for the rule of law by the former antagonists. Depolarization of society is a natural precursor to national unity and reconciliation, and requires reconstruction of institutions that are conducive to a stable and fair political system.[253] Allen contends that while reconciliation conceived as unity is elusive, consensus around the need for rules, laws and procedures is a lower threshold and consequently a more practicable possibility.[254]

Along similar lines, de Greiff has ar gued for a minimalist conception of reconciliation where the primary aspiration is for citizens to trust each other as citizens again. Under such a conception, affection, shared history and co-operation become less important than manifesting suff cient commitment to the norms and values of their ruling institutions.[255] Thicker reconciliation can only take place where antagonistic communities are 'suff ciently conf dent that those who operate those institutions do also on the basis of those norms and values, and are suff ciently secure about their fellow citizen' s commitment to abide by and uphold these basic norms and values'.[256] Here, reconciliation merely requires social relations built on a norm-based trust — transitional justice can help to make the institution trustworthy , even if actual trust may require a later attitudinal change.[257]

While de Greiff examines how the simple process of applying the law can build trust between individuals and communities, Colleen Murphy reminds us in outlining her moral theory of political reconciliation that crimes committed with impunity in the course of systematic state brutality are a moral wrong independent of the wrong in violating an individual' s rights because they undermine the degree to which the state's law can structure and

def ne the contours of the political relationship between rulers and ruled. [258]
Murphy, who like de Greiff and McAdams urges a move from focusing on the
goals of justice to an emphasis on the non-instrumental value in simply
enforcing validly declared rules, argues the erosion of the rule of law 'entails
an erosion of important conditions for relationships to express reciprocity and
respect for agency'. [259] Consequently, she contends that building a mutual
respect for the rule of law amongst ordinary citizens who resent the state for
undermining their reliable expectations of the law through past systematized
impunity is one of the primary tasks of political reconciliation because it can
instantiate the moral value of reciprocity in the relationship between citizens
and off cials.[260] The criticisms of trial as a reconciliatory mechanism are
largely founded on the assumption that the appropriate targets for reconciliation are former antagonists *qua* antagonists. If trials cannot reconcile Hutu
to Tutsi in Rwanda or a Hariri supporter to an anti-Hariri activist in Lebanon
on an individual or community level, then it has failed and may even be
counter-productive. However, if we approach reconciliation at a national level
based around democratic reciprocity, there is a strong argument that the very
process of trial can help reconcile victim communities to the state. V ictim-
desert theories have emphasized how trial can restore the individual to the
state. Hampton, for example, argues that trial by the state can reassert the
victim's value as a human being by negating the evidence of superiority
implied by the wrongdoer' s offence and ref ecting how valuable that
individual is to society .[261] On a less ambitious and individualized level,
punishment can neutralize the society-wide demoralizing effect that arises
when people witness crimes being perpetrated with systematic impunity .[262]
This is particularly important in the context of dehumanizing crimes that the
pre-transitional state either perpetrated or failed to prevent. The impersonal-
ity of the process that the restorative critique emphasizes can in fact vindicate
the victim's humanity and rights because public trial is the most appropriate
forum in which to denounce their violation. [263] Though victim self-respect
should not be presumed to f ow from trial, the public recognition that one
was wronged can redress the massive failure of recognition that undermines
unreconciled societies.[264]

Here, trial serves as an integrative mechanism, even if it is not restorative.
It treats the individual as a citizen to be respected, rather than as a casualty
to be healed. It may provide the reassurance necessary for simple coexistence
or democratic reciprocity, even if it cannot build bridges between perpetrator
and victim. None of this is to argue that reconciliation between individuals
is not important, but failure to develop it should not detract from the
potential of trial to meaningfully contribute to improved relations at a
national level. Demonstrably fair criminal process can potentially create
conditions where the impersonal, unpredictable and unmanageable process of
restoration and reconciliation can take place, and at the same time avoid the
regrettable criticism of the concept of criminal justice that the concern with
reconciliation has hitherto given rise to.

4.5.3 Deterrence and prevention

One of the most commonly cited utilitarian justif cations of transitional trial is deterrence (the proposition that well-def ned punishments with a credible threat of enforcement discourage potential criminal defendants from offending because of the likelihood of punishment). Though recently some have pointed to correlations between trials and the later absence of human rights abuses to assert the plausibility of the deterrent rationale, [265] the causal relationship may run in the opposite direction in that stable transitions are most conducive to trials.[266] Overwhelmingly the literature in the f eld is sceptical – most scholars who examine the issue question whether criminal trial, be it threatened or delivered, can deter the commission of systematic crime by authoritarian regimes, armies or violent non-state groups. [267] During war or repression, analogies with ordinary domestic law are particularly inapt in relation to the instigators of atrocity because those tasked with prosecution may be either coterminous with, or in fear of, those who committed the crimes. Their underlings might take refuge in the safety of numbers (the number of potential indictees will surpass the abilities of even the most competent of judiciaries) and their relative lack of seniority.

After war or repression there is of course a more forward-oriented conception of the deterrence ar gument, the crux which is the frequently expressed hope that indictment, trials and punishments can end an enduring 'cycle of violence' on the basis that impunity emboldens potential future instigators of mass atrocity.[268] The position, perhaps better described as preventive than deterrent, is best expressed by Darehshori, who ar gues that '[t]olerance of impunity can contribute to renewed cycles of violence, both by implicitly permitting unlawful acts and by creating an atmosphere of distrust and revenge that may later be manipulated by leaders seeking to foment violence for their own political ends'. [269] Certainly, to the extent that trial signals to the most destabilizing actors that the law will be enforced, it can contribute to security and long-term peace. It is questionable, however , whether the cycles of violence paradigm is the appropriate one for understanding the preventive impact of trial at the end of war or authoritarianism. Even if it looks unstable in the long term, the very fact of a genuine democratic transition, especially one accompanied by a credible peace-building mission, may mark a distinct causal and contextual break from the previously cyclical nature of violence. The structures that allowed the previous system crimes to occur may have already been broken up, or at least been severely weakened – if they had not, there would not have been a transition. There is a tendency in the literature to look at deterrence in globally prospective terms but to forget that trial applies to a particular state where the balance of power has swung distinctly (but not irreversibly) towards the forces of legality . While deterrence theory can and should be criticized for unref ectively applying a steady-state criminological theory into a dramatically less stable context, there is a danger in going too far in the opposite direction by failing to acknowledge that transitional trial occurs *during* or even *after* transition where the criminality that def ned the state beforehand now f nds a much less conducive environment. A transition strong and stable enough to countenance trial will rarely be one in signif cant danger of short-term reverse. [270] Deterrence in this particular instance is not directed situationally towards changing the decision-making calculus of an identifiable political group or an immediate social danger. After all, deterrence is 'implicit in, and advanced by, the very political reforms attending the transition'. [271] Instead, it should be more sustainability-oriented, signalling that the state has the willingness and ability to maintain accountability in relation to unforeseen future criminality, be it political or ordinary.[272] As such, the deterrent intention of transitional accountability falls somewhere between the steady-state paradigm from which deterrent theory arrives and the conditions of anarchy , war or coercion where it is inapposite, building towards the former while inevitably coloured by the legacy of the latter.

In such a context, the need for convictions as a means to impel changes in the cost-benef t analyses of would-be organizers or perpetrators of destabilizing political crime is of less import to the transition than establishing credible punitive institutions. Sustainably developing judicial and prosecutorial capacity is more important for long-term deterrence than making examples of specif c deviants or specif c groups whose time of inf uence has come and gone. As Greenawalt argues, criminal law deters through its long-term role in shaping, strengthening, and inculcating values, which in turn encourages the development of habitual internal restraints.[273] The inculcation of internal obedience in the average citizen through demonstration of the justice systems' competence and fairness is of greater relevance to the rule of law and transitional liberalization than demonstrating that mass atrocity will be punished. Democratization, reform of security forces, peace-building and disarmament have a greater deterrent effect than even the most punitive series of trials can have. None of this is to argue that trial of past criminals is irrelevant or inadvisable, but policy-makers may benef t from considering the possibility that the most important audience for transitional trial is not the defeated foe of yesterday , but tomorrow's looter or maf oso or insurgent. Snyder and Vinjamuri argue that deterrence requires (a) neutralizing potential spoilers, (b) strengthening a coalition that supports norms of justice, and (c) improving domestic administrative and legal institutions that are needed to implement justice predictably in the long run. [274] Transitional justice discourse has focused too much on (a) by elevating convictions above all else, and not enough on (b) and (c) which emphasize development of a cultural commitment to the criminal justice system and building demonstrably fair and competent institutions. As Stromseth puts it, effective prevention over time requires a more far -reaching approach than prosecuting offenders – institutions and cultural attitudes must be developed along with new patterns of accountability.[275] Instead, however, the conception of successful deterrence is one of non-recurrence of human rights abuses, a tar get that may be either irrelevant or unduly unambitious given the current make-up of the state.

4.6 A mutually acceptable standard of trial

The previous section ar gued for a re-orientation of criminal trial towards more rule of law-centred conceptions of expressivism, reconciliation and deterrence that those involved in justice sector reform and those involved in transitional justice might f nd mutually agreeable. This re-orientation springs from a concern for due process and a fear the criminal justice system will be rigged against a certain category of citizens in its foundational period. Stripped of any retributive and utilitarian purposes, the very practice of trial helps build the rule of law without engaging in questions of political morality as retributivists and utilitarians insist upon. Nevertheless, to insist that trial in and of itself is inherently valuable does not mean it should be pursued in all contexts. The heightened seductiveness of law in transition should not blind policy-makers to the fact that many states are incapable of trial and that grossly inadequate processes (such as those in Rwanda or Ethiopia) are likely to prove counterproductive. Few benef ts can f ow from trials that are manifestly f awed, while they risk bringing the legal system into disrepute at the time of their supposed renascence. So intractable are the dilemmas of victor's justice and so removed from the rule of law are some successor trials, that a minority of writers have advocated their abandonment in certain situations.[276] However, this position mostly originates not from a concern for prospective standards of the rule of law , but rather the risk that obviously partisan or victor's justice trials might undermine social pedagogy or retribution.[277] Siegel, Minow and Holmes suggest that trials should not be pursued where there is no chance for fairness or perception of fairness, a lack of impartiality and competence or where there is a huge disparity between the resources needed to undertake trial and the capacities available. [278] Mendez argues for example that a state like Rwanda should prosecute 'only under rigorous standards of due process',[279] while Ratner contends that impunity is preferable to 'sham justice'.[280] The El Salvador Truth Commission was justi-f ed as the best possible option as no trials were deemed preferable to unfair trials.[281] This is a liberal proceduralist ar gument that rejects any advance in ends if the procedural means are inconsistent with the substantive rule of law On the one hand, such an approach marks a welcome departure from prevailing attitudes that accept or even welcome departures from   fundamental international and constitutional standards provided they merely fall short of show trials or rampant politicization. [282] However, the alternative of doing nothing and sanctioning impunity has an equally detrimental rule of law impact.

It is between the Scylla of unfair trial and the Charybdis of inactivity that there is a role for the UN peace-builders, justice sector reformers and transitional justice practitioners, as acknowledged explicitly or implicitly in the complementarity regime of the Rome Statute (examined in greater detail in the next chapter), the *Rule of Law and Transitional Justice Report* and the growing tendency of bilateral and multilateral partners to participate in the administration of justice. As Kerr and Mobekk ar gue:

> If judicial reform is carried out as part of a holistic approach towards the rule of law in a post-conf ict setting, then a primary obstacle against using domestic trials to redress past crimes is dealt with. [283]

Even if we accept that a formal criminal process is inadvisable without a minimal commitment to fair trial but that this must go beyond mere avoidance of a show trial, this doesn' t answer the question of what standard of trial those involved in supporting national transitional justice and those involved in reforming the state' s justice sector should aim for between the elastic conception of due process implicitly accepted in transitional justice and the more doctrinaire standard of fair trial rule of law reconstruction strains towards.

While there have been unduly demanding expectations of the precondi-tions for domestic transitional trial, the OHCHR establishes a sensible minimum when it calls for criminal proceedings to be conducted 'in accordance with the right to a fair and public hearing by a competent, independent, impartial and duly constituted tribunal'. [284] If such a standard cannot be met, domestic trials are inadvisable. Ratner and Abrams similarly recognize that standards expected in the post-conf ict situation must be realistic, but may go too far in requiring the following four conditions to be present simultaneously:

> A workable legal framework through well-crafted statutes of criminal law and procedure; a trained cadre of judges, prosecutors, defenders and investigators; adequate infrastructure, such as courtroom facilities, investigative off ces, recordkeeping capabilities, and detention and prison facilities; and a culture of respect for the fairness and impartiality of the process and the rights of the accused. [285]

This list at times comes close to being a wishlist more appropriate to a fully functioning industrialized democracy . Nevertheless, it approximates the approach adopted by other constituent bodies of the UN, which applies its own internal standards and international human rights law as providing 'an appropriate framework for establishing and re-establishing and strengthen-ing criminal justice systems'. [286] The UN *Rule of Law and Transitional Justice Report* commits the world body to 'scrupulously comply with international standards for human rights' anywhere it administers justice. [287] However, given the invariably straitened circumstances of the justice system noted in Chapter 2, the fact that the state may barely be able to provide basic services and the limitations of UN, multi-lateral and bilateral budgets, practice on the ground has been less exacting. Peace-builders generally are aware that if best practices are promoted prematurely , they can form obstacles to more sustainable solutions.[288] Conscious that universal standards realistically cannot mesh with the base-line condition of many states, practitioners admit 'the high standards of administration of justice and human rights must be adjusted and brought down to a " *juste niveau*" – a level that is acceptable in the region'.[289]

The better approach may be, as Bayliss suggests, to 'take as a given that trials in post-conf ict countries are likely to be less than optimal in a number of ways'[290] and then ask whether these shortcomings, individually or combined, can be improved or are irredeemable, in which case either impunity, full internationalization (i.e. admissibility before the ICC on the grounds of inability or unwillingness) or grossly inadequate proceedings must take place. It may be the case that the best one can hope for is to give defendants trials that are 'fair enough'. This standard was proposed in the late 1990s by Warbrick who argued that while international fair trial standards are directed at functioning national judicial systems, the absence of a constitutional structure, mechanisms of judicial accountability or a formal notion of the separation of powers in international criminal law meant that international criminal courts were too removed from the conditions that prevail in functioning domestic tribunals to be judged by the same standard that applies there. [291] Of course, as matters transpired, the nascent international tribunals ultimately achieved a generally satisfactory standard of trial that went in the majority of cases well beyond 'fair enough'. However, given the weakness of constitutional structures, mechanisms of accountability and separation of powers in transitional states (to add to the obvious problem of lack of professional capacity), the 'fair enough' argument might prof tably be extended to the conditions of post-conf ict or post-authoritarian judicial systems which are much further removed from the standards of functioning judicial systems than international tribunals.

Warbrick contended that while international human rights law outlined certain standards of fair trial, they were obligations of result (to secure a fair trial for the defendant, as opposed to detailed obligations of process specifying a universal standard means of achieving it), [292] pointing to the relativity of the notion of fair trial and the necessity for assessing it in terms of the materially different circumstances of the judicial mechanism concerned instead of abstract 'fairest of all' standards derived from the standards of functioning courts in industrialized democracies. [293] Because few of the provisions of Article 14 ICCPR are absolute standards, as long as the trial process results in a trial that is 'fair enough', i.e. not doing violence to the rights of the defendant by achieving a satisfactory minimum, the human rights requirements might be deemed to have been satisf ed.[294] Applying such a standard, trials should try to insulate themselves as far as possible from political pressures (though complete dissociation may be impossible), to shield the culpable from bias or overzealous prosecution and to apply at least a base-line level of procedural protection. It can cope with a fexible approach to evidence such as making admissible all evidence of probative value, anonymous witnesses or allowing the mens rea requirement for superiors drop below intentional misconduct in prosecutions where unpunished subordinates exceed military orders, as long as they are consistent with an impersonal rule of law that protects and vindicates the rights of the defendant. Non-prejudicial procedural innovations, such as the conduct of Ar gentina's military junta trials in a single oral proceeding susceptible to television coverage might be acceptable.[295]

On the other hand, if we accept that the criminal procedure expresses the society's fundamental rule of law values, approaches where the state intentionally and systematically tilts the balance of trial against defendant by , for example, extreme inequality of arms, coercive plea-bar gaining, grossly prolonged detention or the sort of creative conspiracy char ges laid at Nuremberg may breach even a minimalist 'fair enough' standard. Space precludes establishing precisely what a 'fair enough' standard would constitute – it is, after all, a job for the international and domestic procedural lawyers who to date have spent more time ar guing for the abandonment of imperfect trials or the pursuit of perfect ones. However , given the prevalent concern with utilitarian punishment that it sacrif ces individual fairness for socio-political welfare, an appropriate standard of trial would give effect to the rule of law's fundamental normative value of the security of the individual against arbitrary legal deprivation of the trial rights. Limiting express or implied political compulsion to secure convictions at all costs through the independent sifting of evidence in an independent court is therefore key . A core dividing line must be a willingness to entertain the possibility of acquittal over institutionally-engineered de facto or de jure presumptions of guilt, even where it would interfere with the retributive or utilitarian purposes of trial. In opposing the 'rigged game' transitional trial so often becomes, Osiel concludes:

> To be sure it is hard to work up much sympathy for a suspected torturer, and meticulous due process in such circumstances may be a virtue that only a lawyer could love. However , it has been precisely this virtue by which liberal societies have long and proudly sought to distinguish themselves from the rest.[296]

The international criminal justice community has largely rejected any role in fostering such standards, and it is to this that attention now turns.

Notes

1 A.J. McAdams, 'Transitional Justice: The Issue That W on't Go Away' (2011) 5 *International Journal of Transitional Justice* 304, 311.
2 C. Offe, 'Disqualif cation, Retribution, Restitution: Dilemmas of Justice in Postcommunist Transitions' (1993) 1 *Journal of Political Philosophy* 17.

3 J.D.Ohlin, 'On the Very Idea of Transitional Justice' (2007)8 *Whitehead Journal of Diplomacy and International Relations* 51, 52.

4 H.Arendt, *The Human Condition* (Chicago: Chicago University Press, 1958), 253.

5 M. Osiel, 'The Banality of Good: Aligning Incentives Against Mass Atrocity' (2005) 105 *Columbia Law Review* 1752, 1807.

6 J. Goldstein and R. Keohane, 'Ideas and Foreign Policy: An Analytical Framework' in J. Goldstein and R. Keohane (eds.), *Ideas and Foreign Policy: Beliefs, Institutions, and Political Change* (Ithaca: Cornell University Press, 1993), 3 at 9–10.

7 J. Rawls, 'Two Concepts of Rules' in R. Baird and S. Rosenbaum (eds.),*Philosophy of Punishment* (Buffalo: Prometheus Books, 1988), 38.

8 I.Kant, *Perpetual Peace – A Philosophical Essay by Immanuel Kant* (London: Allen and Unwin, 1903), 58.

9 For an overall view of utilitarian and consequentialist theory, see C.L. Ten, *Crime, Guilt and Punishment: A Philosophical Introduction* (Oxford: Clarendon Press, 1987), 7–38.

10 E.g. UN Security Council Resolution 955 outlines accountability, deterrence, restoration of peace and reconciliation as the ICTR's purposes (UNSCOR 3453rd Meeting, UN Doc. S/RES/955 of 8 November 1994, Preamble).

11 Ohlin,supra n3, 61.

12 J. Stromseth, 'Introduction: Goals and Challenges in the Pursuit of Accountability' in J. Stromseth (ed.),*Accountability for Atrocities: National and International Responses* (Ardsley, NY: Transnational Publishers, 2003), 6.

13 P. Arthur, 'How "Transitions" Reshaped Human Rights: A Conceptual History of Transitional Justice' (2009) 31 *Human Rights Quarterly* 321, 363.

14 I. Tallgren, 'The Sensibility and Sense of International Criminal Law' (2002) 13 *European Journal of International Law* 561, 591.

15 K.Greenawalt, 'Punishment' (1983) 74 *Journal of Criminal Law & Criminology* 343, 347.

16 C. Nino, *Radical Evil on Trial* (New Haven: Y ale University Press, 1996), 126–127.

17 E.g.Nino, ibid., and J. Malamud-Goti, 'Transitional Government in the Breach: Why Punish State Criminals?' (1990) 12 *Human Rights Quarterly* 1.

18 J. Rabkin, 'No Substitute for Sovereignty: Why International Criminal Justice has a Bleak Future – and Deserves It' in W . Schabas, E. Hughes and R. Thakur (eds.), *Atrocities and International Accountability: Beyond Transitional Justice* (New York: United Nations University Press, 2007), 98 at 128.

19 B.A.Leebaw, '*Transitional Justice* by Ruti Teitel' (Book Review) (2001) *American Journal of Comparative Law* 363, 364.

20 UNSecretary-General, *The Rule of Law and Transitional Justice in Conflict and Post-Conflict Societies* (2004) UN Doc. S/2004/616, para. 39.

21 J. Mendez, 'In Defense of Transitional Justice' in A.J. McAdams (ed.),*Transitional Justice and the Rule of Law in New Democracies* (Notre Dame, London: University of Notre Dame Press, 1997), 1 at 15, R. Kerr and E. Mobekk,*Peace & Justice: Seeking Accountability After War* (Cambridge: Polity Press, 2007), 115.

22 D.Tutu, *No Future Without Forgiveness* (New York: Doubleday, 1999).

23 Off ce of the High Commissioner for Human Rights, 'Rule of Law Tools for Post-Conf ict States: Prosecution Initiatives' (2008) HR/PUB/06/4, 4 at footnote 9.

24 A. Boraine, *A Country Unmasked: Inside South Africa's TRC* (Oxford: Oxford University Press, 2000).

25 M. Ignatieff, *The Warrior's Honor: Ethnic War and the Modern Conscience* (London: Chatto & Windus, 1998), 188.

26 D. Crocker, 'Punishment, Reconciliation and Democratic Deliberation' (2001 – 02) 5 *Buffalo Criminal Law Review* 509, 517–520.

27 M. Minow, *Between Vengeance and Forgiveness: Facing History After Genocide and Mass Violence* (Boston: Beacon Press, 1998), 12.

28 F. Elgesem and G.A. Aneme, 'The Rights of the Accused: A Human Rights Appraisal' in C. Schaefer, G.A. Aneme and K. Tronvoll (eds.), *The Ethiopian Red Terror Trials: Transitional Justice Challenged* (London: James Currey, 2009), 33 and Human Rights Watch, 'Rwanda: Human Rights Developments' in Human Rights Watch, 'World Report 1999' (1999), available: < http://www.unhcr.org/refworld/publisher,HRW,,RWA,3ae6a8b750,0.html>.

29 UNMIK Regulation 2000/64 on the Assignment of International Judges/Prosecutors and/or Change of Venue of 15 December 2000.

30 N. Walker, *Why Punish?* (Oxford: Oxford University Press, 1991), 77.

31 Malamud-Goti, supra n17, 14–15.

32 S. Pillay, 'Conclusion' in C.L. Sriram and S. Pillay (eds.), *Peace Versus Justice?: The Dilemma of Transitional Justice in Africa* (Woodbridge: James Currey, 2010), 347 at 349.

33 E.g. C. Gustafson, 'International Criminal Courts: Some Dissident Views on the Continuation of War by Penal Means' (1998–99) 21 *Houston Journal of International Law* 51, 66, J. Malamud-Goti, 'Human Rights Abuses in Fledgling Democracies: The Role of Discretion' in I. Stotzky (ed.), *Transition to Democracy in Latin America: The Role of the Judiciary* (Boulder: Westview Press, 1993), 225 at 236.

34 Office of the United Nations High Commissioner for Human Rights, supra n23, 3–4.

35 'Serbia Convicts 4 in Killing of Srebrenica Muslims', *International Herald Tribune*, 10 April 2007.

36 S. Cohen, 'State Crimes of Previous Regimes: Knowledge, Accountability , and Policing the Past' (1995) 20 *Law and Social Inquiry* 7, 23.

37 Mendez, supra n21, 1.

38 L. Fletcher and H. Weinstein, 'Violence and Social Repair: Rethinking the Contribution of Justice to Reconciliation' (2002) 24 *Human Rights Quarterly* 573, 595–596.

39 E. Lutz and K. Sikkink, 'The Justice Cascade: The Evolution and Impact of Foreign Human Rights Trials in Latin America' (2001) 2 *Chicago Journal of International Law* 1, 31.

40 Ibid., 24.

41 J. Bodin, *Six Livres de la République: Volume 1* (Paris: Du Pays, 1976), 10.

42 Rabkin, supra n18, 124.

43 M. Osiel, *Mass Atrocity, Collective Memory and the Law* (New Brunswick: Transaction Publishers, 1997), 207.

44 M. Morris, 'The Disturbing Democratic Deficit of the International Criminal Court' (2001) 12 *Finnish Yearbook of International Law* 109, 112–113.

45 R.A. Cobián and F. Réategui, 'Towards Systemic Social Transformation: Truth Commissions and Development' in P. de Greiff and R. Duthie (eds.), *Transitional Justice and Development: Making Connections* (New York: Social Science Research Council, 2009), 142 at 149.

46 Malamud-Goti, supra n17, 11–12.

47 J. Stromseth, 'Justice on the Ground: Can International Criminal Courts Strengthen Domestic Rule of Law in Post-Conf ict Societies?' (2009) 1 *Hague Journal on the Rule of Law* 87 at 92, 96 and 97.

48 R.Teitel, *Transitional Justice* (Oxford: Oxford University Press, 2001), 24.

49 T Olsen, L. Payne and A. Reiter, *Transitional Justice in Balance: Comparing Processes, Weighing Efficacy* (Washington, DC: U.S. Institute of Peace, 2010), 133, S. Landsman, 'Alternative Responses to Serious Human Rights Abuses: Of Prosecutions and Truth Commissions' (1996) 59 *Law and Contemporary Problems* 81, 83.

50 O.Wendell Holmes, 'The Path of Law' (1897) 10 *Harvard Law Review* 457, 459–460.

51 Teitel, supra n48, 3.

52 M. Sieff and L. V injamuri, 'Prosecuting W ar Criminals: An Ar gument for Decentralization' (2002) 2 *Conflict, Security and Development* 103, 111.

53 E.g. Reisman lists prevention, suspension, deterrence, restoration, correction, rehabilitation and reconstruction (W.M. Reisman, 'Institutions and Practices for Restoring and Maintaining Public Order' (1995) 6 *Duke Journal of Comparative and International Law* 175, while Aukerman identif es the following goals in the transition to democracy: desert/retribution/vengeance, deterrence, rehabilitation, restorative justice, communication/social solidarity (M. Aukerman, 'Extraordinary Evil, Ordinary Crimes: A Framework for Understanding T ransitional Justice' (2002) 15 *Harvard Human Rights Journal* 39).

54 See generally R. Henham, 'The Philosophical Foundations of International Sentencing' (2003) 1 *Journal of International Criminal Justice* 64, M. Drumbl, 'Collective Violence and Individual Punishment: The Criminality of Mass Atrocity' (2005) 99 *Northwestern University Law Review* 539 and R. Sloan, 'The Expressive Capacity of International Punishment: The Limits of the National Law Analogy and the Potential of International Criminal Law' (2007) 43 *Stanford Journal of International Law* 39, 39–40.

55 Sentencing Judgment, *Prosecutor v Todorovic*, Case No. IT -95-9/1-S, 31 July 2001, paras. 28–29 and Sentencing Judgment, *Prosecutor v Nikolic*, Case No. IT-02/60/1-S, 2 December 2003, paras. 59 and 90.

56 Judgment,*Prosecutor v Furundzija*, Case No. IT-95-17/1-T, 10 December 1998.

57 Judgment,*Prosecutor v Delalic*, Case No. IT-96-21-T, 16 November 1998, para. 1234.

58 Drumbl,supra n54, 560.

59 Judgment and Sentence, *Prosecutor v Ruggiu*, Case No. ICTR-97-32-I, 1 June 2000, para. 33 and Sentencing Judgment, *Prosecutor v Erdemovic*, Case No. IT-96-22-T, 29 November 1996, para. 21.

60 Ohlin,supra n3, 53–54.

61 Aukerman,supra n53, 75.

62 Kerrand Mobekk, supra n21, 20.

63 For example, Stover has described a tension between the concerns of legal purists and those who would use trials for moral purposes related to social pedagogy (E. Stover, *The Witnesses: War Crimes and the Promise of Justice in The Hague* (Philadelphia: University of Pennsylvania Press, 2005), 23). See also Ohlin, supra n3, 53.

64 Articles 7 and 25 of the African Charter on Human and Peoples' Rights, Articles 8 and 9 of the American Convention on Human Rights, Article 6 of the European Convention on Human Rights.

65 Article 21 ICTY Statute, Articles 63, 64(2), 66–69 Rome Statute.
66 Ohlin,supra n3, 53.
67 J.Elster, *Closing the Books: Transitional Justice in Historical Perspective* (New York: Cambridge University Press, 2004), 86.
68 Ibid.,84.
69 O. Kirchheimer, *Political Justice: The Use of Legal Procedure for Political Ends* (Princeton: Princeton University Press, 1961), 340.
70 Elster, supra n67, 91.
71 Ibid.,88.
72 J. Elster, 'Coming to Terms With the Past: A Framework for the Study of Justice in the Transition to Democracy' (1998) 39 *European Journal of Sociology* 7, 24.
73 Mendez,supra n21, 12.
74 E.Posner and A. Vermeule, 'Transitional Justice as Ordinary Justice' (2004) 117 *Harvard Law Review* 762, 766–767.
75 S. Zappala, 'The Rights of the Accused' in A. Cassese et al. (eds.),   *The Rome Statute of the International Criminal Court: A Commentary: Volume II* (Oxford: Oxford University Press, 2002), 1319 at 1328.
76 Elster, supra n67, 88 and 89.
77 Posnerand Vermeule, supra n74, 813.
78 Ohlin,supra n3, 54.
79 Teitel, supra n48, 222.
80 Off ce of the United Nations High Commissioner for Human Rights, supra n23, 12.
81 Osiel,supra n5, 1758, Aukerman, supra n53, 51.
82 Off ce of the United Nations High Commissioner for Human Rights, supra n23, 12–13.
83 A.B. de Brito et al., 'Introduction' in A.B. de Brito, C. González-Enríquez and P. Aguilar (eds.), *The Politics of Memory: Transitional Justice in Democratizing Societies* (Oxford, New York: Oxford University Press, 2001),1 at 27.
84 D. Joyce, 'The Historical Function of International Criminal Trials: Re-thinking International Criminal Law' (2004) 73   *Nordic Journal of International Law* 461, 470.
85 C. Warbrick, 'International Criminal Courts and Fair T rial' (1998) 3 *Journal of Conflict and Security Law* 45, 53.
86 *Barayagwiza v Prosecutor*, Case No. ICTR-97-19-AR72,   *Decision*, 3 November 1999, para. 61.
87 *Prosecutor v Barayagwiza*, Case No. ICTR-97-19-AR72,   *Decision on Prosecutor's Request for Review or Reconsideration*, 31 March 2000.
88 M. Fedorova, S. Verhoeven and J. Wouters, 'Safeguarding the Rights of Suspects and Accused Persons in International Criminal Proceedings' in C. Ryngaert (ed.), *The Effectiveness of International Criminal Justice* (Intersentia, 2008), 55 at 68.
89 K.C. Moghalu, 'Image and Reality of War Crimes Justice: External Perceptions of the International Criminal Tribunal for Rwanda' (2002) 26 *Fletcher Forum of World Affairs* 21, 29.
90 *Prosecutor v Thomas Lubanga Dyilo*, Case No. ICC-01/04-01/06-1401, *Trial Chamber I, Decision on the consequences of non-disclosure of exculpatory materials covered by Article 54(3)(e) agreements and the application to stay the prosecution of the accused, together with certain other issues raised at the Status Conference on 10 June 2008*, 13 June 2008 and *Decision on the release of Thomas Lubanga Dyilo*, Trial Chamber I, 2 July 2008.

91 Institute for War & Peace Reporting, 'Experts Believe Lubanga T rial May Go Ahead' (2009), available: <http://iwpr.net/report-news/experts-believe-lubanga-trial-may-go-ahead >.

92 Fedorova,Verhoeven and Wouters, supra n88, 85.

93 HumanRights Watch, 'Pinochet Decision Lamented', available: <http://www.hrw.org/news/2001/07/09/pinochet-decision-lamented>.

94 Osiel,supra n43, 106.

95 R.L. Siegel, 'Transitional Justice: A Decade of Debate and Experience' (1998) 20 *Human Rights Quarterly* 431, 448.

96 C.Villa-Vicencio, 'Restorative Justice: Ambiguities and Limitations of Theory' in C. Villa-Vicencio and E. Doxtader (eds.), *The Provocations of Amnesty: Memory, Justice and Impunity* (Trenton, NJ: Africa World Press, 2003), 30 at 35–42.

97 W. Mwangi, 'The International Criminal Tribunal for Rwanda: Reconciling the Acquitted' in Sriram and Pillay (eds.), supra n32, 262, 269–272.

98 Ohlin,supra n3, 53.

99 W. Schabas, 'Balancing the Rights of the Accused with the Imperatives of Accountability' in R. Thakur and P . Malcontent (eds.), *From Sovereign Impunity to International Accountability: The Search for Justice in a World of States* (New York: United Nations University Press, 2004), 154 at 155.

100 Ibid.,154–155.

101 C. Ryngaert, 'Introduction' in Ryngaaert (ed.), supra n88, vii at x.

102 G.A. Knoops, 'The Dichotomy Between Judicial Economy and Equality of Arms Within International and Internationalized Criminal T rials: A Defence Perspective' (2005) 28 *Fordham International Law Journal* 1566, 1566.

103 Off ce of the United Nations High Commissioner for Human Rights, supra n23, 33.

104 C.Rausch (ed.), *Combating Serious Crimes in Postconflict Societies: A Handbook for Policymakers and Practitioners* (Washington, D.C.: USIP Press, 2006), 100.

105 *Prosecutor v Oric*, Case No. IT -03-68 AR73.2 *Interlocutory Decision on Length of Defence Case* (20 July 2005), para. 7.

106 Ibid.

107 J.P.W. Temminck Tuinstra, *Defence Counsel in International Criminal Law* (The Hague: T.M.C. Asser Press, 2009), 159–162.

108 R. Wilson, '"Emaciated" Defense or a T rend to Independence and Equality of Arms in Internationalized Criminal Tribunals?' (2008) 15 *Human Rights Brief* 6.

109 F.F. Basch, 'The Doctrine of the Inter -American Court of Human Rights Regarding States' Duty to Punish Human Rights V iolations and its Dangers' (2007) 23 *American University International Law Review* 195, 210, 213 and 217.

110 C. Doebbler and M. Scharf, 'Will Saddam Get a Fair Trial?' (2005–06) 37 *Case Western Reserve Journal of International Law* 21.

111 M. Tondini, *Statebuilding and Justice Reform: Post-Conflict Reconstruction in Afghanistan* (London: Routledge, 2010), 22.

112 D.M. Amann, 'Impartiality Def cit and International Criminal Judging' in Schabas, Hughes and Thakur (eds.), supra n18, 208.

113 R. Teitel, 'The Law and Politics of Contemporary Transitional Justice' (2005) 38 *Cornell International Law Journal* 837, 848.

114 Elster, supra n67, 98.

115 Henham,supra n54, 79–80.

116 N. Eiskovits, 'Transitional Justice' in E. Zalta et al. (eds.), *Stanford Encyclopaedia of Philosophy* (Stanford: 2009), available: < http://plato.stanford.edu/entries/justice-transitional/>, Section 1.2.3.

117 This trend has not been lost on defence counsel. See J.I. T   urner, 'Defence Perspectives on Law and Politics in International Criminal T   rials' (2008) 48 *Virginia Journal of International Law* 529, 568–569.

118 Stover supra n63, 23.

119 Osiel, supra n43, 59–78.

120 DeBrito et al., supra n83, 27.

121 S. Vandeginste, 'Rwanda: Dealing with Genocide and Crimes Against Humanity in the Context of Armed Conf ict and Failed Political Transition' in N. Biggar (ed.), *Burying the Past: Making Peace and Doing Justice After Civil Conflict* (Washington, D.C.: Georgetown University Press, 2001), 251 at 261–269.

122 De Brito et al., supra n83, 29 and Elgesem and Aneme, supra n28.

123 Gary Bass, *Stay the Hand of Vengeance: The Politics of War Crimes Tribunals* (Princeton: Princeton University Press, 2000), 307.

124 P Novick, *The Resistance Versus Vichy: The Purge of Collaborators in Liberated France* (New York: Columbia University Press, 1968).

125 Elster supra n67, 90.

126 L. Huyse and S. Dhondt, *La Répression des Collaborations 1942–1952: Un Passé Toujours Présent* (Brussels: CRISP, 1993).

127 R. Goldstone, 'Exposing Human Rights Abuses – A Help or Hindrance to Reconciliation?' (1994–95) 22 *Hastings Constitutional Law Quarterly* 607, 609.

128 Elster supra n67, 130–133.

129 J. Cady and N. Booth, 'Internationalized Courts in Kosovo: An UNMIK Perspective' in C. Romano, A. Nollkaemper and J. Kleffner (eds) *Internationalized Criminal Courts and Tribunals: Sierra Leone, East Timor, Kosovo, and Cambodia* (Oxford: Oxford University Press, 2004), 59 at 59.

130 Human Rights Watch, 'Justice at Risk: W ar Crimes Trials in Croatia, Bosnia and Herzegovina, and Serbia and Montenegro' (2004), online: <http://www.hrw.org/en/node/11965>.

131 *Prosecutor v Tadic*, Case No. IT-94-I-T, *Decision on the Prosecutor's Motion Requesting Protective Measures for Victims and Witnesses* (10 August 1995), para. 15.

132 WA. Schabas, *The UN International Tribunals: The former Yugoslavia, Rwanda and Sierra Leone* (Cambridge: Cambridge University Press, 2006), 117.

133 M. Osiel, 'Why Prosecute? Critics of Punishment for Mass Atrocity' (2000) 22 *Human Rights Quarterly* 118, 118.

134 Rule 11*bis* is examined in greater detail in the next chapter.

135 F. Gioia, 'State Sovereignty, Jurisdiction, and "Modern" International Law: The Principle of Complementarity in the International Criminal Court' (2006) 19 *Leiden Journal of International Law* 1095, 1111–1113.

136 K.J. Heller, 'The Shadow Side of Complementarity: The Effect of Article 17 of the Rome Statute on National Due Process' (2006) 17 *Criminal Law Forum* 255. It should be pointed out that Heller, though maintaining the overall correctness of his thesis, has modif ed this position somewhat, positing that a state like Libya in the case of Saif Gaddaf, where a government, by denying any semblance of due process, would make it impossible for an independent judiciary to allow charges to proceed against an alleged perpetrator and as a consequence reducing the likelihood of genuine proceedings or a conviction, might thereby potentially

make the case admissible (K.J. Heller , 'Why the Failure to Provide Saif with Due Process is Relevant to Libya' s Admissibility Charge, Opinio Juris (2012), available <http://opiniojuris.org/2012/08/02/why-the-failure-to-provide-saif-with-due-process-is-relevant-to-libyas-admissibility-challenge/>).

137 M. Arsanjani and W .M. Reisman, 'The Law-in-Action of the International Criminal Court' (2005) 99 *American Journal of International Law* 385, 387–388.

138 N.N.Jurdi, *The International Criminal Court and National Courts: A Contentious Relationship* (Farnham: Ashgate, 2011), 39.

139 Heller, supra n136, 272.

140 ICCOff ce of the Prosecutor, *Informal Expert Paper: The Principle of Complementarity in Practice* (2003) <www.icc-cpi.int/iccdocs/doc/doc654724.PDF>, 15.

141 C. Stahn, 'Taking Complementarity Seriously: On the Sense and Sensibility of "Classical", "Positive" and "Negative" Complementarity' in C. Stahn and M. El Zeidy (eds.), *The International Criminal Court and Complementarity: From Theory to Practice* (Vol. I) (Cambridge: Cambridge University Press, 2011), 233 at 278.

142 Heller, supra n136, 277.

143 R. Mani, 'Does Power Trump Morality? Reconciliation and Transitional Justice', Schabas, Hughes and Thakur (eds.), supra n18, 23 at 33.

144 Drumbl,supra n54, 549.

145 Cohen,supra n36, 10.

146 Ellgren, supra n14, 565–566.

147 P. Akhavan, 'Are International Criminal T ribunals a Disincentive to Peace? Reconciling Judicial Romanticism with Political Realism' (2009) 31 *Human Rights Quarterly* 624, 630.

148 Sloan,supra n54, 41.

149 R. Bhargava, 'Restoring Decency to Barbaric Societies' in R. Rotber g and D. Thompson (eds.), *Truth v. Justice* (Princeton: Princeton University Press, 2000), 45 at 45–50.

150 K. McEvoy, 'Beyond Legalism: Towards a Thicker Understanding of Transitional Justice' (2007) 34 *Journal of Law and Society* 411, 426.

151 Osiel,supra n133, 135.

152 HelenaCobban, *Amnesty After Atrocity?: Healing Nations After Genocide and War Crimes* (Boulder: Paradigm, 2007), 199.

153 Ellgren, supra n14, 590 and 561.

154 P. de Greiff, 'Theorizing T ransitional Justice' in M. W illiams, R. Nagy and J. Elster (eds.), *Transitional Justice* (New York: New York University Press, 2012), 31 at 36.

155 D.Orentlicher, '"Settling Accounts" Revisited: Reconciling Global Norms with Local Agency' (2007) 1 *International Journal of Transitional Justice* 10, 16.

156 H.H. Koh, 'How is International Human Rights Law Enforced?' (1999) 14 *Indiana Law Journal* 1397, 1401.

157 E.g. D. Orentlicher, 'Settling Accounts: The Duty to Prosecute Human Rights Violations of a Prior Legal Regime' (1991) 100 *Yale Law Journal* 2537, 2606, D. Gray, 'An Excuse-Centred Approach to T ransitional Justice' (2005–06) 74 *Fordham Law Review* 2621, 2664, R. Mani, *Beyond Retribution – Seeking Justice in the Shadows of War* (Cambridge: Polity Press, 2002), 32. The key works by these writers are C. Beccaria, *On Crimes and Punishments* (David Young trans) (Indianapolis: Hackett, 1986) which was originally published in 1764 and

J. Bentham, *Introduction to the Principles of Morals and Legislation* (J.H. Burns and H.L.A. Hart eds.) (Oxford: Clarendon Press, 1996) which was originally published in 1789.

158 Gray ibid., 2662.

159 See generally G. Binder , 'Punishment Theory: Moral or Political?' (2002) 5 *Buffalo Criminal Law Review* 321, 333–349.

160 Ibid.,342.

161 Ibid.,347–349.

162 Ibid.,348.

163 M. Lenzen, 'Roads Less Travelled? Conceptual Pathways (and Stumbling Blocks) for Development and Transitional Justice' in de Greiff and Duthie (eds.), supra n45, 76 at 82.

164 P. Akhavan, 'Beyond Impunity: Can International Criminal Justice Prevent Future Atrocities?' (2001) 95 *American Journal of International Law* 7, 10.

165 Nino,supra n16, ix.

166 E. Herman, 'The Banality of Evil' in E. Herman, *Triumph of the Market: Essays on Economics, Politics, and the Media* (Cambridge, MA: South End Press, 1995), 97 at 97.

167 Sloan,supra n54, 42 and 71.

168 M. Drumbl, 'A Hard Look at the Soft Theory of International Criminal Law' in L.N. Sadat and M. Scharf (eds.), *The Theory and Practice of International Criminal Law* (Leiden: Martinus Nijhoff, 2008), 1 at 17.

169 M. Walker, *Moral Repair: Reconstructing Moral Relations After Wrongdoing* (Cambridge: Cambridge University Press, 2006), 190.

170 D. Cassel, 'Why We Need the International Criminal Court' (1999) 116 *The Christian Century* 532, 532.

171 D. Garland, *Punishment and Modern Society: A Study in Social Theory* (Oxford: Clarendon Press, 1990), 67.

172 Osiel,supra n43, 33–34.

173 Ibid.,208.

174 Bass,supra n123, 34.

175 Garland,supra n171, 252.

176 R.Brody, 'Justice: The First Casualty of Truth?', *The Nation*, 30 April 2001.

177 Office of the United Nations High Commissioner for Human Rights, supra n23, 4.

178 Nino,supra n16, 112.

179 Osiel,supra n43, 148.

180 Orentlicher supra n157, 2542.

181 Teitel, supra n48, 43.

182 Akhavan,supra n164, 13.

183 C. Bell, 'Transitional Justice, Interdisciplinarity and the State of the "Field" or "Non-Field"' (2009) 3 *International Journal of Transitional Justice* 5, 25.

184 Opening statement of Chief Prosecutor Jackson in International Military Tribunal, Trial of the Major War Criminals Before the International Military Tribunal (1947), 104.

185 Arthur supra n13, 356.

186 Osiel,supra n43, 5.

187 H. Tajfel and J. Turner, 'An Integrative Theory of Inter group Conf ict' in W. Austin and S. Worchel (eds.), *The Social Psychology of Intergroup Relations* (Monterey: Brooks-Cole, 1979), 33.

188 Payne, Olsen and Reiter fnd that, in the last twenty years, a 'clean break with the past' such as overthrow, collapse or military defeat remains far more conducive to trial than a negotiated transition, with trials being twice as frequent (Olsen, Payne and Reiter, supra n49, 54).

189 WW. Burke-White, 'Regionalization of International Criminal Law Enforcement: A Preliminary Exploration' (2003) 38   *Texas International Law Journal* 729, 736.

190 Minow supra n27, 126.

191 Bass, supra n123, 288–289.

192 M. Klarin, 'The Impact of ICTY T rials on Public Opinion in the Former Yugoslavia' (2009) 7 *Journal of International Criminal Justice* 89, 91.

193 Ibid., 92.

194 Human Rights Center UC Berkeley & Centre for Human Rights, University of Sarajevo, 'Justice, Accountability and Social Reconstruction: An Interview Study of Bosnian Judges and Prosecutors' (2000) 18   *Berkeley Journal of International Law* 102, 147.

195 Fletcher and Weinstein, supra n38, 601.

196 J. Heine, 'All the T ruth but Only Some of the Justice? Dilemmas of Dealing with the Past in New Democracies' in Schabas, Hughes and Thakur (eds.), supra n18, 65 at 66.

197 E. Newman, '"Transitional Justice": The Impact of Transnational Norms and the UN' (2002) 9 *International Peacekeeping* 31, 38.

198 O. Thoms, J. Ron and R. Paris, 'State-Level Effects of Transitional Justice: What Do We Know?' (2010) 4 *International Journal of Transitional Justice* 1, 14.

199 H. van Der Merwe, 'Delivering Justice During Transition: Research Challenges' in H. van der Merwe, V . Baxter and A. Chapman (eds.), *Assessing the Impact of Transitional Justice: Challenges for Empirical Research* (Washington, D.C.: USIP Press, 2009), 115 at 125.

200 J. Andenaes, 'The General Preventive Effects of Punishment' (1965–66) 114 *University of Pennsylvania Law Review* 949, 950.

201 C. Sunstein, 'The Negative Constitution: Transition in Latin America' in Stotzky (ed.), supra n33, 367.

202 Akhavan, supra n164, 13.

203 Bell, supra n183, 25.

204 Mendez, supra n21, 14.

205 J. Ku and J. Nzelibe, 'Do International Criminal Tribunals Deter or Exacerbate Humanitarian Atrocities?' (2007) 84   *Washington University Law Review* 777, 831.

206 Osiel, supra n43, 59.

207 M. Halbertal, 'The Seventh Million: The Israelis and the Holocaust',   *New Republic*, 18 October 1993, 40 at 43.

208 I. Muller, *Hitler's Justice: The Courts of the Third Reich* (Cambridge, MA: Harvard University Press, 1992), 79.

209 Nino, supra n16, 131.

210 K. Andriu, 'Transitional Justice: A New Discipline in Human Rights' (2010) Online Encyclopedia of Mass V iolence, available: < http://www.massviolence. org/IMG/article_PDF/Transitional-Justice-A-New-Discipline-in-Human-Rights.pdf>, 9.

211 Berkeley/Sarajevo Study, supra n194, 127–136 and 147–148.

212Osiel,supra n43, 7.

213J. Malamud-Goti, *Game Without End: State Terror and the Politics of Justice* (Norman: University of Oklahoma Press, 1996), 18–19.

214Osiel,supra n43, 48.

215Ibid.,49.

216Ibid.,50.

217Lenzen,supra n163, 82–83.

218Osiel,supra n43, 300.

219DeGreiff, supra n154, 45.

220Ibid.

221 P. de Greiff, 'T ransitional Justice, Security and Development: Security and Justice Thematic Paper' (2010) W orld Development Report 2011, available: <http://wdr2011.worldbank.org/transitional%20justice>, 10 (footnote 36).

222 C. Offe, 'How Can We Trust Our Fellow Citizens?' in M. Warren (ed.), *Democracy and Trust* (Cambridge: Cambridge University Press, 1999), 42 at 70–71.

223DeGreiff, supra n154, 46.

224M.Ball, *The Promise of American Law* (Athens, GA: University of Georgia Press, 1981), 56.

225For a particularly critical examination, see D. Mendeloff, 'Truth-Seeking, Truth-Telling and Postconf ict Peacebuilding: Curb the Enthusiasm?' (2004) 6 *International Studies Review* 355.

226 C. Campbell and C. T urner, 'Utopia and the Doubters: T ruth, Transition and the Law' (2008) 28 *Legal Studies* 374, 394, suggesting Northern Ireland as an example.

227 I. Furtado de Mendonca, 'Searching for Reconciliation in a Post-Complex Political Emergency Scenario' (2004), paper presented at the Fifth Pan-European International Relations Conference, The Hague, 9–11 September 2004.

228J.P Lederach, *Building Peace: Sustainable Reconciliation in Divided Societies* (Washington, D.C.: United States Institute of Peace Press, 1977).

229 D. Crocker, 'Reckoning With Past Wrongs: A Normative Framework' (1999) 13 *Ethics & International Affairs* 43, 60.

230Crocker supra n26, 528.

231 R. Goldstone, 'Exposing Human Rights Abuses – A Help or Hindrance to Reconciliation?' (1994–95) 22 *Hastings Constitutional Law Quarterly* 607, 615.

232 E. Staub, 'Reconciliation after Genocide, Mass Killing or Intractable Conf ict: Understanding the Roots of Violence, Psychological Recovery and Steps Toward a General Theory' (2006) 27 *Political Psychology* 867, 868.

233 E. Stover and H. Weinstein, 'Introduction: Conf ict, Justice and Reclamation' in E. Stover and H. Weinstein (eds.), *My Neighbor, My Enemy: Justice and Community in the Aftermath of Mass Atrocity* (Cambridge: Cambridge University Press, 2004), 1 at 18.

234M.Mamdani, 'Reconciliation Without Justice' (1996) *Southern African Review of Books* 45.

235Kerrand Mobekk, supra n21, 6.

236 R. Mani, 'Rebuilding an Inclusive Political Community After W ar' (2005) 36 *Security Dialogue* 511, 513.

237Fletcherand Weinstein, supra n38, 637.

238 J. Halpern and H. W einstein, 'Rehumanizing the Other: Empathy and Reconciliation' (2004) 26 *Human Rights Quarterly* 561, 566.

239 Institute for W ar and Peace Reporting, 'The Hague T ribunal and Balkan Reconciliation' (2010) TRI Issue 462, available: < http://iwpr.net/report-news/hague-tribunal-and-balkan-reconciliation>, 1.

240Fletcherand Weinstein, supra n38, 597–598.

241Drumbl,supra n54, 548.

242 J.N. Clark, 'The Three Rs: Retributive Justice, Restorative Justice, and Reconciliation' (2008) 11 *Contemporary Justice Review* 331, 341.

243Pillay supra n32, 353.

244Crocker supra n26, 511.

245Campbelland Turner, supra n 226, 380.

246 B. Roth, 'Peaceful Transition and Retrospective Justice: Some Reservations: A Response to Juan E. Mendez' (2001) 15 *Ethics & International Affairs* 45, 46.

247 D. Bloomf eld, 'Reconciliation: An Introduction' in D. Bloomf eld, T. Barnes and L. Huyse (eds.), *Reconciliation after Violent Conflict: A Handbook* (Stockholm: IDEA, 2003), 10 at 12.

248Ibid.

249B.A.Leebaw, 'The Irreconcilable Goals of Transitional Justice' (2008)30 *Human Rights Quarterly* 95, 105.

250 A. Gutman and D. Thompson, 'Moral Foundations of T ruth Commissions' in Rotberg and Thompson (eds.), supra n149, 22.

251 F. Ní Aoláin and C. Campbell, 'The Paradox of T ransition in Conf icted Democracies' (2005) 27 *Human Rights Quarterly* 172, 185.

252Campbelland Turner, supra n226, 380.

253J. Zalaquett, 'Confronting Human Rights Violations Committed by Former Governments: Principles Applicable and Political Constraints' in N. Kritz (ed.), *Transitional Justice: How Emerging Democracies Reckon With Former Regimes: Volume 1: General Considerations* (Washington, D.C.: United States Institute of Peace, 1995), 3 at 6–9.

254 J. Allen, 'Balancing Justice and Social Unity: Political Theory and the Idea of a Truth and Reconciliation Commission' (1999) 49 *University of Toronto Law Journal* 315.

255DeGreiff, supra n154, 51.

256Ibid.

257Ibid.,52.

258C. Murphy, *A Moral Theory of Political Reconciliation* (Cambridge: Cambridge University Press, 2010), 49 and 47.

259Ibid.,41.

260Ibid.

261 J. Hampton, 'The Moral Education Theory of Punishment' (1984) 13 *Philosophy and Public Affairs* 208 at 209–238.

262Andenaes,supra n200, 950.

263Crocker supra n26, 519.

264DeGreiff, supra n154, 50.

265 E.g. H. Kim and K. Sikkink, 'Explaining the Deterrence Effect of Human Rights Prosecutions for T ransitional Countries' (2010) 54 *International Studies Quarterly* 939, Olsen, Payne and Reiter, supra n49, 133 and 136–146.

266 P. McAuliffe, 'Suspended Disbelief? The Curious Endurance of the Deterrence Rationale in International Criminal Law' (2012) 10 *New Zealand Journal of Public and International Law* (forthcoming).

267 Gray, supra n157, 2663–3677, J. Klabbers, 'Just Revenge? The Deterrence Argument in International Criminal Law' (2001) 12 *Finnish Yearbook of International Law* 249, K. Rodman, 'Darfur and the Limits of Legal Deterrence' (2008) 30 *Human Rights Quarterly* 529, Ku and Nzelibe, supra n205, L. Mjamuri, 'Deterrence, Democracy and the Pursuit of International Justice' (2010) 24*Ethics & International Affairs* 191, D. Wippman, 'Atrocities, Deterrence and the Limits of International Justice' (1999) 23 *Fordham International Law Journal* 473.

268 E.g. Crocker, supra n26, 542–543, N. Kritz, 'Coming to Terms With Atrocities: A Review of Accountability Mechanisms for Mass Violations of Human Rights' (1996) 59 *Law and Contemporary Problems* 127, 129.

269 S. Darehshori, *Selling Justice Short: Why Accountability Matters for Peace* (New York: Human Rights Watch, 2009), 75.

270 See above n188.

271 Teitel, supra n48, 66.

272 E.Mobekk, *Transitional Justice and Security Sector Reform: Enabling Sustainable Peace* (Geneva: Geneva Centre for the Democratic Control of Armed Forces, 2006), 30.

273 K.Greenawalt, 'Punishment' (1983) 74 *Journal of Criminal Law & Criminology* 343, 351.

274 J. Snyder and L. V injamuri, 'Trials and Errors: Principle and Pragmatism in Strategies on International Justice' (2003/4) 28 *International Security* 5, 13.

275 Stromseth, supra n12, 9.

276 E.g. J. Elster, 'On Doing What One Can: An Argument Against Post-Communist Restitution and Retribution' in Kritz (ed.), supra n253, 566.

277 Aukerman, supra n53, 49.

278 Siegel, supra n95, 448, Minow   , supra n27, 50, S. Holmes, 'The End of Decommunization' in Kritz (ed.), supra n253, 116 at 116–120.

279 Mendez, supra n21, 14.

280 S. Ratner, 'New Democracies, Old Atrocities: An Inquiry in International Law' (1998–99) 87 *Georgetown Law Journal* 707, 741.

281 Mani, supra n157, 96.

282 C. Bell, 'The "New Law" of T   ransitional Justice' in K. Ambos, J. Lar   ge, M. Wierda (eds.), *Building a Future on Peace and Justice: Studies on Transitional Justice, Peace and Development* (Berlin: Springer, 2009), 105 at 122.

283 Kerrand Mobekk, supra n21, 106.

284 Off ce of the High Commissioner for Human Rights, 'Impunity', Resolution 2004/72, 21 April 2004, E/CN.4/RES/2004/72, available: < http://www.unhcr.org/refworld/docid/43f313869.html>, para. 13.

285 S. Ratner and J. Abrams, *Accountability for Human Rights Atrocities in Human Rights Law: Beyond the Nuremberg Legacy* (Oxford: Oxford University Press, 2001), 183.

286 *Making Standards Work: Fifty Years of Standard-setting in Crime Prevention and Criminal Justice*, Eleventh United Nations Congress on Crime Prevention and Criminal Justice, UN Doc. A/CONF.203/8, 1 April 2005, para. 43.

287 Para.10.

288 M. Ottaway, 'Rebuilding State Institutions in Collapsed States' (2002) 33 *Development and Change* 1001, 1021.

289 Observations of human rights off cials cited in Mani, supra n157, 77.

290 E. Bayliss, 'Reassessing the Role of International Criminal Law: Rebuilding National Courts Through Transnational Networks' (2009) 50 *Boston College Law Review* 1, 8.

291 Warbrick, supra n85, 51.

292 Ibid.

293 Ibid.,54.

294 Ibid.,54, 55, 62.

295 Osiel,supra n43, 77.

296 Ibid.,272 and 135.

5 Never the twain shall meet?

The challenge of international criminal jurisdiction to justice system reconstruction

Is the world only interested in the prosecution of a handful of notorious criminals while people in the country must continue to make do with a collapsed judicial and the same venal petty off cials who compounded the problems that plagued civil society in the country before, during and after the war? [1]

5.1 Introduction: international rule of law versus domestic rule of law?

Previous chapters have argued that the conf ation of transitional justice with the rule of law has resulted in policies that can do active harm to rule of law reconstruction or merely fail to realize the obvious potential for mutually reinforcing synergies. This tendency is nowhere more apparent than with international criminal law – its application in the aftermath of war or repression is thought to be inherently restorative of the rule of law, regardless of whether it is exercised on the international or domestic plane. Prosecution of a warlord or tyrant in The Hague or in a third state exercising universal jurisdiction is generally presumed to aff rm the principle of legality in the state most concerned, just as domestic prosecutions are believed demonstrate the applicability, relevance and vigour of the corpus of international human rights and humanitarian law. However, though its founding instruments and institutions give lip-service to the desirability of domestic punishment of crimes to which an *erga omnes* obligation to prosecute attaches, international criminal justice, as the most high-prof le iteration of transitional justice, has generally eschewed any responsibility to make this a reality . Indeed, in its failure to integrate perspectives from domestic rule of law reconstruction it is probably the prime example of how the notionally uniform global peace-building community can contradict itself. In this chapter, a number of examples of, and explanations for , this trend will be offered. However , the over-arching reason for this is the failure to harmonize the relatively nebulous international rule of law which underpins international criminal jurisdiction with domestic rule of law reconstruction.

The international rule of law is a very seductive idea, calling to mind an international order based on compliance with law as opposed to the force or expediency that characterized so much of the modern and pre-modern eras. The UN's World Summit in 2005 called for 'universal adherence to and implementation of the rule of law at both the national and international levels' and aff rmed a commitment to 'an international order based on the rule of law and international law , which is essential for peaceful coexistence and cooperation among States'.[2] The concept of an international rule of law is fairly amorphous, but Chesterman divines three possible interpretations. [3] The f rst understands the international rule of law as the application of rule of law principles to relations between the subjects of international law . The second privileges international law over national law where there may be conf ict, for example the prioritization of international human rights obligations over domestic amnesty . The third understanding signals the existence of a normative regime that affects the individual without the mediation of state institutions. The second and third visions are extremely appealing to advocates of international criminal law. If, as few would doubt, sovereign discretion over state security and justice are the shields behind which the atrocities of the last century have hidden, then the extension of Nuremberg's paradigmatic attribution of individual criminal responsibility to state off cials regardless of domestic law is inherently attractive.

The attractiveness of an international rule of law complements the broader faith of international criminal lawyers in their discipline. As Koller ar gues, international criminal law, fundamentally faith-based on account of the lack of empirical verif cation of achievement of the goals it purports to achieve, has developed to a signif cant extent because of the individual and collective identities of those inf uencing the course of international law.[4] Many of those who develop, theorize and practice international law (and international criminal law in particular) are driven by normative ideal that development of the law may progressively catalyse the establishment of f rst an international community and then a cosmopolitan community which would accord all individuals equal moral status, regardless of any national borders. [5] As such, much of international criminal law operates on the basis of a need to depart from international law's past privileging of the state as the unit of normative concern to embrace a broader political identity which in theory values all human beings equally, independent of their national ties. Koller' s argument may go too far in simplifying the numerous, often contradictory, motivations that underlie the policies of actors in the f eld of international criminal law. However, transitional justice has embraced international criminal law as a universal 'global rule of law' for redef ning the relevant community of judgment beyond 'outdated' state-centricity , for its transcendence of traditional political state sovereignty (most notably in relation to heads of state) and for setting in motion normativity among diverse actors beyond the agents or institutions of state. [6] As such, international criminal justice 'underscores state failure', [7] but its self-conception and institutions may deliberately exist at too far a remove from the state to contribute anything towards the rectif cation of it. As this chapter goes on to argue, as international criminal lawyers, judges, scholars and administrators enthusiasticallymediate this new relationship between global institutions and the individual to generate a more cosmopolitan identity, the international criminal institutions themselves have attained paramount importance at the expense of the state' s legal system, which has endured unnecessary and counter-productive neglect in this emerging normative order.

The core crimes which attract *erga omnes* criminal responsibility without the intermediation of national law (war crimes, crimes against humanity   , genocide etc.) do so on three bases that express the international community's interest in a stable and principled world order:

a)   an instrumental international order rationale wherein threats to global peace and security justify the international community in circumventing the hitherto absolute doctrine of sovereign immunity;
b)   a more normative 'collective conscience rationale' justifying the restriction of sovereign prerogatives where crimes by the enemies of mankind exceed the moral boundaries of acceptable conduct;
c)   their manifestation as an element of state policy or omission which is a precondition for lar ge-scale abuse and which implies no alternative forum where abuses can be stopped or punished. [8]

Because these objectives and values combine deep moral resonance with metanational concern, intrusion in the traditional criminal jurisdiction of states is justifed. Too often, leaving enforcement power in the hands of the state has left it subject to prejudicial extra-legal considerations, self-amnesty and delay . The increasing institutionalization of international criminal law in the ad hoc and hybridized tribunals, the ICC and universal jurisdiction has been interpreted as the product of 'cognitive-ideational forces' supplementing the traditional 'material-structural' Westphalian model in a globalized civil society.[9] A triumphalist discourse of international criminal law has emer ged wherein ICC accession is seen as the moral imperative of the times,   [10] as a manifestation of the international community's self-constitutionalization incorporating individuals as 'world citizens',[11] as the triumph of law over barbarism.[12] The best expression of this global rule of law vision is found in the admittedly exceptional circumstances of the seminal *Tadic* jurisdictional decision, when the ICTY Appeals Chamber held that an international criminal tribunal created by the Security Council 'must be endowed with primacy over national courts' because human nature will create 'a perennial danger' of international crimes being character - ized as ordinary crimes or trials being designed to shield the accused. [13] From a perspective of effciency, international courts offer certain advantages – the availability of international assistance should make securing the evidence and suspect easier, an international court would guarantee neutrality , the highest standards of substantive and procedural law would be applied, and the risk of forum-shopping by victims could be curtailed, in addition to their undoubted convenience in the cases of serious cross-border crimes.[14] Above all, the legalistic desire to seal law off from politics (of the domestic variety, at least) through the mechanical, zealous application of an authoritative international criminal apparatus as the path to a more peaceful world, has informed the continuous development of international criminal law from Nuremberg to the ICC.[15]

The vision of a global rule of law underpinning a human-rights-based international community to secure the common good of all human beings is intoxicating. However, the applicability of rule of law principles to the international legal system is highly problematic in relation to international criminal law. While international criminal law meets the Fullerian criteria of prospectivity, clarity etc. in the formation of law,[16] the failure of enforcement at the international level best illustrates the reality that the normative or institutional threshold to justify the use of the term *international rule of law* has not yet been achieved. [17] Simply put, the redistribution of power from states to the international community that would underpin a genuine international rule of law has not occurred. As Broomhall notes, enforcement power of international law remains in state hands, creating a deep divide between the ideal of the international rule of law and its effective realization.[18] Core crimes may transcend mere internal state interest because they amount to an assault on humanity , but effective punishment in all but the most exceptional cases will rely on delegation to individual states. Observing a tension between the vertical international order rationale of international criminal law and the horizontal, state-centric character of the post-Westphalian system,[19] he argues:

> Past failures of enforcement are best explained, and future progress would be best assisted, by f rmly conceiving of international criminal law in the context of the sovereignty-based, diffused peace and security system in which it must develop.[20]

Though the law of atrocity has been globalized, states have been reluctant to grant international judicial institutions primacy . The complementarity regime that emerged in Article 17 (examined in greater detail in Sections 5.5–5.7) established jurisdictional sovereignty as a key principle in the Preamble[21] and in Article 1, where it forms one of three core attributes of the ICC along with permanence and jurisdiction over the most serious crimes. Chapter 4 has ar gued that the state' s assertion of its sovereign duty to prosecute and adjudicate is a core element of restoring national rule of law . This is an ar gument that was highly prominent in the negotiations on the admissibility regime of the Rome Statute. Though there is an element of truth in the ar gument that for many of the states the emphasis on the responsibility of national authorities was a reactive, self-protective measure to ensure contextual solutions could be applied to the dilemmas of conf ict/ transition, it must be acknowledged that for most states complementarity arose out of a genuine belief that emphasis on national responsibility was the only way the putative Rome Statute system could be legitimate and sustainable.[22] From the earliest stages in the negotiation process, states rejected international primacy on the basis that they 'had a vital interest in remaining responsible and accountable for prosecuting violations of their laws'.[23] As noted in the sixth Preambular paragraph, the 'duty of every state to exercise its criminal jurisdiction over those responsible for international crimes' precedes the Rome Statute, deriving from the *aut dedere aut judicare* requirement states accepted in legal instruments such as the Genocide Convention or the Geneva Conventions or from the requirements of international customary law. This duty is realized through genuinely undertaking investigations, followed by a prosecution, trial or extradition where evidence demands. Though newer bases of jurisdiction such as the passive personality principle remain controversial, states undoubtedly have jurisdiction over serious crime committed in their territory and over perpetrators of the state's nationality for crimes committed outside its territory.[24] The reasons already examined in Chapters 2 and 4 why it is imperative for the state to assume responsibility for trying past atrocities were also argued in the negotiations for the ICC, and bear brief repetition. Though judicial sovereignty has been pilloried as a political fetish,[25] it is in fact a central aspect of sovereignty itself – as the ICC Preparatory Committee conceded, the exercise of police power and penal law is a prerogative of states and any ICC jurisdiction could be viewed only as an exception to it.[26] As such, the Statute is a recognition that international crimes are perpetrated first and foremost against the state's legal order and that it remains the most legitimate body to try them.[27]

State delegations in Rome argued that a permanent ICC with unlimited powers to deny states the exercise of these sovereign powers would offend the basic principle of non-intervention,[28] a principle that above all else expresses the democratic thought that sovereignty resides in the community.[29] The demonstrable ability of the transitional state to resolve legal issues domestically is a key element in restoring confidence among the citizenry in the rule of law. In treating the successor trials as legitimate, the population might also treat the institution of courts generally as legitimate. Burke-White offers the example of the Bosnian government's determined efforts to wrest back cases from the ICTY on the basis that the assent of the latter would have a legitimizing effect on the national judiciary, quoting the President of the Court of Bosnia-Herzegovina thus:

> These cases are within our jurisdiction. It is not so much that we want them, but that we have a right to try them. And when the ICTY hands them back to us it validates our work in building this court and expands our credibility.[30]

Referral of cases from the ICTY under the Rule 11 *bis* procedure (examined anon) demonstrated that the nascent Bosnian, Croatian and Serbian criminal justice systems had achieved a certain level of respect and trust amongst the

international community, which in turn bolstered domestic legitimacy .[31]
Similarly, in relation to a putative trial of a Rwandan colonel indicted on
genocide charges, Alvarez argued:

> A local trial for Bagasora, even one subject to extensive international
> observation or even the possibility of appeal to the ICTR, would have
> aff rmed to the world, and most importantly to all Rwandans, that
> Rwanda's institutions, including its judiciary, were capable of rendering
> justice even with respect to formerly exalted public off cials.[32]

To the extent that the ICC might decide a case is not admissible on the basis
of the state's willingness and ability, it might be assumed this would have a
similar legitimating effect on the state concerned.[33] As Newton puts it, it is
only when the state 'accepts the challenges and responsibilities associated
with enforcing the rule of law ... [that] the rule of law is strengthened and a
barrier to impunity is erected'.[34] These arguments accord with sentiment in
the affected states – for example, 51 per cent of interviewees in the Democratic
Republic of the Congo would prefer justice be achieved through the national
justice system over 26 per cent who would prefer the ICC,[35] while population
surveys in Kenya clearly demonstrate a preference for domestic trials over
international criminal justice.[36] The obverse, it should be pointed out, is also
true – to lose jurisdiction would inevitably suggest the inadequacy of the
national justice system at a time when establishing faith in it is paramount.

The f nal argument made by state delegations, one subsequently justif ed
by the ICC's record of one conviction in its f rst ten years of operation, was
that national proceedings offer enormous comparative advantages over more
interventionist international mechanisms in terms of ready availability of
institutions and relevant statutes, the familiarity of procedural rules, punishments and precedents, plus the lack of diff culties in terms of language or
securing evidence and witnesses.[37] In the years after the Rome Conference,
the domestic judiciaries of the former Y ugoslav states would validate this
argument, completing all Rule 11 *bis* cases at f rst instance within f ve years,
a rate of completion far more eff cient than that of the ICTY.[38]

However, in the types of countries this work addresses, where conditions
for prosecution of serious crimes are less than benign, the ad hoc tribunals,
hybrid courts and ICC have attempted to develop solutions which invariably
have erred on the side of international substitution over domestic empower -
ment. The reason for this lies primarily in a discourse of international
criminal law that elevates the global order over the domestic one. Broomhall
exaggerates only slightly when he ar gues scholarship in the f eld of international criminal law implicitly or explicitly presents the reduction of
sovereignty in the name of enforcing international human rights norms as
desirable.[39] The reduction in sovereignty relates not only to the sovereign
discretion of whether or not to prosecute, but the sovereign duty to actually
conduct that prosecution. For every scholar arguing for domestic prosecution,

there are multiples preferring international prosecution on the basis that domestic processes cannot be trusted or that international justice can be fairer, more eff cient, better for victims and less likely to fragment the emerging international criminal jurisprudence.[40] In international criminal legal discourse, there is a pervasive attitude that these self-evidently imper - fect states are incapable of fostering the common good, forcing the world community to step in.[41] As Mégret notes, the diplomats, NGOs and scholars who drove the ICC negotiations were generally unconcerned with ensuring national courts would fulf l their duties under international law and discussed the idea of the Court 'long before they even had given the slightest attention to the issue of relations with national jurisdictions'.[42] In the negotiations for the Rome Statute a number of actors present called for the ICC to serve as the sole venue for prosecuting crimes on the basis that universal jurisdiction rendered certain 'hard-core' crimes outside the exclusive authority of states,[43] while others argued it should enjoy primary jurisdiction with national courts merely exercising residual jurisdiction.[44] Delegates were implored not to let 'outmoded notions of state sovereignty … derail the forward movement' seeking to achieve international peace and order .[45] This chapter goes on to examine how and why the Rome Statute negotiations rejected the   *Tadic-* model supranational primacy and instead prioritized the sovereign duty to prosecute in a later section. However, it should be noted at the outset that its fairly exacting complementarity regime has been decried as an unseemly sacrif ce of justice to sovereignty   [46] and a less than desirable common denominator[47] because it prioritizes the duty of the national criminal justice system over the new international apparatus in The Hague. NGOs, f nding the Court's admissibility requirements 'at variance with the better objectives of international criminal justice' have greeted the complementarity regime with resignation.[48]

It should not be forgotten that when states punish serious crimes, they not only protect the values of the national legal order   , but also those of the international legal community simultaneously .[49] As such, the future of international criminal law and the model that clearly emer   ged from the negotiations on the Rome Statute is not a supranational court with automatic primary jurisdiction over the most serious criminals that would exclude national courts, but rather a model of progressive rapprochement and harmonization of national criminal justice systems with international criminal law vis-à-vis the treatment of mass atrocity .[50] While it is common to view the ICC as a ref   ection of the shortcomings of the international order,[51] the Rome Statute represents a 'principled and pragmatic' way to accommodate the sometimes conf icting but more often mutually-reinforcing imperatives of state sovereignty and a global legal order .[52] In other branches of international law scholars readily accept that the future of international law lies in its ability to 'affect, inf   uence, bolster, backstop and even mandate specif c actors in domestic politics' through checking and monitoring the state's performance of obligations it already accepts.[53] On this view, the goals of international criminal justice are best realized through direct international assistance to domestic justice systems. [54] The shortcomings of states' actions to combat impunity should be remedied (in the parlance of the *Rule of Law and Transitional Justice Report*) not by the substitution of international models, but by the type of solidarity that would foster domestic effectiveness and legitimacy.

If the preference in scholarship and among NGOs for international primacy was merely academic, then their reservations about the pro-sovereignty 'take-it-or-leave-it' jurisdictional regime of international criminal law f nalized at Rome could simply be noted. However , international criminal justice is probably the most obvious area where civil society advocacy and scholarship have impacted on the practice of transitional justice. As V injamuri and Snyder observe:

> Legalists who stress these justif cations for war crimes tribunals have permeated human rights-based nongovernmental organizations (NGOs), international organizations, and universities. More than any other professional class, lawyers have moved freely among these institutions and taken leadership roles in the international tribunals whose creation they have advanced. [55]

Roht-Arriaza, for example, ar gues that once NGOs and human rights organizations began to shift their attention from documenting violations under war or repression to ending impunity for them in transition, the 'f rst result' was the establishment of the ad hoc tribunals. [56] NGOs have been the strongest enthusiasts for international tribunals, most notably the 800 NGOs present in the Coalition for an International Criminal Court at the Rome Conference. [57] In terms of the ICC' s complementarity regime which governs the interaction of domestic rule of law institutions with the Court, actual case-law is greatly outstripped by the volume of scholarly analysis and policy papers that attempt to predict or affect how it is interpreted, making this inf uence even more pronounced.

As Batros notes, international tribunals have internal interests in being active and prominent which are distinct from the external interests of other entities, such as states or peace-building missions[58] The thrust of international criminal justice has coalesced around 'a new culture of human rights and human responsibility, in which there can be no impunity'. [59] This is a goal positioned somewhere between a purely retributive theory of *lex talionis* and a belief in more expansive utilitarian rationales examined in the previous chapter. Simply put, punishment is just and avoidance of such punishment is intolerable. To the extent that some perpetrators, often the most serious, are tried and punished, impunity can be said to have been combated, if not entirely defeated. The more readily attainable opportunity to demonstrate immediate progress in relation to criminal accountability for human rights abuses has trumped a more long-term concern for the viability of the national justice system. This is a phenomenon that has been exacerbated by the noted tendency of the Security Council and donor countries put pressure on international institutions to demonstrate that objectives are being fulf   lled quickly.[60]

The limited ambition of international criminal justice has frustrated many scholars and activists who regret its lack of impact on broader societal conditions, such as the economy and social repair .[61] As this chapter goes on to note, the ad hoc tribunals, hybrid courts and ICC are similarly criticized for their failure to contribute to the development of the rule of law domesti-cally, but this is merely symptomatic of a wider mar ginalization by interna-tional justice policy-makers of purposes not immediately related to ending impunity. Any intention to integrate international criminal trials with holistic rule of law reform has historically remained at the margins of policy-making when formulating and operating internationalized judicial responses to gross human rights violations. [62] Those who negotiated and operated the Nuremberg and Tokyo trials, the ad hoc tribunals, hybrid courts and the ICC have proven more concerned with creating a global culture of accountability or non-impunity as a goal in itself than fostering the domestic rule of law   , and are at best agnostic as to whether international criminal law has a benef cial impact on the national justice system:

> [W]hile other sectors have paid more attention to the idea of building domestic capacity and creating exit strategies, war crimes tribunals have remained largely unconcerned with these projects ... The human rights community has concerns about whether it is even normatively desirable to elevate the goal of capacity-building to the level of other goals of accountability mechanisms. This position assumes that certain important principles intrinsic to fully achieving accountability will be sacrif ced if collaboration increases with domestic institutions and people. [63]

As this chapter goes on to ar gue, because attempts to establish an interna-tional rule of law have systematically taken precedence over developing domestic rule of law, opportunities to harmonize the two perspectives have consistently been squandered. The rest of this chapter goes on to illustrate how this has happened at the ad hoc tribunals, in various hybrid courts and the ICC. Greater emphasis is given to the latter given its permanence.

5.2 The ad hoc tribunals: internationalization unlimited

The ad hoc tribunals for the Former Y   ugoslavia and Rwanda remain the primary examples of the prioritization of the development of international criminal law over the empowerment of national courts. While both statutes recognized national courts would enjoy concurrent jurisdiction with the ad hoc tribunals, the latter would enjoy primacy , meaning that at any stage of the procedure, the ICTY or ICTR could formally request national courts to defer to its competence regardless of how far domestic proceedings had gone or without having to establish inability or bad faith. [64] The language of the global rule of law was very much in evidence – in setting up the tribunals, the Security Council explained that it was acting to put an end to crimes being committed, to bring those responsible to justice, and to maintain peace.[65] As noted above, in the *Tadic* decision primacy was viewed by the ICTY Appeals Chamber as a practical necessity to overcome nationabbstacles to accountability rooted in politics and as a conceptual necessity to refect the nature of the crimes.

The ICTY and ICTR undoubtedly enjoyed some successes, especially in terms of general fairness, development of international criminal and humanitarian law and incapacitation of leaders, as well as paving the way for the ICC. However, by the turn of the century, there emerged a consensus that the emphasis on successful, internationally-driven *outcomes* excluded many other achievable goals that were thought to fow more naturally from, or were made more achievable by , criminal *processes* with greater state ownership. After all, it was the rule of law weaknesses in both areas that compelled the creation of the courts (the technically able former Y ugoslav entities as the paradigmatic examples of politically unwilling states and Rwanda the epitome of the collapsed, unable criminal justice system), but it became apparent that the tribunals would do nothing to rectify these situations. The ICTY's self-identif ed 'Five Core Achievements', namely spearheading the shift from impunity to accountability , establishing a historical record of the conf ict, bringing justice to victims, accomplishments in international law and the strengthening of the (international) rule of law demonstrate the short-term, transitional internality of its interests – longer -term issues of capacity-building, the inculcation of fair trial norms or legitimacy in the domestic courts played little role in this reckoning. [66] Tolbert, in a review of the ICTY, argued that the tribunal suffered from 'a strategic failure in that [it] has not had much impact on the development of courts and justice systems in the region'.[67]

While the ad hoc tribunals' lack of local legitimacy has been extensively catalogued (their lack of domestic control fed allegations of imperialism, [68] their foreign location created a psychological distance from the affected communities,[69] they tended to be seen as ref ecting the goals of the international community over those of Rwanda, Bosnia, Serbia or Croatia), their lack of impact on the national justice systems was less frequently noted. At a time when the peace-building community was trying to reconstruct national institutions in Rwanda and the Balkan states, the international community was very publicly de-legitimizing the national judiciary regardless of the extent to which it was reforming or restructuring by denying them the chance to try local war criminals under the primacy model. A highlyinf uential study in 2000 of Bosnians from every ethnic group in the legal profession of their perceptions of the ICTY found that they were suspicious of its inf uence on perceptions of domestic justice, above all in its procedural and substantive law that diverged from the standards applied domestically .[70] Similar fears were visible in relation to the ICTR. As Alvarez put it:

> Each time the Rwandan legal system is denied the right to put on trial a prominent member of the former regime, the international community is sending an implicit (if perhaps intended) message that Rwandan institutions cannot be trusted or that its judiciary is not ready to implement the rule of law.[71]

This in one sense is not troubling given that there was little indication that national courts at the time were willing and/or able to prosecute with a basic level of competence or fairness. Vindictive, ethnic-based injustice was rife in the former Yugoslav courts,[72] while the Rwandan courts were swamped with genocidaires and unable to attain basic levels of fairness.   [73] However, the stratif ed-concurrent jurisdiction of the courts was fundamentally premised on the fact that the domestic courts would also undertake prosecutions, albeit of f gures at lower levels than those before the ad hoc tribunals.   [74] International criminal justice has never been justif   ed on the basis that international trials of ring-leaders would suff ce – the expectation has always been that any international trials would stimulate and complement national ones.[75]

However, there was little interest on the part of the ad hoc tribunals in developing the justice sector in Rwanda or the Balkan states in their f   rst decade. As noted above, no specifc remit to do so was included in the Statute, and the Tribunals were judged by lar gely internal goals. As such, the actors in the Tribunals had little incentive to invest time or ener   gy in domestic prosecutions since they would have no 'payoff ' as the established criteria of success 'f rmly prioritized international prosecution'.[76] This is best illustrated by the Rules of the Road Programme developed in 1996 to prevent ethnically-motivated prosecutions. This provided that the ICTY had to review case f les from the Bosnia-Herzegovina authorities to ascertain there was suff cient evidence to justify the belief that a suspect may havecommitted a serious violation of international criminal law before domestic indictments could be issued. Though effectively operating as a procedural f   lter to mandate prosecutions for the domestic courts, 'it did little to either improve the skills or capacity of prosecutors or judicial authorities'. [77] Between 1997 and 2005, the ICTY reviewed approximately 1,072 cases involving 3,360 suspects before handing them over to the Bosnian State Prosecutor. However, this resulted in only 94 trials and 73 investigations[78] while doing nothing to alleviate the prevalent bias and corruption. [79]

Indeed, far from developing these domestic capacities, the ICTY might have impeded the process. Because of the sclerosis in the Rules of the Road Programme (referring cases to national authorities attracted little attention and few resources in the ICTY)[80] and the risk that any politically signif cant prosecution could be whisked away from national authorities by the Tibunal, the Programme 'shut down all efforts by Bosnian government authorities to utilize justice to remove war criminals from powerful post-war positions'. [81] The transfer of cases to the domestic judiciary was deemed to lie outside the ICTY's duties and so no budgetary support for national trials was provided from the Tribunal's budget.[82] Burke-White posits that the ICTY generally 'froze out' judicial reform in Bosnia-Herzegovina between its foundation in 1993 and the development of a completion strategy in 2002. The jurisdictional relationship of absolute international primacy which conditioned the exercise of any domestic jurisdiction on aff rmative authorization by the ICTY led domestic authorities to under -invest in the institutional forms necessary to promote an effective judiciary .[83] By the early Noughties, the infantilizing effect of ICTY judicial hegemony was such that Bosnian entity governments neglected to undertake meaningful reform of their judiciaries to deal with human rights abuses because they 'did not believe that state institutions could or should do the job'. [84]

The ad hoc courts had no capacity-building or training remit towards the domestic courts to counteract the disincentives for development imposed by their jurisdiction. The T ribunals were staffed and administered almost exclusively by foreigners. Any contact between the ad hoc courts and the domestic courts has been more about the pursuit of accountability in the former than development of the latter .[85] The lack of any sort of sustainable connection meant that Croatian prosecutors played no part in investigating the crimes with international colleagues, Rwandan judges played no role in adjudicating the trials of their countrymen, and to a lesser extent national defence counsel were side-lined in defendants' trials. This becomes all the more unfortunate when one considers how the sheer size and complexity of the cases and the qualif cations of the staff involved could have trained domestic actors in almost all conceivable skills that a domestic criminal court requires. Instead, lack of integration meant that for the most part, Balkan or Rwandan judges and lawyers did not understand ICTY procedures, which applied a mix of civil and common law procedures unfamiliar to them. Bosnian judges have gone on record to describe their dismay at the lack of impact of the ICTY in the development of the domestic judiciary .[86]

A UN Expert Group established to review the ICTY in 1999 expressed concern at its failure to engage with the states under its jurisdiction and its omission to improve judicial capacity.[87] It would not be until 2002 that the Court began to rectify this with the acceleration of the Completion Strategy's Rule 11*bis* process which began to stimulate local rule of law reconstruction[88] One can ar gue this is a more representative example of how international criminal tribunals interact with justice sector reform. However , as the next section argues in examining the Bosnian W ar Crimes Chamber, the ICTY's assistance was more catalytic than integral, and was guided more by the inter nal demands of its completion strategy than a desire to improve the domestic rule of law. Though there is some suggestion that Rule 11 *bis* should serve as a model for ICC–state interaction in the complementarity regime, Sections

5.5–5.7 go on to demonstrate that the developmental impulses stimulated by the Rule 11*bis* referral bench have no analogue in the present ICC.

It should be remembered that the delegates at the Rome conference rejected international primacy with the geographically- and time-bound ad hoc model f rmly in their minds, explicitly emphasizing the exceptional nature of those institutions [89] and expressing a desire to avoid the bitter jurisdictional disputes that marred the ad hoc tribunals' relationships with the states most concerned. [90] Some even ar gue that the complementarity regime was a retrospective attempt to rectify the aforementioned def ciencies in stimulating accountability domestically .[91] Complementarity for many delegates at Rome was not therefore a 'reluctant concession to realpolitik' as it has been presented, 'but a sound operating rule that recognizes that trials closer to the scene of events at issue have inherent practical as well as expressive value'.[92] Nevertheless, amidst all the later talk of positive complementarity at the ICC there appears to be a form of willed amnesia about the ICTY and ICTR – as Lipscomb notes, few commentators have directly linked the limitations of the ad hoc tribunals to complement justice sector reform with the even weaker structure of ICC when assuming jurisdiction. [93]

5.3 Hybrid courts: a promise unfulfilled

Though hybrid courts were constituted primarily as a response to the shortcomings of domestic courts in the types of transitional states examined in Chapter 2, it was also expected that the 'hybrid' element would also serve to remedy one of the main problems visible in fully international courts, namely their failure to catalyse or stimulate the revitalization of domestic rule of law structures. It was widely predicted that hybrid courts could merge the best elements of both international and domestic systems as a more successful and sustainable means of transitional accountability[94] The primary advantage claimed for hybrid tribunals was that their domestic staff ng (in either a majority or minority) and location within the state avoided the earlier legitimacy def cit identif ed in the ad hoc tribunals. The hybrid courtstructure was posited as a means of importing legitimacy to successor trials in politicized and hostile environments; the presence of international judges and prosecutors in either a majority or minority would alleviate fears of impartiality   , while the trials would enjoy presumptive legitimacy in the eyes of the local population as judges of their own nationality would meaningfully participate as actors in the tribunal. [95] It was anticipated that this sense of ownership would increase the relevancy of the trials for the survivor populations and accord with the emerging consensus that nationally-led strategies were more conducive to sustainable peace-building.[96]

It was furthermore expected that hybrid tribunals would perform a capacity-building function by serving to instruct the domestic court system in how trials should generally be operated, and by developing the abilities of judges, prosecutors, defenders and administrators who might gradually be empowered to assume full responsibility.[97] To adopt a timeworn development cliché, while the ad hoc tribunals f shed for justice, hybrids could teach how to f sh. For example, Cohen ar gued that hybrid composition 'offers unique opportunities for capacity-building in all areas of the court ... T raining and mentoring court actors and administrators ... represent some of the most important contributions that a "hybrid" tribunal can make.' [98] Even if there was no formal mentoring component, it was presumed that on conclusion of hybrid tribunals, local staff returning to the domestic system would have learned valuable lessons and skills from the process. It was furthermore argued that links could be formed between the domestic and hybrid institutions that would inf uence domestic law reform. [99] If the national government had experience of the practical running of a fair and competent special court, it appeared to follow that it could apply these lessons in operating an international-standard domestic system.

Thirdly, it was predicted that having local judges and lawyers participating in high-prof le, foundational trials in their own country would have a benef cial 'demonstration effect' on emerging local legal systems, by offering exemplary standards of independence, impartiality and fair trial norms that would inculcate a cultural commitment among the public to such yardsticks. Writers in the f eld have proposed that hybrid tribunals would allow greater opportunities for public debate,[100] construct networks between international experts and the local judiciary, encourage cross-fertilization of international and domestic norms, and serve as a platform on which the local people 'absorb, apply, interpret, critique and develop' international norms in the national criminal justice system. [101] As such, hybrid tribunals would cross a psychological Rubicon; where something like the right to habeas corpus is seen as imperative in one context within a state, it would assume a validity and force of its own in analogous contexts within that state in future. The UN Secretary's General's *Report on Transitional Justice and the Rule of Law* repeated many of the academic arguments in favour of hybrid structures that emerged after their formation, ar guing that 'specially tailored measures for keeping the public informed and effective techniques for capacity-building, can help ensure a lasting legacy in the countries concerned'. [102]

Notwithstanding their f nancial shortcomings and lack of diplomatic support, the hybrid tribunals for East Timor, Cambodia, Kosovo, Sierra Leone and Bosnia should be commended for establishing accountability where the alternative was systematic impunity in their respective theatres of operation. In Sierra Leone and Cambodia, the leading f gures bearing greatest responsibility for the crimes coming within the jurisdiction of the hybrid tribunals were indicted, prosecuted or convicted by the respective courts. The Timorese Special Panels completed 55 trials in four years, resulting in over 80 convictions, albeit not including the most senior Indonesian organizers of the violence surrounding the 1999 referendum.[103] Kosovo yielded jurisdiction to the ICTY for the prosecution of the most serious criminals from the Kosovar war, but nonetheless completed 23 prosecutions that reversed or re-tried earlier ethnically-biased verdicts.[104] Notwithstanding some disparity in the numbers of indictments, prosecutions and trials, the current and completed tribunals did something revolutionary in each society: they punished egregious breaches of human rights in state courts for the f rst time, when impunity of the sort that could imperil peace had previously been the norm. Beyond this retributive impulse, another limited but essential goal was achieved. By processing criminals in East Timor, Cambodia and Sierra Leone and by reversing unjust convictions in Kosovo, the inf uence of certain individuals and the potency of particular revanchist appeals based on political allegiance or ethnicity was reduced, and the potential for retributive attacks or instability receded in the formative years of the emer ging peace. Though these outcomes f t within the parameters of what transitional criminal trials are traditionally designed to achieve, what is apparent in each tribunal is the consistent failure to go further in developing capacity , inculcating fair trial norms or legitimizing the idea of law in the eyes of the survivor population. The completed hybrid courts have been subject to withering criticism in these respects.[105]

Hopes for capacity-building and for local ownership have continually fallen short of expectations. Initially, it was ar gued that local ownership imported by the hybrid model should be maximized to the extent compatible with fair and competent trials in the pursuit of legitimacy and capacity-building. [106] However, the reality in the years between 2000 and 2003 when hybrid tribunals were in their infancy was that UN off cials were simultaneously vetoing negotiations with Cambodia because local participation was too great,[107] UNMIK was progressively weakening Kosovar participation in the most important trials,[108] and the Sierra Leonean Government was voluntarily relinquishing ever-greater control over the bench and prosecution to internationals.[109] Though it was assumed that hybrid tribunals would be genuinely co-operative, the tendency of both controlling partners (the UN and the domestic governments) in most tribunals has been to transfer as much responsibility to international actors as possible in order to secureconvictions. For example, contrary to the logic of progressive development where international involvement is phased out over time, each phase in UNMIK' s judicial response to insecurity was marked by an increase in international judges. It ran counter to intuitions and early expectations among writers in the area that as the domestic system is strengthened, international involvement would be decreased. Instead, what occurred was a reactive 'linear reverse model' that initially gave responsibility to Kosovars only to then wrest it back. [110] Naarden and Locke argue that international prosecutors 'often had a negative impact on the institutional development of local prosecutorial services, as the decision by an I[nternational] P[rosecutor] to assume a case frustrated the opportunity to "test" the hypothesis that local prosecutors were unable or unwilling to take on that case'. [111] Instead of responding to widespread dismay over ongoing impunity , over time international prosecutors moved from ethnically sensitive prosecutions of war crimes to those gangland crimes local prosecutors were too fearful to take. Similar infantilization was evident in East Timor and to a lesser extent in Sierra Leone. The reluctance of each state (bar Cambodia) to assume ownership of the process increased the likelihood of marginalization of national judges and prosecutors into minor assistance positions, and could only serve to further diminish any sense of ownership the local legal community may have had in the hybrid process. International dominance in hybrid courts undermined any legitimating effect localization of the processes had, reinforcing what Perriello and W ierda call 'the spaceship phenomenon' where the court was seen by the national community as an irrelevant, alien presence.[112]

While domestic authorities were largely marginalized or disengaged from each tribunal, the international staff who dominated the processes were primarily focused on the traditional goal of closing the impunity gap, at the expense of the necessarily time-consuming project of transferring their skills to domestic actors.[113] Mentoring and professional development played little role in any of the mixed tribunals, which were hybrid in form but rarely in ethos. This suggests that professional development and mentoring will invariably suffer diminished roles where successor justice is conceptualized primarily as a matter of combating impunity . Legacy planning was never specif cally incorporated into the mandates of the tribunals, and so was de-prioritized. As an OHCHR policy document on hybrid tribunals puts it:

> Without an explicit mandate on the issue, the interpretation of legacy is, to a large extent, left to the discretion of individual actors. Many will automatically gravitate to an approach which focuses on the eff cient disposing of cases.[114]

Far from catalysing domestic assumption of responsibility , in both East Timor and Kosovo the hybrid tribunals built dependence over time rather than competence. Independent observers of the T imorese justice system which remained dominated by international judges and prosecutors in the years after the Special Panels consistently warned against the dangers of a 'dependency syndrome'.[115] This is notably similar to the position of international authorities in Kosovo, where a decade after the f rst mixed Panels international judges still 'tend[ed] to handle the more challenging cases, including politically-charged crimes and ethnically divisive disputes'. [116] Though the structure of the Extraordinary Chambers in the Courts of Cambodia (ECCC) ref ected an explicit lack of conf dence on the part of the UN in the Cambodian justice system, [117] no systematic effort is being made through the process to improve it. Simply put, the imperative to complete as many cases as possible in the shortest period of time is not consistent with the type of patient, on-the-job integration successful mentoring requires. The experience of the hybrid tribunals counsel a need to be realistic about their domestic capacity-building potential when their focus is so international in nature. The idea that a self-suff cient criminal justice system could arise in such diff cult post-conf ict conditions from a mentoring process in courts with other more pressing short-term requirements is in retrospect obviously over-optimistic and f nds little support in judicial reconstruction literature.

Advocates of the hybrid structure further contended that the very process of trying cases fairly, meeting procedural requirements, applying clear law and generating inarguably just convictions could contribute to the permeation of these legal and human rights norms throughout the national courts. Worryingly given its systematic and institutional nature, of all the elements of a fair trial, inequality of arms is the one where the hybrid courts fell most short. In most hybrid tribunals, the objective of eff ciently prosecuting the mandated number of indictees took precedence over the need to provide anything more (and sometimes less) than the most rudimentary defence structures. While the UN T ransitional Administration in East T imor (UNTAET) passed Regulation 2000/16 governing prosecutors, there was no new legislation to regulate the provision of defence in Special Panel trials, though an under-resourced Defence Lawyers Unit was belatedly created in 2002.[118] As Cohen noted, '[i]t appears simply not to have occurred to the UN administration that provision had to be made for defense, particularly in the post-conf ict situation where no experienced lawyers were available'. [119] Neither Kosovo's Regulation 2000/64 nor its predecessors provided for international defenders or a specialized hybrid defence off ce, even in cases related to war crimes. [120] At the SCSL, a Defence Off ce was created to centralize a number of defence functions in one location. [121] However, even here, defence was merely an 'afterthought' created after the Sierra Leone/UN agreement to establish the Court. [122] The prosecution budget of US$83 million dwarfed the defence's US$4 million at the tribunal's busiest period, demonstrating a greater concern to secure prosecutions than to vindicate the autonomy of the individual before the courts. [123] Equality of arms has improved in the later Khmer Rouge trials – Rule 11 of the Internal Rules of the ECCC outlines the duties of a specialized Defence Support Section (DSS) in supporting the one foreign and one domestic Co-Lawyer each defendant is entitled to, though observers note a consistent problem of short-staff ng, meaning that suspects have been interviewed without the presence of defence lawyers, while the DSS has no role in detention issues.[124] While it is diff cult to point to individual cases where an accused may have been acquitted by better defence (though the Special Panels' coercive plea-bargaining process is a possible exception), [125] the complicity on the part of the international community in the systematic weighting of the court apparatus against defendants suggests that vigorous criminal defence is seen as an impediment to the proper working of the courts rather than an essential element. In addition to inequality of arms, unduly delayed trials were a common factor across all tribunals. This too was in keeping with the shift in human rights law from a defence-based to a prosecution-based perspective, [126] but undermined the example of the tribunals in respecting the fair trial rights of citizens tried before them. All hybrid courts at one stage or another lacked suff cient equipment, security and administrative staff   ng to demonstrate competent trials in action due to lack of resources. [127] While all have been criticized for failing to exemplify commonly accepted international fair trial standards, it could hardly be otherwise given the lack of resources and the need to co-opt under-qualif ed domestic lawyers and judges whose failure to attain such standards was the *raison d'être* of the tribunals in the f rst place.

The impact of a trial process on the domestic justice system remains in a subordinate position in the normative hierarchy of priorities of those in supranational organizations tasked with responding judicially to gross violations of human rights and the laws of war . Although it has also been argued that hybrid tribunals could achieve their more holistic promise through greater investment in resources, [128] a thorough re-orientation of purpose is what is most required. The Bosnian W ar Crimes Chamber shows what can be achieved when a more sustainable mindset applies, and represents the best reconciliation of the global rule of law with the domestic to date. Indeed, it has been hailed as a belated rectif cation of the ICTY's non-involvement in national legal orders.[129] As with Kosovo, fears over the loss of skilled judges since the war , bias, unfair arrests and ethnic prosecutions motivated the internationalization of domestic processes of accountability in Bosnia,[130] though the primary motivation was the ICTY'   s completion strategy. Security Council Resolution 1503 (2003) ur ged the T ribunal to complete all trial activities by the end of 2008 and all of its work in 2010.[131] The process was to be facilitated by focusing 'on the prosecution and trial of the most senior leaders suspected of being responsible for crimes' while 'transferring cases involving those who may not bear this level of responsibility to competent national jurisdictions', specifying a special chamber within the State Court of Bosnia-Herzegovina.[132] Rule 11*bis* of the ICTY's amended Rules of Procedure and Evidence enabled the transfer of cases to national authorities by an ICTY referral panel of judges after considering the gravity of the crimes, whether the accused could be guaranteed a fair trial, and whether or not the death penalty would be applied. [133]

In 2005 a Bosnian W ar Crimes Chamber (BWCC) was created within the State Court and a Special Department for War Crimes was established within the State Prosecutor's Off ce. Until 2008, there were f ve trial panels and two appellate panels containing two international judges and one domestic judge. The Special Department for W ar Crimes was also of mixed composition. After 2008, the composition switched to two Bosnians and one international,[134] with the ultimate aim of becoming fully national by 2009 (later extended to 2012).[135] Though conceived as a joint initiative of the ICTY and Off ce of the High Representative, the or ganizing principle of the Chamber was that accountability remains the responsibility of the Bosnian people. [136] This principle had a more sustainable effect on national capacity-building because the BWCC was to be a permanent national structure with a six-phase plan to transition from international dependence to a fully-functioning national court. Certainly by comparison to the other hybrid courts, the

BWCC model was a more appealing model of sustainability and ownership. Within two years, there were 41 national judges to 7 international ones. Commendably, international judges and prosecutors have deliberately played a 'behind-the-scenes role', deferring to their national counterparts in all bar the initial Rule 11 *bis* referrals.[137] One judge claimed that '[i]t is good that nationals take responsibility ... In the long-term it is the only way to restore public confidence in the judiciary.'[138] Indeed, the mentoring relationship in Bosnia has been reversed, with international judges being assigned local mentors.[139] This has not been at the expense of productivity – between 2005 and 2010, the BWCC handed down trial verdicts in over 60 cases of war crimes, crimes against humanity and genocide that arose during the war.[140]

Bosnification has not been accelerated to the detriment of fair trial, even if issues endure over lenient sentencing, prison escapes and defendants with mental health issues.[141] The ICTY confirmed that the Chamber was fully capable of providing the defendant Radovan Stankovic with a fair trial in the first referral by the Appeals Chamber to Sarajevo,[142] and subsequent trials have been generally endorsed as fair.[143] International actors have increased awareness of international human rights instruments and fair trial rights.[144] Judges writing judgments and prosecutors formulating indictmentsregularly refer to the European Convention on Human Rights, adding force to the Bosnian Constitution's provision in Article 2(2) that the Convention shall apply directly in Bosnia and Herzegovina and 'shall have priority over all other law'.[145] Judges and prosecutors are deliberately recruited from the three main ethnic groups, helping to draw a line in the sand from the era of biased prosecutions and convictions. Criminal defence has mostly been by Bosnians, spurring an extraordinary amount of training by the BWCC' s Criminal Defence Support Section – within the first two years, it had trained approximately 350 lawyers.[146] After the overall Bosnian Criminal Procedure Code was revolutionized in 2003 to switch from an accusatorial system to a more common law adversarial process, international staff in the Chamber were commended for contributing to the capacity of local legal professionals in applying it.[147]

It might therefore be argued that the BWCC points the way forward in international criminal law. It certainly demonstrates a commitment to sustainability and domestic ownership that international criminal justice has hitherto not distinguished itself by. A number of scholars and practitioners have argued that the Rule 11*bis* model should be adopted by the ICC in some form in order to regulate the interaction or division of labour between domestic and international fora.[148] However, closer inspection suggests an enduringly insular preoccupation with international criminal law that calls into question the BWCC' s general applicability to other peace-building ecologies, while the context in which the BWCC operated is so *sui generis* that its relevance may be questioned.

To begin with, the BWCC was born not of a need to develop the domestic rule of law, but was instead mostly a continuance of the ICTY' s priorities.

Resolution 1503 certainly spurred Bosnia's Peace Implementation Council to prioritize justice sector reconstruction, [149] and court f gures argue national development was an ancillary goal.[150] However, it is widely accepted that the BWCC was 'born primarily as a result of a drive to ensure the completion of the work of the ICTY ... it would appear that, were it not for the ICTY Completion Strategy, national capacities such as those which are now in existence may never have been created'.[151] While standards of trial have been high, most cases have dealt with war crimes and crimes against humanity which will have limited application to the other branches of the Bosnian legal system in an era of peace and stability. As Ortega-Martin and Herman note, '[t]his makes it less important that the [B]WCC or State Court, in general, participate in direct capacity-building to the rest of the members of the judiciary'.[152] The capacity it sought to develop was entirely limited to war crimes, and as such the skills it has developed, the legitimacy for the rule of law it has garnered and the fair trial norms it has inculcated may be ring-fenced in war crime trials indef nitely – the National War Crimes Prosecution Strategy states that around 8,000 people remain under investigation.[153] Most assistance by the ICTY has been in the transfer of evidence and materials, as opposed to know-how and skills. [154] While it is undoubtedly useful for a Bosnian justice system to punish war crimes in the long-term, an approach of merely dividing labour with the ICTY is perhaps less ambitious than the hopes many advocates entertained for the capacity-building potential of hybrid tribunals. It also is worth remembering that the ICTY may only defer to national proceedings if the crimes and responsibility of the accused involve intermediate or lower -level indictees[155] – notwithstanding justice sector reform and willingness to prosecute, the ICTY in *Milosevic* reiterated that certain cases are better placed before an international forum whereas as other less important cases would also be suitable for trial by national courts. [156] Increases in national trial competence were never matched with an increase in international willingness to allow the state courts to establish their ability to try the most serious cases. In Rwanda, despite granting requests for transfer to other countries' courts, the ICTR has repeatedly denied applications for transfer to Kigali notwithstanding efforts by the Government to meet the requirements for a successful transfer to a domestic jurisdiction set forth in Rule 11*bis* through legislated judicial reform.[157]

One can of course ar gue that a more general development of the criminal courts through the BWCC is unnecessary given the parallel work being done in rule of law reconstruction in Bosnia. It is worth remembering that the BWCC is merely one of three Chambers of mixed-international composition operating within the Criminal Division of the State Court of Bosnia, the others being Or ganized Crime and General Crime Chambers. Indeed, the judges may sit simultaneously in the different chambers. Each project is intended to be fully absorbed into the national courts. As one observer points out, 'although it contains a signif cant international component, the [B]WCC is essentially a domestic institution operating under international law'. [158]

This difference is worth remembering when examining its superior perfor -
mance relative to the other hybrid courts. Bosnia-Herzegovina has existed as
a de facto protectorate of the EU's Off ce of the High Representative, whose
policy objective is 'a stable, viable, peaceful and multiethnic BiH, cooperat-
ing peacefully with its neighbors and irreversibly on track towards EU
membership'.[159] To the extent it has performed better than other hybrid
tribunals or international courts, it may be as a result of the signif   cant
advantages it enjoyed and that may not be replicated in African, Asian or
Latin American states, most notably the amount of European support. Former
ICTY judge Fausto Pocar admits that the EU's interest in developing Balkan
judiciaries effectively meant all BWCC work could remain off the ICTY' s
books.[160] While Rule 11*bis* in theory put the ICTY in a position to monitor
the quality of the domestic judiciary , its inquiry generally consists of an
extremely superf cial determination of whether an adequate legal framework
for a fair trial exists,[161] while ongoing monitoring pursuant to Rule 11 *bis*(D)
is primarily performed by the OSCE.[162] Though generally enthusiastic about
the Chamber, Ivanisevic warns that the Bosnian model may not be applied
easily elsewhere because '[t]he creation of the War Crimes Chamber has taken
place 10 years after the end of the war , in a country with a functioning
infrastructure and administration, skilled human resources, a strong and
powerful international presence under the political authority of the OHR
[Off ce of the High Commissioner]'.[163]

5.4 The Rome Statute system of justice: help or hegemon?

Chapter 4 argues that the domestic state is generally the most appropriate
forum for the prosecution of serious crimes committed within it in the past.
However, as the experience of Rwanda, the Balkans and the hybrid courts
demonstrate, in the societies of most interest to the ICC some or all of the
prerequisites for competent trial will rarely be present. Many states will prove
unable or unwilling to fulf l their sovereign duty . As a result, the desire
expressed by some states in the ICC's negotiation process for national *primacy*
even if proceedings lacked competence or were intended to shield defendants
was not realized.[164] What instead emer ged was a *preference* for domestic
proceedings, as seen in the Preambular references to effective prosecution
being ensured by taking measures at national level   [165] and the duty of
states to exercise their criminal jurisdiction.   [166] Under Article 17, for a
case to be admissible before the ICC, the Court must be satisf   ed that
domestic authorities have not pursued or are not pursuing the case. If
they have pursued it or are pursuing it, the Court must satisfy itself that
these efforts are/were the product of genuine willingness and ability to investigate or prosecute. [167] In terms of unwillingness, the Court examines
whether:

(a) The proceedings were or are being undertaken or the national decision was made for the purpose of shielding the person concerned from criminal responsibility for crimes within the jurisdiction of the Court …;

(b) There has been an unjustified delay in the proceedings which in the circumstances is inconsistent with an intent to bring the person concerned to justice;

(c) The proceedings were not or are not being conducted independently or impartially, and they were or are being conducted in a manner which, in the circumstances, is inconsistent with an intent to bring the person concerned to justice.[168]

In terms of ability, the Court may inquire as to whether the state is able to undertake proceedings based on a consideration of 'whether due to a total or substantial collapse or unavailability of its national judicial system, the state is unable to obtain the accused or the necessary evidence and testimony or otherwise unable to carry out its proceedings'.[169] If the national proceedings are non-existent or not genuine, then the Office of the Prosecutor (OTP) may proceed with an investigation. The test applies at two phases of activity by the OTP; firstly, in the situational phase when the Prosecutor makes the initial decision to investigate a particular situation which requires a general examination of the national justice system's efforts to investigate or prosecute the same general circumstances, and secondly at the case stage when a certain suspect(s) and conduct have been identified, which requires a more categorical analysis of prosecutorial activity at the national level involving that suspect and conduct.

The standards set for a declaration of admissibility , though broad, are deliberately set quite high to secure states' priority over investigation and prosecution from ICC intrusion.[170] Indeed, in the *Katanga Admissibility Decision*, Trial Chamber II held that complementarity 'is designed to protect the sovereign rights of states to exercise their jurisdiction in good faith when they wish to do so'.[171] In the years between 1998 and the first actual prosecutions, there was a common understanding that the Court would operate in a merely residual manner as a 'last resort'[172] or as a 'safety net'.[173] Nevertheless, the Rome Statute strikes a balance between this sovereign duty and the need for effective international supervision. Sovereignty, though vindicated, is now fundamentally limited because the possibility of inactivity is removed from the realm of sovereign discretion, and actual activity is monitored to ensure it meets certain criteria.[174] The Court, and not the state, is the ultimate arbiter. However, states retain all rights not expressly transferred to the ICC, while Articles 18 and 19 place express further limits on the admissibility of cases to the Court. If the principle of complementarity operates as an integrated check on state sovereignty, then its precise statutory form represents a check on this check.[175] As such, the Rome Statute reflects neither the old state-voluntarist idea that all international law is sovereign-created nor the international human rights community's oft-stated belief that the content of sovereignty is def ned by international law . Instead, it ref ects a vision of sovereignty (as enjoying the primary duty) and international law (the supervising f nal arbiter) as mutually constituted.[176]

Admissibility determinations appear to revolve around cases where the state's legal and administrative structures are too weak to attempt prosecutions (the unable state) or where judicial institutions are restrained from exercising its jurisdictional competence (the unwilling state). If sovereignty , then, is to some degree conditioned on its proper usage, it follows that the ICC has a greater legitimate interest in encouraging and facilitating states to exercise their jurisdiction to make the international criminal justice system effective than to assume this responsibility itself.[177] As Lipscomb puts it:

> Arguably, it is maintaining effective judicial systems and stabilizing the rule of law, not ending [global] impunity, that enables nations emerging from conf ict to establish orderly systems that ensure protection of individual rights ... and prevent nations from sliding back into conf ict.[178]

This seemed to be the understanding of the f rst ICC Prosecutor when he emphasized in a much-quoted statement that the success of the Court would be determined not by its number of prosecutions, but by the number of international prosecutions avoided because of increased functioning of domestic legal systems.[179] The Assembly of States Parties at the Kampala Review Conference of the ICC in 2010 passed a resolution conf rming that the struggle against impunity required frst and foremost that states prosecute serious crimes committed in their territory or by their nationals.[180] However, they emphasized the need for practical steps to be taken to ensure that states willing but unable to do so were provided with necessary assistance to assume this duty[181] and for more coordination between international justice and rule of law actors at country level.[182]

As this section goes on to ar gue, there are solid reasons for believing the complementarity regime *could* play a key role in positively inf uencing the direction of domestic rule of law development. The concepts of inability and unwillingness closely map the concepts of institutional weakness and culture of illegality. Before the f rst glut of complementarity decisions were made in the closing years of the Noughties, scholars posited that the necessity for national governments to respond to ICC pressure would motivate and shape judicial reform efforts and that the Article 17 provisions would provide a skeletal blueprint for this work.[183] It should be noted that it is diff cult to state categorically what the Court's position on all elements of the distribution of rights and duties in Article 17 is given the paucity of illuminating case-law. Of the cases that have progressed furthest, the Uganda, DR Congo, and Central African Republic cases that have dominated the Court's workload have all reached the Court via effective self-referrals under Article 12(3), while the Sudan case arrived as a result of a Security Council referral. None of these states are transitional in the sense explored by this book.

These cases, characterized by excessive deference to the Court in the former examples and outright hostility in the latter, say little about how the Court can assist a state in a period of genuine transition that wishes to remedy its willingness or ability deficit. Because the Court largely operates in ongoing conflicts or severely conflicted democracies, only two genuinely transitional states have come to the attention of the Court, namely Libya (Security Council referral) and Côte d'Ivoire (a convoluted self-referral), which at the time of writing have not progressed very far. Kenya's challenge to the admissibility of cases pursuant to Article 19 in 2011 was the first time a State Party challenged admissibility by making reference to national proceedings.[184] Inferences drawn from the practice of the Court and the policy papers of the OTP about the impact of the complementarity regime on transitional states who wish to develop their capacity or will to try cases themselves are purely conjectural. Nevertheless, the case law that has emerged in the first ICC cases suggests a Court no more concerned with catalysing domestic rule of law reform than its predecessor tribunals in The Hague and Arusha, notwithstanding the roots of the Court in the institutional and cultural context of domestic impunity.

Complementarity was the 'deal-breaker' in negotiations on the creation of the ICC[185] and the drafters deliberately left as little opportunity as possible for later reinterpretation of the Statute[186] lest support for the Statute be unravelled.[187] However, far from working constructively to achieve the end of improved domestic fulfilment of their legal obligations, greater attention has been given to how to make the Court a more relevant and efficient actor in the international legal order. The Preambular declarations that the Court's purpose is to 'put an end to impunity' and 'contribute to the prevention of crimes' have operated to offer endless scope for the Statute to be reinterpreted teleologically in the light of these objects and purposes, above all to reflect a 'modern' model of international relations between states that would affirm the advantages of the *Tadic* approach and reject restrictive interpretations of the Statute that might limit ICC jurisdiction.[188] NGOs and scholars have preferred to retrospectively mend the Statute to reflect a more 'progressive' view than the Rome Conference's consensus.[189] They are helped in this by the fact that the phrase 'complementarity' itself is somewhat opaque – it is not mentioned in the Statute and appears in no dictionaries, seemingly leaving space to infer more proactive visions of the Court.[190]

Notwithstanding the deluge of commentary on the drafting processes, scholars have been able to find infinite vagueness, ambiguity and unclearness in the provisions of Article 17.[191] The Oxford English Dictionary understands its derivative 'complement' as meaning the completion or perfection of something else or as the supply of the other's deficiencies. Though Kleffner interprets this as implying the ICC and national courts naturally form a unit in the enforcement of ICC crimes, there is a fundamental difference between the ICC completing something as one (superior) half of a whole and the ICC as a replacement for the deficiencies of the state.[192] The latter view emphasizes the 'safety net/last resort' vision seemingly agreed upon in Rome. The former interpretation opens up something more expansive. As Jurdi (somewhat pejoratively) puts it, there is a negative view of complementarity among jurists which sees the ICC merely as a substitute for national trials when the national justice system fails to prosecute, and a positive view wherein Article 17 is only ever of relevance where there is a clash between the ICC and a state' s criminal jurisdiction. [193] This latter view would permit states to renounce the duty to prosecute and encourage the Court to take up the burden. This conf ict between 'strict' and 'liberal' interpretations contin- ues throughout the Statute, with diametrically opposed views of the role of the state. [194] For example, El Zeidy demonstrates a conf ict between Article 19(4)'s fortif cation of the state's duty to prosecute and Article 19 (8–11)' s reinforcement of the Court's ability to intervene, arguing that an emphasis by the Court on the former would suggest the Rome vision of complementarity had succeeded, while an emphasis on the latter would show the ICC emeging as a supranational institution 'with implied primacy which, although not ref ected in its statute, is ref ected in its practices'. [195]

If, as observers suggested just after the ICC came into effect, there is a balance to be struck between minimalism and over -assertiveness, the Court has erred on the side of the latter .[196] This development was not entirely unpredictable. As Judge Alvarez noted in the ICJ case on *Membership in the United Nations*, 'an institution, once established, acquires a life of its own, independent of the elements that gave birth to it, and must develop not in accordance with the views of those who created it, but in accordance with the requirements of international life'.[197] At the ad hoc tribunals, Schabas noted their 'diff culty of knowing when to stop … They may develop momentum of their own that soon becomes unhinged from the rationale that justif ed their creation in the f rst place.'[198] As the latter half of this chapter goes on to examine, with its policies on self-referrals, the same conduct test, the doctrine of positive complementarity and the growth of burden-sharing, the Court has moved towards a primacy model. Early predictions that Article 17' s require- ments 'may chafe an ICC prosecutor that sees them as an overly restrictive manifestation of arcane sovereignty principles' have been vindicated.[199]

Paradoxically, this self-assertiveness may be a ref ection of the Court' s general insecurity. Operating on a small annual budget (the 2010 allocation was €103.6m, signif cantly less than that enjoyed by the ad hoc tribunals at an equivalent stage, notwithstanding their narrower remits) and acting without the support of three of the fve permanent Security Council members, the Court has existed in a permanent state of weakness that belies earlier hopes for the Court. In its f rst six years there were only two suspects in custody, while the maximum workload envisaged in the next three was a paltry two to three trials per year.[200] States like Sudan, Uganda and Colombia have to varying degrees thumbed their noses at the Court with impunity The ICC Prosecutor's claim that the success of the Court would be determined not by its number of prosecutions, but by the number of domestic trials appeared to resolve the problem identif ed in the ad hoc tribunals of international judicial institutions lacking motivation to improve the domestic justice system. However, this deference to national jurisdiction has diminished in practice given the ICC's consistent need to justify its budget and avoid the type of inactivity that would 'kill' the Court. [201] As Schabas notes:

> The suggestion that the Court might measure its success by a paucity of cases was not a very compelling message for States Parties, who were investing large sums of money in the institution and who expected to see trials and convictions.[202]

The ICC's one-sided and enthusiastic collaborations with the relatively repressive governments of Uganda and DR Congo who appear to be using the Court to marginalize political rivals particularly have been seen as indicating a desperation for trials. [203] This assertiveness has had two main consequences. Firstly, the judges as gate-keepers of their docket may construe the Statute opportunistically to generate activity.[204] Secondly, they may favour retention of cases even where the state becomes willing or able. [205] There exists a risk (one possibly already realized) that the Court will operate on a cynical model of 'an inwardly focused court whose primary concern is not the well-being of societies recovering from mass atrocities, but instead the maintenance of a docket that will maximize the Court's own visibility and prestige'. [206] Seils and Schabas have criticized the Court for a mindset of 'looking for business' that has severely limited the Court's impact on national proceedings[207] and for working more to attract cases for prosecution than insisting states fulf l their obligations.[208]

Complementarity in practice is signif cantly different to complementarity in principle as enunciated in the Rome Conference:

> In treatment and conceptualization, the concept of complementarity has undergone a dynamic transformation. At the Rome Conference, complementarity was traditionally associated with the protection of domestic jurisdiction ... This focus has gradually shifted in the light of the f rst policies and practice of the Court, which were largely dictated by ideas of 'partnership', 'dialogue', and the promotion of co-operation by states. [209]

The rest of this chapter examines the consequences of this shift for the fruitful interaction of rule of law reconstruction with the ICC. It does so following two of the main axes of analysis already outlined in the book – institutional capacity-building and cultural commitment to the rule of law.

5.5 The ICC and domestic institution-building

As noted above, for a case to be admissible before the ICC on account of national inability, one of three disabling circumstances (total collapse of the judicial system, substantial collapse, or unavailability) must be present, notwithstanding domestic claims that the national system can manage a prosecution. These disabilities must then render the state unable to obtain evidence or the accused or otherwise unable to carry out proceedings. This final criterion of 'otherwise unavailable' covers most types of institutional weakness. The test is fact-driven, objective and not related to the quality of the trial or the risk of the state being overburdened by prosecutions. Circumstances where inability will be in question will typically be those of the type examined in Chapter 1 – state failure, war, post-authoritarian purge.

The distinction between total collapse and substantial collapse is difficult to define. Total collapse of the judiciary (i.e. failure to exist or operate) will usually follow the collapse of the state in a situation like East Timor or Somalia – its logical conclusion is complete inaction, automatically making the case admissible. [210] While reconstruction in such cases is imperative, internationalization of accountability is the only reasonable response given that basic functionality might be a decade away. Substantial collapse raises different possibilities. Though obviously indicating a serious degree of institutional weakness, the state may argue it has sufficient quality and/or quantity of personnel to prosecute successfully. International assistance to develop these capacities if the OTP or Pre-Trial Chamber deems them lacking could help secure competent trial if the state continues to be willing. Without it, the national judiciary will prove too dysfunctional to try the case. Unavailability, by contrast, refers to a situation where the administration of justice generally exists and would ordinarily be able to prosecute genuinely were it not for specific legal and factual impediments such as having too many trials to conduct, absence of jurisdiction under domestic law, the existence of an amnesty, lack of safety, etc.[211]

To successfully investigate or prosecute a case at national level requires a basic degree of functionality in analysis-based investigation, prosecution and judging even in the presence of defects in the criminal code or in victim- and witness-protection. Infrastructure is key – as Holmes notes, the presence of a functioning law enforcement mechanism is a prerequisite for a successful prosecution.[212] Because most case-law has dealt with self-referrals or unwilling Security Council referees, the Court has had little cause to consider inability. However, some consideration has gone into examining how the ICC can assist states to try cases. Though inability relates to the entire criminal justice system,[213] it is invariably conceived of in terms of investigation, prosecution, criminal statute reform and related issues such as witness and victim protection or physical infrastructure that facilitate convictions – the judiciary, defence and court administration are largely ignored.[214]

Two main theories for how the ICC could stimulate domestic institutional reform in the justice sector have been advanced. The first is through the ordinary, carrot-and-stick approach of classical/passive complementarity. This approach applies equally to cases of unwillingness and therefore is examined later in Section 5.6. The second posits a more activist ICC that uses its provisions to lend assistance to domestic transitional accountability.

Some have labelled this *positive complementarity*, but as we will see, positive complementarity is a phrase that means many different things to many different people. After Rome, there was cautious optimism that the ICC's complementarity regime would require the re-enforcement of national judicial systems for the purpose of reducing the impunity gap. [215] As one national representative put it, complementarity would allow the Court to 'play a twofold role: f rst, in motivating states to strengthen their judicial mechanisms; and secondly, in assisting states, especially weakened states, during or after a conf ict, for instance in delivering justice in accordance with the Rome Statute'.[216] It was believed that complementarity would be tied to other rule of law efforts in the affected state [217] and that the permanency of the ICC would better facilitate the transfer of know-how to national jurisdictions.[218] In a global society reliant more on the management of domestic duties than actual enforcement by supranational bodies, capacity-building through direct co-operation, technical training, benchmarks and standards would be more sustainable and effective.[219] States have always taken this view of complementarity, from early Working Group proposals[220] to the Kampala Review Conference in 2010. Here, the Assembly of States Parties argued that the capacity and will to carry out effective prosecutions of Rome Statute crimes require as a foundation the basic outlines of competent courts, independent judges, a professional bar and functioning judicial infrastructure, even if more specif c tools were also needed given the complexity of the crime.[221] Later initiatives by States Parties, the UN and INGOs have emphasized the need for co-ownership of complementarity by development and justice sector reform actors. [222]

Though the Court has no specif c mandate to engage in capacity-building, it is easy to ar gue the Court possesses an implied power under the terms of the Preamble and complementarity provisions to reinvigorate a national state's judicial system.[223] Article 93(10) which provides that the Court 'may, upon request, co-operate with and provide assistance to a State Party conducting an investigation into or trial in respect of conduct which constitutes a crime within the jurisdiction of the Court' provides an attractive way for the Court to lend technical assistance to a state to overcome problems of 'inability' or 'unavailability'.[224] As Gioia notes, the potential for assistance in this article is discretionary , tellingly less detailed than the provisions on assistance from states to the ICC (hence its characterization as 'reverse complementarity') and its non-exhaustive list of measures envisages the article as primarily relating to evidentiary matters, leaving it an open question as to whether it should be used for capacity-building functions. [225]

However, the organs of the ICC appear unwilling to interpret the Statute so constructively. The ICC Prosecutor' s 2009–2012 Prosecutorial Strategy makes clear that the ICC will encourage national prosecutions but only 'without involving the Off ce directly in capacity building or f nancial or technical assistance'.[226] The f rst Prosecutor consistently emphasized the Court is not a 'development agency', [227] somewhat confusingly stating that 'complementarity is not about training judges, we passing information, we building capacity. No, complementarity is what others are doing.' [228] While this evinces international criminal justice's traditionally greater concern with the symptoms of impunity than with its roots, there is also a concern that any involvement in domestic capacity-building could compromise admissibility litigation in future if it did not succeed. [229] The ICC OTP and Registry have instead accepted a more catalytic role as coordinators of assistance by states, INGOs and NGOs to f ll the void they perceive in the Statute as regards building the capacity of states to prosecute international crimes.   [230] Rather than directly assist the domestic justice sector , the OTP intends to function as the hub of a network of capacity-building efforts by these other actors. [231] Given its own meagre resources (the f nancial impact of adding capacity-building to the Court's role is one that is often mentioned)[232] and the variety of available NGOs and development agencies with superior experience in remedying capacity def cits, this is seen as a more eff cient and cost-effective approach.[233] The presumption is that if crimes are committed in a state over which the ICC has jurisdiction, the Court could draw attention to the need for trials and convene actors interested in progressing the state towards trial.[234]At Kampala, it appeared that States Parties were happy that other stakeholders such as states and INGOs would undertake capacity-building roles (direct and indirect 'horizontal complementarity'), obviating the need for the Court to undertake a major capacity-building role. [235]

The ICC has functioned at times as a focal point for rule of law reform action by development practitioners and peace-builders. The EU Action Plan of the ICC suggests that states 'should support training programmes and other such activities as may be necessary for fostering the professionalism of national judges, prosecutors, off cials, other staff, or experts needed for the effective functioning of the ICC complementarity system'. [236] The European Commission announced at the Kampala Review Conference that it would develop a toolkit for the promotion of domestic prosecutions. At Kampala, INGOs like Advocats Sans Frontieres, No Peace W ithout Justice and the Institute of Legal Practice were commended for their capacity-building activities,[237] which can complement the work of familiar actors like UNDP , OSCE and UNODC. Groups like the Open Society Justice Initiative have formulated realistic, budget-conscious types of training for judges and prosecutors, drawing on existing advisory and training models.   [238] At Kampala a 30-page compilation of examples of state and NGO projects aimed at strengthening domestic jurisdictions to deal with Rome Statute crimes was issued and makes for impressive reading.   [239] However, little interest has been apparent in more ambitious proposals for a permanent inteᵣ national institute dedicated to capacity-building for states dealing with serious international crimes that would give advice and provide monitoring. [240]

While the foregoing examples constitute positive developments, progress should not be over-stated. Capacity-building in states where the ICC is active has been more ad hoc than strategic, [241] while assistance projects themselves focus more on the interests of the ICC than the national justice sector as a whole. In accordance with a restrictive reading of Article 93(10), most assistance is evidence-based and not necessarily related to improving the judiciary's ability to use that evidence. The OTP's 2009–2012 Strategy envisages an extremely limited form of 'positive complementarity' prioritizing the provision of information collected by the Offce to national judiciaries upon their request pursuant to Article 93(10) and sharing databases of non-confdential materials and crime patterns. [242] The OTP's much-trumpeted Law Enforcement Network's threefold mandate to share information and evidence, facilitate legal and technical assistance for investigations and prosecutions and to support knowledge transfer will leave domestic judiciaries, administration and defence structures largely untouched. The Registry has been more ambitious than the OTP. Recognizing that basic skills need to be developed and explicitly wishing to 'harness itself within, not duplicate' existing rule of law initiatives, it has been active in building local capacity[243] However, the projects pursued such as witness protection programmes, public information and outreach, extradition, witness/victim protection and implementing substantive criminal legislation construct national ability very narrowly.[244] The Registry's comprehensive online knowledge system (The 'Legal Tools Project') relates exclusively to serious crimes, while some of its capacity-building relates to helping states co-operate with ICC prosecutions as opposed to undertaking their own. [245] Any more intensive process of training, oversight or presence by international personnel is expressly disavowed.[246]

There is a risk that complementarity can distort domestic priorities, by aiming for ICC standards in areas of ICC relevance at the expense of more mundane but essential areas of rule of law reform. Many scholars and practitioners argued that the Rome Statute would provide a framework for justice sector reform and lead to consistency in systems and procedures between the domestic jurisdiction and the Court in The Hague. The literature is rife with references to setting common standards for acceptable national trials [247] and harmonization of national justice systems around common international criteria established by ICC judges. [248] Much work has gone into developing frameworks on criminal procedure.[249] However, the prospects for standardization have suffered because states have been content to reap the reputational and fnancial rewards of ratifcation but signifcantly lag behind in implementation.[250] After more than a decade, only three of the thirty African states who signed the Rome Statute had enacted legislation to incorporate the state's provisions into domestic law.[251]

While some have lamented the potentially homogenizing infuence of the ICC,[252] the greater risk might be that identifed by Witte, namely that states 'might be tempted to seek ICC-inspired high-tech upgrades and complicated solutions where low tech and simple solutions will suffce and be more sustainable'.[253] For example, though the Registry and OTP both show a commendable concern for the protection of victims and witnesses in keeping with the ambitious and progressive Rome Statute, in building capacity in these areas for crimes of immediate concern they disregard the fact that the state in question might be a generation away from being able to replicate any such facilities. Uganda has modelled its War Crimes Court on the ICC on the basis of a mistaken belief that this is necessary to preclude the admissibility of Lord's Resistance Army (LRA) cases in The Hague and may alter its victim participation rules to copy the Rome Statute.[254] Some may welcome this as a benefcial reform, but it can detract resources from other areas of training and development and may not set a sustainable precedent for the rest of the justice system there. Few would go as far as Pocar who argues that 'the goal of the domestic court should indeed be that of applying the same standards as the international court',[255] but the Rome system appears to promote 'domestic ICCs' in respect of Rome Statute crimes at a time when other actors are trying to create something entirely more sustainable.[256] Rule of law reconstruction, by contrast, emphasizes the need to match reforms to the state's 'absorptive' capacity, as measures which impose unrealistic demands may do more to undermine than strengthen the justice sector.[257]

One sees in the literature a general presumption that the needs of domestic jurisdictions relating to international justice overlap with other rule of law needs or that developing the capacity for very complex crimes automatically bolsters capacity for lesser ones,[258] but this will not always be the case. The panoply of fair trial rights and legislative provisions states will be assisted in developing may merely constitute empty husks if attention is not paid to local context:

> One should not under-estimate the drain on the resources of relatively weak and already overburdened legislatures, for example on some countries in the Global South, that could be caused by the sort of comprehensive [ICC legal] package that is now being held up as necessary to adopt.[259]

Incorporating Rome Statute provisions domestically does not risk overburdening states alone. It also risks overwhelming rule of law reconstruction. For example, the Registry explicitly states its goal is to 'push' the inclusion of mechanisms for prosecuting serious crimes into rule of law reform initiatives[260] and indeed has expressed concern that resources could be diverted to other rule of law activities.[261] Any signifcant improvement in domestic capacity to try serious crime will be undertaken by rule of law actors, as opposed to the ICC:

> Overwhelmingly, the task of developing the will and capacity to deal with international crimes falls not to the international justicecommunity, but to the traditional rule-of-law development community. The latter's much greater network of international organizations, aid agencies, and other donor and implementing bodies offers extensive programs already

in place around the world, as well as vast experience and expertise in fostering the rule of law . Any attempt by the international justice community to establish parallel efforts would cause confusion, create ineff ciencies, and take longer to produce results. In short, fostering the conditions necessary to address international crimes is such a signif cant task that only the rule-of-law development community has the scope to undertake it.[262]

As Witte suggests, even if there is a commitment to some form of transitional accountability, many involved in rule of law reconstruction may question the value of integrating a Rome Statute vision of justice into their already strained programmes.[263]

5.6 The ICC and domestic rule of law culture

In examining the willingness of states to conduct prosecutions, issues of rule of law culture among the state' s leadership and judicial autonomy will be paramount. The types of 'unwilling' state the Court will deal with can run the gamut of willingness from formalized impunity in non-transitional states (e.g. Sudan, Indonesia) to the garden-variety peace versus justice or truth versus justice dilemmas in genuine but precarious transitions (e.g. the Latin American or W est African transitions) that dominate transitional justice literature. Only the latter are of interest in this chapter. In the Rome Statute system, otherwise unwilling states are believed to be aware of the risk of ICC admissibility with the consequent possibility that they will commence investigations and prosecutions to preclude it. Unwillingness is not def ned in the Rome Statute. As noted earlier , Article 17(2) instead outlines an exhaustive but porous list of situations that may assist the Court in determin- ing it. Article 17(2)(a) requires proof that a domestic proceeding was under - taken for the purpose of shielding the accused. This demands a subjective assessment of the quality of justice delivered and proof by the Prosecutor of 'devious intent on the part of the state, contrary to its apparent actions'.[264] By contrast, Article 17(2)(b) and (c) require either an unjustif ed delay in the proceedings or proceedings not being conducted independently or impar - tially, which in either circumstance is inconsistent with an intent to bring the person concerned to justice, and so do not require this subjective element.

Given that many of the cases the Court has been concerned with are self- referrals or Security Council referrals (Sudan refuses to acknowledge the Court's jurisdiction, Libya ostensibly prosecutes with alacrity), surprisingly little jurisprudence has developed in relation to unwillingness. No standards for a 'bad faith' prosecution have been developed beyond the broad Article 17 criteria, even if the ECtHR, IACtHR, ad hoc tribunal jurisprudence and international standards of judicial independence referred to in Chapter 1 are expected to form the core of the inquiry.[265] What is clear is that mere activity by the state is not enough. The Article 17(2) inquiry begins when there exist

212 Transitional justice and rule of law reconstruction

reasons to believe the domestic proceedings are not genuinely directed towards delivering justice. As Jurdi notes, the test will incorporate normative and empirical factors.[266] Both require a systemic inquiry into the institutional autonomy of the courts, including laws, procedures for appointment or dismissal, and political links to government. An Informal Expert Paper on complementarity in practice outlined the factors it will take into account when examining the autonomy of national proceedings. These include:

- Constitutional role, separation of powers, and powers attributed to institutions of the criminal justice system;
- Parameters of prosecuting powers and discretion;
- Degree of de jure and de facto independence of judiciary , prosecutors, investigating agencies;
- Jurisdictional territorial divisions; special jurisdictional regimes (military tribunals);
- Integrity/corruptibility of staff and institutions;
- Patterns of political interference in investigation and prosecution;
- Patterns of trials reaching preordained outcomes;
- Commonality of purpose between suspected perpetrators and state authorities involved in investigation, prosecution or adjudication;
- Delay in various stages of the proceedings in comparison with normal delays in the national system for cases of similar complexity.[267]

In short, examining potential state unwillingness would involve inquiry into many of the same issues peace-builders concerned with buttressing the autonomy of the courts are interested in.

Because these issues exist on the political plane, it is more diff cult to identify how the Court can bolster the autonomy of the domestic justice system than it is to see where institutional capacities can be improved. However, because unwillingness is a political issue it does not suffer from resource def cit as capacity-building does. While capacity-building f ts uncertainly within the Rome Statute and is a complex task the ICC itself is institutionally unsuited to undertaking, the Court is specif cally mandated to deal with unwillingness in Articles 15, 18, 19 and 53. These articles govern the carrot-and-stick vision of complementarity in which the ICC defers to the state's retained duty to investigate, prosecute and punish core crimes unless these proceedings prove not to be genuine. This vision of complementarity , variously given the misleading titles of 'negative', 'classical' or 'passive' complementarity, is a mechanism for inducing compliance in the Statute. It encapsulates a vision of the Court as a catalyst for action and a monitor of that action. The OTP's 2003 Informal Expert Paper labelled these two guiding principles as 'partnership' and 'vigilance'. [268] Partnership was interpreted conservatively as encouraging the state to undertake national proceedings (though it made the then-novel suggestion that this might also include burden-sharing, an issue addressed later), while vigilance referred to the principle that the OTP could gather and request information on national proceedings to ensure they were genuine.[269]

Though it has been ar gued by the OTP itself and scholars that any role beyond a passive Court (i.e. merely awaiting state inactivity or failure) in encouraging or monitoring state action amounts to 'positive complementarity',[270] inspection of the Preamble and relevant articles suggests that the Statute never intended to separate national and international jurisdiction and instead envisaged a process of formalized interaction, even when credible domestic proceedings were being undertaken.[271] Though the Rome Statute prioritized the state's duty to prosecute, it never envisaged ICC passivity. As the Court put it in the *Kony* admissibility case:

> Considered as a whole, the corpus of these provisions delineates a system whereby the determination of admissibility is meant to be an ongoing process throughout the pre-trial phase, the outcome of which is subject to review depending on the evolution of the relevant factual scenario.[272]

The framework of complementarity envisages an active court operating as a catalyst for states who might otherwise be reluctant to allow their judicial institutions to investigate, prosecute and try cases.[273] The catalysing process can be seen as encouragement or as antagonism depending on the timing and manner in which interaction occurs, but at all stages there is an implied or express threat that the case might be made admissible. The state is the 'f rst mover' who can determine to investigate or prosecute before the OTP is even aware of the crimes, but the decision is made fully conscious of the possibility of ICC action.[274] The very existence of the ICC might motivate states to allow their institutions of justice to start a trial and do so credibly . In certain situations, the ICC could insulate governments from the political cost of undertaking prosecutions against powerful or destabilizing elements by stressing to domestic audiences the inevitability of prosecution at The Hague if they do not commence proceedings.[275] The ICC becomes involved in Article 53(1) and (2) which require the Prosecutor to evaluate whether a case would be admissible before proceeding with an investigation, which will involve inquiry into domestic proceedings. It is inconceivable that the state would not be aware of such an assessment. Indeed, at this stage and at the Article 15 stage where the Prosecutor may initiate preliminary investigations *proprio motu* on the basis of information on crimes within the jurisdiction of the Court, the OTP has made its activities public to notify states of a potential full investigation and to encourage them to take action themselves.[276] From the requirements in Article 18 (preliminary rulings regarding admissibility) for the Prosecutor to provide notice of a pending investigation[277] through Article 19 (challenges to the jurisdiction of the Court or the admissibility of a case), states are given ample opportunity to commence effective proceedings that would lead to the suspension of ICC activity . At this stage, interaction between OTP and state is more antagonistic than the earlier 'encouragement' process, but the underlying presumption remains the same – that the state will commence genuine proceedings to avoid international embarrassment or loss of control over the case. Once it has initiated a case, the OTP is entitled to specify benchmarks for domestic proceedings under its Article 54(1)(b) mandate to ensure the effective investigation and prosecution of crimes. The most obvious example is the Agreed Minutes outlined between the OTP and Kenya which establish timelines and indicators for domestic proceedings to foster compliance. [278]

Where action has been catalysed and the state ostensibly undertakes proceedings, Articles 18 and 19 allow the Court to monitor them for genuineness under the criteria def ned in Article 17, with admissibility permitted where the proceedings fail. Space precludes a detailed examination of these provisions, but opportunities for the state to challenge admissibility [279] are balanced by monitoring opportunities for the Prosecutor in reviewing defer - rals,[280] challenging a f nding of admissibility,[281] conducting parallel investigations[282] and above all being kept informed on domestic ones. [283] As noted earlier, the normative and empirical dimensions of this supervisory function allows the ICC system to identify and highlight areas where the criminal justice system is restrained by the executive or is self-restraining. It is likely that the process of scrutiny will fall short of the type of system-wide examination found in the aforementioned Rule 11 *bis* (D)(iv) process (Drumbl, for example, notes the 'searing reviews' undertaken in relation to Rwanda'   s judicial system).[284] As always, international criminal justice is more concerned with impunity in the case at hand than the general conditions that permit it – complementarity analysis will be case-specif   c and not state/ situation specif c so there will be no overall evaluation of the national judiciary.[285] Indeed, the former Prosecutor was at great pains to deny that any admissibility proceedings would serve as a judgment on the national justice system.[286] The ICC Appeals Chamber in Kenya' s appeal against the earlier admissibility f nding was dismissive of Kenya's claims that judicial reforms were underway that would render its stated intention to try post-2007 election violence cases credible. [287] The short timelines for state action imposed by Articles 15, 17, 18 and 19 make it highly unlikely any or gan of the ICC would adopt what Jalloh calls a 'let's take a big picture'[288] approach with a state who requested time to undertake judicial reform before trials. As a result, the ICC may not induce states to establish training programmes or appoint experienced off cials to handle serious crimes cases as eventually occurred in the Balkans after Rule 11   *bis*.[289] Nevertheless, even this more narrow inquiry can throw an unfor giving and off cial light on impediments to judicial autonomy. This could serve a valuable service in developing the autonomy of the Courts as a high prof le and independent evaluation exercise.

Encouragement, threat and monitoring by the ICC has catalysed some action in most of the states it is involved in, such as pledges from Uganda to commence special tribunals and the actual creation or activation of criminal processes in Sudan, Libya and the DRC. However   , in all of these cases (including Kenya) and in the cases of Colombia and the Central African Republic, neither encouragement nor threats have prompted states to prosecute genuinely, instead yielding a 'perverse complementarity' of Potemkin proceedings to forestall or mitigate ICC scrutiny .[290] This disappointing trend above all demonstrates the political limitations of the Court in dealing with states that are themselves complicit in crime or negotiating peace with groups that are – as Batros observes, it can encourage or threaten states, but it cannot force them.[291] However, it also suggests that pushing for compliance in illiberal or non-transitional states will often prove a fool's errand. The rule of law cannot be imposed from outside, but must inhere in the state itself.

Bearing this in mind, the Rome Statute allows the Court to exercise political pressure on the state beyond its own complementarity limitations. Just as it aspires to serve as a hub for capacity-building, the OTP envisages providing information about the judicial work of the Office to those involved in political mediation such as the UN and other envoys who might exert pressure on reluctant states [292] and to mainstream ICC issues at the Security Council and regional groupings to maximize co-operation by states.[293] Given that a reluctant state is never a monolithic entity , the Court can support reform constituencies domestically in its interactions with the state by identifying and empowering reformers within the government and judiciary, building support for and co-operating with reformist elements in civil society, publicly identifying political obstacles to justice, and pressing for aid to be made conditional on reform. [294] Only this aggressive use of diplomacy and outreach, it is submitted, goes above and beyond the provisions of the statute to constitute genuinely positive complementarity . Though it is suggested that any form of encouragement to the state to commence prosecutions constitutes positive complementarity ,[295] such communications are inherent in any practical reading of the Statute. Labelling communications merely incidental to the ordinary operation of complementarity as 'positive' denies the concept any independent purpose.

5.7 Positive for whom? Interrogating 'positive' complementarity

An examination of the Court' s decade of practice demonstrates that this vision of positive complementarity , of the Court pressing aggressively through diplomacy and pressure to give effect to domestic rule of law principles (in addition to the encouragement/threats implicit in the Statute), has not been realized. Neither has the vision the States Parties outlined at Kampala, which defined positive complementarity as 'all activities/actions whereby national jurisdictions are strengthened and enabled to conduct genuine national investigations and trials of crimes included in the Rome Statute'.[296] Far from empowering or enabling states to conduct prosecutions, the vision of complementarity that has emer ged is less one of ensuring national compliance with legal obligations, but rather a diametrically opposed one in which the Court assumes as much responsibility as possible for combating impunity. Since the OTP's Informal Expert Paper in 2003, it has conceived positive complementarity as a 'partnership' policy based less on transfer of assistance from the Court to the state than that of a 'consensual division of labour' in which cases are transferred from the state to the Court.[297] This approach has found great support in the literature. Though the provisions of the Statute clearly suggest otherwise, classical complementarity is typically presented as inherently inert[298] or as inevitably involving ruinous antagonism between the Court and the state.[299] By contrast, a greater role for the Court in trying cases is justif ed in unobjectionable terms as more co-operative,[300] more amicable,[301] more consistent[302] and more effective in combating impunity.[303] Employing this false dichotomy , the Prosecutor argued he would not compete for cases with states but rather would adopt a policy of coordinated action between the ICC and state to ensure crimes did not go unpunished. Initially, the presumption was that this would only apply to states that were unable or unwilling after ICC assistance. As the OTP' s *Paper on Some Policy Issues before the Office of the Prosecutor* (2003) put it:

> [T]he Court and a territorial State incapacitated by mass crimes may agree that a consensual division of labour is the most logical and effective approach. Groups bitterly by conf ict may oppose prosecutions at each others' hands and yet agree to a prosecution by a Court perceived as neutral and impartial.[304]

Stahn cites this paper , issued at a time before the Court had ever even commenced a trial, as the point at where the ICC stopped being viewed as the last resort.[305] While defensible perhaps in cases of ongoing war , in the context of a transitional state such an approach treats unwillingness or inability as irreversible in the short to medium term, the very time when establishing the *bona fides* of the national justice system is most imperative. The def ning feature of the rule of law is a willingness on the part of the state to deal with sensitive cases through its own mechanisms, not a willingness to f nd an alternative venue, even if Benzing is correct in ar guing that such a transfer would fulf l the state's *aut dedere aut judicare* obligations.[306]

Over time, this vision of a division of labour has shifted from one where the Court assumed the duties of a particular state where it is inactive, unable or unwilling to a more interventionist policy of encouraging any division of labour that achieves the primary goal of the Statute in ending impunity , regardless of the circumstances of the state. This is most evident in the system of self-referrals in which the state refers a situation itself, makes explicit its inaction in all or certain def ned cases, and refrains from contesting admissibility.[307] Though not mentioned expressly in the Statute and seemingly rejected as a policy option in the negotiations for the Statute for its tendency to undermine the effectiveness of national justice systems, [308] self-referrals f t within the regime of State Party referrals in Article 13(a). [309] Though critics have argued that where national courts are willing and able to prosecute any relinquishing of jurisdiction is impermissible, [310] Article 17 clearly makes a case admissible where for any reason it is not being investigated by the state, achieving the same effect as a self-referral.[311] The voluntary acceptance of ICC admissibility by states was welcomed by the OTP on the basis that it would lead to more effective justice on account of the ICC's expertise and the likelihood of co-operation with the state.[312] Indeed, the Prosecutor actively sought them out, expressly warning the states in the f rst three situations that came before the Court (DR Congo, Uganda and Central African Republic) that he might open an investigation *proprio motu* if they did not refer the situations to him under Article 13(a).[313] In 2011, the non-State Party Côte d'Ivoire indicated that it wished the Prosecutor to initiate an investigation under his *proprio motu* powers into core crimes taking place in that country since 19 September 2002, indicating that the Ivorian courts are not up to the task of prosecuting these crimes. The Appeals Chamber has recognized that 'there may be merit' in the consensual decision of a state to relinquish its jurisdiction in favour of the Court, f nding that this is consistent with the objective of eradiating impunity for international crimes. [314]

Because with self-referrals the state relinquishes its duty to exercise jurisdiction, the OTP and Court' s encouragement of inactivity has been criticized. At a time when the national judiciary should be establishing its credentials, it creates a 'pernicious incentive' to do nothing in terms of post-conf ict justice other than externalize the responsibility .[315] The policy has been criticized for running contrary to the ethos of the Rome Statute which prioritized the state duty to prosecute and for contradicting the Prosecutor' s stated policy to encourage national prosecutions.   [316] While the initial presumption was that the modalities of the complementarity regime would serve to force states to develop an ability to exercise jurisdiction, it instead encourages 'laziness' on the part of the state' s judicial apparatus. [317] Indeed, self-referrals are presented as a form of collaboration and assistance to the national justice system, the virtue of which is that it obviates the need for the Prosecutor to act as an 'interfering watchdog' to spur state activity through *proprio motu* investigations.[318] Far from critically examining the state's reasons for inactivity, the Appeals Chamber in *Katanga* held that regardless of how functional and well-regarded a national judicial system is, if a statedetermines that it does not want to pursue the case then the reasons for this decision are not deemed relevant to the admissibility decision.   [319] This has served to preclude any analysis of the relative merits of national versus international jurisdiction.[320] Perhaps most worryingly, the superf cial deference to national judiciaries 'facilitates the abdication domestic prosecutorial authority'.[321] The 2009–2012 Prosecutorial Strategy's concept of positive complementarity is entirely silent as to the use of threat of investigation or prosecution to encour age national governments to pursue accountability . As Burke-White argues, the Court appears to have renounced its most powerful tool, namely the ability to 'incentivize, nudge or cajole' reluctant national governments to undertake domestic prosecutions.[322]

This trend was made clear in the self-referrals by the DR Congo and Uganda. In the former, the Pre-Trial Chamber in the *Lubanga* case accepted a self-referral by Kinshasa, though ultimately the admissibility decision was founded on national inaction on the basis that the arrest warrants issued by national authorities did not refer to Lubanga's alleged responsibility for recruiting child soldiers.[323] Even though there are serious problems in the Congolese judiciary overall,[324] Lubanga, Ngudjolo Chui and Katanga were all either in custody or ready for prosecution by authorities in the Ituri region where an EU justice capacity-building programme had yielded considerable progress in terms of abilities, the UN's Stabilization Mission (MONUC) provided protection to judges, and several war crimes prosecutions had already taken place.[325] As Schabas notes, the Congolese justice system was doing a better job of prosecuting than the ICC because it was prosecuting Lubanga for crimes of greater gravity than recruitment of child soldiers.[326] Indeed, the Prosecutor has conceded that Congolese courts are capable of undertaking prosecutions.[327] As Jurdi argues, the ICC could have made a more effective contribution to combating impunity in the DR Congo by helping amend the national indictments to include recruitment of child soldiers or by encouraging the national judiciary to assume primary responsibility and monitoring the trials thereafter.[328] Instead of supporting national trials, the ICC superseded them. Though the OTP has argued that 'voluntary acceptance of ICC admissibility does not necessarily presuppose or entail a loss of national credibility',[329] it effectively constitutes a high-profle admission that the state lacks faith in its judicial institutions:

> [Removal of the *Lubanga* and *Katanga* cases from the DRC] undermines the confdence of domestic judiciaries; it sends a message that they might be trying to reform themselves and might be trying to deal with very complicated justice questions, but that's not necessarily going to stop an international body from intervening.[330]

Uganda's self-referral refected the fact that it was unable to gain physical custody of its indictees and that there were politico-military factors that made using the ICC to pressure the LRA attractive. The logic of complementarity would dictate that should the indictees return to Uganda or be captured elsewhere, the case should be inadmissible before the ICC[331] given that the Ugandan justice system is highly functional, relatively independent and has successfully prosecuted members of the LRA in the past.[332] Though there are sensible reasons in terms of the interests of justice, general state practice and the underlying premise of complementarity to allow withdrawal of a self-referral,[333] on two occasions the ICC Prosecutor stated that Joseph Kony and the other LRA indictees would have to be tried in The Hague.[334] As Seils notes, this position appears to 'discount completely the possibility that the Ugandan prosecutions initiative could pass muster under the Statute'.[335] Though there are policy-based justif cations that support this position based on use of resources, timing of cases and independence of the OTP,[336] to deny the Ugandan courts jurisdiction in any future case of the LRA indictees would represent the privileging of the Court' s internal interests over the domestic responsibility the Statute attempted to enshrine. Some suggest that ICC dominance has actually discouraged the Ugandan courts from taking cases domestically due to the reinforcement of the norm that international justice is better justice.[337]

None of this is to suggest self-referrals should never be entertained. The weaknesses of the Central African Republic' s legal system are such that its Court of Appeal's self-declaration of admissibility should be accepted at face value.[338] However, this instance is distinct from the position of an ostensibly democratizing and relatively developed Côte d'Ivoire, which would benef t more from undertaking domestic trial with direct international participation or monitoring than from subcontracting its responsibility to The Hague. Far from stimulating the rule of law by buttressing the independence of the judiciary, the ICC has been complicit in a handful of states in undermining their independence by presuming judicial autonomy does not exist, while crystallizing choice over accountability as lying with the executive and not the institutions of justice. Self-referrals are justif ed purely on the basis that, as the Appeals Chamber put it in *Katanga*, it may be more 'opportune' for the Court to carry out the investigation or prosecution of sensitive cases. [339] However, cultivating a culture of the rule of law will often require the state to risk inopportune consequences like risking the displeasure of certain powerful groups in society.

The ICC's attempts to establish itself as a global actor in the f ght against impunity has tended to diminish empowerment-based perspectives premised on the need to build a domestic rule of law culture, ref ecting more the concurrence structure of the ad hoc tribunals than the initial model of complementarity.[340] While there was some suggestion that the early glut of self-referrals could be explained as a temporary measure for a Court needing to justify its existence,[341] burden-sharing based on voluntary relinquishment of jurisdiction has become the dominant paradigm. The OTP now states that it 'will initiate prosecutions of the leaders who bear the most responsibility for the crimes. On the other hand, it will encourage national prosecutions, where possible, for the lower-ranking perpetrators.'[342]

The ICC's activities in Uganda, DR Congo and Central African Republic have all been presented by the OTP as forms of burden-sharing, notwithstanding the almost complete lack of prosecutions by the states in question of those at lower levels.[343] Though it is not mentioned in the Statute at any stage and is not to be found anywhere in the *travaux préparatoires* (negotiations on complementarity were premised on the notion that the ICC was not inher - ently superior and specif cally designed to avoid ICC micromanagement),[344] scholarship has worked hard to justify this approach. Though Article 17 appears clear in its prescriptions, Stahn agues that this is just aninstitutional, dispute resolution dimension of complementarity . There is, he ar gues, a second, broader, 'systemic' dimension that or ganizes a distinct legal system in which the ICC and domestic jurisdictions reinforce each other to institutionalize accountability for mass crimes.[345] This system of justice isstructured around four fundamental components, namely forum selection, vertical and horizontal dialogue, mutual co-operation and incentive-based compliance under which a decision about the proper forum for justice is not exclusively based on national failure, but can instead take into account the comparative advantages of domestic and international forums in dividing labour .[346] Similarly, Gioia contends that the Statute set up a pluralist system in which national and international elements are meant to enrich and inf uence one another, in which complementarity operates as a device to allow joint pursuance of the ultimate goal of ending impunity.[347] Robinson, though acknowledging that the Statute represents a systemic preference for national prosecutions, refers to the Preambular aims to 'end impunity', ensure crimes 'must not go unpunished' and 'enhancing international cooperation', to demonstrate that the Statute shows concern for effectiveness at any level. [348] He argues that in any case falling short of a state undertaking effective prosecutions without political, logistical, f nancial or political barriers, a managerial approach where the choice of forum is decided by comparative advantages should apply.[349]

When weighing up a case-hungry ICC against a shattered national justice sector, the comparative advantage will invariably lie with the former , especially if the concerns of the international justice community in highest-quality trial, victim involvement, consistency with the corpus of international law etc. are prioritized. This comparative advantage may explain the general support for the self-referrals from the willing and able DRC and Uganda – though most advocates of a burden-sharing system preface their support by acknowledging an able and willing state can and should proceed alone, it is usually accompanied by support for the practice of self-referrals in which national willingness and ability have thus far been disregarded. From the perspective of a global system of justice, allocation of senior criminals to The Hague and less serious criminals to the state is both a rational and preferable division. It is hard to ar gue against co-operation, fairness and non-impunity, while the presumption must be that burden-sharing is consented to by the state and not expressly prohibited by the Statute.

However, while Stahn argues that effectiveness 'played an important, if not dominant, role in the justif cation of complementarity',[350] this runs contrary to the historical record of what the states agreed in the Statute negotiations. State delegations rejected the initial International Law Commission inclusion of 'effectively' in what became Article 17 because they worried that a concern with effectiveness would allow the Court to intervene wherever it believed it could investigate, prosecute or try more eff caciously than the state. [351] The qualif er 'genuinely' in relation to investigation and prosecution was preferred to a concept of effectiveness to preclude the ICC from assuming jurisdiction simply because it could undertake proceedings with greater competence or speed.[352] Nevertheless, the operative presumption now seems to be that the ICC can deal with the most serious cases better and is therefore the most appropriate venue. For a number of writers, the main reason for developing national capacity is not because it would develop the rule of law domestically but rather because the ICC's resource constraints and policy of prosecuting only those who bear greatest responsibility means that it can only prosecute a few senior leaders.[353] On such a view, jurisdiction appears to travel from the Court to the state and not the other way around. As former ICC judge Politi puts it:

> What is then the ultimate purpose of complementarity? There is no doubt that one important goal is to establish a division of labour between national jurisdictions and the ICC, under which the Court should essentially concentrate on those who have a major responsibility for the crimes involved.[354]

However, on a reading of the Statute's provisions and the *travaux préparatoires*, it is clear that the shared goal of the ICC and the States Parties in ending impunity does not necessarily equate to a shared task – there is quite clearly a tiered allocation of responsibility with the state at the top regardless of how serious the crime or criminal is.[355]

While burden-sharing might be legally permissible as the Court implicitly agreed in *Katanga*,[356] it is necessary to look at the wisdom of the policy as well as the legality. If it continues to form an organizing principle of the ICC, it is likely the Court will have no greater an impact domestically than its ad hoc and hybridized predecessors. Not only does it undermine any process of buttressing the autonomy of the national courts in transition, it may make capacity-building less, rather than more, imperative. Advocates of burden-sharing miss one obvious point – if the state feels unable or unwilling to try a case of a major criminal or is found to be so, how then can it be prepared to try someone only slightly further down the criminal hierarchy? Even if a division is drawn between complex 'big f sh' and less complex 'small f sh' cases (though given the ICC's stated ambition to try only a handful of cases, the division would probably be one between big f sh and slightly smaller ones), the state cannot be presumed to be equipped to cope with the latter , which will still involve immense technical diff culties and may prove equally sensitive politically. As Glasius argues:

> There is a logical inconsistency at the heart of the positive complementarity doctrine: complementarity teaches that the ICC is only supposed to take up situations where states are 'unable' or 'unwilling' to investigate or prosecute – but positive complementarity in situation countries demands that the same states suddenly recover their ability and willingness with regard to all the perpetrators the ICC does not have capacity to try .[357]

Any capacity-building a scheme of burden-sharing would generate would be ring-fenced into the prosecution of serious crimes and divorced from wider justice sector reconstruction.[358] However, assistance may not even go that far – though the OTP has committed to 'assisting' and 'encouraging' states to undertake these more minor prosecutions, the earlier survey of the ICC's capacity-building role demonstrates a lack of will and imagination to facilitate any improved responsiveness or ability in the national justice systems in question. Given that any burden-sharing with the state will require assistance from that state, it may be the case that capacity-building will relate more to enabling the transfer of witnesses, victims and evidence to The Hague than improving the national judiciary.[359] Indeed, off cers in the ICC have expressed concern that *any* type of capacity-building could detract resources from direct investigations and prosecutions.[360] While the ICC argues that its intervention should 'trigger more, not less' efforts to address issues of judicial capacity and independence,[361] it is just as likely that the unwilling or unable state might assume that they are absolved of responsibility for any criminals not brought before the ICC given the ICC's implicit lack of interest in them.[362] Though a number of observers have ar gued that the Bosnian War Crimes Chamber might prove an appropriate model for assistance to national jurisdictions,[363] the more strained relationship visible in the early Rules of the Road era is the more likely result given the reality that the ICC's 'myopic' focus on a handful of perpetrators precludes more long-term engagement with the domestic sector.[364] Stahn describes the logical end-point of burden-sharing when he ar gues that '[e]ncouraging domestic proceedings *should therefore not be seen as an absolute goal of "positive" complementarity. It only provides a means to an end, i.e. an instrument to strengthen the goals and impact of the Court*' (emphasis added).[365] On such a view, an international rule of law manifested in temporary, superf cial interventions in troubled states takes precedence over developing the apparatus of state to sustainably combat impunity.

Burden-sharing may be desirable in cases where states are genuinely incapacitated or where there is good reason to believe that a domestic trial would prove too divisive. It should not, however, serve to weaken national and international motivation to resolve these problems in situations where there is scope for reconstructive engagement. In genuinely transitional states, the state will benef t more from international assistance to develop national capacity or from international pressure to see investigations through to their conclusion than the assumption of this responsibility by foreign actors. However, initial practice suggests the ICC may evince a greater concern for its future than that of the national justice sector. Though the desire for burden-sharing is born of an understandable desire to prevent unwilling states from delaying or obstructing justice, it has operated thus far to pressure states that are willing and/or able (DR Congo, Côte d'Ivoire, Uganda) to abdicate responsibility. A lar ge, multi-layered, multi-skilled system of international criminal justice achieving a common goal of non-impunity is attractive if one assumes a global community is a more appropriate frame of reference than a national one, but it is not what was agreed at Rome, where only a residual primacy was left to the ICC. Burden-sharing does not represent the realization of complementarity, but rather its failure.

5.8 Conclusion

States Parties at Kampala noted a diver   gence of interest between justice sector reformers and the ICC, the former having long-term interests with the latter more short-term in nature, the former taking a sector-wide approach to development in contradistinction to narrower remit of the latter , the former relying on collaborative relationships with governments and the latter more likely to suffer lack of co-operation or readier to operate without it. [366] This has been apparent in the f rst ten years of the Court, where the complemen-tarity regime has served less as a procedural tool aimed at facilitating proper performance of the state's obligations than as a means to assert the superiority of pristine international justice over the grubbier process of domestic accountability. To observers of the ad hoc tribunals and hybrid courts, the prioritization of international criminal justice's internal concerns once more in the ICC would come as no surprise. As Mégret puts it:

> The problem with much of the rhetoric surrounding international criminal justice is that it has been focused on outcome (the repression of given criminals, the f ght against impunity, the establishment of the foundations of a new legal regime) rather than process ... T ypically the emphasis has been on the ability of any given mechanism to achieve successful prosecutions that would lead to those desired results. [367]

There is ample scope for co-operative, mutually re-enforcing syner   gies between the ICC and rule of law reconstruction in states that attract its attention. However, as actors in the SCSL belatedly realized, 'a positive legacy is not a self-fulf lling prophecy, but must be carefully designed and produced'.[368] International criminal justice is justif ed on the basis of its contribution to the rule of law, but that rule of law is conceived on a global level with priorities markedly different from those working to build the institutional, cultural and normative elements of the domestic justice system. An emphasis on the global rule of law emphasizes the status and legacy of the international criminal justice institutions themselves, at the expense of building the capacity of national courts or fostering a responsible approach to justice on the part of state authorities. A pristine trial for Joseph Kony in the Netherlands may satisfy the global community but does nothing to make Uganda better able to try other Konys in future, nor does it do anything to build faith among the population that the national court system can ever be trusted to do so.

Notes

1 L. Gberie, 'Brief ng: The Special Court of Sierra Leone' (2003) 102 *African Affairs* 637, 643.
2 2005 World Summit Outcome Document, UN Doc. A/RES/60/1 of 16 September 2005, para. 134.
3 S. Chesterman, 'An International Rule of Law?' (2008) 56 *American Journal of Comparative Law* 331, 355–356.
4 D. Koller, 'The Faith of the International Criminal Lawyer' (2008) 40 *NYU Journal of International Law and Politics* 1019, 1021 and 1023.
Ibid., 1050.
R. Teitel, *Global Transitional Justice* (Washington, D.C.: Centre for Global Studies Working Paper, 2010), 5, 11 and 14.
Ibid., 13.
8 B. Broomhall, *International Justice & the International Criminal Court: Between Sovereignty and the Rule of Law* (New York: Oxford University Press, 2003), 41–51.
9 E. Leonard, 'Global Governance and ICC Effectiveness: The Current State of Humanitarian Law', paper presented at the International Studies Association Meeting, New York, 15–18 February 2009, available <http://citation.allacademic. com/meta/p_mla_apa_research_citation/3/1/1/9/1/pages311915/p311915-1. php>, 5.
10 F. Mégret, 'Why Would States Want to Join the ICC? A Theoretical Exploration Based on the Legal Nature of Complementarity' in J. Kleffner and G. Kor (eds.), *Complementary Views on Complementarity* (The Hague: TMC Asser Press, 2006), 1 at 3.
11 B. Fassbender, 'Comments on Chapters 1 and 2 of Frédéric Mégret and Gerben Kor' in Kleffner and Kor (eds.), ibid., 73 at 75.
12 P. Akhavan, 'International Justice in the Era of Failed States: The ICC and the Self-Referral Debate' in C. Stahn and M. El Zeidy (eds.) *The International Criminal Court and Complementarity: From Theory to Practice* (Vol. I) (Cambridge: Cambridge University Press, 2011), 283 at 302.
13 *Prosecutor v Tadic*, Case No. IT-94-AR72, *Appeals Chamber Decision on the Defence Motion for Interlocutory Appeal on Jurisdiction* (2 October 1995), para. 59.
14 F. Gioia, 'State Sovereignty, Jurisdiction, and "Modern" International Law: The Principle of Complementarity in the International Criminal Court' (2006) 19 *Leiden Journal of International Law* 1095, 1107–1109.
15 J. Czarnetzky and R. Rychlak, 'An Empire of Law? Legalism and the International Criminal Court' (2003) 79 *Notre Dame Law Review* 55, 61–62.
16 Broomhall, supra n8, 54.
17 Chesterman, supra n3, 358.
18 Broomhall, supra n8, 61 and 43.
19 Ibid., 185–192
20 Ibid., 54.
2 Paragraph 10.
22 R. Rastan, 'Complementarity: Contest or Collaboration' in M. Ber gsmo (ed.), *Complementarity and the Exercise of Universal Jurisdiction for Core International Crimes* (Oslo: Torkel Opsahl, 2010), 83 at 132 and Mégret, supra n10, 23.
23 Ad Hoc Committee on the Establishment of an International Criminal Court, *Report of the Ad Hoc Committee on the Establishment of an International Criminal Court*, UN Doc. A/50/22 of 6 September 1995, 31.

24 B. Brown, 'Primacy or Complementarity: Reconciling the Jurisdiction of National Courts and International Criminal Tribunals' (1998) 23 *Yale Journal of International Law* 383, 391–392.

25 'Round Table: The ICC Relationship With National Jurisdictions: What Future?' in M. Politi and F . Gioia (eds.), *The International Criminal Court and National Jurisdictions* (Aldershot: Ashgate, 2008), 133 at 136.

26 Preparatory Committee on the Establishment of an International Criminal Court, *Report of the Preparatory Committee on the Establishment of an International Criminal Court*, UN Doc. A/51/22, 1996, 332.

27 Mégret, supra n10, 51.

28 Rastan, supra n22, 107.

29 Brown, supra n24, 384.

30 WW. Burke-White, 'The Domestic Infuence of International Criminal Tribunals: The International Criminal Tribunal for the Former Yugoslavia and the Creation of the State Court of Bosnia & Herzegovina' (2008) 46 *Columbia Journal of Transnational Law* 279, 324.

31 O. Bekou, 'Rule 11*bis*: An Examination of the Process of Referrals to National Courts in ICTY Jurisprudence' (2009–10) 33 *Fordham International Law Journal* 723, 790–791.

32 J. Alvarez, 'Crimes of State/Crimes of Hate: Lessons From Rwanda' (1999) 24 *Yale Journal of International Law* 365, 402.

33 J. Charney, 'Editorial Comments: International Criminal Law and the Role of Domestic Courts' (2001) 95 *American Journal of International Law* 95, 122.

34 M. Newton, 'Harmony or Hegemony? The American Military Role in the Pursuit of Justice' (2004) 19 *Connecticut Journal of International Law* 231, 252.

35 P Vinck et al., *Living With Fear: Population-Based Survey on Attitudes about Peace, Justice and Social Reconstruction in Eastern Democratic Republic of Congo* (Human Rights Center, UC Berkeley and International Center for Transitional Justice, 2008), 46.

36 C. Bjork and J. Goebertus, 'Complementarity in Action: The Role of Civil Society and the ICC in Rule of Law Strengthening in Kenya' (2011) 14 *Yale Human Rights and Development Law Journal* 205, 210.

37 Ad Hoc Committee on the Establishment of an International Criminal Court, supra n23, 31.

38 D. Tolbert and A. Kontic, 'The International Criminal T ribunal for the former Yugoslavia ("ICTY") and the Transfer of Cases and Materials to National Judicial Authorities: Lessons in Complementarity' in Stahn and El Zeidy (eds.) (V ol. II), supra n12, 888 at 910.

39 Broomhall, supra n8, 58.

40 L.N. Sadat and S.R. Carden, 'The New International Criminal Court: An Uneasy Revolution' (2000) 88 *Georgetown Law Journal* 381, 385, L.S. Bickley , 'U.S. Resistance to the International Criminal Court: Is the Sword Mightier than the Law?' (2000) 14 *Emory International Law Review* 213, 272–275.

41 Czarnetzkyand Rychlak, supra n15, 111.

42 Mégret, supra n10, 39.

43 M.C. Bassiouni (ed.), *Legislative History of the International Criminal Court: An Article-by-Article Evolution of the Statute from 1994–1998* (The Hague: Kluwer Law International, 1999), 62.

44 S. Williams, 'Article 17: Issues of Admissibility' in O. Tiffterer (ed.), *Commentary on the Rome Statute of the International Criminal Court* (Baden-Baden: Nomos Verlagsgesellscaft, 1999), 383 at 385–386.

45 Benjamin Ferencz, Address to the UN Diplomatic Conference of Plenipotentiaries on the Establishment of the International Criminal Court, 16 June 1998.

46 Gioia,supra n14, 1096.

47 P Dascalopoulou-Livada, 'The Principle of Complementarity and Security Council Referrals' in Politi and Gioia (eds.), supra n25, 57 at 57.

48 F. Mégret, 'T oo Much of a Good Thing? Implementation and the Uses of Complementarity' in Stahn and El Zeidy (eds.) (Vol. I), supra n12, 361 at 374.

49 J. Kleffner, *Complementarity in the Rome Statute and National Criminal Jurisdictions* (Oxford: Oxford University Press, 2008), 1, 26, 32.

50 M. Delmas-Marty, 'Interactions between National and International Criminal Law in the Preliminary Phase of Trial at the ICC' (2006) 4 *Journal of International Criminal Justice* 2, 7.

51 N.N. Jurdi, *The International Criminal Court and National Courts: A Contentious Relationship* (Farnham: Ashgate, 2011), 266.

52 R. Philips, 'The International Criminal Court Statute: Jurisdiction and Admissibility' (1999) 10 *Criminal Law Forum* 61, 64.

53 A. Slaughter and W .W. Burke-White, 'The Future of International Law is Domestic (or, The European W ay of Law)' (2006) 47 *Harvard International Law Journal* 327, 350.

54 J. Stromseth, 'The International Criminal Court and Justice on the Ground' (2009)43 *Arizona State Law Journal* 427, 442.

55 L. Vinjamuri and J. Snyder 'Advocacy and Scholarship in the Study of International War Crimes Tribunals and Transitional Justice' (2004) 7 *Annual Review of Political Science* 345, 358.

56 N. Roht-Arriaza, 'Role of International Actors' in A.B. De Brito et al. (eds.), *The Politics of Memory: Transitional Justice in Democratizing Societies* (Oxford, New York: Oxford University Press, 2001), 40 at 56.

57 The obvious example being the Coalition for International Criminal T ribunals, though Amnesty International, Human Rights W atch and scores of region- and context-specif c organizations have been highly prominent.

58 B. Batros, 'The Evolution of the ICC Jurisprudence on Admissibility' in Stahn and El Zeidy (eds.) (Vol. I), supra n12, 558 at 595.

59 R. Zacklin, 'The Failings of Ad Hoc International T ribunals' (2004) 2 *Journal of International Criminal Justice* 541, 541.

60 J. Beauvais, 'Benevolent Despotism: A Critique of UN State-Building in East Timor' (2001) 33 *NYU Journal of International Law & Policy* 1101, 1166.

61 L. Fletcher and H. W einstein, 'Violence and Social Repair: Rethinking the Contribution of Justice to Reconciliation' (2002) 24   *Human Rights Quarterly* 573, 580.

62 D. Joyce, 'The Historical Function of International Criminal T rials: Re-thinking International Criminal Law' (2004) 73 *Nordic Journal of International Law* 461, 465.

63 V. Hussain, 'Sustaining Judicial Rescues: The Role of Judicial Outreach and Capacity-Building Efforts in War Crimes Tribunals' (2005) 45 *Virginia Journal of International Law* 547, 551.

64 ICTY Statute, Article 9(1) and (2) and ICTR Statute, Article 8(1) and (2).

65 UN Security Council Resolution 808, UN Doc. S/RES/808 of 22 February 1993, Preambular paras. 8–9 and UN Security Council Resolution 955, UN Doc. S/RES/955 of 8 November 1994, Preambular paras. 5–6.

66 The list is taken from one of the ICTY' own documents (http://www.icty.org/x/f le/Outreach/view_from_hague/jit_accomplishments_en.pdf), and has been referred

to, *inter alia*, in *Report to Secretary-General of the Commission of Experts to Review the Prosecution of Serious Violations of Human Rights in Timor-Leste (then East Timor) in 1999* (26 May 2005) UN Doc S/2005/45825, para. 31.

67 D. Tolbert, 'The International Criminal T ribunal for the Former Y ugoslavia: Unforeseen Successes and Foreseeable Shortcomings' (2002) 26 *Fletcher Forum of World Affairs* 5, 12.

68 *Prosecutor v Slobodan Milosevic*, Case No. IT-02-54, Transcript of Initial Appearance.

69 Human Rights Center UC Berkeley & Centre for Human Rights, University of Sarajevo, 'Justice, Accountability and Social Reconstruction: An Interview Study of Bosnian Judges and Prosecutors' (2000) 18 *Berkeley Journal of International Law* 102, and P. Ironside, 'Rwandan Gacaca: Seeking Alternative Means to Justice, Peace and Reconciliation' (2002) 15 *New York International Law Review* 21, 31.

70 Berkeley/SarajevoStudy, ibid., especially 136–140.

71 Alvarez,supra n32, 466.

72 M. Ellis, 'Bringing Justice to an Embattled Region – Creating and Implementing the "Rules of the Road" for Bosnia and Herzegovina' (1999) 17 *Berkeley Journal of International Law* 1, 4–6.

73 C. Ferstman, 'Rwanda' s Domestic T rials for Genocide and Crimes Against Humanity' (1997) 5 *Human Rights Brief* 1.

74 M.C. Malaguti, 'Can the Nuremberg Legacy Serve Any Purpose in Understanding the Modern Concept of "Complementarity"?' in Politi and Gioia (eds.), supra n25, 113 at 121.

75 Tolbert, supra n67, 13.

76 Burke-White,supra n30, 305.

77 D. Tolbert and A. Kontic, 'The International Criminal T ribunal for the former Yugoslavia: Transitional Justice, the T ransfer of Cases to National Courts, and Lessons for the ICC' in C. Stahn and G. Sluiter (eds.), *The Emerging Practice of the International Criminal Court* (Leiden: Brill N.V., 2009), 135 at 145.

78 Tolbert and Kontic, supra n38, 897–898.

79 F Donlon, 'Rule of Law: From the International Criminal Tribunal for the Former Yugoslavia to the W ar Crimes Chamber of Bosnia and Herzegovina' in D.F. Haynes (ed.), *Deconstructing the Reconstruction: Human Rights and Rule of Law in Postwar Bosnia and Herzegovina* (Aldershot: Ashgate, 2008), 257 at 264.

80 Ellis,supra n72, 19.

81 P. Williams and P. Taft, 'The Role of Justice in the Former Y ugoslavia: Antidote or Placebo for Coercive Appeasement?' (2003) 35 *Case Western Reserve Journal of International Law* 219, 253–254.

82 Tolbert and Kontic, supra n77, 143.

83 Burke-White,supra n30, 299.

84 Donlon, supra n79, 283. A similar point is made by Burke-White, ibid., 316.

85 J.Stromseth, M. Wippman and R. Brooks, *Can Might Make Rights? Building the Rule of Law After Military Interventions* (Cambridge: Cambridge University Press, 2006), 273.

86 Berkeley/SarajevoStudy, supra n69.

87 ExpertGroup, *Report of the Expert Group to Conduct a Review of the Effective Operation and Functioning of the International Tribunal for the former Yugoslavia and the International Criminal Tribunal for Rwanda*, UN Doc. A/54/634 of 22 November 1999.

88 Rule11*bis* was adopted on 12 November 1997 at the conclusion of the 14th plenary session of the Tribunal, President of the ICTYFifth Annual Report of the International Tribunal, UN Doc. S/1998/737, A/53/219 of 10 August 1998, para. 105.

89 J. Holmes, 'Complementarity: National Courts versus the ICC' in A. Cassese, P. Gaeta and J. Jones, (eds.), *The Rome Statute of the International Criminal Court: A Commentary* (Oxford: Oxford University Press, 2002), 667 at 670.

90 P. Clark, 'Chasing Cases: The ICC and the Politics of State Referral in the Democratic Republic of the Congo and Uganda' in Stahn and El Zeidy (eds.) (Vol. II), supra n12, 1180 at 1184.

91 J. Alvarez, 'The New Dispute Settlers: (Half) Truths and Consequences' (2003) 38 *Texas International Law Journal* 405, 438–439.

92 Ibid.,437.

93 R. Lipscomb, 'Restructuring the ICC Framework to Advance Transitional Justice: A Search for a Permanent Solution in Sudan' (2006) 106 *Columbia Law Review* 182, 194.

94 A small, indicative but infuential sample includes L. Dickinson, 'The Promise of Hybrid Courts' (2003) 97 *American Journal of International Law* 295, E. Higonnet, 'Restructuring Hybrid Courts: Local Empowerment and National Criminal Justice Reform' (2006) 23 *Arizona Journal of International & Comparative Law* 347, J.I. Turner, 'Nationalising International Criminal Law' (2005) 41 *Stanford Journal of International Law* 1.

95 B. Hall, 'Using Hybrid Tribunals as Trivias: Furthering the Goals of Post-Confict Justice While Transferring Cases from the ICTY to Serbias Domestic War Crimes Tribunal' (2005) 13 *Michigan State Journal of International Law* 39, 57.

96 UNSecretary-General, *The Rule of Law and Transitional Justice in Conflict and Post-Conflict Societies* (2004) UN Doc. S/2004/616, para. 15.

97 Higonnet,supra n94, 377.

98 D. Cohen, '"Hybrid" Justice in East Timor, Sierra Leone and Cambodia: 'Lessons Learned" and Prospects for the Future' (2007) 43 *Stanford Journal of International Law* 1, 37.

99 Off ce of the High Commissioner for Human Rights, 'Rule of Law T ools for Post-Conf ict States: Maximizing the Legacy of Hybrid T ribunals' (2008), HR/PUB/08/02, 37–39.

100 WW. Burke-White, 'Regionalization of International Criminal Law Enforcement: A Preliminary Exploration' (2003) 38 *Texas International Law Journal* 729, 737.

101 Dickinson,supra n94, 304.

102 *Rule of Law Report*, supra n96, para. 44.

103 UN Secretary-General, Letter dated 24 June 2005 from the Secretary General addressed the President of the Security Council, UN Doc. S/2005/458, Annex II, *Report to Secretary-General of the Commission of Experts to Review the Prosecution of Serious Violations of Human Rights in Timor-Leste (then East Timor) in 1999*, of 25 May 2005, para. 120.

104 UNMIK Department of Justice f gures, cited in Amnesty International, 'The UN in Kosovo – A Legacy of Impunity' (2006), available: http://www.amnesty.org/en/library/info/EUR70/015/2006 >, 5.

105 E.T. Perriello and M. Wierda, *Lessons Learned From the Deployment of International Judges and Prosecutors in Kosovo* (New York: International Center for Transitional Justice, 2006), C. Reiger and M. Wierda, *The Serious Crimes Process in Timor-Leste: In Retrospect* (New York: International Center for Transitional Justice, 2006), 40.

106 Cohen, supra n98, 36–37, Dickinson, supra n94, 307, A. Cassese, 'The Role of Internationalized Courts and T ribunals in the Fight against International Criminality' in C. Romano, A. Nollkaemper and J. Kleffner (eds.),

Internationalized Criminal Courts and Tribunals: Sierra Leone, East Timor, Kosovo, and Cambodia (Oxford: Oxford University Press, 2004), 3 at 6.

107 On 8 February 2002, the UN withdrew from negotiations, declaring that it had 'come to the conclusion that the Extraordinary Chambers, as currently envisaged, would not guarantee the independence, impartiality, and objectivity that a court established with the support of the United Nations must have'.

108 UNMIK Regulation 2000/64 gave the accused, defence, prosecutor or Department of Justice the right to ask UNMIK to intervene in a case and assign international judges or prosecutors to it, whereas the previous regulations 2000/6 and 2000/34 preserved Kosovar majorities (Special Representative of the Secretary-General, *On the Assignment of International Judges/Prosecutors and/or Change of Venue*, UNMIKOR, 2000, UN Doc UNMIK/REG/2000/64).

109 The Freetown Government went so far as to amend the Agreement establishing the SCSL to replace the words 'Sierra Leone judges' with 'judges appointed by the government of Sierra Leone', choosing to appoint only three national judges out of the possible four appointees they could make.

110 M. Hartmann, *International Judges and Prosecutors in Kosovo: A New Model for Post-Conflict Peacekeeping* (Washington, D.C.: United States Institute of Peace Special Report, 2003), 14.

111 G. Naarden and J. Locke, 'Peacekeeping and Prosecutorial Policy: Lessons From Kosovo' (2004) 98 *American Journal of International Law* 727, 729.

112 T Perriello and M. Wierda, *The Special Court for Sierra Leone Under Scrutiny* (New York: International Center for Transitional Justice, 2006), 2.

113 See generally Hussain, supra n63.

114 OHCHR, supra n99, 7.

115 UNDP Mid-term Evaluation Team, 'UNDP Strengthening the Justice System in Timor-Leste Programme: Independent/External Mid-Term Evaluation Report September 2007' (2008), available: ‹http://www.norad.no/en/Tools+and+publications/Publications/Publication+Page?key=109793›, 59.

116 International Crisis Group, 'The Rule of Law in Independent Kosovo' (2010) Europe Report No 204, available < http://www.crisisgroup.org/~/media/Files/europe/balkans/kosovo/204%20The%20rule%20of%20Law%20in%20Independent%20Kosovo.ashx>, 15.

117 OHCHR, supra n99, 24.

118 M. Othman, *Accountability for International Humanitarian Law Violations: The Case of Rwanda and East Timor* (Berlin: Springer, 2005), 103.

119 Cohen, supra n98, 16.

120 In cases involving international judges and prosecutors, the Kosovar Department of Judicial Administration and the Ministry of Public Services paid defence teams.

121 Rule 45 of the Rules of Evidence and Procedure.

122 Cohen supra n98, 8–9.

123 J. Cockayne, 'The Fraying Shoestring: Rethinking War Crimes Tribunals' (2005) 28 *Fordham International Law Journal* 616, 671.

124 R. Skilbeck, 'Defending the Khmer Rouge' (2008) 8 *International Criminal Law Review* 423, 440–441.

125 S. Linton and C. Reiger, 'The Evolving Jurisprudence and Practices of East Timor's Special Panels For Serious Crimes on Admissions of Guilt, Duress and Superior Orders' (2001) 4 *Yearbook of International Humanitarian Law* 1.

126 W. Schabas, 'Balancing the Rights of the Accused with the Imperatives of Accountability' in R. Thakur and P. Malcontent (eds.), *From Sovereign Impunity to International Accountability: The Search for Justice in a World of States* (New York: United Nations University Press, 2004), 154 at 155.

127 T. Ingadottir, 'The Financing of Internationalized Criminal Courts and Tribunals' in Romano, Nollkaemper and Kleffner (eds.), supra n106, 271.

128 P.K. Mendez, 'The New Wave of Hybrid Tribunals: A Sophisticated Approach to Enforcing International Humanitarian Law or an Idealistic Solution With Empty Promises?' (2009) 20 *Criminal Law Forum* 53, 55.

129 Bekou, supra n31, 790.

130 Human Rights Watch, 'Justice at Risk: War Crimes Trials in Croatia, Bosnia and Herzegovina, and Serbia and Montenegro' (2004) available < http://www.hrw.org/en/node/11965>.

131 Resolution 1503 (2003), SC RES 1503, UNSCOR, 2003, UN Doc. S/RES/1503 (2003), para. 7.

132 Ibid., Preamble.

133 Rule 11*bis*(A).

134 Office of the High Representative, 'War Crimes Chamber Project: Project Implementation Plan – Registry Project Report' (2004), online: < http://www.ohr.int/ohr-dept/rule-of-law-pillar/pdf/wcc-project-plan-201004-eng.pdf >, 8.

135 Office of the High Representative, 'Decision Enacting the Law on Amendment to the Law of the Court of Bosnia and Herzegovina' (2009), online: < http://www.ohr.int/decisions/judicialrdec/default.asp?content_id=44283>, Article 1.

136 Office of the High Representative, 'War Crimes Chamber Project: Project Implementation Plan – Registry Progress Report' (2004), online: <http://www.ohr.int/ohr-dept/rule-of-law-pillar/pdf/wcc-project-plan-201004-eng.pdf >, 4.

137 B.Ivanisevic, *The War Crimes Chamber in Bosnia and Herzegovina: From Hybrid to Domestic Court* (New York: International Center for Transitional Justice, 2008), 11–12.

138 Ibid.,11.

139 Ibid.,40.

140 C.Garbett, 'Localising Criminal Justice: An Overview of National Prosecutions at the War Crimes Chamber of the Court of Bosnia and Herzegovina' (2010) 10 *Human Rights Law Review* 558, 558.

141 Bekou, supra n31, 724–725.

142 *Prosecutor v Radovan Stankovic*, Case No. IT-96-23/2-AR11*bis*1, *Decision on Rule 11 bis referral* (ICTY Appeals Chamber, 1 September 2005), para. 30.

143 Ivanisevic, supra n137, 1.

144 Human Rights Watch, 'Looking for Justice: The War Crimes Chamber in Bosnia and Herzegovina' (2006), available < http://www.hrw.org/en/reports/2006/02/07/looking-justice-0>, 10.

145 Ivanisevic, supra n137, 41.

146 HumanRights Watch, supra n144, 24.

147 Ibid.,10.

148 D. Tolbert, 'International Criminal Law: Past and Future' (2009) 30 *University of Pennsylvania Journal of International Law* 1281, 1294, M. El Zeidy, 'From Primacy to Complementarity and Backwards: (Re)-Visiting Rule 11 *bis* of the Ad Hoc Tribunals' (2008) 57 *International and Comparative Law Quarterly* 403, 405, F. Donlon, 'Positive Complementarity in Practice: ICTY Rule 11*bis* and the

Use of the Tribunal's Evidence in the Srebrenica Trial before the Bosnian War Crimes Chamber' in El Zeidy and Stahn (eds.), Vol. II, supra n12, 920.
149 Donlon, ibid., 922.
150 Burke-White, supra n30, 320, Bekou, supra n31, 789.
151 T. Abdulhak, 'Building Sustainable Capacities – From an International Tribunal to a Domestic War Crimes Chamber for Bosnia and Herzegovina' (2010) 9 *International Criminal Law Review* 333, 335.
152 O. Ortega-Martin and J. Herman, 'Hybrid Tribunals and the Rule of Law: Notes from Bosnia & Herzegovina & Cambodia' (2010), JAD-PbP Working Papers Series No. 7, online <http://www.uel.ac.uk/chrc/documents/WP7.pdf>, 20.
153 M. Bergsmo et al., *The Backlog of Core International Crimes Case Files in Bosnia and Herzegovina* (Oslo: International Peace Research Institute, 2009), Annex 2, 183.
154 Elbert and Kontic, supra n38, 915.
155 Rule 11*bis*(C).
156 *Prosecutor v Milosevic*, Case No. IT-98-29/1-PT, *Decision on Referral of Case Pursuant to Rule 11bis* (8 July 2005), para. 18.
157 J Melman, 'The Possibility of Transfer(?): A Comprehensive Approach to the International Criminal Tribunal for Rwanda's Rule 11*bis* to Permit Transfer to Rwandan Domestic Courts' (2010) 79 *Fordham Law Review* 1271.
158 HumanRights Watch, supra n144, 2.
159 Council Joint Action 2008/130/CFSP of 18 February 2008, Extending the Mandate of the European Union Special Representative in Bosnia and Herzegovina Article 2, online: < http://eur-lex.europa.eu/LexUriServ/LexUriServ.do?uri=OJ:L:2008:043:0022:0025:en:PDF>.
160 Quoted at 'Round Table', supra n25, 159.
161 Bekou, supra n31, 770.
162 Elbert and Kontic, supra n38, 904.
163 Ivanisevic, supra n137, 39.
164 Holmes, supra n89, 673.
165 Preamble para. 4.
166 Preamble, para. 6.
167 Article 17(1).
168 Article 17(2).
169 Article 17(3).
170 Holmes, supra n89, 675.
171 *Prosecutor v Katanga and Ngudolo*, ICC-01/04-01-07-1213-tENG, para. 78.
172 M. Benzing, 'The Complementarity Regime of the International Criminal Court: International Criminal Justice between State Sovereignty and the Fight against Impunity' (2003) 7 *Max Planck Yearbook of United Nations Law* 591, 599.
173 M.C. Bassiouni, 'The ICC – Quo Vadis?' (2006) 4 *Journal of International Criminal Justice* 421, 422.
174 Benzing, supra n172, 600.
175 L.C. Dembowski, 'The International Criminal Court: Complementarity and its Consequences' in J. Stromseth (ed.), *Accountability for Atrocities: National and International Responses* (Ardsley, NY: Transnational Publishers, 2003), 135 at 141.
176 Mégret, supra n10, 49–51.
177 Benzing, supra n172, 596.
178 Lipscomb, supra n93, 184.

179 Luis Moreno-Ocampo, Statement at the Ceremony for the Solemn Undertaking of the Chief Prosecutor of the ICC, 16 June 2003.

180 International Center for Transitional Justice, 'Meeting Summary of the Retreat on "Complementarity after Kampala: The W ay Forward"' (2010), available <http://ictj.org/sites/default/f les/ICTJ-Global-Complementarity-Greentree-2010-English.pdf>, 1.

181 Ibid.

182 E.Witte, *International Crimes, Local Justice: A Handbook for Rule-of-Law Policymakers, Donors and Implementers* (New York: Open Society Justice Initiative, 2011), 21.

183 WW. Burke-White, 'Complementarity in Practice: The International Criminal Court as Part of a System of Multi-Level Global Governance in the Democratic Republic of Congo' (2005) 18 *Leiden Journal of International Law* 557, 575.

184 *Prosecutor v Ruto et al.* and *Prosecutor v Muthaura et al.*, Case Nos. ICC-01/09–01/11 and ICC-01/09–02/11, *Application of the Government of the Republic of Kenya Pursuant to Article 19 of the ICC Statute*, 31 March 2011.

185 K. Miskowiak, *The International Criminal Court: Consent, Complementarity and Cooperation* (Copenhagen: DJOF Publishing, 2000), 40.

186 M. Arsanjani and W .M. Reisman, 'The Law-in-Action of the International Criminal Court' (2005) 99 *American Journal of International Law* 385, 389, footnote 18.

187 J. Holmes, 'The Principle of Complementarity' in R. Lee (ed.), *The International Criminal Court: The Making of the Rome Statute, Issues Negotiations and Results* (The Hague, Boston: Kluwer Law International, 1999), 41 at 74.

188 Gioia,supra n14, 1097, 1101 and 1122.

189 Mégret,supra n48, 375, Kleffner, supra n49, 160.

190 David Tolbert, quote taken from Foreword, in Jurdi, supra n51, xxi.

191 E.g. Batros, supra n58, 589, C. Stahn, 'Taking Complementarity Seriously: On the Sense and Sensibility of "Classical", "Positive" and "Negative" Complementarity' in Stahn and El Zeidy (eds.), Vol. I, supra n12, 233 at 241 and 244.

192 Kleffner, supra n49, 100.

193 Jurdi,supra n51, 164–165.

194 A. Muller and I. Stegmiller , 'Self-Referrals on Trial: From Panacea to Patient' (2010) 8 *Journal of International Criminal Justice* 1267, 1288.

195 M.El Zeidy, *The Principle of Complementarity in International Criminal Law* (Leiden: Martinus Nijhoff, 2008), 274.

196 J. Kleffner, 'The Impact of Complementarity on National Implementation of Substantive International Criminal Law' (2003) 1 *Journal of International Criminal Justice* 86, 86 (Abstract).

197 *Conditions of Admission of a State to Membership in the United Nations (Article 4 of Charter)*, Advisory Opinion of 28/05/1947-8, 67–68, cited in El Zeidy , supra n195, 303.

198 W Schabas, *The UN International Criminal Tribunals: The Former Yugoslavia, Rwanda and Sierra Leone* (New York: Cambridge University Press, 2006), 40.

199 M.Newton, 'Comparative Complementarity: Domestic Jurisdiction Consistent with the Rome Statute of the International Criminal Court' (2001) 167 *Military Law Review* 20, 68.

200 ICC-OTP, Prosecutorial Strategy 2009–2012 (2010), available <http://www.icc-cpi.int/NR/rdonlyres/66A8DCDC-3650-4514-AA62-D229D1128F65/281506/OTPProsecutorialStrategy20092013.pdf>, 7.

201 This concern was best expressed at a Round Table in June 2004, when Theodor Meron noted that without a critical mass of cases, States Parties would question whether the Court was worth sustaining and Mauro Politi acknowledged that it was diffcult to convince ambassadors to support the Court when it only had one trial ('Round Table', supra n25, 135 and 156).

202 W. Schabas, 'The Rise and Fall of Complementarity' in Stahn and El Zeidy (eds.), Vol. I, supra n12, 150 at 156.

203M.Drumbl, 'Policy Through Complementarity: The Atrocity Trial as Justice' in Stahn and El Zeidy (eds.), supra n12, 197 at 214 and 221, Clark, supra n90, 1201–1202.

204 W. Schabas, 'Prosecutorial Discretion v. Judicial Activism at the International Criminal Court' (2008) 6 *Journal of International Criminal Justice* 731, 761.

205Drumbl,supra n203, 202–203.

206A.Greenawalt, 'Complementarity in Crisis: Uganda, Alternative Justice, and the International Criminal Court' (2009–10) 50 *Virginia Journal of International Law* 107, 160.

207 P. Seils, 'Making Complementarity Work: Maximizing the Limited Role of the Prosecutor' in Stahn and El Zeidy (eds.) (Vol. II), supra n12, 989 at 989.

208W Schabas, 'Complementarity in Practice: Some Uncomplimentary Thoughts' (2007) 19 *Criminal Law Forum* 5, 6.

209C.Stahn, 'Perspectives on Katanga: An Introduction' (2010) 23 *Leiden Journal of International Law* 311, 311.

210Kleffner supra n49, 154.

211 Benzing, supra n172, 614, S. Nouwen, 'Fine-T uning Complementarity' in B. Brown (ed.), *Research Handbook On International Criminal Law* (Cheltenham: Edward Elgar, 2011), 206 at 218–219.

212Holmes,supra n187, 49.

213Kleffner supra n49, 154.

214ICCAssembly of States Parties, *Report of the Bureau on Stocktaking: Complementarity*, UN Doc. ICC-ASP/8/51 of 18 March 2010, paras. 8–18.

215Hans-PeterKaul, quoted at 'Round Table', supra n25, 150.

216 Permanent Representative of Liechtenstein to the United Nations in 2003, quoted in Kleffner, supra n49, 309.

217 Tolbert and Kontic, supra n38, 899, M. Newton, 'The Quest for Constructive Complementarity' in Stahn and El Zeidy (eds.), Vol. I, supra n12, 304 at 340.

218 F. Gioia, 'Complementarity and "Reverse Cooperation"' in Stahn and El Zeidy (eds.), ibid., 807 at 827–828.

219Slaughterand Burke-White, supra n53, 339.

220 As early as 1992 the W orking Group on the Question of an International Criminal Court argued the need for strengthening national courts to enable them to deal more effectively with international crimes (cited in El Zeidy, supra n195, 300).

221E. Witte, *Putting Complementarity into Practice: Domestic Justice for International Crimes inDRC, Uganda, and Kenya* (New York: Open Society Justice Initiative, 2010).

222 ICTJ, UNDP, Ministries of Foreign Affairs of Denmark and South Africa, 'Supporting Complementarity at the National Level: An Integrated Approach to Rule of Law' (2011), available < http://www.ictj.org/sites/default/f les/ICTJ-Global-Greentree-Two-Synthesis-Report-2011.pdf>, 1.

223Kleffner supra n49, 330.

224Stahn,supra n191, 267 and Gioia, supra n218, 807.

225Gioia,ibid., 807–812.

226ProsecutorialStrategy 2009–2012, supra n198, 5.

227*Report of the Bureau on Stocktaking*, supra n214, para. 42.

228Quoted at Consultative Conference on International Criminal Justice, 9–11 September 2009, cited in Bjork and Goebertus, supra n36, 213.

229 Seils, supra n207, 1012, C. Hall, 'Positive Complementarity in Action' in Stahn and El Zeidy (eds.), Vol. II, supra n12, 1014 at 1031.

230ProsecutorialStrategy 2009–2012, supra n198, 2–3.

231Ibid.

232 ICTJ, supra n180, 4, Hall, supra n229, 1031, 'Round Table', supra n25, 139.

233J.I.Turner, 'Transnational Networks and International Criminal Justice' (2006–07) 105 *Michigan Law Review* 985.

234Burke-White,supra n30, 96.

235Hall,supra n229, 1049.

236 Council Decision 2011 O.J. L 76/56 168 (21 March 2011).

237Hall,supra n229, 1050.

238Witte, supra n182, 64, 84, 88–89.

239*Focal points' compilation of examples of projects aimed at strengthening domestic jurisdictions to deal with Rome Statute Crimes*, Review Conference Doc. RC/ST/CM/INF.2 of 30 May 2010.

240 As proposed, for example, by M. Ellis, 'International Justice and the Rule of Law: Strengthening the ICC through Domestic Prosecutions' (2009) 1 *Hague Journal on the Rule of Law* 79, 81–82.

241Open Society Justice Initiative, 'Promoting Complementarity in Practice – Lessons from Three ICC Situation Countries' (2010), available < http://www.issafrica.org/anicj/uploads/OSJIComplementaritycasestudies.pdf>, 2.

242ProsecutorialStrategy 2009–2012, supra n198, 5.

243 S. Arbia and G. Bassy , 'Proactive Complementarity: A Registrar' s Perspective and Plans' in Stahn and El Zeidy (eds.) Vol. I, supra n12, 52 at 56.

244 Ibid., and M. Ber gsmo, O. Bekou and A. Jones, 'Complementarity and the Construction of National Ability' in Stahn and El Zeidy (eds.), V ol. II, supra n12, 1052.

245Begsmo, Bekou and Jones, ibid., 1053, 1056, 1059.

246Ibid.,1066.

247 Czarnetsky and Rychlak, supra n15, 97, Drumbl, supra n203, 212.

248Delmas-Marty supra n50, 4, El Zeidy, supra n195, 299.

249T Abdulhak, 'Complementarity of Procedures: How to Avoid Reinventing the Wheel' in Stahn and El Zeidy (eds.), Vol. II, supra n12, 955 at 961.

250 M. du Plessis, 'Complementarity and Africa: The Promises and Problems of International Criminal Justice' (2008) 17 *African Security Review* 154, 165.

251 C. Ero, 'Understanding Africa's Position on the International Criminal Court' in P. Clark (ed.), *Oxford Transitional Justice Research: Debating International Justice in Africa* (Oxford: FLJS, 2010), 11 at 12.

252Drumbl,supra n203, 197.

253Witte, supra n182, 13.

254S.Nouwen, 'Complementarity in Uganda: Domestic Diversity or International Imposition?' in Stahn and El Zeidy (eds.), Vol. II, supra n12, 1120 at 1138–1148.

255 Quoted in 'Round Table', supra n25, 152.

256 DuPlessis, supra n250, 156.

257 R. Sannerholm, *Rule of Law after War and Crisis: Ideologies, Norms and Methods* (Cambridge: Intersentia, 2012), 240.

258 As summarized by Witte, supra n182, 13 and 29.

259 Mégret, supra n48, 387.

260 Arbia and Bassy, supra n243, 64.

261 Begsmo, Bekou and Jones, supra n244, 1061.

262 Witte, supra n182, 21.

263 Ibid., 21.

264 L. Arbour and M. Bergsmo, 'Conspicuous Absence of Jurisdictional Overreach' (2009) 1 *International Law Forum du Droit International* 13, 14.

265 El Zeidy, supra n195, 175–178, Kleffner , supra n49, 129 and 139 and Jurdi, supra n51, 42 and 45.

266 Jurdi, ibid., 38.

267 ICC Off ce of the Prosecutor, *Informal Expert Paper: The Principle of Complementarity in Practice* (2003) <www.icc-cpi.int/iccdocs/doc/doc654724.PDF>, Annex 4.

268 Ibid., 3.

269 Ibid., 3–4.

270 E.g. the OTP' s 'Report on Prosecutorial Strategy 2006' (2006), available <http://www.f dh.org/IMG/pdf/OTPProsecutorialStrategy_2006-2009.pdf>, 5 and Hall, supra n229, 1019, who see a number of mundane communications that arise incidentally from the Statute as forms of positive complementarity.

271 1Delmas-Marty supra n50, 2, Kleffner, supra n49, 91.

272 *Prosecutor v Kony et al., Decision on the Admissibility of the Case Under Article 19(1) of the Statute*, ICC-02/04-01/05-377 (10 March 2009), para. 52.

273 J. Kleffner, 'Complementarity as a Catalyst for Compliance' in Kleffner and Kor (eds.), supra n10, 79 at 82, Hall, supra n229, 1017.

274 Burke-White, supra n30, 300.

275 WW. Burke-White, 'Reframing Positive Complementarity' in Stahn and El Zeidy (eds.), Vol. I, supra n12, 341 at 345. For example, Kenya' s Commission on Inquiry into the Post-Election V iolence referred to the ICC in its report to encourage the Government to pursue domestic accountability.

276 Annex to ICC Off ce of the Prosecutor , 'Paper on Some Policy Issues before the Off ce of the Prosecutor ' (2003), available < http://www.amicc.org/docs/OcampoPolicyPaper9_03.pdf>, 4.

277 Article18(1).

278 Offce of the Prosecutor, *Agreed minutes of the meeting between Prosecutor Moreno-Ocampo and the Delegation of the Kenyan Government*, The Hague, 3 July 2009.

279 Most notably Articles 18(2), 18(4), 18(7), 19(2), 19(4) and 19(7).

280 Article18(3).

281 Article19(10).

282 Articles18(6) and 19(8).

283 Articles18(5) and 19(11).

284 Drumbl, supra n203, 202.

285 Ibid., 204, El Zeidy, supra n195, 162, Benzing, supra n172, 603.

286 L. Moreno-Ocampo, 'A Positive Approach to Complementarity: The Impact of the Off ce of the Prosecutor' in Stahn and El Zeidy (eds.), V ol. I, supra n12, 21 at 23.

287*Situation in the Republic of Kenya*, Case No. ICC-01/09-02/11-274, *Judgment on Kenya's Appeal of Decision Denying Admissibility*, 30 August 2011.

288 C.C. Jalloh, 'Situation in the Republic of Kenya' (2012) 106 *American Journal of International Law* 118, 124.

289Elbert and Kontic, supra n77, 151.

290Hall,supra n229, 1021 and 1037.

291Batros,supra n58, 599.

292ProsecutorialStrategy 2009–2012, supra n198, 5.

293*Report of the Bureau on Stocktaking*, supra n214, Recommendations 50, 62 and 66.

294 Witte, supra n182, 18–19. See also du Plessis, supra n250, 159.

295ElZeidy, supra n195, 299.

296*Report of the Bureau on Stocktaking*, supra n214, para. 16.

297InformalExpert Paper, supra n267, 4.

298 E.g. Arbia and Bassy, supra n243, 54, B. Batros, 'The Judgment on the Katanga Admissibility Appeal: Judicial Restraint at the ICC' (2010) 23 *Leiden Journal of International Law* 343, 359.

299Hakan Friman, quoted in 'Round Table', supra n25, 148, C. Stahn, 'Complementarity: A Tale of Two Notions' (2008) 19*Criminal Law Forum* 87, 102.

300InformalExpert Paper, supra n267, 3.

301Stahn,supra n191, 236.

302Abdulhak,supra n249, 959.

303Seils,supra n207, 1011.

304*Paper on Some Policy Issues*, supra n276, 5.

305Stahn,supra n299, 102.

306Benzing,supra n172, 630.

307 Though the Prosecutor and Court are still obliged to examine the admissibility of any purported waiver (El Zeidy, supra n195, 275).

308 Ad Hoc Committee on the Establishment of an International Criminal Court, supra n23, 47.

309 It provides: The Court may exercise its jurisdiction with respect to a crime referred to in Article 5 in accordance with the provisions of this Statute if: (a) A situation in which one or more of such crimes appears to have been committed is referred to the Prosecutor by a State Party in accordance with Article 14.

310E.g.Arsanjani and Reisman, supra n186, Schabas, supra n204.

311D.Robinson, 'The Mysterious Mysteriousness of Complementarity' (2010) 21 *Criminal Law Forum* 67.

312InformalExpert Paper, supra n267, 19.

313 Hall, supra n229, 1018, P. Gaeta, 'Is the Practice of Self-Referrals a Sound Start for the ICC?' (2004) 2 *Journal of International Criminal Justice* 949, 950.

314*Prosecutor v Germain Katanga and Mathieu Ngudjolo Chui*, Appeals Chamber, *Judgment on the Appeal of Mr Katanga against the Trial Decision of Trial Chamber II of 12 June 2009 on the Admissibility of the Case*, ICC-01/04-01/07-1497, 25 September 2009, para. 85.

315Drumbl,supra n203, 200.

316 Jurdi, supra n51, 177–178 and 180, Clark, supra n90, 1203.

317Jurdi,ibid.,180.

318Gaeta,supra n313, 950.

319*Judgment on the Appeal of Mr Katanga against the Trial Decision of Trial Chamber II*, paras. 78–80, 82 and 85.

320 Batros,supra n298, 361.

321 Newton,supra n217, 319.

322 Burke-White,supra n275, 347.

323 ElZeidy, supra n195, 231.

324 M. Glasius, 'A Problem, Not a Solution: Complementarity in the Central African Republic and Democratic Republic of Congo' in Stahn and El Zeidy (eds.), Vol. II, 1204 at 1213–1214.

325 Clark,supra n90, 1192–1193.

326 Schabas,supra n204, 743.

327 *Prosecutor v Lubanga* (Case No. ICC-01/04-01/06-8), *Prosecutor's Warrant for Warrant of Arrest*, para. 35.

328 Jurdi,supra n51, 264.

329 InformalExpert Paper, supra n267, 19.

330 Phil Clark, as quoted in S. Sacouto and K. Cleary'The Katanga Complementarity Decisions: Sound Law but Flawed Policy' (2010) 23*Leiden Journal of International Law* 363, 372–373.

331 W.W. Burke-White and S. Kaplan, 'Shaping the Contours of Domestic Justice: The International Criminal Court and an Admissibility Challenge in the Uganda Situation' (2009) 7 *Journal of International Criminal Justice* 257, 259.

332 Jurdi,supra n51, 149–161 and 170.

333 A. Maged, 'Withdrawal of Referrals – A Serious Challenge to the Function of the ICC' (2006) 6 *International Criminal Law Review* 419, 422.

334 Seils,supra n207, 1001–1002.

335 Ibid, 1002.

336 G. Gaja, 'Issues of Admissibility in Case of Self-Referrals' in Politi and Gioia (eds.), supra n25, 49 at 50.

337 S. Nouwen, 'The Catalysing Effect of the International Criminal Court in Uganda', presentation at ISA Annual Meeting, New Y ork, 16 February 2009, cited in Drumbl, supra n203, 215.

338 Glasius,supra n324, 1208–1209.

339 *Prosecutor v Germain Katanga, Judgment on Appeal of Mr Germain Katanga against the Oral Decision of Trial Chamber II of 12 June 2009 on the Admissibility of the Case*, ICC-01/04-01/07 0A8, 25 September 2009, para. 79.

340 Clark,supra n90, 1203.

341 Stahn,supra n191, 277–278.

342 *Paper on Some Policy Issues*, supra n276, 3.

343 E.g. 'Statement of the Prosecutor Luis Moreno-Ocampo to Diplomatic Corps', The Hague, 12 February 2004, available: < http://www.iccnow.org/documents/ OTPStatementDiploBrief ng12Feb04.pdf>, 4.

344 Newton,supra n199, 72.

345 Stahn,supra n299, 90–91.

346 Stahn,supra n191, 239–240 and 264.

347 Gioia,supra n14, 1106, 1115 and 1116.

348 Robinson,supra n311, 96.

349 Ibid.,99.

350 Stahn,supra n191, 276.

351 K.J. Heller, 'The Shadow Side of Complementarity: The Effect of Article 17 of the Rome Statute on National Due Process' (2006) 17 *Criminal Law Forum* 255, 273.

352 Holmes, supra n89, 674.

353 As argued by Glasius, supra n324, 1205, Jurdi, supra n51, 56–57, Arbia and Bassy, supra n243, 53, Bjork and Goebertus, supra n36, 211.

354 M. Politi, 'Refections on Complementarity at the Rome Conference and Beyond' in Stahn and El Zeidy (eds.), Vol. I, supra n12, 145.

355 As Judge Politi's colleague Judge Philippe Kirsch put it at the same Round Table (supra n25):'It is only in extreme cases that the international community should intervene … The business of the Court is not to second guess domestic proceedings.'

356 *Prosecutor v Katanga and Ngudjolo*, ICC-01/04-01/07-1497, 25 September 2009, paras. 82–85.

357 Glasius, supra n324, 1218.

358 Drumbl, supra n203, 209–210.

359 Begsmo, Bekou and Jones, supra n244, 1056.

360 Ibid., 1063.

361 ProsecutorialStrategy 2009–2012, supra n198, 15.

362 Kleffner supra n273, 93–94.

363 Supra n148 and surrounding text.

364 Greenawalt, supra n206, 144.

365 Stahn, supra n191, 277.

366 ICTJ, supra n180, 3.

367 F. Mégret, 'In Defence of Hybridity: T owards a Representational Theory of International Criminal Justice' (2005) 38 *Cornell International Law Journal* 725, 741–742.

368 UNDevelopment Programme and International Center for Transitional Justice, 'The "Legacy" of the Special Court for Sierra Leone', unpublished paper cited by Higonnet, supra n94, 368.

6 Restorative justice, traditional law, and justice sector reform

Many scholars have cautioned against seeking to combine [formal justice and informal justice], given the risk that informal justice systems may undermine fundamental rule of law principles, for example by perpetuating discriminatory social norms. Others have argued that, given the resilience of informal systems and their potential to support state processes, the best way may be to seek to create synergies between the two.[1]

International actors often must contend, therefore, not only with customary law in its varied forms and indefinite substance, but also with the vestiges of post-independence legal systems and varieties of legal pluralism. Understandably, it is not an easy task for them to understand and integrate these within their rule of law reform efforts. Nevertheless, it is a responsibility they cannot shirk.[2]

6.1 Introduction: pluralism and restoration

Previous chapters have examined how the practice and theory of transitional justice has failed to engage with perspectives from rule of law reconstruction. While the use of amnesty and truth commissions to circumvent the courts has formed a key element of transitional justice debates since the field's earliest days, the headlong pursuit of transitional justice dividends from trial has resulted in forms of administering criminal justice that depart paradigmatically from the model of fair, depoliticized justice those reconstructing the judiciary would wish to inculcate. International criminal justice in particular has frequently ignored or undermined national judicial reform. However, it is in the employment of traditional justice mechanisms that the failure to integrate perspectives from rule of law reconstruction is most pronounced, as actors in both fields attempt to make the legal state and the socio-logical nation of ethnic or linguistic or regional groupings cohere. Before proceeding, it is necessary to explain the choice of the term 'traditional justice'. One of the recurring problems in this area is adopting a suitable common term for the plethora of dispute resolution mechanisms that fall outside the scope of the formal justice system. Actors in the field have used terms such as *customary, non-state, subnational, indigenous, non-state, informal* and *popular* to define them, though all such categorizations at a certain level risk cultural insensitivity and do an injustice to the complexity of the concept. 'Traditional' is the descriptor used to describe the justice mechanisms employed herein. Huyse, among others, suggests that the term may be unsuitable, arguing that it may connote a static, unresponsive body of rules and custom that ignores the continuous change these mechanisms evince in responding to changing political, social and economic circumstances. [3] However, this warning presumes too conservative a view of the term – the def nition used here merely indicates dispute resolution processes rooted in local tradition (which may in fact be of relatively recent provenance) but does not presume inertia, and should be read as fully compatible with a realistic appreciation of their capacity to adapt in accordance with changing social, economic and political circumstance. The characteristics of what I label traditional justice are many, but among the key attributes are the following:

- Those tasked with responsibility for delivering justice are appointed from within a subnational community (usually quite small and based on geography or ethnicity) on the basis of lineage, status or (less frequently) election
- They enjoy a degree of historical, charismatic and/or popular legitimacy
- Crimes and disputes are viewed as relating to the entire community , as opposed to only the parties most immediately involved. There is a high degree of public participation
- Decisions are arrived at after consultation, often with an emphasis on reconciliation, social harmony and reparation
- The process is voluntary, even if enforcement of decisions requires social pressure from the community
- Legal representation is not allowed and there are no formal rules of evidence
- Participants may feel a stronger loyalty to the micro-community than to the state.

Familiar examples from within the transitional justice literature would include the *mate oput* of Uganda, *nahe biti* of East Timor, *gacaca* in Rwanda. Other forms of atraditional grassroots transitional justice such as monuments or memory projects are not considered.

Practitioners and scholars in the f elds of both transitional justice and rule of law reconstruction have embraced traditional mechanisms of dispute resolution as part of their national strategies after initially dismissing them as irredeemably inimical to modernity . However, neither f eld has been enriched by the practice or theory of the other . Most of the ample literature on traditional justice is anthropological in nature, with a marked focus on legal pluralism.[4] As a theory, legal pluralism in essence is a concept used to analyse interactions between legal and social rule systems embedded at various layers in the state.[5] However, as Hinton notes, anthropology has been 'largely silent' on the topic of transitional justice, engaging little with overall theory even if there are particularized studies of individual transitional justice processes that employ customary mechanisms. [6] The reason he gives for this disengagement is transitional justice's teleological impetus towards democratization and modernization which implicitly deprecates ostensibly more 'backward' or even 'barbaric' traditional practices in a manner reminiscent of the civilizing missions of colonialism[7] This hesitation is somewhat misplaced; if anything, as this chapter goes on to show, traditional justice has more often been idealized in transitional justice literature. However, it is clear that most works in rule of law reconstruction literature by scholar -practitioners on traditional justice mechanisms in post-conf ict scenarios pay short shrift to issues of transitional justice, which is generally either ignored completely or mentioned only in passing.[8]

This indifference is reciprocated in transitional justice scholarship, with more damaging consequences. As Griff ths argues, legal pluralism is more a fact, i.e. an inescapable social state of affairs, than a mere doctrine or theory.[9] It is a pervasive element of life in most countries, in particular those likely to attract the operation of transitional justice. However , the few links between transitional justice and anthropology 'have been tangential or indirect through related literatures on the anthropology of genocide, political violence, human rights, social suffering, and international law'.[10] In his 2005 study of embedded transitional justice, Gready noted that legal pluralism has not been seriously addressed in the main works on localizing transitional justice.[11] In the intervening years, some writers in the feld have looked at the relation between traditional justice as transitional justice and processes whereby transitional states attempt to regulate their relationship with subnational legal or customary orders. Notable examples include Nagy (examining how scholars and practitioners of transitional justice should approach the problem of interacting with different legal orders within the state), [12] Huyse and Salter (whose edited volume is the f rst sustained attempt to place transitional justice in a pluralist state justice reconstruction context),[13] Clark (placing traditional justice more holistically within post-conf ict reconstruction processes),[14] and Kerr and Mobekk (examining the use of informal justice mechanisms to deal with past atrocities and their interaction with the formal justice system).[15] These works take cognisance of the complexities of the interaction between traditional justice as transitional justice and rule of law reconstruction. However , elsewhere in the bur geoning literature on transitional justice, traditional mechanisms are generally evaluated in the context of universalized human rights concerns, transitional trial or truth commissions. Consequently, the literature tends to assume the form of simplif ed, dichotomized debates on subsets of the hackneyed restorative justice versus criminal justice debate: African justice versus Western justice,[16] justice for the people versus justice as a tool of the state,[17] local culture versus universalized principles,[18] local community versus the nation. [19] As a result, it replicates many of the short-term, exceptionalist and anti-formalist emphases of transitional justice scholarship, to the exclusion of perspectives on more mundane issues of legal pluralism which form the basis for the understanding of traditional justice in long-term rule of law reconstruction.

This dichotomic presentation tends to obscure the commonalities of interest between transitional justice and more national rule of law reconstruction processes in post-conf ict states, most notably in the pressing debate on whether and/or how traditional justice mechanisms can be integrated into state-level justice sector reform. As Shaw points out, '[m]ost post-conf ict states of the global South have dualist legal systems: formal state law and informal customary law'. [20] However, the place of traditional justice in a dualist national legal system is a question transitional justice scholarship has largely ignored. Copious quantities of ink have been spilt on whether and how the use of traditional justice processes might complicate admissibility of cases to the ICC or jeopardize peace in Sudan; [21] the degree to which they might f t within the criminological templates of transitional justice; [22] the risk of human rights abuses in employing them to account for mass crimes;[23] or the ethical superiority of localized mechanisms vis-à-vis positivistic secular law.[24] These debates, essentially revolving around the clash between local culture and universal principles, can lead only to impasse. By contrast, little or no attention is given to more practical issues of the relationship between these mechanisms and simultaneous domestic rule of law reconstruction. For example, transitional justice scholarship is greatly concerned about whether the *mato oput* tradition of Uganda's Acholi people can bring peace or satisfy the ICC's complementarity requirements.[25] However, from the point of view of rule of law reconstruction, the more important issue in the long term may be what the use of *mato oput* for serious crimes says about Article 2 of the Ugandan constitution on consistency of custom with state law or the relevance of Article 129 that allows subordinate courts to operate at regional and village level, [26] or the prevailing national consensus that customary fora are appropriate for land and family-related disputes but not for serious violations of criminal law .[27] In Burundi, a clash has emer ged between international donors and NGOs who attempt to rehabilitate the traditional *bashingantahe* process for the purposes of transitional justice on the one hand, and the national government who are opposed to using it in this way, on the other.[28] Given the simplistic assumption one sees in transitional justice that traditional justice is of automatic utility in addressing past human rights violations (see Section 6.4), it is unclear how much thought, if any , has been given to whether the employment of these mechanisms for serious crimes can or should be accommodated within the national rule of law strategy of a transitional government whose attitude to customary law may or may not be as accommodating. This may be a function of the widely disparate interests of transitional justice policy-makers and their brethren in justice sector reform. The metrics by which the use of customary law as transitional justice is judged, such as trust between antagonistic groups, empathy for the other' s position, psychosocial healing and democratic dialogue are far removed from the more prosaic types of questions justice sector reformers ask when they approach traditional justice: how should and do the plural legal orders within the state interact? How should jurisdiction be divided between a standardizing, centralizing state justice sector and pluralist, decentralized traditional mechanisms? To what extent should individual rights guaranteed by the state take precedence over restorative and collective principles? What frameworks should inform resolution of conf   icting principles and practices? W   ill integration of formal and informal systems prove mutually benef   cial or mutually corrosive?

As Section 6.4 goes on to examine, there is great optimism that traditional justice can capture the meaning of conf ict in ways that more remote, state- or international-based processes cannot. However , if these mechanisms are to make a long-term, sustainable impact beyond the transitional moment, greater attention must be given to how their employment in this context might interact with the national rule of law strategy overall. If traditional justice is to be integrated better into overall transitional justice strategies, the vast literature on state legal pluralism recently incorporated into rule of law reconstruction policy would be an ideal place to start. It is a commonplace of rule of law reconstruction that formal and informal justice 'form part of a large organic justice system in which different systems interact'   [29] – as Plunkett notes, the art of re-establishing the state is to understand how to harmonize 'micro rule of law systems' outside the state within one larger national rule of law.[30] However, the view of these micro rule of law systems in transitional justice process tends to be an atomized one where potential interaction with the formal state justice sector is either ignored or disparaged. This may be a function of the tendency for the complexity of legal pluralism to be 'invisible' to outsiders,[31] though as far as transitional justice is concerned the problem is more a tendency to see just one side of the picture. As Section 6.4 goes on to argue, in transitional justice discourse customary justice mechanisms tend to be seen through a primarily restorative lens. In stable states, those applying a restorative lens to the provision of justice have traditionally struggled to deal with the public dimensions of crime. [32] It remains to be seen whether this challenge can be surmounted in the transitional context.

Of course, many in the transitional justice f   eld will disagree with an approach explicitly premised on 'thinking like the state' or entertaining any top-down control given that traditional justice has been valorized as an example of 'justice from below'.[33] However, many of the issues that concern those who advocate the use of customary law as a response to past violence such as the risk of human rights violations, the treatment of minorities, their lack of accountability and their susceptibility to political manipulation, can only be rectif ed with a large role for the state. This necessity tends to be dismissed in a literature that all too often assumes glibly that formal state structures are automatically too distant or illegitimate. It is common to see transitional justice scholarship urging 'a deep understanding of local culture'[34] or advising practitioners to tailor programmes to the environments in which grassroots transitional justice takes place. [35] However, as this chapter goes on to demonstrate, the process of understanding and tailoring traditional justice mechanisms to the transitional context tends to ignore one very salient element of that context, namely the simultaneous process of regulating the plural national legal and normative orders. As a result, transitional justice practitioners and rule of law reconstructors reach very different conclusions about the merits of integration with the state, the role of the executive and the importance of 'restoration'.

This disparity between the interests of transitional justice and rule of law reconstruction can be explained to a signif cant degree by the different roots of their consideration of the f eld. Transitional justice's engagement with traditional justice draws to a signif cant degree on W estern theories of restorative justice as an antidote to formalist state/international criminal justice mechanisms. Consequently, it has been esteemed as a bottom-up alter native to elitist bargains and presented in idealized terms, and in the process has frequently disdained the role of the state in supervising or monitoring it. By contrast, rule of law reconstructors view traditional and formal justice in less dichotomized terms and embed the discussion in a broader national and temporal framework. There is an awareness that traditional justice mechanisms present a 'clash of two goods' – respect for local customs and practices, on the one hand, and the goals of sustainable, rights-based, non-discriminatory state-building on the other .[36] The emphasis has always been on how to integrate traditional systems with the emer ging state legal system. This viewpoint takes a role for the state as both legitimate and inevitable. In the process of integrating traditional justice with the formal system, the empha- sis is 'to build mutually benef cial linkages between the systems ... T o harness the positive aspects of each system and mitigate the negative.' [37] Transitional justice discourse, by contrast, presents traditional justice mecha- nisms as laudably antithetical alternatives to formal justice and tries to divorce the two as far as possible. Transitional justice is to be commended for rejecting the applicability of idealized formal systems to post-conf ict ecologies one saw so frequently in the earlier literature and appreciating the value of the previously caricatured customary systems. However, in so doing, it has often merely reversed tropes, idealizing the latter and caricaturing the former. To simplify generally but not inaccurately, in transitional justice the main value attached to any subnational justice process is its inherent restora- tive potential, not its capacity to f ll rule of law gaps. By contrast, the main value attached to traditional justice mechanisms in rule of law reconstruction is its ability to close rule of law gaps, and not their restorative nature.

This chapter does not attempt to synthesize debates between the suspicious detractors and romantic advocates of traditional justice as a form of transitional accountability. It instead ar gues that when customary law is being employed as a form of transitional justice it should complement, or at least not contradict, the invariably contemporaneous process by which the state and peace-builders attempt to accommodate these customs in a weak national justice system. The ability of traditional justice to advance reconciliation and restoration is lar gely overestimated and hostage to a number of fortunes. By contrast, traditional justice as transitional justice can take advantage of its high prof le, the involvement of NGOs and the undoubted f exibility of custom in periods of political f ux to serve a more immediately realizable, sustainable and more prosaic role as a model for the interaction of non-state and state-based justice. Section 6.2 examines the roots of this disparity and examines why practitioners in the f elds of transitional justice and rule of law reconstruction take such different approaches. Sections 6.3 and 6.4 then examine why this has led to differing views of the merits of integration with the formal justice system and the role of the transitional government in supervising traditional justice. Section 6.5 then concludes by examining how transitional justice offers an opportunity to sensibly and sustainably ground standards of human rights, accountability and non-discrimination in traditional justice.

6.2 Parallel conversations: why customary mechanisms are viewed differently in rule of law reconstruction and transitional justice

It is surprising that this disparity has emer ged. After all, the emphasis one sees in both rule of law reconstruction and transitional justice on customary methods of dispute resolution is of relatively recent provenance. The legal pluralism which informs the use of traditional justice in rule of law recon-struction became popularized in socio-legal studies in the 1990s,[38] as did the restorative justice theories that have formed the intellectual underpinning for transitional justice's engagement with non-state law.[39] It was only in the late 1990s and early 2000s that the use of traditional mechanisms was main-streamed in both f elds after earlier falling foul of their hitherto-dominant universalizing, formalist perspectives. The emphasis on traditional justice in both transitional justice and justice sector reform is the result of a consensus that top-down, national-level processes alone were suffcient neither to reckon with the past nor build a better future, and that more bottom-up perspectives with national ownership were essential to empower vulnerable groups and create access to justice. Nevertheless, the engagement of both justice sector reformers and transitional justice practitioners with customary law was to a certain extent more the product of circumstances in the post-conf ict or post-authoritarian states to which they deployed than conscious policy . In transi-tions from authoritarian rule to democratic rule, there will usually be some continuity between the old and new legal dispensations. Even in the most fragile and war-torn of transitions of the sort examined in Chapter 1, a *tabula rasa* in relation to rules and norms is unlikely to obtain. Though there may be a vacuum in terms of formal legal structures, highly resilient and histori-cally or socio-culturally embedded forms of traditional justice usually f ll the gaps until the point where their competences are snapped. Endemically weak states will often co-exist with strong traditional society (for example, eight

years after the f rst democratic elections, Malawi' s 9 million people at one
stage shared 24,000 traditional justice mechanisms and only 300 lawyers), [40]
and may even facilitate it:

> It is frequently assumed that the collapse of state structures, whether
> through defeat by an external power or as a result of internal chaos, leads
> to a vacuum of political power. This is rarely the case. The mechanisms
> through which political power are exercised may be less formalized or
> consistent, but basic questions of how best to ensure the physical and
> economic security of oneself and one' s dependents do not simply
> disappear when the institutions of the state break down. Non-state actors
> in such situations may exercise varying degrees of political power over
> local populations. [41]

The existence in the transitional environment of these systems, invariably
more entrenched, legitimate and accessible than the formal justice system for
the reasons described in Chapter 1, is something every peace-building process
has to grapple with. At the most basic peace-building level, it was obvious
that rapidly resolving small local problems could prevent them from
mushrooming into lar ger regional ones, while removing local justice
measures (if this were at all possible) might create a security vacuum. [42] In
these contexts, non-recognition of customary justice is entirely unrealistic as
people will use it anyway or the structures will operate under ground beyond
the inf uence of the state or peace-builders. As the rule of law is gradually
reconstructed, formalizing links and jurisdictional spheres with these
proliferating and fragmenting non-state processes is an immediate necessity
and a key part of soldering the state back together. [43]

Similarly, transitional justice also has to reckon with a pre-existing
traditional justice sector more readily available than the ad hoc mechanisms
it can formulate. Refusal to engage with customary law has generally proven
impossible, given the tendency of traditional mechanisms to pre-empt state-
level transitional justice processes in the likes of Rwanda [44] and East Timor [45]
(in signif cantly different form to later more formalized employments), as
well as in the likes of Burundi,[46] Peru[47] and Mozambique,[48] though it should
be pointed out that local communities will often reach some form of *modus
vivendi* ('Don't-bother-me-and-I-won't-bother-you') even in the absence of
customary reconciliation. [49]

One sees in the literature, policy documents and practice of those in justice
sector reform and transitional justice shared assumptions about the strengths
and weaknesses of traditional justice. In terms of strengths, both viewpoints
accept the necessity of informal justice given the formal system' s chronic
weakness – previous association with an illegitimate regime, human rights
abuses and the sheer lack of qualif ed professionals in formal institutions
of justice mean the reconstructing state cannot penetrate below state level.
Even where the justice system has not been decimated, it may have little

coverage outside of the major cities. For example, in 2011 Mozambique only had two district courts with full-time judges in a territory twice the area of Italy.[50] Even in non-conficted or non-transitional countries in the developing world, remarkably consistent fgures of around 80–90 per cent of all legal disputes are resolved outside the formal system.[51] However, this reliance on traditional law cannot be explained by the weakness of the justice sector or the gap between community and the state alone. Customary mechanisms should not be regarded merely as poor substitutes. As Isser notes, 'customary law, like any other system of law, is not just a set of rules but a deeply contextual and socially embedded regulatory system'.[52] To begin with, traditional justice might have spiritual roots such as Mozambique's *magamba* spirit system where spirits of victims of abuses against the local order can infect the realm of the living if justice is not secured,[53] or in East Timor where society is based on a 'refned socio-cosmic system' in which dispute resolution is characterized through replacement of values to stabilize the cosmic fow to ensure continued harmony within the community.[54] Even without this spiritual aspect, traditional mechanisms present many practical advantages.[55] Above all, the emphasis on consultation, debate, compromise and compensation tends to foster the type of social harmony (or the absence of social acrimony) which is necessary in economically marginal, interdependent localities – a dispute does not simply exist between two or three parties, but is viewed as a potential source of community-wide disorder. Stability rather than penalization is often the primary goal of indigenous justice. Wongdoing is considered not as a crime to be punished, but an action against the social order or circulation of values which must be rebalanced. In areas of Colombia, vigilantism and mob violence are fve times more likely than in places where informal mechanisms continue to function.[56] By contrast, the innocent/guilty binary of the formal system risks exacerbating animosity, and if it results in imprisonment robs both the community of someone economically productive and the victim of compensation for the wrongdoing.[57] Traditional justice systems tend to deal with the crimes that are of greatest concern to local people such as personal security, property (land and livestock), family and community disputes, including socially-divisive matters the criminal justice system cannot deal with like divorce and witchcraft.[58] Finally, traditional justice tends to be more accessible and responsive. Both advocates and detractors would admit that it is far quicker than formal justice because of its informality and proximity, which also tend to make it far cheaper. The value of traditional justice can be demonstrated by a well-worn stolen chicken anecdote. Though both formal and local systems could resolve the case of a woman's stolen chicken, reporting the matter to a criminal court would take days or weeks to resolve, might require hundreds of miles of travel and would cost infnitely more than the chicken is worth.[59] Informal processes, by contrast, can be initiated within 24 hours and generally require little or no payment. These processes are also conducted in a language familiar to all parties which may not be the case in national judicial systems.

However, while traditional justice mechanisms are popular ,[60] it does not necessarily follow that those who rely on them are blindly committed to them. Though there are a number of particularized criticisms of traditional justice, two of the most recurring general complaints relate to their tendency to reinforce power hierarchies and the frequency of human rights abuses. While much is made of their harmonizing potential, 'not all customary laws are necessarily benign, as they have undergone their own troubled history and evolution, and their content may not necessarily be uniformly acceptable to all citizens or communities in the country'. [61] The concept of community at the root of local justice processes needs to be interrogated given the tendency of traditional justice, like all systems of justice, to reinforce the power of existing hierarchies. Those who administer customary law often tend to be older men from dominant lineages who enjoy material wealth, while the absence of any separation of powers between executive and judicial functions may increase the risk of abusing their power .[62] By contrast, less powerful groups like women, the young and the indigent fnd themselves marginalized by a system that is rarely sensitive to their needs. As Merry puts it, informal justice processes inevitably ref ect 'what the stronger is willing to concede and the weaker can successfully demand'.[63] Wojkowska offers the example of Somalia, where militarily strong clans may openly refuse to comply with a judgment that favours a weaker clan.   [64] In this context, the search for consensus and harmony may in fact result in smothering legitimate grievance unfairly.

A further problem is that of reach. T raditional justice systems may work well internally but struggle when trying to restrain bodies outside the community like the government, civil service or corporations.[65] If the society is heterogenous in terms of language, ethnicity or religion, then customary law may be of little utility when some groups consider themselves outside of its remit or the traditional leaders consider certain groups to be excluded. As scholars argue in relation to Afghanistan, '[w]here customary law fails entirely is where it was never meant to go: solving disputes among people who do not see themselves as part of a common community'.[66] As Section 6.4 examines in greater detail, traditional justice is generally unsuited to very serious crimes like murder or or ganized crime which expose the limits of community solidarity. Here it is often recognized by the communities themselves that the formal system' s emphasis on rights, adversarialism and punitive sanctions may be more appropriate.

Human rights tend to be the most potent source of criticism of traditional justice. In many customary systems, the individual is less the bearer of rights than the embodiment of certain social values that must 'f ow' in the right direction.[67] Due process complaints are the most frequent – because of the hierarchical organization of those tasked with adjudicating, an individual traditional justice mechanism might attract allegations of 'miscarriage of justice, favouritism, coercion, arbitrary imprisonment or extended detention without trial'.[68] The greater concern lies with the list of punishments employed wherever a mechanism departs from restorative principles, to the extent they were ever present. Among the reasons why donors have proven reluctant to fund these mechanisms are the harsh physical punishments (for example, torture[69] and lynchings[70] have been reported in places like East Timor and Guatemala) and banishments employed, particularly when they are used in a discriminatory manner .[71] Even where restorative methods are preferred, these systems can still uphold traditional practices that violate the rights of women. Feminists have long protested use of local law as a means of restricting women's rights.[72] As noted above, women rarely administer traditional justice. Male dominance is compounded when issues of security and peace arise.[73] Traditional justice tends to undermine the socio-economic status of women. For example, in many places in sub-Saharan Africa, women may not be able to own, control or inherit land except through a male relative, while widows and divorcees are mar ginalized.[74] Indeed, even the spirits can be biased – in Mozambique's *magamba* system, only spirits of men can return to the sphere of the living to reclaim justice. [75] In a number of countries, women may be forced to marry their rapists, be punished for suffer ing sexual abuse or see compensation given to their kin group collectively for her loss in marital value.[76] It is with women's rights in particular that ideal-ized scholarly attachments to indigenous cultures most frequently bows to more individual-oriented state laws on issues like property , sexual offences, child custody, and support payments.[77] Justice sector reformers have ar gued for a role for the state to '(a) identify the social mechanisms present within customary systems that permit women to exert inf uence and have a voice, (b) take care lest its policies constrain these mechanisms, and, where possible, (c) seek to reinforce them'.[78]

The other criticisms of local justice also have a marked rule of law bent. Traditional mechanisms make no distinction between civil and criminal cases as both are considered social disturbances, while the punishment of supernatural crimes like witchcraft necessarily involves signif cant departures from even the most basic rules of evidence. Pressure to confess crimes and lack of appeal are also pertinent criticisms. The fact that law is unwritten allows for a degree of f exibility which conduces to deliberation and consensus, but may also serve to reduce certainty and transparency as identical cases receive disparate treatments. Above all, there is little to stop a traditional justice mechanism reaching a decision which f atly contradicts the law of the land.[79] Grenfell summarizes a number of reasons why traditional justice is seen to challenge ordinary intuitions about the rule of law: (i) it does not emanate from the state and so lies outside its domain, (ii) it competes with state law , (iii) it is unwritten and therefore unpredictable, (iv) it is not applied uniformly across the state, (v) it is frequently not accountable to a higher authority, and (vi) its norms may contradict human rights norms. [80] As Lubkeman et al. point out, these limitations might better be characterized as trade-offs, given that some of the elements that contradict the rule of law (inequality, lack of human rights standards) may facilitate other rule of law goals like legitimacy, security, flexibility and non-violent conflict resolution.[81] However, even advocates of these mechanisms admit that they are frequently 'paradigmatically contradictory' to modern systems of rule of law.[82]

6.3 From ignored to indispensable – traditional justice in rule of law reconstruction

As noted above, when peace-builders and transitional governments come to tackle the rule of law deficit in post-conflict states, it is less a question of whether to engage with traditional justice and more one of how to interact with on-going processes given the unwillingness or inability of local communities to wait for the rectification of the shattered formal justice structures. Initially, peace-builders were slow to acknowledge this reality given the rule of law shortcomings canvassed above. Some argued that they were so far removed from the goals of the rule of law that 'justice strategies should seek to replace rather than engage them ... [a]ccording to this argument, any official recognition of customary systems is tantamount to sanctioning human rights violations'. [83] Normative structures outside the state were variously viewed as 'disorderly , corrupt, unimportant or even potentially subversive'.[84] The UN Transitional Administration in Cambodia made no effort either to dismantle or incorporate informal legal structures they found in operation.[85] In the early years of transition from Taliban rule in Afghanistan, the donor community focused exclusively on the formal legal system, notwithstanding the vibrancy (and dangers) of traditional systems based on tribal and Islamic law.[86] Successive peace-building missions in East Timor developed no strategy for identifying desirable spheres of jurisdiction between the nascent formal legal sector and traditional justice mechanisms in which as many as 99 per cent of all social disputes were resolved, though Civilian Police (CivPol) pragmatically employed them on an ad hoc basis. [87] In all cases, traditional justice emerged more as a competitor than a complement to the formal justice sector , while ongoing discriminatory or abusive practices went unchallenged. The failure of the rule of law in East Timor in particular highlighted the inadequacies of approaches that revolved exclusively around the state justice sector .[88] This state-formalist emphasis on strengthening the institutions of government, in addition to normative emphasis on human rights and due process, marginalized subnational processes which were always juxtaposed against judicial bodies seen in functional states.[89] As Chapter 2 examined, over time policy-makers and practitioners realized this narrow technical formalism could not ground the rule of law as it neglected the socio-political dynamics of the social order The accessibility, legitimacy and popularity of a traditional justice system meant it regulated how a majority of people actually ordered their lives:

> In these contexts, in short, the 'rule of (state) law' is only a small subset of the overall 'rules of the game' and as such, an exclusive concentration

on state law by development practitioners is unlikely to yield the results hoped for.[90]

As Barfeld et al. note, pragmatism over capacity gaps emer ged as the lead approach.[91] Organizing the traditional justice system was simply acknowledged as the most effective means of fostering and overseeing access to justice. Integration of traditional and state systems of justice now forms a core element of UN peace-building, as recognized in the *Rule of Law and Transitional Justice Report*:

> [D]ue regard must be given to indigenous and informal traditions for administering justice or settling disputes, to help them to continue their often vital role and to do so in conformity with both international standards and local tradition. Where these are ignored or overridden, the result can be the exclusion of lar ge sectors of society from accessible justice. Particularly in post-conf ict settings, vulnerable, excluded, victimized and mar ginalized groups must also be engaged in the development of the sector and benef t from its emerging institutions.[92]

Consequently, this *volte-face* should not be mistaken for a turn towards restorative justice, justice from below as something meritorious in itself or a rejection of a role for the state at local level.

It should be noted that much like its references to integrating transitional justice with rule of law reconstruction, little guidance is given in the *Report* about how this might be achieved or how conf icting ends might be prioritized. This concentration on justice gaps was allied to a greater emphasis in peace-building on access to justice (def ned as 'the ability of people to seek and obtain a remedy through formal or informal institutions of justice, and in conformity with human rights standards')[93] for disadvantaged people, who suffer the most if injustices cannot be remedied in a timely fashion. As peace-builders recognized that past peace-building initiatives touched the lives of very few people,[94] support to traditional justice mechanisms began to form a key premise of development programmes at multilateral [95] and bilateral levels.[96] Given the levels of public participation, it is assumed that traditional justice is inherently more empowering for people who can collaboratively control local justice where otherwise they risk subordination in larger, more formal processes. [97] However, even the foremost apostles of the legal empowerment approach such as Golub and Faundez argue that customary justice 'operates best when it integrates activities so that the whole is greater than the sum of its parts', most notably through interaction with other types of legal services and law reform. [98] The UNDP similarly encourages the strengthening of linkages between formal and informal structures as a means of mainstreaming the socio-legal concerns of the poor .[99]

At the same time as the formal justice system would be made more competent, legitimate and rights-respecting, the parallel traditional justice system would be made more progressive and accountable. However , given that (re)construction of the rule of law can take anything from f ve years to decades to emerge, integration of indigenous mechanisms with the formal sector is neither a side issue nor an interim tactic, but rather a core part of any effective rule of law strategy:

> The general view among leading policy-makers is that customary law should not only be recognized and applied by the traditional institutions but should be the main source of legislation and governance in all areas except those where modern exigencies require adopting from outside sources. This is a radical departure from earlier approaches that relegated customary law to a subordinate position. [100]

This focus is relentlessly pragmatic. Projects in the area typically mix training and education (on human rights, constitutional and other municipal law, mediation and arbitration) and institutional support (building infrastructure like computers, buildings, administration), but will often formalize the mechanisms by recording decisions or codifying the law in a manner that makes them more cognizable or assimilable for state oversight mechanisms. Notwithstanding some formalization, the key is 'to build mutually benef cial linkages between the systems without threatening the integrity of either'. [101] Some of the uniqueness and f exibility of the law is regrettably lost in this way , but this is an inevitable by-product of using traditional mechanisms to fulf l rule of law functions the state is unable to provide in a manner that is accountable and standards-driven. In response, the state must demonstrate greater sensitivity to local socio-political structures and co-operate with them strategically and sustainably in delineating the blurry lines between formal and informal law.

Embracing traditional justice can relieve pressure on the nascent justice system,[102] but this makes manifest the paradoxical nature of traditional justice as something of pressing immediate utility that may over time become obsolete given the hoped-for trajectory of rule of law reconstruction in a consolidated, legitimate and rights-respecting justice sector. In the same way that formal justice is unequipped to compete with customary law in weak states, as the state strengthens and modernizes, many cases and disputes will outstretch the competence and experience of local fora. [103] Pluralist perspectives aspire towards different forms of integration ranging from obsolescence of traditional justice over time to simple co-existence to full integration. Much will depend on the attitude of the national government, which shows great disparity among different states and different transition types. Just as pre-colonial traditional law changes under colonial rule, so too does its relations with national government evolve after independence or transition. After colonialism, some governments embraced traditional justice as a forum aff rming an independent national identity and left it untouched. Sometimes in transition, new national identity often demands that discrete indigenous practices are sacrif ced in the interests of unifying homogeneity , even if this exposes justice gaps – the diversity of normative systems may be seen as potentially divisive, and states move either to supervise traditional justice or to abolish it. [104] Educated, modernized elites frequently view customs as backwards and unable to address the needs of a rapidly modern- izing society.[105] This is all the more so when the new government sees these mechanisms as being aligned against them. For example, the more left-wing, statist Frelimo leaders of post-independence and post-transitional Mozambique historically opposed customary law for being anti-modern, discriminatory and more aligned with their political rivals Renamo until it recognized local law in the mid-1990s.[106] Similarly, the Timorese government that took over from UNTAET (made up of a largely urban mestizo elite with a def nite pro- modernization agenda) initially marginalized traditional justice as antitheti- cal to a formal, Portuguese-speaking formal system. [107] The predominantly Hutu government of Burundi is mistrustful of *bashingantahe* because of the inf uence of Tutsi at that level,[108] much as Guatemalan state policies formu- lated by the mestizo government marginalizes traditional Mayan law.[109]

Beyond the particular biases of the government, the nature of conf ict or authoritarianism before transition will have a signif cant effect on approaches to traditional justice after it. Sometimes the trauma of war will signif cantly affect the functioning and legitimacy of customary law , even if the diversity of experience precludes even the most generalized observations. Because war is synonymous with forced relocations in affected rural areas to towns or refugee camps (it is important to remember that some areas remain completely untouched by virtue of geography , ethnicity or poverty of resources), indigenous social structures might be ruptured, as occurred in Sierra Leone,[110] indigenous leaders might be lost, as occurred in Guatemala,[11] or traditional ceremonies become impossible, as in Uganda. [112] The savagery of war may see taboos disregarded and sacred places def led,[113] while the weaponization of disputes might make previously quiescent groups or individuals unwilling to compromise. For example, militia leaders in Afghanistan commandeered customary justice previously applied by the traditional *jirgas*.[114] Traditional authorities may have been complicit in war crimes, such as in Rwanda where 15.7 per cent of the *gacaca* judges had to be replaced by 2005 because of suspicion of complicity in genocide, [115] or failed to prevent them, as in Burundi. [116] Traditional justice itself may be a signif - cant motivating factor for conf ict – the patrimonial exclusion of young men has been found to be one of the primary reasons why young rural men joined Sierra Leone's RUF (indeed, they specif cally targeted customary authority f gures during the war),[117] while traditional rites have been used to frame the worldview of young recruits to the LRA in Uganda. [118] In authoritarian regimes, traditional justice might also be degraded – Malawi' s chiefs were discredited by the role they played in consolidating undemocratic rule by the post-colonial regime,[119] just as customary law was used by Ian Smith' s Rhodesian regime to shore up its rule.[120]

On the other hand, traditional justice might emerge stronger from conflict, such as in South Sudan where the post-independence government promotes traditional justice as a central facet of the new state after it formed a core aspect of the national identity in the war of liberation in contradistinction to Khartoum's use of *sharia*.[121] Traditional justice might enjoy sufficient legitimacy to form an explicit part of a peace settlement, such as the Juba Agreement in Uganda (integrating *mato oput* ceremonies into national transitional justice policy), Guatemala's peace accords (where the Government agreed to recognize and integrate indigenous law, though this was later defeated in a referendum), Burundi's Arusha accords which speak of rehabilitating *bashingantahe* or the Rwandan RPF's enthusiastic reclamation of *gacaca* as a key part of the national social fabric.

However, the impact of past conflict on the state's attitude to traditional justice might pale in comparison to that of state-building. If traditional justice is strongest where the state is weak, then it may decline in importance as the state develops judicial capacity that extends across the whole national territory Though some optimists argue that development of the justice sector might spur the customary system to adapt to stay relevant,[122] Brown has argued that generally 'customary law is not equipped to compete with the monolithic strength of introduced law systems and will be the inevitable loser in any circumstances where there is a choice between the systems'.[123] For example, by the time of the gencocide, *gacaca* in Rwanda had almost completely died as people preferred the state courts.[124] In the types of state examined in this book, the point where the formal justice system can compete with local processes is very far off. Many relatively well-functioning justice systems like Botswana retain a significant role for customary authorities. Nevertheless, changes in politics and economics will change behaviour and alter demand as the distribution of rights, responsibilities and resources is re-ordered. Some prerogatives will be lost over time, particularly in relation to criminal law where risks of human rights abuses and the desire for state control are greatest. However, beyond the mere fact of state intrusion, modernity, globalization and capitalism might have the biggest impact on traditional justice.[125] Increases in income level, literacy, migration to economic centres and technology will inevitably erode traditional values and mean that traditional leaders stop being the sole sources of information or authority. Some customary practices simply become 'dysfunctional' in modern states.[126] Even if peace-builders and most states have moved beyond regarding traditional law as a problem to be remedied, if transition is ultimately successful, customary mechanisms will have to adapt by dividing jurisdiction with the state, being accountable to the state through some form of judicial review and to those who use it. The alternatives may ultimately be repression or obsolescence.

The degree to which peace-builders will succeed depends to a significant extent on the attitude of the transitional government to customary law. Most dualist states, and in particular those emerging from conflict, tend to maintain that dualism primarily because they have no choice given the parlous state of the formal legal system. Pluralism is a fact of national life and its management is only avoidable if alternative forms of justice are abolished. Schemes to do so rarely succeed when state capacity is minimal. However, there are two more positive cases to be made for integrating traditional mechanisms, which might loosely be described as political and institutional capacity-building. It is better to begin with the former as ultimately the question of integration is more a political than a technical one. As political structures become more state-like, macro-political units historically have co-opted localized and sub-state mechanisms to varying degrees. During the colonial era, imperial powers would f rstly employ indigenous leaders and processes in a lar gely hands-off manner as a means of indirect rule before formalizing the relationship when colonial rule was extended. Jurisdiction would be divided over issues of government, commerce and serious crime (the state) and issues of family , some property , religion and minor crime (traditional mechanisms).[127] It should be pointed out that there would be wide variation within this rough division, and that similar processes were observed in states that were not subject to colonialism. [128] After colonialism, newly independent states would view increased supervision of these mechanisms as a key element of modernization, both as a means of legitimizing the new regime as something distinctly national/non-colonial and of bolstering the power of the state. [129] Here, legal pluralism operated essentially as a framework for state control. [130] The extent to which the state recognizes (or does not) the various customary mechanisms within its borders has implications for national public order as it determines the reach of the state at local level and how that reach is exercised. Some degree of control, supervision or co-operation may allow the state leadership to check local power structures and assert its monopoly on the legitimate use of force given the aforementioned risk of arbitrary and abusive punishment. Of course, state authority is best established through effective institutionalized implementation and enforcement of the law. Given the inevitable interaction between state and non-state systems, the choice the government faces is effectively one of conf ict or coherence. States building the rule of law may justif ably be wary of alternative venues for the provision of justice where abusive or discriminatory practices are prevalent. On the other hand, they may be keen to use them to extend or decentralize the state justice system where they are not on the basis of the simple principle that two (or three, or four) justice systems may be better than a single weak one.

Isser outlines a number of advantages of linkages between state and non-state systems:

- Alleviation of case-loads in the overburdened formal system
- Promotion of the relevance of the state
- Oversight of the customary system
- Mitigation of the effects of forum-shopping
- Recognition of multiculturalism.[131]

Others with equal optimism posit that linkages will ensure that what happens at formal court level can be 'fed back' into the local communities, thereby enhancing justice at both levels. [132] Connolly has identif ed four general ways in which states engage with non-state mechanisms.[133] The f rst, increasingly rare, is *abolition*, where the state explicitly abolishes informal justice systems through legislation to build legal uniformity. A diametrically opposed approach is *full incorporation*, where the formal state system incorporates a def ned role for customary rules into its decision-making processes. Traditional mechanisms may comprise a lower echelon of the justice system hierarchy, while arrangements are established to hear disputes arising from the application of customary law. Between these extremes are *non-incorporation* and *partial incorporation*. In the former, the state justice system coexists with the free and independent application by local communities of their local norms and customs on the basis of strict jurisdictional boundaries drawn between the two. In the latter , the relationship is much the same but with localized processes receiving recognition, assistance and oversight from the state, essentially splitting the difference between full incorporation and non-incorporation.

Considerations of space preclude a detailed survey of the ways in which state and non-state law are interpenetrated. There is no ideal ratio of state to customary mechanisms peace-builders or state governments should aspire to. However, one can look to a number of South American and African constitutions to see how states can balance the right of indigenous and local communities to govern themselves according to their own norms with the duty of the state to ensure consistency with national rule of law values. [134] Which of the four approaches is taken will be a ref ection of the history and politics of the state, the relative strengths of formal and informal mechanisms, the vagaries of transition and the ideological leanings of the government. At the most integrative end of the spectrum, governments might engage in the codif cation of customary laws or registration of decisions in traditional mechanisms, undertake human rights and technical training, fund traditional processes or even depute state off cials to take part. At a more basic level (assuming they do not intend on abolition), governments will have to clarify the role of alternative justice mechanisms in jurisdictional terms, assess their conformity with the emeging or revived constitutional order andnternational human rights law. This may constitute a permanent settlement of the state/non-state justice sector relationship, though often the state will fully absorb many traditional functions as it consolidates and expands its functionality.

6.3.1 *Jurisdiction*

Given the state's lack of capacity, detailed criteria will need to be developed to determine which of the state or traditional mechanisms should assume responsibility for dealing with a certain offence, and how jurisdictional disputes should be resolved procedurally . At least in the early days, it is unrealistic to assume that all but the most major crimes should be dealt with at national level. The process may be as much about collaboration as competition 'as different institutions and actors negotiate the boundaries of their jurisdiction based on their power, interests, and different notions of justice'.[135] Overall, however, the jurisdictional divide will typically resemble the post-colonial one where the state retains jurisdiction over issues of government, commerce and serious crime and non-state processes cover some family   , property and religious disputes, in addition to minor crime. This should serve to eliminate the risks of indeterminacy which f ow from forum-shopping. In successful models of jurisdictional allocation, the formal legal system should defer to customary principles and rules, subject only to a collateral review of decisions in light of constitutional and human rights guarantees or any deviations from the established procedures and remedies of the mechanism in question.[136] It should be pointed out that even where the state reserves the right to punish anything above a given level of crime, it should not necessarily mean that there will be no community sanction. Pluralist legal regimes can accommodate both the state's monopoly over punishment and the community's need to resolve tensions the offence has caused.

6.3.2 Human rights

Because the state remains the primary duty-bearer in relation to human rights and because human rights is generally central to its modernization process, a state that recognizes the resolutions of traditional mechanisms tends to do so (in theory if not always in practice) to the extent that they comply with constitutional human rights guarantees. As such, international human rights norms represent a more defensible modern spin on old colonial repugnancy clauses.[137] Given the aforementioned risks of abuse of power   , overly-harsh punishment and unaccountable decision-making, those subject to traditional processes will benef t from human rights guarantees to at least mitigate the risks of abuse. T raditional mechanisms will not require the whole panoply of procedural rights guaranteed in the formal system, and full compliance with constitutional or international human rights guarantees may be impossible, but with integration of the systems progress can be made. Corradi, for example, ar   gues that development of formal justice systems can improve standards at local level by providing competition or 'negotiation resources' when those responsible for administering customary law interpret it.[138]

6.3.3 Mutually beneficial integration?

As Section 6.4 later illustrates, in transitional justice discourse interference by the state in indigenous justice is typically presented as compromising the pristine, restorative nature of localized justice processes. However   , local populations take a more pragmatic view and recognize a role for state primacy or oversight in relation to crimes that seriously strain the social order In most pluralist states, sophisticated moral economies of justice apply to questions of jurisdiction. For example in East Timor 69 per cent of people would use local justice and 13 per cent the formal system for theft; for serious assault by a family member 33 per cent would use local justice and 47 per cent the formal system, while 91 per cent recognize the formal system as the appropriate mechanism for murder trials.[139] Liberians generally believe that cases should progress upwards from customary mechanisms where resolution at this level proves impossible, while offences above a threshold seriousness should only be dealt with by state courts.[140] Malawians value the availability of the formal system given the risk of corruption and bias at local level. [141] This translates into the application of transitional justice – for example, surveys of Ugandans show a willingness for senior commanders to be prosecuted while those of lesser rank go through more restorative processes. [142]

However, one sees in transitional justice literature a distinct sense that those who administer and rely on traditional mechanisms resent state encroachment on their processes as corrupting and illegitimate, which underlies a misleading conception of traditional justice as a bastion of resistance to the state Leviathan. Certainly, there is a risk that hard rules can reduce the necessary flexibility of customary remedies and temper the sense of ownership, while the legitimacy of traditional authorities may be diminished if they are seen as too close to an unpopular state.[143] Furthermore, the state itself can be abusive and cynically use traditional justice to consolidate local power bases, while traditional mechanisms may enjoy their own checks and balances for flawed decisions, independent of state supervision. However, on the other side of the ledger, traditional mechanisms 'benefit by securing state funding and by enjoying the boost of status and authority (and sometimes coercive backing) that follows from state recognition'. [144] Local mechanisms may benefit from the fact that state courts can uphold their decisions if appealed,[145] while accountability to the state may in fact bolster their legitimacy .[146] Of course, successful integration is easier said than done. Faundez notes that most interaction of state with non-state justice systems 'generally does not yield improvements on the rule of law or produce results that further good governance',[147] while Chirayath et al. note that the changes introduced by successive regimes often increase the conflict between rule systems. [148] Nevertheless, transparent, accountable and mutually agreed integration can yield modest benefits, ironing out certain persistent problems even if some remain unremedied, without detracting from the traditional goals of customary law. As Isser argues, '[j]ustice reform strategies should not seek premature answers but should try to set the stage for a constructive process of working towards a locally designed and inclusive system of justice'. [149] However, the failure of transitional justice to engage with this constructive state process means that opportunities for individual local processes of responding to past atrocity to set standards for human rights, non-discrimination or community-state interaction are severely diminished. It is to this that attention now turns.

6.4 Restoration and idealization: the transitional justice view

While peace-builders must grapple with the nature of traditional mechanisms (location, status, strength), their position in transition (more legitimate, less legitimate, enduring or ravaged) and the attitude of the government (opposition, toleration, recognition, control), there is little evidence that such contingencies inform policy where international actors working in transitional justice apply or assist in the application of customary law to the legacy of war or authoritarianism. Though idealism has given way to pragmatism in justice sector reform, it retains a strong infuence in transitional justice. The advocacy of traditional mechanisms as a response to confict stems less from the justice gap or pluralist perspectives than from a belief in the value of restorative justice, which in turn is derived less from an appraisal of the generic needs of developing and post-confict states than it is from contemporary scholarship on the need to revolutionize the way Western states respond to crime and socially-disruptive behaviour. Indeed, the mainstreaming of restorative justice considerations into both national criminal law and transitional justice theory can be pinpointed to the late 1990s.[150] The inspiration is the less the makeshift, pluralist responses to the absence of state justice one sees in Central America or sub-Saharan Africa than restorative police cautioning schemes, family group conferences and victim-offender mediation employed in North America and Europe which superfcially mirror the ideal traditional justice principles of communication between victim and perpetrator, reparation of harm etc. Eminent transitional justice scholars such as Dyzenhaus, Mani, Huyse and Leebaw have located the attraction of transitional justice to customary law in the application of law by aboriginal groups in stable societies (most notably Canada, Australia and New Zealand),[151] the 'informal justice' movement of the 1970s that emerged due to dissatisfaction with the state criminal justice system [152] and alternative dispute resolution practices like indigenous courts and juvenile justice programmes.[153] These programmes have been born of a belief that the rationales for state law in the West, and in particular criminal law, are unsatisfactory, counter-productive and remote from the needs of victims – in short, criminal punishment 'isn't working'.[154] While of undoubted application to laudable Western transitional justice initiatives like Northern Ireland's Ardoyne Commemoration Project [155] or the Greensborough Truth and Reconciliation Commission in the US, [156] Western notions of restorative justice have been too readily and unquestioningly accepted as the primary frame of reference for the employment of customary norms in transitional justice. It by no means follows that because the 'hollowed-out' state in the West might be divesting itself of responsibility for justice for minor crimes in favour of discursive solutions at community level, [157] it should serve as a frame of reference for transitional countries with comparatively little state to hollow out in dealing with comparatively far more serious crimes.

Traditional justice mechanisms are never consciously created as a reaction to, or alternative to, functioning formal justice systems. Historically , they pre-exist the formal system and then endure where that formal justice system is weak or non-existent. Nevertheless, the use of transitional justice for past human rights abuses is legitimized in the literature by references to trends in the West.[158] As a result, traditional justice is lauded in transitional justice discourse for its greater ability than formal justice to wrestle with the multi-faceted complications of justice in developing, post-conf ict states but in so doing ignores one of the key relationships these mechanisms must cultivate, namely that with the formal justice sector . The turn towards traditional justice was motivated by the commendable realization that decontextualized attempts to replicate the ideal of W estern justice in post-conf ict states were doomed to failure.[159] However, in so doing, it has drawn on ideal applications of restorative justice in that W estern milieu, which are of questionable relevance to dualist states.

This framework from Western restorative justice principles has interacted with various strands of the transitional justice critique of formalist responses. As Nagy notes, the rationale for embracing *gacaca*, like other traditional mechanisms, 'is perhaps best understood against the foil of what has not worked'.[160] The inf uence of W estern restorative justice theory is most evident in the tendency to criticize the formal justice system, to valorize distance from it, and to resist any role of the state in guiding, overseeing or standardizing the application of customary law to the problems of transition. The f rst strand of thought is one already examined in Chapter 4, namely the tendency to conceive of reconciliation primarily in personal, psycho-social terms. Though reconciliation was a stated aspiration of early truth commissions, it was only with the South African TRC that it stopped being regarded as a f g-leaf to justify the impunity outgoing regimes were able to secure from criminal trial. Over time a more principled defence of TRCs as the best response to past atrocity emer ged that emphasized their reconciliatory potential.[161] At its essence was a threefold commitment to human dignity , accountability for harm and the creation of social conditions in which human rights would be respected. However , as Kiss points out, these justif cations were also encapsulated by formal justice.[162] The added value of truth commissions, it was ar gued, was that they established an additional, superior , reconciliatory dimension of restorative justice 'concerned not so much with punishment as with correcting imbalances, restoring broken relationships – with healing, harmony and reconciliation'. [163] Employing language that was highly ambitious in terms of social transformation and highly derogatory towards criminal justice, [164] the transitional justice movement became 'blindly besotted' with restorative language. [165] Signif cantly, the restorative jargon of indigenous *ubuntu* was preferred to the more Judaeo-Christian or liberal theorizing that previously under girded reconciliatory processes, [166] pointing the way to a later valorization of indigenous custom. Over time, the SATRC would be acknowledged to have fallen short of what the early claims promised (famously, a Nielsen-Market Research Africa survey concluded that two-thirds of South Africans questioned believed the Commission led to a deterioration of race relations). [167] However, this did not call the restorative principle into question. Instead, scholars would ar   gue that top-down processes of national reconciliation were inferior and less useful than more localized, day-to-day reconciliation among intimate (former) antagonists who must live side by side. [168] For example, the failure of the Sierra Leone T ruth Commission to employ local traditional mechanisms of integration and purif cation in all but the most superf cial forms was regretted.[169]

This critique corresponded with a parallel critique of formal criminal mechanisms. As examined in Chapter 5, the exorbitant cost and slowness of the ad hoc tribunals, coupled with the legitimacy def cit that came with the exclusion of national involvement at all levels made them the paradigmatic examples of remote, irrelevant justice from above. Furthermore, formal systems were criticized for failures to give voice to victims' experiences (or instrumentalizing them where they did), to resolve contested truths or to address broader structural causes of human rights abuses. [170] The dependence of criminal law on f xed categories of perpetrator and victim and fxed catego- ries of guilt or innocence was deemed inapt to reckon with the grey areas, mixed motives and ambiguities of complicity relating to bystanders, prof teers or forcibly recruited soldiers. Implicit in this critique was the notion that these universalist, formalist methods excluded more legitimate, participatory and effective indigenous or *in situ* modalities that respected the constructive agency of those most affected.[171] This echoed the core restorative justice argument that trial of crime by the state privileges law and 'steals' the property of conf ict from the excluded victim and immediate community to whom it belongs.[172] A marked turn towards localization followed,[173] perhaps best framed by Gready' s distinction between 'embedded' and 'distant' justice.[174] The embrace of restoratively-inf uenced reconciliation and localiza- tion interacted with a third strand of transitional justice scholarship which emphasized the need for holistic, multi-faceted responses to atrocity and ref ected the inf uence of wider inter -disciplinary perspectives. As the f eld passed its f rst decade, it was gradually accepted that old binary choices between truth and justice had generated 'unhelpful and overly simplistic solutions',[175] a disruptive orthodoxy that gave way to a more enlightened preference for transitional justice as a spectrum of mutually-supportive mechanisms harmonizing as many perspectives as possible over the previous hierarchical understandings.[176] In this more open intellectual climate, indig- enous systems of justice in particular found favour for their local reach and potential synthesis of the values of criminal trial and truth commissions.

The evolving embrace of traditional justice measures was further catalysed by the reality alluded to earlier that it was happening anyway . Indeed, some of the more principled justif cations for a role for indigenous processes in dealing with past atrocity might best be considered as *post hoc* rationalizations of what was already happening on the ground. Most scholars accept that the

Rwandan government's turn towards *gacaca* was the starting point for the embrace of non-formal justice mechanisms – 'a hype was born', as Huyse puts it.[177] While much work would subsequently go into rationalizing and explaining *gacaca*'s position in transitional justice (the international community was generally sceptical at f rst over human rights concerns, but by around 2002 had changed tack and became more supportive, [178] until there emerged a backlash against this backlash), it was designed more to redress a capacity gap in the treatment of thousands of political prisoners than a legitimacy gap from the formal justice system. Likewise, in East T imor, traditional justice was embraced

> not because it was seen as virtuous or culturally appropriate in itself, but because the formal justice sector was struggling to address large numbers of perpetrators. It was only after traditional justice was utilised that arguments could be heard for its ostensible merits: as community based, or culturally appropriate.[179]

These more normative arguments about traditional justice would eventually drown out initial pragmatic justif cations based on the rule of law gap. As they did so, they would manifest a certain idealization of restorative justice and disparagement of the formal sector.

Def ning the widely contested concept of restorative justice is a diff cult task. As Roche admits, it tends to 'mean all things to all people'. [180] This problem is exacerbated by the fact that there is no agreement on whether it should be viewed as a process or as an outcome, whether it is a set of values or practices, and, if the latter , what particular practices can be included within its orbit.[181] What one is left with is a grab-bag of characteristics and aspirations. Overall, restorative justice

> revolves around the idea that crime is, in essence, a violation of a person by another person (rather than a violation of legal rules); that in responding to a crime our primary concerns should be to make offenders aware of the harm they have caused, to get them to understand and meet their liability to repair such harm and to ensure that further offences are prevented; that [this] should be decided collectively by offenders, victims and members of their communities through constructive dialogue in an informal and consensual process; and that efforts should be made to improve the relationship between offender and victim to re-integrate the offender into the law-abiding community.[182]

The values associated with restorative justice are ones few would quibble with – responsibility, respect, equality, inclusion, honesty, humility, empathy, care and trust.[183] However, most of the literature in the area is written by its proponents.[184] Its critics point out with force that this literature is lar gely 'aspirational' in character, conf ating exaggerated ideals and enthusiasm with coherent models of general practice. [185] After a period of untrammelled enthusiasm, even some of its most avid advocates began to admit the optimistic claims made have not been substantiated by empirical research.[186]

As noted above, much of the theory on traditional justice's applications in transition are drawn from restorative justice literature.[187] If anything, restorative theory becomes more attractive when applied in the context of developing states because the meso-social structures of moral community and communal coercion that make truly restorative justice untenable in industrialized democracies are to be found only in societies without the modern state justice apparatus.[188] While restorative justice is accepted only at the margins of criminal justice in the W est, it has assumed a central role in our understanding of transitional justice.

> There has been a tendency in international interventions to equate the concept of 'traditional' with 'fair', 'good' and 'impartial', particularly in situations where international interveners are sensitive to stepping on the culture of the country.[189]

That transitional justice practitioners should have such an aff nity for traditional mechanisms is not surprising – practitioners in both f elds often emerge from a realm of civil society that is voluntary , based on shared ideals and def ned by their autonomy from the state. When allied to the rootedness of traditional justice in indigenous culture and its assumed 'bottom-up' authenticity, the potential for making grandiose claims about what it can achieve in a transitional context are obvious. As a result, the treatment of customary dispute resolution by its enthusiasts in transitional justice is replete with repeated injunctions not to over-eulogize[190] or romanticize[191] it and to beware its seductive appeal [192] in light of the legitimacy and human rights concerns that attach to customary law. However, despite these caveats, the potential use and impact of traditional mechanisms has been reviewed more favourably than their modest record would suggest appropriate – 'awareness of the many weaknesses was not lacking, but they were too often kept in the shade'.[193] The sense one gets is that traditional justice *is* restorative justice. Community-based healing in Mozambique is credited (along with amnesty) in ending cycles of violence there, [194] the integrative practice of Peruvian *campesinos* is seen as 'several steps' ahead of that at national level,[195] *gacaca* is viewed as 'inherently a participatory and communal enterprise' and 'an important mechanism for promoting democratic values'.[196] At various stages it has been asserted unproblematically that Balkan codes regulating blood feuds [197] or *gacaca*[198] would provide a national foundation the rule of law. Chakravarty, Longman and Uvin all argued that the means by which a defendant could put forward his case in *gacaca* and the open play of argument and counter-argument could amount to a fair trial the equal of what one would receive before a criminal court.[199] Though Meyerstein points out that many of the more generous analyses of *gacaca* were undertaken before the trial phase took place, this in itself is indicative of a pronounced tendency towards wishful thinking.[200]

Over time, much of the romantic received wisdom regarding traditional justice's applicability in transition has given way to more realistic appraisals of the empirical record. The literature on *gacaca* which dominates so much of the thinking in the area in particular has retrospectively been characterized as overly positive.[201] The most obvious realization is one alluded to earlier , namely that traditional mechanisms are frequently very punitive. While traditional justice in the likes of Mozambique and East T imor followed a restorative template, physical punishments were employed in places like Sierra Leone and Liberia. Where ostensibly restorative modes of justice were pursued, they diver ged signif cantly from facile W estern imaginings of communitarian harmony. If, as Daly suggests, restorative justice assumes a generous, empathetic, rational and supportive human spirit, it has often been lacking after mass atrocity.[202] While W estern restorative justice is victim-centred, stability emerged in many traditional mechanisms as the paramount value – the search for consensus tends to favour the interests of the commu-nity as a whole over those of victims, and is often coercive towards them. [203] Though Mozambique is seen as the paradigmatic example of restorative traditional justice, the mechanisms employed were based more on for getting than forgiving.[204] The 'cool heart' emphasized in Sierra Leonean traditional justice is also more about for getting and moving on than repairing relation-ships.[205] In a Ugandan survey, only 9 per cent of those interviewed associated traditional ceremonies with reconciliation.[206] Compromise must satisfy both parties, raising obvious diff culties if one of them has caused egregious harms. Any emphasis on for giveness asks far more of victims than offenders, a problem exacerbated where confessions and apologies by defendants are insincere, formulaic or partial.[207] Overall, where some measure of reconcilia-tion arises, it is usually closer in Galtungian terms to a negative peace where community cohesion amounts to the mere absence of violence than a positive peace in which relationships are restored and remaining disputes are resolved constructively.[208] Superf cial reintegration of offenders into communities and 'pretended peace' on the part of victims have been the order of the day in many communities.[209] For the reasons described in Section 6.2, many of the communities are so sundered by conf ict that past presumptions that local leaders enjoy legitimacy are misplaced.[210] Though most forms of customary law rely on reparations if relationships are to be rebuilt, those responsible for the transgression are rarely in any position to do so by reason of their poverty relative to the number of victims or the scale of the violation. [211]

Finally, traditional justice' s perpetual inability to deal with situations involving people from different communities, recalcitrant f gures with guns, and government off cials is compounded by the way mass conf ict operates. Expectations that traditional justice can play a signif cant part in transition are premised on the notion that much violence is of a horizontal neighbour -against-neighbour nature. However, most conf ict is instead vertical in nature, originating from or against the state security apparatus, crossing and re-crossing the internal borders that mark the limits of communities or the applications of a given mechanism. Conf icts are often fought between ethnic, religious or linguistic groups who do not have the common bonds that under gird tradi-tional justice. Customary mechanisms have struggled to reckon with crimes that have cross-regional dimensions such as those committed by roving *Interahamwe* in Rwanda[212] or between Acholi and Langi in Uganda, [213] above all because victims cannot identify perpetrators. Furthermore, these mecha-nisms are unsuited to the types of violence perpetrated. Though suited to restoring harmony when property disputes, family disturbances or minor crime upset community relations, unprecedented crimes of war or repression when visited on a small community may not merely unbalance the social order, but may very well destroy it. At various points, those familiar with *gacaca*[214] or *bashingantahe*,[215] or *mato oput*[216] have argued that these mechanisms are unsuited to dealing with serious crimes, and outside of Rwanda rarely have done so. The obvious implication is that there must be some role for the state justice system in deciding which crimes can be devolved to the local level and which cannot. However, little attention is given to this in the literature.

Allen's argument that scholars accept too readily the potential for restora-tion in the Acholi community's mechanisms[217] is one that is gaining ground in other contexts also – in an era where transitional justice is open to greater empirical scrutiny, the 'myth-making',[218] 'blanket support'[219] and 'oversell-ing'[220] that has characterized the f eld is now being criticized. However , in diagnosing why traditional justice has failed, great emphasis has been placed on Rwanda's *gacaca*, from which most empirical studies were drawn. As this section goes on to illustrate, the blame for the failures here were placed not on the sheer improbability of healing and reconciliation after a genocide, nor on the inappropriateness of employing *gacaca* to this end, but more on the retributive nature of the process and the instrumentalization of it by the Rwandan government. The danger is no longer that traditional justice will be idealized, but rather that the formal justice system or a role for the state in oversight of the mechanisms continues to be disparaged.

The general belief in transitional justice literature that customary law should not be retributive or instrumentalized by government builds on a recurrent trope in Western restorative justice theory, namely the misrepresen-tation of criminal justice systems. Restorative justice has always been explained by a dichotomized contrast with a formal justice system invariably essentialized as retributive. [221] As one prominent advocate of restorative approaches puts it, the 'retributive' lens sees harm as the breaking of rules as opposed to damage to people, ignores the needs of victims, obscures the nature of crime and def nes injustice in purely technical terms. [222] In this presentation, state justice, it would appear, 'has only interfered with people's innate desire to reconcile and for give one another'.[223] What is important is that this binary opposition works along grossly simplif ed lines of 'restorative justice, good; everything else, bad' and 'distort[s] the real meaning of retributive justice, our understanding of what modern criminal justice systems do'.[224] This bias, to the extent that it is replicated in relation to indigenous systems of justice, is not conducive to a considered appraisal of what societies may need in the context of transition. Justice sector reformers argue that similar scattergun critiques of liberal legalism too often leads to a 'state law bad, folk law good' attitude which not only obscures the harm of some customary practices, but also unduly fetters ability of that state law to mitigate these harms.[225] Even restorative justice scholars now concede that the polarization of restorative and formal justice, so useful rhetorically , is misleading and obscures the common ground between them.[226]

Space precludes a detailed examination of the dangers of valorizing traditional justice at the expense of formal state-based processes, but a few points should be made at this point, all of which fow from the fundamental premise of legal pluralism that different legal orders exist and perform different, complementary (as opposed to antagonistic) roles:

- Victims are not the only relevant constituency in transitional justice. The perspectives of other ordinary members of society are also relevant. For example, one cannot look at the justice preferences of the Acholi people in isolation – people in distant South Uganda have a legitimate interest in the state punishing organized state and non-state violence.[227] From a wider national perspective, reconciliation between individuals and micro-communities may be 'personally helpful but socially and politically irrelevant ... individual persons ... for give, but states seek justice'.[228] Furthermore, the emphasis on the restorative, interpersonal and therapeutic may do a disservice to victims who would prefer to consider themselves as citizens entitled to justice from the state than patients in need of healing.[229]

- An over-emphasis on the importance of localized justice risks misrepresenting the nature of the conflict – for example, Latigo ar gues that '[a] fundamental weakness of the application of *mato oput* as a remedy is that, conceptually, it wrongly projects the LRA insur gency as a local Acholi affair. In reality this war had inherent national and international dimensions'.[230] Serious conflict is not caused by atomized individuals or isolated communities, nor can general security be created by them. None of this is to argue traditional mechanisms are inappropriate, but the state can give guarantees that local mechanisms cannot.

- Arguments that, for example, '[m]any Rwandans have also felt that the ability of courts to contribute to reconciliation is limited, since their activity is removed from the general population', are unduly simplistic and narrow.[231] As Chapter 4 ar gued, criminal justice for past human rights violations can do much to reconcile the individual with the state, even if it does little to restore individual relationships. A functioning criminal justice system is a grassroots need, even where it has few immediate grassroots applications.

- Too much is made of the fact that the formal justice system is 'divorced from social practice and local conceptions'[232] and that criminal trials 'do not translate well across different cultural contexts'. [233] As Section 6.3 illustrated earlier, in legally pluralist societies citizens have sophisticated moral economies of justice. It may be that the crime in question lies outside social conceptions of what traditional justice can deal with. Judging any tribunal by its lack of connection to daily lives [234] grossly mischaracterizes what people expect from the formal criminal justice system, which in any state is primarily used for those exceptional crimes that lie outside the daily lived experiences of people. It is difficult to conceive of a citizenry anywhere which expects trials that do not concern them personally to touch their lives.

- Too much also is made of the illegitimacy of formal trial compared to the popularity and legitimacy of traditional mechanisms. [235] Firstly, state mechanisms are likely to be unpopular not because the idea of state justice is illegitimate *per se*, but because justice has been administered badly in the past. Citizens' institutional preferences for justice are guided less by an established legal culture than by the options available to them. [236] As Chapter 2 argued, a society's perception of the judicial system changes if it is seen to work.[237] Avoiding the criminal justice system because people do not have faith in it risks becoming self-perpetuating. Only by using these tribunals in periods of political flux can they demonstrate their greater credibility. Secondly, this popularity may be the product of past treatment of minor, everyday breaches of the social order, and therefore says little about attitudes to contemporary or future treatment of more serious offences.

- Consequently, criticism of formal justice is more related to the outcomes of trial than its processes. The perceived outcome gap between transitional justice and local needs includes things like healing, rectification of root causes of conflict and micro-communal harmony that formal mechanisms have never been designed to guarantee and that traditional mechanisms can deliver only exceptionally for serious crimes, if at all. The restorative ambitions scholars and practitioners have for traditional mechanisms are hostage to many fortunes in transition (the personalities of the victim and perpetrator, who 'won' and who 'lost', the ethics of justice that apply therein) while some violations such as the death or rape of a child or spouse are such that even the most minimal restoration is unimaginable.

- Finally, much is made in the literature of how the failures of ad hoc tribunals and the ICC have spurred the turn towards local justice. [238] However, one must be careful not to confuse the shortcomings of inter - national tribunals with those of national justice systems. The rare and exceptional nature of the exercise of international criminal law make it a questionable comparator for any other system of justice.

Nevertheless, most analyses in academia and journalism of the applicability of traditional justice in transition are premised on a romanticized (some might say caricatured) endorsement of customary mechanisms as authentically African/Amerindian/Asian and therefore better at dealing with the past than 'Western' and 'retributive' justice.[239] To begin with the latter categorization, when drawing comparisons between what the formal system and traditional justice can offer , the formal system is invariably described as retributive or punitive [240] and contrasted with alternative systems that are unquestioningly presented as restorative, reconstructive or community-building.[241] The most famous example of this is the South African Truth and Reconciliation Commission's founding legislation which synonymized criminal justice with vengeance and retaliation, providing that 'there is a need for understanding but not for vengeance, a need for reparation but not for retaliation, a need for *ubuntu* but not for victimization'.[242] As Wilson puts it, the Commission unfairly 'portrays retributive justice as bloodlust and "wild justice" and as an affront to democratization and the new constitutional order'.[243]

State-based justice is also generally described as 'W estern',[244] implying a foreign imposition utterly removed from the needs of the nation as a whole (this may of course come as some surprise to states in East Asia and the Muslim world who have had state justice systems in some form for centuries). For example, Chopra et al. warn that 'a new justice system will become dominated by elites unfamiliar with local realities or intent on introducing a foreign and inaccessible justice system'. [245] This approach casts traditional justice and the supposedly W estern notion of state law as irreconcilably separate phenomena, and implicitly delegitimizes the latter . The problem with this is that it is not the justice system which is alien, but the idea of a state acting as a state and fulf lling the duties of one. Debates over the legitimacy of the imported state (*l'etat importé*) have raged for decades, but the salient fact that all involved in transitional countries must grapple with is that the process of importation will not be reversed. The conf icts that give rise to transition are usually over control of that state, not the legitimacy of it. A state justice system is 'imposed' or 'foreign' only to the extent that the concept of the state itself is. Given that the state is not going to disappear , a formal justice system is a reality that cannot be wished away . This brings us to a second, related problem, which is that this image of the state as foreign and inappropriate is not how citizens in these states view the formal justice system. For example, as Allen ar gues in the context of Uganda, local people do not reject the use of formal justice (though they have legitimate concerns that it might imperil peace, much like ordinary people in Latin America and Eastern Europe) and would in fact welcome the types of conventional legal apparatus that applies to modern states.[246] As Section 6.3 demonstrated, most communities with traditional justice mechanisms willingly concede a role for the state and expect a pragmatic division of labour with formal justice systems. Allen goes on to argue that there is no reason to believe that Africans are more inclined towards reconciliation than other people — surveys of South Africans suggest they f nd retribution as important as reconciliation, [247]

Ethiopia and Rwanda have pursued the most centralized and retributive prosecutions since World War II, and the surprising number of self-referrals to the ICC from Africa suggests there is nothing alien about formalist responses. Citizens have valid concerns about state justice systems (those examined in Chapter 2), but the simplistic idealization of traditional mechanisms as inherently superior in transition in developing states poses a distinct risk of Orientalism by constructing and essentializing traditional mechanisms as entirely outside of the national political and legal context [248] or presenting their communities as ahistorical and unchanging. [249] The tendency of most case-studies of indigenous mechanisms as a form of transitional justice to focus on single-community cases (often a single village or region) does little to assuage this myopia. Perspectives from pluralist states and peace-building illustrate a more complex picture.

This presentation of state criminal law as inherently retributive or Western f ows from, and re-enforces, the rigidly stratif ed images of traditional justice as bottom-up and state justice as top-down that dominates the view of customary law in transitional justice. While the intention to avoid universalist presumptions or undue retaliation is laudable, it tends to lead to an unhelpfully isolated view of the mechanisms in a post-conf ict environment. 'From below' perspectives are generally welcomed for their 'resistant' and 'mobilizing' character in response to powerful hegemonic political, social or economic forces.[250] As McEvoy and McGregor note, the emphasis on bottom-up approaches builds on earlier subaltern studies that reasserted the agency of persons who are socially , politically, and geographically excluded from a society's established structures for political representation, in place of an earlier emphasis on the dispositions of 'elites'.   [251] Certainly, the roots of transitional justice in bar gains between unaccountable power blocs, the tendency to instrumentalize the participation of victims and the lack of impact at community level makes the f   eld apt for such a perspective. However, there is a risk of throwing yet another baby out with the bathwater The problem with valorizing 'from below' perspectives which, as they point out, are normally assumed to operate outside of the structures of the state, [252] is that employing alternative mechanisms as a site of resistance to the state is seen as imperative regardless of the transitional context – a premium is *prima facie* placed on autonomy from governmental inf uence regardless of whether the government is elected, consensual, majoritarian or merely disguised authoritarianism; regardless of whether that government intends to oppose, tolerate, welcome or control alternative forms of justice; regardless of whether that particular brand of justice from below is tolerant, abusive, exclusionary or inclusionary. For example, Daly ar gues that employing traditional justice as a form of transitional accountability would allow people to def ne justice for themselves as opposed to having it def ned and imposed on them from above, thereby shifting power from central government to the people.   [253] Lundy and McGovern uncontroversially emphasize the value of local owner - ship and control, but do so because it transfers power 'from the dominant, decision-making people and institutions to those who are subordinated during the process'.[254]

This presumption that the citizens of a state are automatically subordinated by involvement of that state in transitional justice is one that needs to be interrogated for the reasons described earlier in Section 6.3. Likewise, the common, dismissive and highly pejorative usage of 'elites' to describe any and all transitional governments regardless of how representative, legitimate or accountable they may be is one that needs to be examined as it connotes a degree of disconnection or antipathy to local community initiatives that may be entirely inappropriate.[255] Scholars warn generally of 'the risks of political capture',[256] the 'dissemination of state authority',[257] the need 'to keep a safe distance from formal power under the state'[258] and the risk that a given mechanism might benef t elites more than local communities,[259] but these admonitions are based on three very questionable assumptions – that interests of state and local communities share no overlap, that state involvement is inherently domineering, and that the remote state presents a greater threat to the individual or community cohesion than local dispute resolution practices. On this presentation, the division of the state into disengaged elites and disempowered locals begins to look every bit as simplistic as the division of humankind into victims and perpetrators that sparked the search for alternative forms of justice in the f rst place.

Much of the blame for this attitude may lie with the operation of *gacaca* in Rwanda, which casts a lar ge shadow over analysis of traditional mechanisms given the volume of the literature on it relative to other examples of traditional justice in action. Space precludes a detailed examination of the process or the voluminous literature on it, but it is undeniable that the practices most associated with it (forced participation, the coercive plea system, lack of application to the RPF) have tended to legitimize a very repressive and vindictive Kagame/RPF regime. *Gacaca* has been criticized justly as a form of social engineering and for tightening the control of a minority government.[260] Other criticisms of *gacaca*, however, are misplaced. There is nothing inher - ently wrong with a traditional process facilitating the centralization of a government,[261] given that many states weakened by regional factions need to centralize. Nor indeed is there anything inherently wrong with traditional justice being used to consolidate state power,[262] given that most national variants of transitional justice tend to do this. Political 'elites' may commandeer transitional justice to secure their impunity , buttress their political control over rivals or facilitate corruption.[263] Equally, however, they may do so because modernizing states need to monitor parallel sources of potentially abusive power. Even in Rwanda, few could quibble with a role for the state in f ltering the Category 1 genocidaires or monitoring trials carefully given that upwards of 10,000 people a month were being processed in a procedure with a distinct potential to exacerbate community tensions. States have a legitimate interest in overseeing the operation of customary law , checking local power imbalances and asserting legitimate authority . Meyerstein presents dichotomies of traditional justice (i) as either a 'means of social control or forward-looking attempts to build the country' and (ii) as either 'courts of the people or tools of the state', but depending on the context the options may not be mutually exclusive.[264] As noted above in relation to South Sudan, many African states have historically aimed to resuscitate and monitor traditional mechanisms.[265] *Gacaca* itself was always well-integrated into a relatively highly centralized state even before colonialism. [266] Though the lessons of *gacaca* are sobering, it is hardly typical of how transitional governments in developing states deal with traditional mechanisms – the initial indifference of transitional East Timor and Guatemala or the relatively proactive integration seen in Uganda or South Sudan present far more typical models of interaction. What depends most of all is the type of government in power or type of state being transitioned to. For example, Liberians may well fear the integration of local justice with state law on the basis that it echoes past discriminatory impositions by the Monrovian elite (as Lubkeman et al. argue)[267] but it plainly matters whether that 'elite' is Charles Taylor's autocracy or Ellen Johnson Sirleaf's democratically elected government, for all its faults. Any judgments on the merits of top-down versus bottom-up initiatives require a careful assessment of that top and of that bottom. Local authorities cannot be presumed to be rights-respecting, legitimate and democratic, while government cannot be presumed to be exploitative or intolerant of local diversity.

Nevertheless, there is resistance to an assertive role for the state in the regulation of traditional mechanisms. McEvoy, who regrets the institutionalization of transitional justice into state-like structures, argues that the tendency towards 'seeing like the state' may undermine developing lines of ownership and accountability to the communities they were bound to serve. [268] Though the danger is real, a role for the state does not automatically mitigate against ownership and may augment existing local accountability.[269] To use the metaphor of cycling, in extreme cases like Rwanda the government may steer the bike, but more often the state's role is to act as a stabilizer. Injunctions that the state should not co-opt local justice, [270] formalize it[271] or 'administratize' it[272] when dealing with past human rights abuses may fall on deaf ears if the state wants to harness customary mechanisms to fill rule of law gaps, rein in the influence of abusive local elites or tackle discrimination at community level. The presumption that weakening the role of government may enhance the trust that people have in the process[273] or that there is merit in leaving 'as much power as possible' to those outside the central state power structure [274] may reflect the concerns of Western restorative justice more so than the needs of women, the young and the 'other' in communities where customary law applies.

6.5 Conclusion: opportunities lost? The value of integration

If all that was at issue was merely a difference of opinion, the divergence between transitional justice and rule of law reconstruction in terms of how both sectors approached traditional justice would be unfortunate, but of purely academic interest. After all, transitional justice actors might try to insulate the projects they support from state involvement, but bottom-up processes established explicitly in opposition to state involvement can rarely resist encroachment if the government so wishes. [275] Forceful criticism of top-down justice appears to do little to diminish the popular desire for a functioning legal sector. However, the failure to integrate perspectives from rule of law reconstruction into support from NGOs, scholars, activists and aid agencies for using traditional mechanisms to engage with past human rights violations means that the benef cial innovations they bring to traditional processes for the purposes of reckoning with past abuses may not be sustained. It is with customary law that T eitel's argument that transitional justice can instigate a normative shift while maintaining stability is most appropriate.[276] No examination of traditional mechanisms is complete without reference to their inherent f exibility and predisposition to evolve in light of changing social circumstances, which in this respect above all others it surpasses formal justice systems.[277] As noted earlier , traditional justice, like all culturally informed practices, is socially situated and must change meaning and appearance over time.[278] This inevitability of change is exacerbated by transition. As noted above in Section 6.2, traditional mechanisms usually enter transition either compromised by their role in the old order or enjoying a renewed legitimacy in the new. They may be strengthened through identity with the victors or through the legitimacy that comes from preventing abuses during conf ict, or weakened by the breakdown in community structures, the diminution of temporal and spiritual authority or the prevalence of armaments. In either case, the role of transitional processes in the new state order is ripe for reconsideration. For example, in the aftermath of Burundi'   s National Reconciliation Policy, a commission on national unity recommended that *bashingantahe* be adopted to the needs of the modernizing state.[279] Since then, greater government support and capacity-building have been forthcoming, even if the Bujumbura government is reluctant to extend *bashingantahe*'s role to transitional justice.[280] The Sierra Leone TRC recommended changes to the relationship between chiefs and the state [281] and was followed in recent years by draft legislation to regulate customary law in relation to gender , children and appointments of traditional authorities.[282] The use of *gacaca* was revived and reconsidered by the Kigali government as a key part of establishing a new Rwandese identity, for good or ill. Whether change is compelled by socio-economic change, by ref nement of the formal justice system or by transition, the challenge for the state and peace-builders is to ensure that any monitor - ing, integration or alteration of customary law should proceed sensibly . The challenge, as Shaw and Waldorf note, is to achieve a pragmatic pluralism that facilitates day-to-day choices on the part of the population but which prevents abuse.[283]

Development agencies typically warn that donor engagement is not appropriate where non-state justice systems violate basic human rights. [284]

Two noteworthy (but by no means universal) conclusions peace-builders have drawn in addressing this issue have been that (a) reforms resulting from internal critique are more effective than blatantly top-down dictats, [285] and (b) where this internal critique occurs, traditional leaders tend to be responsive to changing normative attitudes as failure to do so might undermine their level of respect in the community .[286] Transitional justice has served as an excellent opportunity for the all-important task Merry identif   es of translating human rights ideas into frameworks that are relevant to the communities observing their procedures. [287] Where traditional mechanisms are employed as a form of transitional justice, they tend to incorporate human rights and non-discrimination standards in a way that would accord with the interests of those working to integrate customary law fruitfully into the national legal order . As Oomen notes, the operation of   *gacaca* attracted unprecedented amounts of funding from bilateral and multilateral donors that would otherwise not have gone to Rwanda.[288] NGOs tend to emphasize human rights and gender equality – the strings attached to this funding generally emphasize training, human rights education, outreach and monitoring, all of which will benef t indigenous systems in the long run. [289] For example, transitional justice has been at the vanguard of gender mainstreaming customary law – women have headed localized truth-seeking projects in Sierra Leone, [290] seen more involvement in Rwanda's *gacaca* than was traditionally allowed, [291] while in East T   imor stipulations that a minimum 30 per cent of all Regional Commissioners be women and that people have 'appropriate gender representation' were observed in the CA VR (Timor-Leste Commission for Reception, T   ruth and Reconciliation) Community Reconciliation Process. Once given this push, communities 'willingly appointed female representatives'.[292] However, where the interaction of transitional justice activists, training and funding emphasizes a jealous, splendid isolation from the state, it becomes less likely that these processes are sustainable.

One pertinent example is East T   imor's aforementioned Community Reconciliation Process (CRP) which employed traditional reconciliation ceremonies but integrated itself with the hybrid national criminal tribunal system in a mutually benef cial way. Before giving a statement to the CRP , deponents were informed that information included in the statements would be sent to the Off ce of the General Prosecutor (OGP) and could be used in future criminal proceedings if the OGP so chose.   [293] Statements were forwarded to the OGP who decided on the basis of clear criteria whether to prosecute or return the case to the CRP , whereupon the OGP's authority to initiate criminal proceedings was stayed pending compliance with CRP hearing procedures. The possibility existed to isolate minor crimes from serious ones as the CRP would hear the former without prejudice to the OGP's jurisdiction over the latter . While the implementing legislation imposed no legal obligations on deponents to enter into a Community Reconciliation Agreement, once one had been signed the deponent was legally obliged to fulf l the obligations outlined therein. Failure to perform them constituted a criminal offence punishable by a maximum prison sentence of a year or a maximum f ne of $3,000, or both. On the other hand, completion of the required acts meant the deponent received legal notif ca-tion of his legal immunity from criminal and civil liability . Proof of the effectiveness of this link to the OGP is apparent in the fact that only one deponent failed to comply with a Community Reconciliation Agreement.

Thus we see at all stages a process where a CRP adopting and adapting local justice processes acted as both a complement and an alternative to the formal justice system. The CRP benefted from the OGP's ability to prosecute non-compliance with Community Reconciliation Agreements and the remit of the formal courts to monitor them for adherence to human rights. The OGP certainly benef ted in that the CRP 'effectively averted the need for police investigation, the preparation of indictments by prosecutors, judicial hearings and an expanded court administration and prison system to deal with these cases'.[294] Though the OGP had paramount authority , at the core of the relationship between them was the effective upward delegation of jurisdiction for borderline serious crimes from the CRP to the OGP. Though it may have been wiser given the enormous case-backlogs in the state for jurisdiction to instead run downwards from the state level to the community, it could have served as a valuable model for the future operation of an integrated, pluralistic legal system in East Timor. Instead, the CRP ended in mid-2004, and no comparable integration has since occurred despite growing backlogs and a permanently weak court system. Within three years there was a conservative estimate of 4,700 pending cases in the T imorese justice system.[295] Backlogs remain in existence to this day.

The Timorese experience sums up the short-term view of transitional justice praxis as it relates to customary processes. T ransitional justice actors are good at facilitating training and internalizing human rights and non-discrimination, but only the state can sustain it in the long term. It is not enough to incorporate a general transitional justice strategy 'that encom-passes bottom-up local efforts as well as top-down state-driven or internation-ally driven ones' if such a perspective means they continue to exist in splendid isolation from each other.[296] The key is to allow the top inf uence the bottom and vice-versa in the most mutually-benef cial way, even if a degree of impre-cision and inconclusiveness between plural legal and normative orders will endure for years (it may even be welcome). Only with a greater awareness of the wider dilemmas of integrating traditional justice processes on the part of those promoting customary justice as a form of transitional justice can bene-f cial innovations be made to endure.

Notes

1 C. Bull, *No Entry Without Strategy: Building the Rule of Law Under UN Transitional Administration* (New York: United Nations University Press, 2008), 56.

2 R. Mani, *Beyond Retribution – Seeking Justice in the Shadows of War* (Cambridge: Polity Press, 2002), 83.

3 L.Huyse, 'Introduction: Tradition-based Approaches in Peacemaking, Transitional Justice and Reconciliation Policies' in L. Huyse and M. Salter (eds.), *Traditional Justice and Reconciliation After Conflict: Learning from African Experience* (Stockholm: International Institute for Democracy and Electoral Assistance, 2008), 1 at 7.

4 Ibid.,10.

5 The most useful and most widely cited introductions to legal pluralism are S. Merry 'Legal Pluralism' (1988) 22 *Law and Society Review* 869 and J. Griff ths, 'What is Legal Pluralism?' (1986) 24 *Journal of Legal Pluralism and Unofficial Law* 1.

6 A.L. Hinton, 'Introduction: T oward an Anthropology of T ransitional Justice' in A.L. Hinton (ed.), *Transitional Justice: Global Mechanisms and Local Realities after Genocide and Mass Violence* (New Brunswick: Rutgers University Press, 2010), 1 at 6.

7 Ibid.,6–7.

8 A good example is the excellent D. Isser (ed.), *Customary Justice and the Rule of Law in War-Torn Societies* (Washington, D.C.: USIP, 2011) which presents a magisterial overview of the issues related to the use of traditional justice in rule of law reconstruction, but which does not mention transitional justice once.

9 Griffths, supra n5, 4 and 12.

10 Hinton,supra n6, 6.

11 P Gready, 'Reconceptualising Transitional Justice: Embedded and Distanced Justice' (2005) 5 *Conflict, Security and Development* 3, 17.

12 R. Nagy, 'Transitional Justice and Legal Pluralism in T ransitional Context: The Case of Rwanda's Gacaca Courts' in J. Quinn (ed.), *Reconciliation(s): Transitional Justice in Postconflict Societies* (Montreal: McGill-Queen' s University Press, 2005), 86.

13 Huyseand Salter, supra n3.

14 P. Clark, 'Hybridity, Holism and "T raditional Justice": The Case of the Gacaca Courts in Post-Genocide Rwanda' (2007) 39 *George Washington International Law Review* 765.

15 R.Kerr and E. Mobekk, *Peace & Justice: Seeking Accountability After War* (Cambridge: Polity Press, 2007), 151–172.

16 Nagy supra n12, 103, rejecting this dichotomy.

17 A. Meyerstein, 'Between Law and Culture: Rwanda' s Gacaca and Postcolonial Legality' (2007) 32 *Law and Social Inquiry* 467, 495.

18 R. Shaw and L. Waldorf, 'Introduction: Localizing Transitional Justice' in R. Shaw, L. Waldorf and P. Hazan (eds.), *Localizing Transitional Justice: Interventions and Priorities after Mass Violence* (Stanford: Stanford University Press, 2010), 3 at 25.

19 K. Theidon, 'Justice in Transition: The Micropolitics of Reconciliation in Postwar Peru' (2006) 50 *Journal of Conflict Resolution* 433, 456.

20 Shawand Waldorf, supra n18, 15.

21 Kerrand Mobekk, supra n15, 165–166.

22 E.g. M. Drumbl, 'Punishment Post-Genocide: From Guilt to Shame to Civis in Rwanda' (2000) 75 *New York University Law Review* 1221.

23 The best example is the debate between H. Cobban, 'The Legacies of Collective Violence: The Rwandan Genocide and the Limits of Law' (2002) 27(2) *Boston Review*, 4–15 and K. Roth and A. Des For ges, 'Justice or Therapy? A Discussion on Helena Cobban's Essay on Crime and Punishment in Rwanda' (2002) 27 (3–4) *Boston Review*, 21–29.

24 J.O. Latigo, 'Northern Uganda: Tradition-Based Practices in the Acholi Region' in Huyse and Salter (eds.), supra n3, 85 at 101.

25 For example L. Hovil and J. Quinn, 'Peace First, Justice Later: Traditional Justice in Northern Uganda' (2005) Refugee Law Project, Working Paper, available <http://www.refugeelawproject.org/working_papers/RLP.WP17.pdf> and A. Branch, 'Uganda's Civil War and the Politics of ICC Intervention' (2007) 21 *Ethics and International Affairs* 179.

26 Onthe relevant provisions see generally D. Mukholi, *A Complete Guide to Uganda's Fourth Constitution: History, Politics, and the Law* (Kampala: Fountain Publishers, 1995).

27 S. Callaghan, 'Overview of Customary Justice and Legal Pluralism in Uganda', paper given at Customary Justice and Legal Pluralism in Post-Confict and Fragile Societies conference, 17–18 November 2009, Washington, D.C.

28 B. Ingelaere and D. Kohlhagen, 'Situating Social Imaginaries in Transitional Justice: The *Bashingantahe* in Burundi' (2012) 6 *International Journal of Transitional Justice* 40, 41.

29 D. Isser, 'Understanding and Engaging Customary Justice Systems', in Isser (ed.), supra n8, 325 at 336.

30 M. Plunkett, 'Rebuilding the Rule of Law' in W. Maley, C. Sampford and R. Thakur (eds.), *From Civil Strife to Civil Society: Civil and Military Responsibilities in Disrupted States* (Tokyo, New York: United Nations University Press, 2003), 207 at 212–213.

31 L.Chirayath, C. Sage and M. Woolcock, *Customary Law and Policy Reform: Engaging with the Plurality of Justice Systems* (Washington, D.C.: World Bank, 2006), 4.

32 L. Walgrave, 'Integrating Criminal Justice and Restorative Justice' in G. Johnstone and D.W. Van Ness (eds.), *Handbook of Restorative Justice* (Cullompton: Willan Publishing, 2007), 559 at 560.

33 K. McEvoy, 'Letting Go of Legalism: Developing a "Thicker" Version of Transitional Justice' in K. McEvoy and L. McGregor (eds.),*Transitional Justice from Below: Grassroots Activism and the Struggle for Change* (Portland: Hart Publishing, 2008), 15 at 25–28.

34 J.Ramji-Nogales, 'Designing Bespoke Transitional Justice: A Pluralist Process Approach' (2010) 32 *Michigan Journal of International Law* 1, 65.

35 A. Iliff, 'Root and Branch: Discourses of "Tradition" in Grassroots Transitional Justice' (2012) 6 *International Journal of International Justice* 253, 273.

36 T. Barfeld, N. Nojumi and J.A. Thier, 'The Clash of Two Goods: State and Nonstate Dispute Resolution in Afghanistan' in Isser (ed.), supra n8, 159 at 185.

37 Ibid.,189.

38 E. Melissaris, 'The More the Merrier? A New Take on Legal Pluralism' (2004) 13 *Social & Legal Studies* 57.

39 D. Roche, 'Retribution and Restorative Justice' in Johnstone and Van Ness (eds.), supra n32, 75 at 76–77.

40 L. Piron, 'Time to Learn, Time to Act in Africa' in T. Carothers (ed.), *Promoting the Rule of Law Abroad: In Search of Knowledge* (Washington, D.C.: Carnegie Endowment for International Peace, 2006), 275 at 291.

41 S. Chesterman, M. Ignatieff and R. Thakur, 'Introduction: Making States Work' in S. Chesterman, M. Ignatieff and R. Thakur (eds.), *Making States Work: State Failure and the Crisis of Governance* (New York: United Nations University Press, 2005), 1 at 1.

42 D. Brinkerhoff, 'Rebuilding Governance in Failed States and Post-Conflict Societies: Core Concepts and Cross-Cutting Themes' (2005) 25 *Public Administration and Development* 3, 11.

43 A.Potter, *The Rule of Law as the Measure of Peace? Responsive Policy for Reconstructing Justice and the Rule of Law in Post Conflict and Transitional Environments* (Geneva: Centre for Humanitarian Dialogue, 2004), 9.

44 B. Ingelaere, 'The Gacaca Courts in Rwanda' in Huyse and Salter (eds.), supra n3, 25 at 34.

45 T. Chopra, C. Ranheim and R. Nixon, 'Local-Level Justice Under Transitional Administration: Lessons from East Timor' in Isser (ed.), supra n8, 119 at 137.

46 A. Naniwe-Kaburahe, 'The Institution of Bashingantahe in Burundi' in Huyse and Salter (eds.), supra n3, 149 at 161.

47 K.Theidon, supra n19.

48 A. Honwana, 'Healing and Social Integration in Mozambique and Angola' in E. Skaar, S. Gloppen and A. Suhrke (eds.), *Roads to Reconciliation* (Lanham: Lexington Books, 2005), 83.

49 D. Peachey, 'The Elusive Quest for Reconciliation in Northern Uganda' in N. Palmer, P. Clark and D. Granville (eds.), *Critical Perspectives in Transitional Justice* (Cambridge: Intersentia, 2012), 289 at 305.

50 S. Lubkeman, H.M. Kyed and J. Garvey, 'Dilemmas of Articulation in Mozambique: Customary Justice in Transition' in Isser (ed.), supra n8, 13 at 39.

51 Usage levels between 80–90 per cent are cited in, *inter alia*, B. Tamanaha, 'The Rule of Law and Legal Pluralism in Development' (2011) 3 *Hague Journal on the Rule of Law* 1, 4, E. Wojkowska, *Doing Justice: How Informal Systems Can Contribute* (Oslo: UNDP Oslo Governance Centre, 2006), 11, UNDP , 'Access to Justice: Practice Note' (2004), available < http://www.undp.org/content/undp/en/home/librarypage/democratic-governance/access_to_justiceandruleoflaw/access-to-justice-practice-note.html>, 9.

52 Isser, supra n29, 327.

53 V. Igreja, 'The Politics of Peace, Justice and Healing in Post-war Mozambique: "Practices of Rupture" by Magamba Spirits and Healers in Gorongosa' in C.L. Sriram and S. Pillay (eds.), *Peace Versus Justice? The Dilemma of Transitional Justice in Africa* (London: James Currey, 2009).

54 T Hohe and R. Nixon, *Reconciling Justice: 'Traditional' Law and State Judiciary in East Timor* (Washington, D.C.: United States Institute of Peace, 2003), 2.

55 For a list of ideal or typical attributes of traditional justice mechanisms see Penal Reform Initiative, *Access to Justice in Sub-Saharan Africa: The Role of Traditional and Informal Justice Systems* (London: Penal Reform Initiative, 2002), 112.

56 Wojkowska, supra n51, 14.

57 J. Hessbruegge and C.F.O. Garcia, 'Mayan Law in Post-Conflict Guatemala' in Isser (ed.), supra n8, 77 at 95.

58 Departmentfor International Development (DFID), 'Briefing: Non-state Justice and Security Systems' (2004), available < http://www.gsdrc.org/docs/open/SSAJ101.pdf>, 1 and 10.

59 A. Harrington, 'Institutions and the East Timorese Experience' (2005) 3 *East Timor Law Journal* 1, 13.

60 Seebelow n234.

61 Mani,supra n2, 40.

62 DFID,supra n58, 20–21.

63 S. Merry, 'The Social Or ganization of Mediation in Non-Industrial Societies: Implications for Informal Community Justice in America' in R. Abel (ed.), *The Politics of Informal Justice* (New York: Academic Press, 1982), 17 at 23.
64 Wojkowska, supra n51, 20.
65 Ibid., 23, Kerr and Mobekk, supra n15, 162, Isser, supra n29, 331.
66 Barfeld, Nojumi and Thier, supra n36, 174–175.
67 Chopra,Ranheim and Nixon, supra n45, 126.
68 F. Deng, 'Customary Law in the Cross Fire of Sudan' s War of Identities' in Isser (ed.), supra n8, 285 at 316.
69 Bull,supra n1, 230.
70 Mani,supra n2, 75.
71 Piron,supra n40, 292.
72 H. Charlesworth and M. W ood, 'Women and Human Rights in the Rebuilding of East Timor' (2002) 71 *Nordic Journal of International Law* 325, 336.
73 T. Chopra, 'W omen's Rights and Legal Pluralism in Post Conf ict Societies: An Analytical Agenda', paper given at Customary Justice and Legal Pluralism in Post-Conf ict and Fragile Societies conference, 17–18 November 2009, Washington, D.C.
74 Chirayath,Sage and Woolcock, supra n31, 4.
75 V. Igreja, 'Restorative Justice and the Role of Magamba Spirits in Post-Civil War Gorongosa, Central Mozambique' in Huyse and Salter (eds.), supra n3, 61 at 80.
76 Kerr and Mobekk, supra n15, 159.
77 K.O. Adinkrah, 'Folk Law is the Culprit: W omen's "Non-Rights" in Swaziland' (1990–91) 30–31 *Journal of Legal Pluralism* 223.
78 Lubkeman,Kyed and Garvey, supra n50, 69.
79 Kerr and Mobekk, supra n15, 159.
80 L. Grenfell, 'Legal Pluralism and the Challenge of Building the Rule of Law in Post-conf ict States: A Case Study of T imor-Leste' in Isser (ed.), supra n8, 157 at 171–172.
81 Lubkeman, Kyed and Garvey, supra n50, 33. They later point out that popular sentiment 'arguably prizes a hard-won peace over the f ner niceties of the rule of law' (at 65).
82 Hohe and Nixon, supra n54, 2.
83 As described in Isser, supra n29, 341.
84 J. Faundez, 'Legal Pluralism and International Development Agencies: State Building or Legal Reform?' (2011) 3 *Hague Journal on the Rule of Law* 18, 18.
85 Bull,supra n1, 110.
86 C. Rausch (ed.), *Combating Serious Crimes in Postconflict Societies: A Handbook for Policymakers and Practitioners* (Washington, D.C.: USIP Press, 2006), 25.
87 Bull,supra n1, 229–230.
88 J. Chopra and T. Hohe, 'Participatory Intervention' (2004) 10 *Global Governance* 289.
89 Isser supra n29, 326–327.
90 C. Sage, N. Menzies and M. Woolcock, *Taking the Rule of the Game Seriously: Mainstreaming Justice in Development* (Washington, D.C.: W orld Bank Justice & Development Working Paper Series, 2009), 3.
91 Barfeld, Nojumi and Thier, supra n36, 183.
92 UN Secretary-General, *The Rule of Law and Transitional Justice in Conflict and Post-Conflict Societies*, UN Doc. S/2004/616, of 3 August 2004, para. 3.

93 UNDP, 'Programming for Justice: Access for All: A Practitioner' s Guide to a Human-Rights-Based Approach to Access to Justice' (2005), available < http://www.unrol.org/doc.aspx?d=2311>, 5.

94 J.Stromseth, M. Wippman and R. Brooks, *Can Might Make Rights? Building the Rule of Law After Military Interventions* (Cambridge: Cambridge University Press, 2006), 341.

95 See UNDP, supra n92, and the World Bank's Justice for the Poor (J4P) Program.

96 E.g.Danida (Denmark), *Evaluation: Danish Support to Promotion of Human Rights and Democratisation, Volume 2: Justice, Constitution and Legislation* (Copenhagen: Evaluation Secretariat, Ministry of Foreign Affairs, 2000, DFID, supra n58.

97 See generally S. Golub, 'Beyond Rule of Law Orthodoxy: The Legal Empowerment Alternative' (2003) 25 Carnegie Endowment for International Peace Paper No. 41 (Rule of Law Series) available < http://www.carnegieendowment.org/f les/wp41.pdf>.

98 Ibid.,35. Faundez, supra n83, 20.

99 UNDP supra n51, 3.

100Deng,supra n68, 314.

101Barfeld, Nojumi and Thier, supra n36, 189.

102Bull,supra n1, 56.

103 R. Daniels and M. T rebilcock, 'The Political Economy of Rule of Law Reform in Developing Countries' (2004) 26 *Michigan Journal of International Law* 99, 120–121.

104 L. Waldorf, 'Mass Justice for Mass Atrocity: Rethinking Local Justice as Transitional Justice' (2006) 79 *Temple Law Review* 1, 11–12.

105Deng,supra n68, 285.

106 Be Sousa Santos, 'The Heterogenous State and Legal Pluralism in Mozambique' (2006) 40 *Law and Society Review* 39, 64.

107 P. McAuliffe, 'East T imor's Community Reconciliation Process as a Model for Legal Pluralism in Criminal Justice' (2008) 2 *Journal of Law, Global Justice and Social Development* 1, 7.

108 C. Deslaurier, 'Le "Bushingantahe"; Peut-il Réconcilier le Burundi?' (2003) 92 *Politique Africaine* 76.

109Hessbrueggeand Garcia, supra n57, 78.

110 J. Alie, 'Reconciliation and Traditional Justice: Tradition-based Practices of the Kpaa Mende in Sierra Leone' in Huyse and Salter (eds.), 123 at 140.

111Hessbrueggeand Garcia, supra n57, 96.

112Hoviland Quinn, supra n25, 26.

113 L. Huyse, 'Conclusion and Recommendations' in L. Huyse and M. Salter (eds.), supra n3, 181 at 183.

114Barfeld, Nojumi and Thier, supra n36, 172.

115Ingelaere,supra n44, 48.

116 Naniwe-Kaburahe, supra n46, 161, though it is noted that some traditional leaders also saved some people and prevented atrocities.

117SierraLeone Truth and Reconciliation Commission, *Witness to Truth, Vol. 3A, Historical Antecedents to the Conflict*, 8.

118. TAllen, 'Ritual (Ab)use? Problems With Traditional Justice in Northern Uganda' in N. Waddell and P. Clark (eds.), *Courting Conflict? Justice, Peace and the ICC in Africa* (London: Crisis States Research Centre, 2006), 47 at 50.

119DFID,supra n58, 10.

120 D. Lan, *Guns and Rain: Guerrillas and Spirit Mediums in Zimbabwe* (Berkeley: University of California Press, 1985).

121 Deng, supra n68, 285–291.

122 Isser supra n29, 355.

123 K. Brown, 'Customary Law in the Pacif c: An Endangered Species' (1999) 3 *Journal of South Pacific Law*, no page numbers.

124 J. Sarkin, 'The Tension Between Justice and Reconciliation in Rwanda: Politics, Human Rights, Due Process and the Role of the *Gacaca* Courts in Dealing with the Genocide' (2001) 45 *Journal of African Law* 143, 159–160.

125 'The spread of capitalism visits sweeping changes on cultures and societies: drawing people from the country to the city   , bringing women into the workplace, imposing work discipline, controlling the daily rhythm, providing money to families and communities from external sources, offering a broader range of goods for consumers, increasing exposure to mass media, and much more' (Tamanaha, supra n51, 12).

126 S. Rose-Ackerman, 'Establishing the Rule of Law' in R. Rotber g (ed.), *When States Fail: Causes and Consequences* (Princeton: Princeton University Press, 2004), 182 at 208.

127 Tamanaha, supra n51, 6.

128 Ibid.

129 Chirayath, Sage and Woolcock, supra n31, 8.

130 On this, see H.M. Kyed, 'The Politics of Legal Pluralism: State Policies on Legal Pluralism and their Local Dynamics in Mozambique' (2009) 59 *Journal of Legal Pluralism and Unofficial Law* 87.

131 Isser supra n29, 359.

132 Kerrand Mobekk, supra n15, 161.

133 B. Connolly, 'Non-State Justice Systems and the State: Proposals for a Recognition Typology' (2005) 38 *Connecticut Law Review* 239.

134 Article 8 of ILO Convention No. 169 Addressing Indigenous and T   ribal Peoples in Independent Countries gives traditional communities the right to retain their own institutions and customs provided they are not incompatible with fundamental rights as def ned by the state legal system or the corpus of international human rights. The African Commission on Human and Peoples' Rights observed the problems in the area, ar guing that '[t]raditional courts are not exempt from the provisions of the African Charter relating to fair trial'.

135 Lubkeman, Kyed and Garvey, supra n50, 51.

136 D. Pimentel, 'Rule of Law Reform Without Cultural Imperialism? Reinforcing Customary Justice Through Collateral Review in Southern Sudan' (2010) 2 *Hague Journal on the Rule of Law* 1.

137 Ibid., 16–17.

138 G. Corradi, 'Human Rights Promotion in Post Conf ict Sierra Leone: Coming to Grips With Plurality in Customary Justice' (2010) 60 *Journal of Legal Pluralism and Unofficial Law* 73. 93.

139 P. Pigou, *The Community Reconciliation Process of the Commission for Reception, Truth and Reconciliation* (Dili: UNDP Timor-Leste, 2004), 34.

140 S. Lubkeman, D. Isser and P. Banks III, 'Unintended Consequences: Constraint of Customary Justice in Post-Conflict Liberia' in Isser (ed.), supra n8, 193 at 219.

141 Piron, supra n40, 292.

142 Peachey supra n49, 301.

143 J. Stevens, *Traditional and Informal Justice Systems in Africa, South Asia and the Caribbean* (Paris: Penal Reform International, 1998), 44.

144 Tamanaha, supra n51, 9.

145 J. Adoko and S. Levine, 'How Can W e Turn Legal Anarchy into Harmonious Pluralism? Why Integration is a Key to Legal Pluralism in Northern Uganda', paper given at Customary Justice and Legal Pluralism in Post-Conf ict and Fragile Societies conference, 17–18 November 2009, Washington, D.C.

146 Kerrand Mobekk, supra n15, 158.

147 Faundez, supra n83, 20.

148 Chirayath, Sage and Woolcock, supra n31, 9.

149 Isser supra n29, 352.

150 G. Johnstone and D. Van Ness, 'The Meaning of Restorative Justice' in Johnstone and Van Ness (eds.), supra n32, 5 at 5–6.

151 D. Dyzenhaus, 'Judicial Independence, T ransitional Justice, and the Rule of Law' (2003) 10 *Otago Law Review* 345, 367, L. Huyse, *All Things Pass Except the Past* (Van Halewyck: Kessel-Lo, 2009), 190–191.

152 Mani, supra n2, 36–37.

153 B.A.Leebaw, 'The Irreconcilable Goals of Transitional Justice' (2008)30 *Human Rights Quarterly* 95, 104.

154 K. McEvoy, 'Beyond Legalism: Towards a Thicker Understanding of Transitional Justice' (2007) 34 *Journal of Law and Society* 411, 437.

155 P. Lundy and M. McGovern, 'Whose Justice? Rethinking T ransitions From the Bottom Up' (2008) 35 *Journal of Law and Society* 265.

156 L.Magarrell and J. Wesley, *Learning from Greensboro: Truth and Reconciliation in the United States* (Philadelphia: University of Pennsylvania Press, 2008).

157 T Longman, 'Justice at the Grassroots? *Gacaca* Trials in Rwanda' in N. Roht-Arriaza and J. Mariezcurrena (eds.), *Transitional Justice in the Twenty-First Century: Beyond Truth Versus Justice* (New York: Cambridge University Press, 2006), 206 at 213–214, P. Clark, 'The Rules (and Politics) of Engagement: The Gacaca Courts and Post-Genocide Justice, Healing and Reconciliation in Rwanda' in P. Clark and Z. Kaufman (eds.), *After Genocide: Transitional Justice, Post-Conflict Reconstruction and Reconciliation in Rwanda and Beyond* (New York: Columbia University Press, 2009), 297 at 300, P . Uvin and C. Mironko, 'W estern and Local Approaches to Justice in Rwanda' (2003) 9 *Global Governance* 219.

158 E.g.Waldorf, supra n103, 14–16, Huyse, supra n3, 20–21.

159 McEvoy supra n33, 41–42.

160 Nagy supra n12, 91.

161 E. Kiss, 'Moral Ambition Within and Beyond Political Constraints: Ref ections on Restorative Justice' in R. Rotber g and D. Thompson (eds.), *Truth v. Justice: The Morality of Truth Commissions* (Princeton: Princeton University Press, 2000), 68, 68–69.

162 South Africa Truth and Reconciliation Commission, *Final Report* (Cape Town, 1998) Vol. I, Chapter 5, para. 89.

163 Ibid.,para. 54a.

164 Kiss,supra n160, 81.

165 R. Brody, 'Justice: The First Casualty of Truth' (2001) 272 (17) *The Nation* 4.

166 Kiss,supra n160, 86.

167 D. Crocker, 'Punishment, Reconciliation and Democratic Deliberation' (2001 –02)5 *Buffalo Criminal Law Review* 509, 542.

168E.g.Theidon, supra n19, 455–456.

169 M. Schotsmans, '"Blow Your Mind and Cool Your Heart": Can Tradition-Based Justice Fill the Transitional Justice Gap in Sierra Leone?' in Palmer , Clark and Granville (eds.), supra n49, 263 at 280. The Statute establishing the Commission authorized it to 'seek assistance from traditional and religious leaders to facilitate its public sessions and in resolving local conf icts arising from past violations or abuses or in support of healing and reconciliation' (T ruth and Reconciliation Commission Act, 2000, para. 7.2).

170Ramji-Nogales,supra n34, 10–11.

171M.Drumbl, 'Collective Violence and Individual Punishment: The Criminality of Mass Atrocity' (2005) *Northwestern University Law Review* 539, 597.

172 J. Larson Sawin and H. Zehr, 'The Ideas of Engagement and Empowerment' in Johnstone and Van Ness (eds.), supra n32, 41 at 42, echoed in McEvoy' s claim that transitional justice seems to 'belong' less to victims than to 'lawyers, policy makers and state off cials' (McEvoy, supra n153, 413).

173 E.g. Shaw, Waldorf and Hazan (eds.), supra n18, E. Stover and H. W einstein (eds.), *My Neighbor, My Enemy: Justice and Community in the Aftermath of Mass Atrocity* (Cambridge: Cambridge University Press, 2004).

174Gready supra n11.

175Offce of the United Nations High Commissioner for Human Rights, 'Rule of Law Tools for Post-Conf ict States: Prosecution Initiatives' (2008), HR/PUB/06/04.

176 Ramji-Nogales, supra n34, 4, N. Roht-Arriaza, 'The New Landscape of Transitional Justice' in Roht-Arriaza and Mariezcurrena (eds.), supra n156, 1 at 8.

177Huyse,supra n3, 1.

178 B. Oomen, 'Donor-Driven Justice and its Discontents' (2005) 36*Development and Change* 887, 902.

179 C.L. Sriram, 'Justice as Peace? Liberal Peacebuilding and Strategies of Transitional Justice' (2007) 21 *Global Society: Journal of Interdisciplinary International Relations* 579, 590.

180D.Roche, 'The Evolving Def nition of Restorative Justice' (2001)4 *Contemporary Justice Review* 341, 342.

181 K. Daly, 'The Limits of Restorative Justice' in D. Sullivan and L. Tifft (eds.), *The Handbook of Restorative Justice: A Global Perspective* (New York: Routledge, 2006), 134 at 135.

182G. Johnstone, *Restorative Justice: Ideas, Values, Debates* (Cullompton: W illan Publishing, 2002), ix.

183 K. Pranis, 'Restorative Values' in Johnstone and Van Ness (eds.), supra n32, 59 at 61–62.

184 G. Johnstone, 'Critical Perspectives on Restorative Justice' in Johnstone and Van Ness, ibid., 598 at 598.

185 A. Von Hirsch, A. Ashworth and C. Shearing, 'Specifying Aims and Limits for Restorative Justice: A "Making Amends" Model' in A. V on Hirsch et al. (eds.), *Restorative Justice and Criminal Justice: Competing or Reconcilable Paradigms?* (Oxford: Hart Publishing, 2003), 21.

186J. Braithwaite, 'Restorative Justice: Assessing Optimistic and Pessimistic Accounts' (1999) 25 *Crime and Justice* 1, 107.

187 Reciprocally, many locate the origins of restorative justice in customary law traditions, e.g. R. Ross, *Returning to the Teachings: Exploring Aboriginal Justice* (Canada: Penguin Books, 1996).

188Daly supra n180, 137.

189Kerrand Mobekk, supra n15, 167.

190 P. Lundy and M. McGovern, 'The Role of Community in Participatory Transitional Justice' in McEvoy and McGregor (eds.), supra n190.

191L.Arriaza and N. Roht-Arriaza, 'Social Reconstruction as a Local Process' (2008) 2 *International Journal of Transitional Justice* 152, 161, Huyse, supra n3, 8, Nagy, supra n12, 100, Shaw and Waldorf, supra n18, 15.

192Mani,supra n2, 38.

193Huyse,supra n3, 6.

194Cobban,supra n23.

195Theidon,supra n19, 456.

196E. Daly, 'Between Punitive and Reconstructive Justice: The *Gacaca* Courts in Rwanda' (2002) 30 *New York University Journal of International Law and Politics* 355, 375–376. See also A. W   ierzynska, 'Note: Consolidating Democracy Through Transitional Justice: Rwanda's Gacaca Courts' (2004) 79 *New York University Law Review* 1934.

197 R. Ehrenreich Brooks, 'The New Imperialism: Violence, Norms and the 'Rule of Law'' (2003) 101 *Michigan Law Review* 2275, 2335.

198 J. Widner, 'Courts and Democracy in Post-Conf   ict Transitions: A Social Scientist's Perspective on the African Case' (2001) 95 *American Journal of International Law* 64, 66 and E. Daly, supra n195, 376.

199 A. Chakravarty, 'Gacaca Courts in Rwanda: Explaining Divisions within the Human Rights Community' (2006) 1 *Yale Journal of International Affairs* 132, 135 and 140, P. Uvin, 'Case Study: The Gacaca T ribunals in Rwanda' in D. Bloomf eld, T. Barnes and L. Huyse (eds.), *Reconciliation After Violent Conflict: A Handbook* (Stockholm: International Institute for Democracy and Electoral Assistance, 2003), 116 at 119, Longman, supra n156, 219.

200Meyerstein,supra n17, 470.

201Ibid.,470 and Waldorf, supra n103, 44–46.

202Daly supra n180, 134.

203Arriazaand Roht-Arriaza, supra n190, 161.

204S.Gibbs, 'Postwar Social Reconstruction in Mozambique: Reframing Children's Experiences on Trauma and Healing' in K. Kumar (ed.), *Rebuilding Societies After Civil War: Critical Roles for International Assistance* (Boulder: L ynne Rienner, 1997), 227.

205R. Shaw, 'Memory Frictions: Localising the Truth and Reconciliation Commission in Sierra Leone' (2007) 1 *International Journal of Transitional Justice* 183, 194–196.

206 H. Weinstein et al., 'Stay the Hand of Justice: Whose Priorities Take Priority?' in Shaw, Waldorf and Hazan (eds.), supra n18, 27 at 42.

207 L. Waldorf, 'R wanda's Failing Experiment in Restorative Justice' in Sullivan and Tifft (eds.), supra n180, 422 at 429.

208J.Galtung, *Peace by Peaceful Means: Peace and Conflict, Development and Civilization* (Oslo: International Peace Research Institute, 1996).

209Nagy supra n12, 96.

210Kerrand Mobekk, supra n15, 157.

211Meyerstein,supra n17, 486.

212Longman,supra n156, 220.

213Huyse,supra n112, 189.

214 Rwandan experts rejected the notion gacaca could be used to process genocide cases because in the past it could not even be used for homicide (UNHCR, *Gacaca: Le Droit Coutumier de Rwanda* (1996)).

215 Ingelaereand Kohlhagen, supra n28, 52.

216 Latigo,supra n24, 114.

217 Allen,supra n117, 47.

218 Huyse,supra n3, 6.

219 Kerrand Mobekk, supra n15, 161.

220 McEvoy supra n33, 30.

221 J. Braithwaite, *Restorative Justice and Responsive Regulation* (New York: Oxford University Press, 2002), 5, C. Cuneen, 'Reviving Restorative Justice Traditions?' in Johnstone and Van Ness (eds.), supra n32, 113 at 117.

222 H.Zehr, *Changing Lanes* (Scottsdale: Herald Press, 1990), 184–185.

223 Roche,supra n39, 80.

224 Ibid.,81 and 77.

225 M.Trebilcock and R. Daniels, *Rule of Law Reform and Development: Charting the Fragile Path of Progress* (Cheltenham: Edward Elgar, 2008), 36.

226 H Zehr, *The Little Book of Restorative Justice* (Intercourse, PA: Good Books, 2002), 59.

227 'Using "traditional" justice risks implying that the government and the rest of the country have nothing to do with the northern confict, and also that northern Ugandans need their own special justice measures, because they are not yet ready for modern ones' (Allen, supra n117, 47).

228 L.G. Jones, *Embodying Forgiveness: A Theological Analysis* (Grand Rapids: Erdemans, 1995), 239 and 267, cited in Kiss, supra n160, 87.

229 Kiss,ibid., 73.

230 Latigo,supra n24, 114.

231 Longman,supra n156, 206.

232 Chopra,Ranheim and Nixon, supra n45, 121.

233 Ramji-Nogales,supra n34, 11.

234 E.g. B. Oomen, 'Justice Mechanisms and the Question of Legitimacy: The Example of Rwanda's Multi-layered Justice Mechanisms' in K. Ambos, J. Large, M. Wierda (eds.), *Building a Future on Peace and Justice: Studies on Transitional Justice, Peace and Development* (Berlin: Springer, 2009), 175 at 182 and Ramji-Nogales, ibid., 27–28.

235 The popularity of these mechanisms is evident in surveys like T . Longman, P. Pham and H. Weinstein, 'Connecting Justice to Human Experience: Attitudes Toward Accountability and Reconciliation in Rwanda' in Stover and Weinstein (eds.), supra n172, 206 and Pigou, supra n138, 79–87.

236 Oomen,supra n233, 180.

237 For example, Schedler ar gues supportive habits can be stimulated through introduction of new judicial structures (A. Schedler , 'Measuring Democratic Consolidation' (2001) 36 *Studies in Comparative International Development* 66, 75).

238 J.N. Clark, 'The Three R' s: Retributive Justice, Restorative Justice, and Reconciliation' (2008) 11 *Contemporary Justice Review* 331, 345.

239 In making this ar gument I paraphrase Nagy , supra n12, at 97 who makes a similar observation but solely in relation to Rwanda.

240 E.g. Cobban, supra n23, Latigo, supra n24, 109, Oomen, supra n233, 187, C. Villa-Vicencio, 'Transitional Justice, Restoration, and Prosecution' in Sullivan and Tifft (eds.), supra n180, 387 at 387.

241E.g.E. Daly, supra n195, 367 and 378.

242Promotionof National Unity Act 1995, Preamble.

243R.Wilson, *The Politics of Truth and Reconciliation in South Africa: Legitimizing the Post-Apartheid State* (New York: Cambridge University Press, 2001), 207.

244 E.g. Hovil and Quinn, supra n25, 22, Iliff, supra n35, 264, Longman, supra n156, 218, Peachey, supra n49, 306.

245Chopra,Ranheim and Nixon, supra n45, 155.

246Allen,supra n117, 85.

247 J. Gibson and A. Gouws, 'Support for the Rule of Law in the Emer ging South African Democracy' (1997) 49 *International Social Science Journal* 173.

248 A danger noted by Cuneen, supra n220, 116, Oomen, supra n177, 903.

249Nagy supra n12, 100.

250 K. McEvoy and L. McGregor , 'Transitional Justice From Below: An Agenda for Research, Policy and Praxis' in McEvoy and McGregor (eds.), supra n33, 1 at 3.

251Ibid.,4–5.

252Ibid.,6.

253E.Daly, supra n195, 376.

254Lundyand McGovern, supra n109.

255 The word is used, for example, by Arriaza and Roht-Arriaza, supra n190, 153, Huyse, supra n3, 10, Iliff, supra n35, 262, Waldorf, supra n206, 426.

256Ramji-Nogales,supra n34, 54.

257Iliff,supra n35, 261.

258Latigo,supra n24, 111.

259Waldorf, supra n206, 426.

260Oomen,supra n177, 906.

261Ibid.

262Nagy supra n12, 10.

263 Ramji-Nogales, supra n34, 19, Barf eld, Nojumi and Thier, supra n36, 187.

264Meyerstein,supra n17, 481 and 495.

265 D. Pimentel, 'Legal Pluralism and the Rule of Law: Can Indigenous Justice Survive?' (2010) 32(2) *Harvard International Review* 32, 35.

266Chirayath,Sage and Woolcock, supra n31, 17.

267Lubkeman,Isser and Banks III, supra n139, 203.

268McEvoy supra n33, 28.

269 It should be pointed out that McEvoy and McGregor note a need to manage/ regulate justice from the bottom up lest they reify existing discriminatory practices (McEvoy and McGregor, supra n249, 10).

270Waldorf, supra n103, 9.

271Arriazaand Roht-Arriaza, supra n190, 170.

272Meyerstein,supra n17, 486.

273E.Daly, supra n195, 377.

274Ibid.,376–377.

275 On the evidence of the states examined in this chapter , Merry's argument that 'Popular justice established in opposition to the state tends to die out or be colonized by state law' is one that applies beyond the United States (S. Merry , 'Sorting Out Popular Justice' in S. Merry and N. Milner (eds.), *The Possibility of Popular Justice: A Case Study of Community Mediation in the United States* (Ann Arbor: University of Michigan Press, 1993), 31 at 31–32).

276R.Teitel, *Transitional Justice* (Oxford: Oxford University Press, 2001), especially Chapters 1 and 7.

277 E.g. Alie, supra n109, 133, Chirayath, Sage and W   oolcock, supra n31, 2, Pimentel, supra n135, 6.

278S.Finnstrom, *Living with Bad Surroundings: War, History, and Everyday Moments in Northern Uganda* (Durham, NC: Duke University Press, 2008), 299.

279Naniwe-Kaburahe,supra n46, 161.

280Ibid.,162 and 168.

281Schotsmans,supra n168, 279.

282Corradi,supra n137, 87–90.

283Shawand Waldorf, supra n18, 22.

284DFID,supra n58, 4.

285 J.M. Kane, O. Onyango and A. T   ejan-Cole, 'Reassessing Customary Law Systems as a V ehicle for Providing Equitable Access to Justice for the Poor' (2005), paper presented at Arusha Conference, New Frontiers of Social Policy 12–15 December, 2005, available: < http://siteresources.worldbank.org/ INTRANETSOCIALDEVELOPMENT/Resources/Kane.rev.pdf>.

286 T. Mennen, 'Putting Theory into Practice – Improving Customary Justice', paper given at Customary Justice and Legal Pluralism in Post-Conf   ict and Fragile Societies conference, 17–18 November 2009, Washington, D.C.

287S. Merry, *Human Rights and Gender Violence: Translating International Law into Local Justice* (Chicago: University of Chicago Press, 2006), 219.

288Oomen,supra n177, 906.

289Kerrand Mobekk, supra n15, 160.

290Alie,supra n109, 133.

291Ingelaere,supra n44, 52.

292Pigou,supra n138, 83.

293Seegenerally McAuliffe, supra n106.

294 Commission for Reception, Truth and Reconciliation in East Timor, *Chega! The Final Report of the Commission for Reception, Truth and Reconciliation in East Timor Part 9* (2005), 40.

295UNSecretary-General, *Letter dated 16 May 2008 from the Secretary-General to the President of the Security Council, UN Doc. S/2008/329, Annex (Report of the Expert Mission to Timor-Leste on policing, 17 to 27 March 2008)*, para. 41.

296Arriazaand Roht-Arriaza, supra n190, 153.

Conclusion

Foundational justice and transitional justice, the pragmatic and the profound

As f elds of study, both transitional justice and rule of law reconstruction are relatively young and undertheorized. As concepts, both transitional justice and rule of law reconstruction are amorphous, expansionist and prone to conf ation with other laudable ends. As a result, the types of operational diff culties sketched in Chapter 1 and the conceptual divergences explored in Chapters 2 and 3 should not be surprising. Nevertheless, the observable tendencies of transitional justice and rule of law reconstruction to operate simultaneously in splendid isolation from each other , to pull in distinctly different directions and make little contribution to each other's ends *do* seem to surprise, and then disappoint, the regrettably small number of practitioners and scholars minded to consider their interaction. This surprise f   ows inevitably from the f awed but widely-shared presumption that transitional justice is inherently conducive to rebuilding the rule of law in post-authoritarian and post-conf ict states. This presumption in turn f ows from the failure to acknowledge that the rather nebulous concept of the rule of law means very different things to those whose primary concern is rebuilding the justice sector, on the one hand, and those whose primary concern is addressing human rights abuses of the past to create a better future, on the other   . The former conceptualize the rule of law as a programme of institutions, culture and norms where sustainable and exemplary standards of good practice must be fostered sedulously in the foundational period of the emerging polity. On this view , it would appear that there are obvious areas of convergence with transitional justice. However, transitional justice discourse emphasizes a distinctly transitional rule of law presented as a progressist narrative which serves to legitimize departures from the institutions, values and norms that underpin the reconstructing justice sector in the hope (often justif ed) that these compromises will pave the way for the conditions in which the rule of law can thrive in future, or at least symbolize a minimal prospective commitment to the rule of law   . There is something almost messianic in transitional justice' s self-presentation. Its goals are so self-evidently good, its advocates so obviously well-intentioned and the surrounding circumstances so demonstrably bleak that the tendency to minimize doubts over the empirical record, the questionable assumptions and the contradictions inherent in its mechanisms lest they slow the impetus towards creating a better society is understandable. However , in this more sceptical era of transitional justice scholarship, there is much to be gained from paying attention to the f eld's blind-spots that went unobserved in earlier , more exuberant theorizing. This book has ar gued that transitional justice has not paid the requisite attention to the institutions, culture and norms that need to be fostered in a justice system in transition. Rejecting the existence of an excusatory, contingent transitional rule of law that has justif ed this inatten-tion and ar guing that the potential benef ts of transitional justice are exaggerated, it urges policy-makers to re-balance the compromises inherent in transitional justice mechanisms against the foundational demands of rule of law reconstruction. Prioritizing achievable and pragmatic justice sector reform objectives over the more profound but potentially unobtainable political ends that dominate transitional justice theory, the book recommends that a more clear-eyed vision of costs and benef ts, risks and opportunities is required when decisions are made to employ, circumvent or complement the transitional state's institutions of justice.

This agenda might best be described as a foundational approach to transi-tional justice. If due regard is f nally paid to the long-term interests of the reconstructing state justice sector, some of the assumptions that have under -pinned transitional justice practice to such underwhelming effect might prof tably be revised. For example, Chapter 4 examined how the profound objectives of transitional trial (retribution, deterrence, reconciliation, politi-cal expressivism) have frequently operated to turn transitional trial into an imbalanced, punitive model that wilfully disregards the standards of due process peace-builders might wish to inculcate in the court system. Questioning whether these aspirations can ever be achieved in the radically imperfect conditions of transition, a more pragmatic approach that elevates judicial process over political product may not only avoid the spectre of systematically imbalanced trials in the period when the state lays the founda-tions for its future administration of criminal justice, but may also generate modest retributive, reconciliatory, deterrent and expressivist effects. Chapter 5 examined the most high-prof le example of transitional justice, namely international criminal law. In one sense, it should come as little surprise that something so global in outlook should have so minimal a legacy domestically However, all international criminal institutions established since the 1990s have been justif ed at least in part by those establishing them for their poten-tial to catalyse, interact with or promote domestic justice sector reform. That international criminal law has consistently failed to do so, and at times gone so far as to infantilize and undermine nascent national justice systems, is largely attributable to the profound desire on the part of practitioners, advo-cates and scholars in the area to substantiate a global rule of law in preference to the more prosaic forms of assistance to transitional and developing crimi-nal justice systems that was ur ged by the States Parties at the Kampala

Review Conference of the ICC. Finally, Chapter 6 explored how the valorization of traditional justice mechanisms as inherently restorative, bottom-up sites of resistance to the state in transitional justice conficts with the emphasis of rule of law reconstructors on employing customary law to plug rule of law gaps, facilitating state oversight and integrating these subnational structures with the formal justice system. The many benefcial reforms in terms of rights, non-discrimination and accountability that transitional justice can bring to traditional processes may be lost due to this short-term outlook.

It should be remembered, however, that the book merely proposes that foundational concerns for the rule of law in transition should be given greater weight when designing transitional justice responses, be they trials domestically, in The Hague, a truth commission or a traditional hearing in a village. It does not propose that the long-term interests of the rule of law should operate as trumps or exercise determinative infuence. Reconstructing the rule of law is a vast undertaking and hostage to so many independent, inter-related fortunes that the ultimate infuence of transitional justice on it, for good or ill, may be minimal. It is unwise, given the diversity of transitional justice responses that have helped advance transition, to argue that trials must always occur and must always be exemplarily fair, that the Rome Statute's admissibility regime should respond only to complete national inertia or that traditional justice mechanisms should always be tightly integrated with the state. All transitional justice policy must be context-specifc, and this will depend on the nature of the prior regime, its legal culture, contemporary political circumstances, the type of transition under-gone, the most pressing contemporary social needs and, not least of all, the human factors motivating those who are responsible for co-ordinating justice policy. The context may be such that convictions should be secured rapidly, the international community should assume complete control or localized processes should be divorced entirely from the state. However, in certain post-confict ecologies, it will be clear that policy-makers should focus on the process of transitional justice and how it serves a model for future practice in the justice sector as much as on the outcome. In particular, where the transition is one to something resembling a democratic government committed at least minimally to the rule of law, policy-makers need to ask whether a proposed process helps develop the emergent institutions of justice, binds the people to those institutions, fosters respect among the political leadership for their autonomy or exemplifes the manner in which those institutions should treat citizens in future. Given the idiosyncrasies of transition, the only defnite proposal the book can make is that policy-makers in transitional justice and rule of law reconstruction should ground their initiatives on a solid empirical and comparative approach alive to the blind-spots, contradictions and opportunities for mutually-benefcial synergies these chapters have highlighted.

Bibliography

Books/monographs

Ambos K., Large, J. and Werda, M. (eds.) *Building a Future on Peace and Justice: Studies on Transitional Justice, Peace and Development* (Berlin :Springer, 2009)

Bell C., *Peace Agreements and Human Rights* (Oxford, New York: Oxford University Press, 2000)

Bosire L., *Overpromised, Underdelivered: Transitional Justice in Sub-Saharan Africa* (New York: ICTJ ,2006)

Bowden B., Charlesworth H. and Farrall J. (eds.), *The Role of International Law in Rebuilding Societies after Conflict: Great Expectations* (New York: Cambridge University Press, 2009)

Bull C., *No Entry Without Strategy: Building the Rule of Law Under UN Transitional Administration* (New York: United Nations University Press, 2008)

Call C., (ed.), *Constructing Justice and Security After War* (Washington, D.C.: United States Institute of Peace, 2007)

Carothers T., (ed.), *Promoting the Rule of Law Abroad: In Search of Knowledge* (Washington, D.C.: Carnegie Endowment for International Peace, 2006)

Chesterman S., Ignatieff M. and Thakur R. (eds.), *Making States Work: State Failure and the Crisis of Governance* (New York: United Nations University Press, 2005)

Chirayath L., Sage C. and Wolcock, M. *Customary Law and Policy Reform: Engaging with the Plurality of Justice Systems* (Washington, D.C.: World Bank, 2006)

De Brito, A.B. , González-Enríquez C. and Aguilar P. (eds.), *The Politics of Memory: Transitional Justice in Democratizing Societies* (Oxford, New York: Oxford University Press, 2001)

De Greiff, P. and Duthie R. (eds.), *Transitional Justice and Development: Making Connections* (New York: Social Science Research Council, 2009)

Huyse L., and Salter M. (eds.), *Traditional Justice and Reconciliation After Conflict: Learning from African Experience* (Stockholm :International Institute for Democracy and Electoral Assistance, 2008)

Isser D. (ed.), *Customary Justice and the Rule of Law in War-Torn Societies* (Washington, D.C.: USIP, 2011)

Kerr R. and Mobekk E. *Peace & Justice: Seeking Accountability After War* (Cambridge : Polity Press, 2007)

Mani R., *Beyond Retribution – Seeking Justice in the Shadows of War* (Cambridge Polity Press, 2002)

McEvoy K. and McGregor L. (eds.), *Transitional Justice from Below: Grassroots Activism and the Struggle for Change* (Portland :Hart Publishing, 2008)

Olsen T, ,Payne, L. and Reiter, A., *Transitional Justice in Balance: Comparing Processes, Weighing Efficacy* (Washington, D.C.: U.S. Institute of Peace, 2010)

Osie M. *Mass Atrocity, Collective Memory and the Law* (New Brunswick :Transaction Publishers, 1997)

Paris R. *At War's End: Building Peace After Civil Conflict* (New York: Cambridge University Press, 2004)

Potter A. *The Rule of Law as the Measure of Peace? Responsive Policy for Reconstructing Justice and the Rule of Law in Post Conflict and Transitional Environments* (Geneva : Centre for Humanitarian Dialogue, 2004)

Sannerholm R. ,*Rule of Law after War and Crisis: Ideologies, Norms and Methods* (Cambridge :Intersentia ,2012)

Schedler A. , Diamond L. and Plattner M. (eds.), *The Self-Restraining State: Power and Accountability in New Democracies* (Boulder :Lynne Rienner Publishers, 1999)

Shaw R. , Waldorf, L. and Hazan P. (eds.), *Localizing Transitional Justice: Interventions and Priorities after Mass Violence* (Stanford: Stanford University Press, 2010)

Sriram C., I Martin-Ortega , O and Herman , J(eds.), *Peacebuilding and Rule of Law in Africa* (Oxford :Routledge ,2011)

Stahn C.,and E Zeidy, M (eds.), *The International Criminal Court and Complementarity: From Theory to Practice* (Vol. I)(Cambridge :Cambridge University Press, 2011)

Stover E. and Weinstein, H. (eds.), *My Neighbor, My Enemy: Justice and Community in the Aftermath of Mass Atrocity* (Cambridge: Cambridge University Press, 2004)

Stromseth J, ,Wippman, M. and Brooks, R., *Can Might Make Rights? Building the Rule of Law After Military Interventions* (Cambridge :Cambridge University Press, 2006)

Teitel, R. *Transitional Justice* (Oxford :Oxford University Press, 2001)

Trebilcock, M. and Daniels R. ,*Rule of Law Reform and Development: Charting the Fragile Path of Progress* (Cheltenham Edward Elgar, 2008)

van der Merwe, H. , Baxter V. and Chapman A. (eds.), *Assessing the Impact of Transitional Justice: Challenges for Empirical Research* (Washington, D.C.: USIP Press, 2009)

Wojkowska, E. *Doing Justice: How Informal Systems Can Contribute* (Oslo :UNDP Oslo Governance Centre, 2006)

Yusuf, H. ,*Transitional Justice, Judicial Accountability and the Rule of Law* (London : Routledge ,2010)

Journal articles

Aukerman M. 'Extraordinary Evil, Ordinary Crimes: A Framework for Understanding Transitional Justice' (2002)15 *Harvard Human Rights Journal* 39

Bell, C., 'Transitional Justice, Interdisciplinarity and the State of the "Field" or "Non-Field"' (2009)3 *International Journal of Transitional Justice* 5

Brinkerhoff D. ;'Rebuilding Governance in Failed States and Post-Conf ict Societies: Core Concepts and Cross-Cutting Themes' (2005) 25 *Public Administration and Development* 3

Burke-White W.W. ,'The Domestic Inf uence of International Criminal Tribunals: The International Criminal Tribunal for the Former Yugoslavia and the Creation of the State Court of Bosnia & Herzegovina' (2008) 46 *Columbia Journal of Transnational Law* 279

Connolly, B. ,'Non-State Justice Systems and the State: Proposals for a Recognition Typology' (2005)38 *Connecticut Law Review* 239

Daniels, R. and Trebilcock, M. ,'The Political Economy of Rule of Law Reform in Developing Countries' (2004)26 *Michigan Journal of International Law* 99

Dickinson, L. ,'The Promise of Hybrid Courts' (2003) 97 *American Journal of International Law* 295

DuBois, F., and Czarnota, A. ,'The Transitional Rule of Law' (1999)24 *Alternative Law Journal* 9

Dyzenhaus, D., 'Judicial Independence, Transitional Justice and the Rule of Law' (2003)10 *Otago Law Review* 345

Faundez, J. ,'Legal Pluralism and International Development Agencies: State Building or Legal Reform?' (2011) 3 *Hague Journal on the Rule of Law* 18

Fletcher, L., Weinstein, H. and Rowen, J., 'Context, Timing and the Dynamics of Transitional Justice: A Historical Perspective'(2009) 31 *Human Rights Quarterly* 163

Gray, D. ,'An Excuse-Centred Approach to Transitional Justice' (2005–06) 74 *Fordham Law Review* 2621

Gready, P. , 'Reconceptualising Transitional Justice: Embedded and Distanced Justice' (2005)5 *Conflict, Security and Development* 3

Hussain, V., 'Sustaining Judicial Rescues: The Role of Judicial Outreach and Capacity-Building Efforts in War Crimes Tribunals' (2005) 45 *Virginia Journal of International Law* 547

Lambourne, W. , 'Transitional Justice and Peace-building After Mass Violence' (2009)3 *International Journal of Transitional Justice* 28

Leebaw, B.A. ,'The Irreconcilable Goals of Transitional Justice' (2008)30 *Human Rights Quarterly* 95

McAuliffe, P., 'Transitional Justice and the Rule of Law: The Perfect Couple or Awkward Bedfellows?' (2010)2 *Hague Journal on the Rule of Law* 110

McAuliffe, P., 'UN Peace-Building, Transitional Justice and the Rule of Law in East Timor: The Limits of Institutional Responses to Political Questions' (2011) 58 *Netherlands International Law Review* 103

McEvoy, K. ,'Beyond Legalism: Towards a Thicker Understanding of Transitional Justice' (2007)34 *Journal of Law and Society* 411

Merry, S. ,'Legal Pluralism' (1988)22 *Law and Society Review* 869

Ní Aoláin, F. and Campbell, C. ,'The Paradox of Transition in Conficted Democracies' (2005)27 *Human Rights Quarterly* 172

Ohlin, J.,D. ,'On the Very Idea of Transitional Justice' (2007)8 *Whitehead Journal of Diplomacy and International Relations* 51

Peerenboom, R., 'Human Rights and the Rule of Law: What's the Relationship?' (2005)36 *Georgetown Journal of International Law* 809

Pimentel, D., 'Legal Pluralism and the Rule of Law: Can Indigenous Justice Survive?' (2010)32 (2)*Harvard International Review* 32

Raz, J, ,'The Rule of Law and its Virtue' (1977)93 *Law Quarterly Review* 195

Sannerholm, R. ,'Legal, Judicial and Administrative Reforms in Post-Confict Societies: Beyond the Rule of Law Template' (2007) 12 *Journal of Conflict and Security Law* 65

Snyder, J. and Vinjamuri, L. ,'Trials and Errors: Principle and Pragmatism in Strategies on International Justice' (2003–04) 28 *International Security* 5

Stromseth, J., 'Justice on the Ground: Can International Criminal Courts Strengthen Domestic Rule of Law in Post-Confict Societies?' (2009) 1 *Hague Journal on the Rule of Law* 87

Subotic J., ,'The Transformation of International Transitional Justice Advocacy' (2012)6 *International Journal of Transitional Justice* 106

Tamanaha, B. ,'The Rule of Law and Legal Pluralism in Development' (2011)3 *Hague Journal on the Rule of Law* 1

Thoms Q., Ron J. and Paris R. ;'State-Level Effects of Transitional Justice: What Do We Know?' (2010)4 *International Journal of Transitional Justice* 1

Waldorf, L., 'Mass Justice for Mass Atrocity: Rethinking Local Justice as Transitional Justice' (2006)79 *Temple Law Review* 1

Widner, J. ;'Courts and Democracy in Post-Conf ict Transitions: A Social Scientist's Perspective on the African Case' (2001) 95 *American Journal of International Law* 64

Chapters in edited volumes

Bergsmo, M., Bekou, O. and Jones, A., 'Complementarity and the Construction of National Ability' in Stahn C. and El Zeidy, M. (eds.), *The International Criminal Court and Complementarity: From Theory to Practice* (Vol. II)(Cambridge :Cambridge University Press, 2011),1052

Burke-White W.W. , 'Reframing Positive Complementarity' in Stahn C. and El Zeidy, M. (eds.), *The International Criminal Court and Complementarity: From Theory to Practice* (Vol. I)(Cambridge :Cambridge University Press, 2011),341

Call C., ;'Conclusion: Constructing Justice and Security after War' in Call C. (ed.), *Constructing Justice and Security After War* (Washington, D.C.: United States Institute of Peace, 2007),375

Carothers T., ,'Steps Towards Knowledge' in Carothers T. (ed.), *Promoting the Rule of Law Abroad: In Search of Knowledge* (Washington, D.C.: Carnegie Endowment for International Peace, 2006),327

De Greiff, P., 'Articulating the Links Between Transitional Justice and Development: Justice and Social Integration' in de Greiff, P. and Duthie R. (eds.), *Transitional Justice and Development: Making Connections* (New York: Social Science Research Council, 2009),28

De Greiff, P. ,'Theorizing Transitional Justice' in Williams, M. , Nagy R. and Elster J. (eds.), *Transitional Justice* (New York: New York University Press, 2012),31

Donlon, F., 'Rule of Law: From the International Criminal T ribunal for the Former Yugoslavia to the W ar Crimes Chamber of Bosnia and Herzegovina' in Haynes, D.F. (ed.), *Deconstructing the Reconstruction: Human Rights and Rule of Law in Postwar Bosnia and Herzegovina* (Aldershot :Ashgate ,2008),257

Farrall, J., 'Impossible Expectations? The UN Security Council' s Promotion of the Rule of Law after Conf ict' in Bowden B. , Charlesworth H. and Farrall J. (eds.), *The Role of International Law in Rebuilding Societies after Conflict: Great Expectations* (New York: Cambridge University Press, 2009),134

Hall C., ;'Positive Complementarity in Action in Stahn, C and El Zeidy, M(eds.), *The International Criminal Court and Complementarity: From Theory to Practice* (Vol. II)(Cambridge :Cambridge University Press, 2011),1014

Hinton A.L. ,'Introduction: Toward an Anthropology of Transitional Justice' in Hinton A.L. (ed.), *Transitional Justice: Global Mechanisms and Local Realities after Genocide and Mass Violence* (New Brunswick: Rutgers University Press, 2010),1

Huyse L., ;'Introduction: Tradition-based Approaches in Peacemaking, Transitional Justice and Reconciliation Policies' in Huyse L. and Salter, M. (eds.), *Traditional Justice and Reconciliation After Conflict: Learning from African Experience* (Stockholm : International Institute for Democracy and Electoral Assistance , 2008), 1

IsserD. ,'Understanding and Engaging Customary Justice Systems' in   D.Isser (ed.), *Customary Justice and the Rule of Law in War-Torn Societies* (Washington, D.C.: USIP, 2011),325

Jensen, E., 'The Rule of Law and Judicial Reform: The Political Economy of Diverse Institutional Patterns and Reformer's Responses' in   Jensen E. and Heller T. (eds.), *Beyond Common Knowledge: Empirical Approaches to the Rule of Law* (Stanford : Stanford Law and Politics, 2003),336

KritzN. ,'The Rule of Law in the Post-Conflict Phase' in   CrockerC. and   Hamson , F. (eds.), *Managing Global Chaos* (Washington, D.C.: USIP, 2006),587

KritzN. ,'Policy Implications of Empirical Research on Transitional Justice' in   van der Merwe, H. ,   Baxter V. and   Chapman A. (eds.), *Assessing the Impact of Transitional Justice: Challenges for Empirical Research* (Washington, D.C.: USIP Press, 2009),13

O'DonnellG. ,'Horizontal Accountability in New Democracies' in   Schedler A. ,   Diamond L. and   Plattner M. (eds.), *The Self-Restraining State: Power and Accountability in New Democracies* (Boulder :Lynne Rienner Publishers, 1999),29

OffeC. ,'Designing Institutions in East European Transitions' in   GoodinR. (ed.), *The Theory of Institutional Design* (Cambridge: Press Syndicate of the University of Cambridge, 1996),199

PlunkettM. ,'Rebuilding the Rule of Law' in   MaleyW., SampfordC. and   Thakur R. (eds.), *From Civil Strife to Civil Society: Civil and Military Responsibilities in Disrupted States* (Tokyo, New York: United Nations University Press, 2003),207

PulverR. ,'Rule of Law, Peacekeeping and the United Nations' in   Sriram C.L. ,   Martin-OrtegaO. and   HermanJ. (eds.), *Peacebuilding and Rule of Law in Africa* (Oxford :Routledge ,2011),60

RichmondO. ,'The Rule of Law in Liberal Peace-Building' in   SriramC.L. ,   Martin-Ortega, O. and   HermanJ. (eds.), *Peacebuilding and Rule of Law in Africa* (Oxford : Routledge ,2011),44

Roht-ArriazaN. ,'The New Landscape of Transitional Justice' in   Roht-ArriazaN. and   MariezcurrenaJ. (eds.), *Transitional Justice in the Twenty-First Century: Beyond Truth Versus Justice* (New York: Cambridge University Press, 2006),1

SchedlerA. ,'Restraining the State: Conflicts and Agencies of Accountability'   in   SchedlerA. ,   DiamondL. and   PlattnerM. (eds.), *The Self-Restraining State: Power and Accountability in New Democracies* (Boulder :Lynne Rienner Publishers, 1999),333

ShawR. and   Wldorf, L. ,'Introduction: Localizing Transitional Justice' in   ShawR. ,   Wldorf, L. andHazan, P. (eds.), *Localizing Transitional Justice: Interventions and Priorities after Mass Violence* (Stanford: Stanford University Press, 2010),3

SriramC.L. ,   Martin-OrtegaO. and   HermanJ. ,'Just Peace? Lessons Learned and Policy Insights' in   Sriram C.L. ,   Martin-Ortega O. and   Herman J. (eds.), *Peacebuilding and Rule of Law in Africa* (Oxford :Routledge ,2011),197

Stahn, C., 'Taking Complementarity Seriously: On the Sense and Sensibility of "Classical", "Positive" and "Negative" Complementarity' in   Stahn C. and   El Zeidy, M. (eds.), *The International Criminal Court and Complementarity: From Theory to Practice* (Vol. I)(Cambridge :Cambridge University Press, 2011),233

ZartmanW. ,'Introduction: Posing the Problem of State Collapse' in   ZartmanW. (ed.), *Collapsed State: The Disintegration and Restoration of Legitimate Authority* (Boulder :Lynne Rienner, 1995),6

Index